elevate science

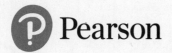 **Pearson**

Boston, Massachusetts   Chandler, Arizona
Glenview, Illinois   New York, New York

You're an author!

As you write in this science book, your answers and personal discoveries will be recorded for you to keep, making this book unique to you. That is why you are one of the primary authors of this book.

✏ **In the space below, print your name, school, town, and state. Then write a short autobiography that includes your interests and accomplishments.**

YOUR NAME ....

SCHOOL ....

TOWN, STATE ....

AUTOBIOGRAPHY ....

....

....

....

....

....

....

Your Photo

The cover photo shows a white-legged damselfly.

Pearson Education, Inc. 330 Hudson Street, New York, NY 10013

ISBN-13:   978-0-328-94854-3
ISBN-10:   0-328-94854-3
2 18

Program Authors

ZIPPORAH MILLER, Ed.D.

Coordinator for K-12 Science Programs, Anne Arundel County Public Schools
Dr. Zipporah Miller currently serves as the Senior Manager for Organizational Learning with the Anne Arundel County Public School System. Prior to that she served as the K-12 Coordinator for science in Anne Arundel County. She conducts national training to science stakeholders on the Next Generation Science Standards. Dr. Miller also served as the Associate Executive Director for Professional Development Programs and conferences at the National Science Teachers Association (NSTA) and served as a reviewer during the development of Next Generation Science Standards. Dr. Miller holds a doctoral degree from the University of Maryland College Park, a master's degree in school administration and supervision from Bowie State University and a bachelor's degree from Chadron State College.

MICHAEL J. PADILLA, Ph.D.

Professor Emeritus, Eugene P. Moore School of Education, Clemson University, Clemson, South Carolina
Michael J. Padilla taught science in middle and secondary schools, has more than 30 years of experience educating middle-school science teachers, and served as one of the writers of the 1996 U.S. National Science Education Standards. In recent years Mike has focused on teaching science to English Language Learners. His extensive experience as Principal Investigator on numerous National Science Foundation and U.S. Department of Education grants resulted in more than $35 million in funding to improve science education. He served as president of the National Science Teachers Association, the world's largest science teaching organization, in 2005–6.

MICHAEL E. WYSESSION, Ph.D

Professor of Earth and Planetary Sciences, Washington University, St. Louis, Missouri
Author of more than 100 science and science education publications, Dr. Wysession was awarded the prestigious National Science Foundation Presidential Faculty Fellowship and Packard Foundation Fellowship for his research in geophysics, primarily focused on using seismic tomography to determine the forces driving plate tectonics. Dr. Wysession is also a leader in geoscience literacy and education; he is the chair of the Earth Science Literacy Initiative, the author of several popular video lectures on geology in the *Great Courses* series, and a lead writer of the *Next Generation Science Standards**.

---

*Next Generation Science Standards is a registered trademark of Achieve. Neither Achieve nor the lead states and partners that developed the Next Generation Science Standards were involved in the production of this product, and do not endorse it. NGSS Lead States. 2013. *Next Generation Science Standards: For States, By States*. Washington, DC: The National Academies Press.

REVIEWERS

Program Consultants

Carol Baker
Science Curriculum

Dr. Carol K. Baker is superintendent for Lyons Elementary K-8 School District in Lyons, Illinois. Prior to this, she was Director of Curriculum for Science and Music in Oak Lawn, Illinois. Before this she taught Physics and Earth Science for 18 years. In the recent past, Dr. Baker also wrote assessment questions for ACT (EXPLORE and PLAN), was elected president of the Illinois Science Teachers Association from 2011–2013, and served as a member of the Museum of Science and Industry (Chicago) advisory board. She is a writer of the Next Generation Science Standards. Dr. Baker received her B.S. in Physics and a science teaching certification. She completed her master's of Educational Administration (K-12) and earned her doctorate in Educational Leadership.

Jim Cummins
ELL

Dr. Cummins's research focuses on literacy development in multilingual schools and the role technology plays in learning across the curriculum. *Elevate Science* incorporates research-based principles for integrating language with the teaching of academic content based on Dr. Cummins's work.

Elfrieda Hiebert
Literacy

Dr. Hiebert, a former primary-school teacher, is President and CEO of TextProject, a non-profit aimed at providing open-access resources for instruction of beginning and struggling readers, She is also a research associate at the University of California Santa Cruz. Her research addresses how fluency, vocabulary, and knowledge can be fostered through appropriate texts, and her contributions have been recognized through awards such as the Oscar Causey Award for Outstanding Contributions to Reading Research (Literacy Research Association, 2015), Research to Practice award (American Educational Research Association, 2013), and the William S. Gray Citation of Merit Award for Outstanding Contributions to Reading Research (International Reading Association, 2008).

Content Reviewers

Alex Blom, Ph.D.
Associate Professor
Department Of Physical Sciences
Alverno College
Milwaukee, Wisconsin

Joy Branlund, Ph.D.
Department of Physical Science
Southwestern Illinois College
Granite City, Illinois

Judy Calhoun
Associate Professor
Physical Sciences
Alverno College
Milwaukee, Wisconsin

Stefan Debbert
Associate Professor of Chemistry
Lawrence University
Appleton, Wisconsin

Diane Doser
Professor
Department of Geological Sciences
University of Texas at El Paso
El Paso, Texas

Rick Duhrkopf, Ph.D.
Department of Biology
Baylor University
Waco, Texas

Jennifer Liang
University of Minnesota Duluth
Duluth, Minnesota

Heather Mernitz, Ph.D.
Associate Professor of Physical Sciences
Alverno College
Milwaukee, Wisconsin

Joseph McCullough, Ph.D.
Cabrillo College
Aptos, California

Katie M. Nemeth, Ph.D.
Assistant Professor
College of Science and Engineering
University of Minnesota Duluth
Duluth, Minnesota

Maik Pertermann
Department of Geology
Western Wyoming Community College
Rock Springs, Wyoming

Scott Rochette
Department of the Earth Sciences
The College at Brockport
State University of New York
Brockport, New York

David Schuster
Washington University in St Louis
St. Louis, Missouri

Shannon Stevenson
Department of Biology
University of Minnesota Duluth
Duluth, Minnesota

Paul Stoddard, Ph.D.
Department of Geology and Environmental Geosciences
Northern Illinois University
DeKalb, Illinois

Nancy Taylor
American Public University
Charles Town, West Virginia

Teacher Reviewers

Jennifer Bennett, M.A.
Memorial Middle School
Tampa, Florida

Sonia Blackstone
Lake County Schools
Howey In the Hills, Florida

Teresa Bode
Roosevelt Elementary
Tampa, Florida

Tyler C. Britt, Ed.S.
Curriculum & Instructional
 Practice Coordinator
Raytown Quality Schools
Raytown, Missouri

A. Colleen Campos
Grandview High School
Aurora, Colorado

Ronald Davis
Riverview Elementary
Riverview, Florida

Coleen Doulk
Challenger School
Spring Hill, Florida

Mary D. Dube
Burnett Middle School
Seffner, Florida

Sandra Galpin
Adams Middle School
Tampa, Florida

Margaret Henry
Lebanon Junior High School
Lebanon, Ohio

Christina Hill
Beth Shields Middle School
Ruskin, Florida

Judy Johnis
Gorden Burnett Middle School
Seffner, Florida

Karen Y. Johnson
Beth Shields Middle School
Ruskin, Florida

Jane Kemp
Lockhart Elementary School
Tampa, Florida

Denise Kuhling
Adams Middle School
Tampa, Florida

Esther Leonard, M.Ed. and L.M.T.
Gifted and talented Implementation Specialist
San Antonio Independent School District
San Antonio, Texas

Kelly Maharaj
Challenger K–8 School of Science
 and Mathematics
Spring Hill, Florida

Kevin J. Maser, Ed.D.
H. Frank Carey Jr/Sr High School
Franklin Square, New York

Angie L. Matamoros, Ph.D.
ALM Science Consultant
Weston, Florida

Corey Mayle
Brogden Middle School
Durham, North Carolina

Keith McCarthy
George Washington Middle School
Wayne, New Jersey

Yolanda O. Peña
John F. Kennedy Junior High School
West Valley City, Utah

Kathleen M. Poe
Jacksonville Beach Elementary School
Jacksonville Beach, Florida

Wendy Rauld
Monroe Middle School
Tampa, Florida

Anne Rice
Woodland Middle School
Gurnee, Illinois

Bryna Selig
Gaithersburg Middle School
Gaithersburg, Maryland

Pat (Patricia) Shane, Ph.D.
STEM & ELA Education Consultant
Chapel Hill, North Carolina

Diana Shelton
Burnett Middle School
Seffner, Florida

Nakia Sturrup
Jennings Middle School
Seffner, Florida

Melissa Triebwasser
Walden Lake Elementary
Plant City, Florida

Michele Bubley Wiehagen
Science Coach
Miles Elementary School
Tampa, Florida

Pauline Wilcox
Instructional Science Coach
Fox Chapel Middle School
Spring Hill, Florida

Safety Reviewers

Douglas Mandt, M.S.
Science Education Consultant
Edgewood, Washington

Juliana Textley, Ph.D.
Author, NSTA books on school science safety
Adjunct Professor
Lesley University
Cambridge, Massachusetts

TOPIC 1

The Cell System 1

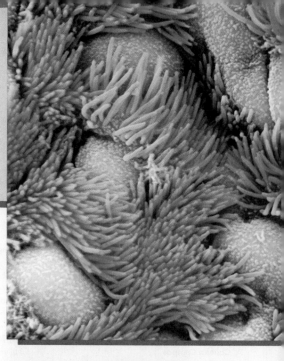

The Essential Question How does the structure of cells determine their function?

Quest KICKOFF Cells on Display 2

MS-LS1-1, MS-LS1-2, MS-LS1-3, MS-LS1-6, MS-LS1-7, MS-LS2-3

 Go to PearsonRealize.com to access your digital course.

 VIDEO
  • Illustrator

 **INTERACTIVITY**
  • Through a Microscope • Functions of All Cells • A Strange Specimen • Structure Function Junction • Build a Cell • Specialized Cells • Cell Transport • Entering and Leaving the Cell • A Cell Divides • How Does a Broken Bone Heal? • The Cell Cycle • Making Food for Cells • From Sunlight to Sugar • Making Energy for Cells

 **VIRTUAL LAB**

ASSESSMENT

eTEXT

APP

HANDS-ON LABS

ИConnect What Can You See?

ИInvestigate
  • Observing Cells
  • Comparing Cells
  • Egg-speriment with a Cell
  • Modeling Mitosis
  • Energy From the Sun
  • Exhaling Carbon Dioxide

ИDemonstrate
Design and Build a Microscope

Go to PearconRealize.com to access your digital course.

▶ **VIDEO**
• Nutritionist

👆 **INTERACTIVITY**
• Human Body Systems • Interacting Systems • Balancing Act
• Communication and Homeostasis
• Joints • A Variety of Symptoms
• Bits and Pieces • Investigating Cells and Homeostasis • A Day in the Life of a Cell • Body Highways and Byways
• Testing a Training Plan • Circulatory System • Body Systems Revisited
• Humans vs. Computers • Flex Your Reflexes

📱 **VIRTUAL LAB**

☑ **ASSESSMENT**

📖 **eTEXT**

📱 **APP**

HANDS-ON LABS

uConnect How is Your Body Organized?

uInvestigate
• Observing Cells and Tissues
• Parts Working Together
• Measuring Calories
• Body Systems Working Together
• Parts of the Nervous System

uDemonstrate
Reaction Research

TOPIC 3

Reproduction and Growth

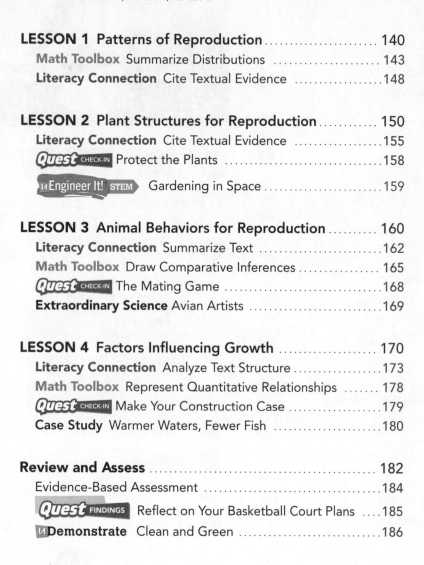

Go to PearsonRealize.com to access your digital course.

▶ **VIDEO**
  • Zookeeper

👆 **INTERACTIVITY**
  • Inheritance of Traits
  • Animal Reproduction
  • Twin Studies
  • Designer Flowers
  • Plants and Pollinators
  • They're Acting Like Animals
  • Fireflies
  • See How They Grow
  • Breeding Bigger Bovines
  • Growing Crops

📱 **VIRTUAL LAB**

☑ **ASSESSMENT**

📖 **eTEXT**

📱 **APP**

HANDS-ON LABS

uConnect To Care or Not to Care

uInvestigate
  • Is It All in the Genes?
  • Modeling Flowers
  • Behavior Cycles
  • Watching Roots Grow

uDemonstrate
Clean and Green

TOPIC
4

Go to PearsonRealize.com
to access your digital course.

VIDEO
• Environmental Engineer

INTERACTIVITY
• There's No Place Like Home
• An Ecological Mystery
• Factors Affecting Growth
• Energy Roles and Flows
• Living Things in an Ecosystem
• A Changing Ecosystem
• Cleaning an Oil Spill
• Cycles of Matter
• Earth's Recyclables

VIRTUAL LAB
• Chesapeake Bay Ecosystem Crisis

ASSESSMENT

eTEXT

APP

HANDS-ON LABS

иConnect Every Breath You Take

иInvestigate
• Elbow Room
• Observing Decomposition
• Following Water

иDemonstrate
Last Remains

Populations, Communities, and Ecosystems 232

The **Essential Question** How do living and nonliving things affect one another?

Quest KICKOFF To Cross or Not to Cross 234

MS-LS2-1, MS-LS2-2, MS-LS2-3, MS-LS2-4, MS-LS2-5

Go to PearsonRealize.com
to access your digital course.

▶ **VIDEO**
• Field Biologist

👆 **INTERACTIVITY**
• Symbiotic Relationships
• Life on a Reef
• Shared Interactions
• Succession in an Ecosystem
• A Butterfly Mystery
• Biodiversity in the Amazon
• Human Impacts on Biodiversity
• Maintaining Healthy Ecosystems
• Preventing Soil Erosion
• Walk This Way

📱 **VIRTUAL LAB**

✓ **ASSESSMENT**

📖 **eTEXT**

📱 **APP**

HANDS-ON LABS

uConnect How Communities Change

uInvestigate
• Competition and Predation
• Primary or Secondary
• Modeling Keystone Species
• Ecosystem Impacts

uDemonstrate
Changes in Ecosystems

Go to PearsonRealize.com to access your digital course.

▶ **VIDEO**
- Geophysicist

👆 **INTERACTIVITY**
- Distribution of Fossil Fuels
- Using Renewable Resources
- Biogas Farming
- Distribution of Minerals
- Distribution of Water Resources
- Wetland Restoration
- Water Worth

📱 **VIRTUAL LAB**

☑ **ASSESSMENT**

📖 **eTEXT**

📱 **APP**

HANDS-ON LABS

uConnect What's in a Piece of Coal?

uInvestigate
- Fossil Fuels
- The Power of Wind
- Cool Crystals
- An Artesian Well

uDemonstrate
To Drill or Not to Drill

Human Impacts on the Environment 334

Essential Question How does human activity impact Earth's systems?

Quest KICKOFF Trash Backlash 336

MS-ESS3-4

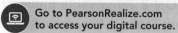
Go to PearsonRealize.com
to access your digital course.

▶ **VIDEO**
• Water Engineer

INTERACTIVITY
• Modern Life
• Human Population Growth
• Sources of Resources
• Damage From the Skies
• Sources and Solutions of Air Pollution
• Farming Lessons
• Ride the Light Rail
• Water Cycle Interrupted
• Mutation Mystery
• Wetland Restoration
• Research Water Pollution

VIRTUAL LAB

☑ **ASSESSMENT**

eTEXT

APP

HANDS-ON LABS

uConnect Finding a Solution for Your Pollution

uInvestigate
• Doubling Time
• It's All in the Air
• Mining Matters
• Getting Clean

uDemonstrate
Washing Away

TOPIC 8

Waves and Electromagnetic Radiation 388

 Go to PearsonRealize.com to access your digital course.

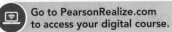 **VIDEO**
• Lighting Designer

INTERACTIVITY
• Modeling Waves
• Making Waves
• Describe the Properties of Waves
• Model Wave Interactions
• Use Models to Describe Wave Behavior
• Reflection, Transmission, and Absorption of Sound Waves
• Sound
• Doppler Effect
• Build an Electromagnetic Wave
• Models of Light
• Describe Electromagnetic Waves
• Describe the Behavior of Light
• Blinded by the Light
• Predict the Behavior of Light Rays

VIRTUAL LAB

ASSESSMENT

eTEXT

APP

HANDS-ON LABS

uConnect What Are Waves?

uInvestigate
• Waves and Their Characteristics
• Wave Behavior
• Understanding Sound
• Build a Wave
• Light Interacting with Matter

uDemonstrate
Making Waves

TOPIC 9 Electricity and Magnetism 450

Essential Question What factors affect the strength of electric and magnetic forces?

Quest KICKOFF Light as a Feather 452

MS-PS2-3, MS-PS2-5, MS-PS3-2

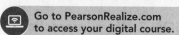

Go to PearsonRealize.com to access your digital course.

▶ **VIDEO**
• Electrical Engineer

☝ **INTERACTIVITY**
• Theremin
• Electric Currents
• Charged Interactions
• Interactions of Magnetic Fields
• Model Magnetic Forces
• Electricity and Magnetism
• Electromagnetism
• Electromagnetic Evidence
• Electric Motors
• Generators
• Electricity, Magnets, and Motion

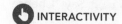

📱 **VIRTUAL LAB**

☑ **ASSESSMENT**

📖 **eTEXT**

📱 **APP**

HANDS-ON LABS

иConnect Magnetic Poles
иInvestigate
• Detecting Charges
• Detecting Fake Coins
• Electric Currents and Magnetism
• Electric, Magnetic Motion
иDemonstrate
Planetary Detective

TOPIC

10 Information Technologies 500

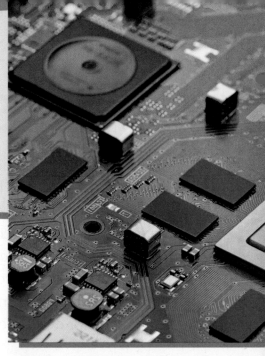

MS-PS4-3

Go to PearsonRealize.com to access your digital course.

▶ **VIDEO**
• Network Administrator

☞ **INTERACTIVITY**
• Electric Circuits
• How Can You Light the Lights?
• Analog and Digital Signals
• I've Got to Take This Call
• Digitized Images
• Film Cameras and Digital Cameras
• Technology and Communication
• Signal Reliability

▣ **VIRTUAL LAB**

☑ **ASSESSMENT**

▥ **eTEXT**

▢ **APP**

HANDS-ON LABS

Connect Continuous or Discrete?

Investigate
• Electric Current and Voltage
• Constructing a Simple Computer Circuit
• Let the Music Play

Demonstrate
Over and Out

Elevate your thinking!

Elevate Science takes science to a whole new level and lets you take ownership of your learning. Explore science in the world around you. Investigate how things work. Think critically and solve problems! *Elevate Science* helps you think like a scientist, so you're ready for a world of discoveries.

Explore Your World

Explore real-life scenarios with engaging Quests that dig into science topics around the world. You can:

- Solve real-world problems
- Apply skills and knowledge
- Communicate solutions

Make Connections

Elevate Science connects science to other subjects and shows you how to better understand the world through:

- Mathematics
- Reading and Writing
- Literacy

Quest KICKOFF

What do you think is causing Pleasant Pond to turn green?

In 2016, algal blooms turned bodies of water green and slimy in Florida, Utah, California, and 17 other states. These blooms put people and ecosystems in danger. Scientists, such as limnologists, are working to predict and prevent future algal blooms. In this problem-based Quest activity, you will investigate an algal bloom at a lake and determine its cause. In labs and digital activities, you will apply what you learn in each lesson to help you gather evidence to solve the mystery. With enough evidence, you will be able to identify what you believe is the cause of the algal bloom and present a solution in the Findings activity.

Math Toolbox

Graphing Population Changes

Ohio's Deer Population

Changes in a population over time, such as white-tailed deer in Ohio, can be displayed in a graph.

Deer Population Trends, 2000–2010

Year	Population (estimated)	Year	Population (estimated)
2000	525,000	2006	770,000
2001	560,000	2007	725,000
2002	620,000	2008	745,000
2003	670,000	2009	750,000
2004	715,000	2010	710,000
2005	720,000		

Relationships Use the data

| READING CHECK | **Determine Central ideas** |

What adaptations might the giraffe have that help it survive in its environment?

Academic Vocabulary

Relate the term *decomposer* to the verb *compose*. What does it mean to compose something?

Build Skills for the Future

- Master the Engineering Design Process
- Apply critical thinking and analytical skills
- Learn about STEM careers

Focus on Inquiry

Case studies put you in the shoes of a scientist to solve real-world mysteries using real data. You will be able to:

- Analyze Data
- Test a hypothesis
- Solve the Case

Case Study

MS-LS2-1

THE CASE OF THE DISAPPEARING

Cerulean Warbler

The cerulean warbler is a small, migratory songbird named for its blue color. Cerulean warblers breed in eastern North America during the spring and summer. The warblers spend the winter months in the Andes Mountains of Colombia, Venezuela, Ecuador, and Peru in northern part of South America.

Enter the Lab

Hands-on experiments and virtual labs help you test ideas and show what you know in performance-based assessments. Scaffolded labs include:

- STEM Labs
- Design Your Own
- Open-ended Labs

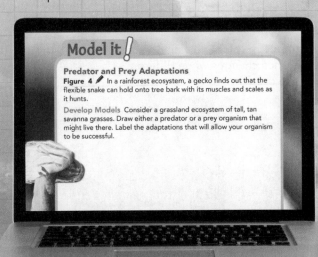

Model it

Predator and Prey Adaptations
Figure 4 In a rainforest ecosystem, a gecko finds out that the flexible snake can hold onto tree bark with its muscles and scales as it hunts.

Develop Models Consider a grassland ecosystem of tall, tan savanna grasses. Draw either a predator or a prey organism that might live there. Label the adaptations that will allow your organism to be successful.

HANDS-ON LAB

Investigate Observe how once-living matter is broken down into smaller components in the process of decomposition.

The Cell Systems

HANDS-ON LAB

uConnect Explore how an object's
appearance changes when different
tools are used.

NGSS PERFORMANCE EXPECTATIONS

MS-LS1-1 Conduct an investigation to
provide evidence that living things are made
of cells; either one cell or many different
numbers and types of cells.

MS-LS1-2 Develop and use a model to
describe the function of a cell as a whole and
ways parts of cells contribute to the function.

MS-LS1-3 Use argument supported by
evidence for how the body is a system of
interacting subsystems composed of groups
of cells.

MS-LS1-6 Construct a scientific explanation
based on evidence for the role of photosynthesis in the cycling of matter and flow of
energy into and out of organisms.

MS-LS1-7 Develop a model to describe
how food is rearranged through chemical
reactions forming new molecules that
support growth and/or release energy as this
matter moves through an organism.

MS-L2-3 Develop a model to describe the
cycling of matter and flow of energy among
living and nonliving parts of an ecosystem.

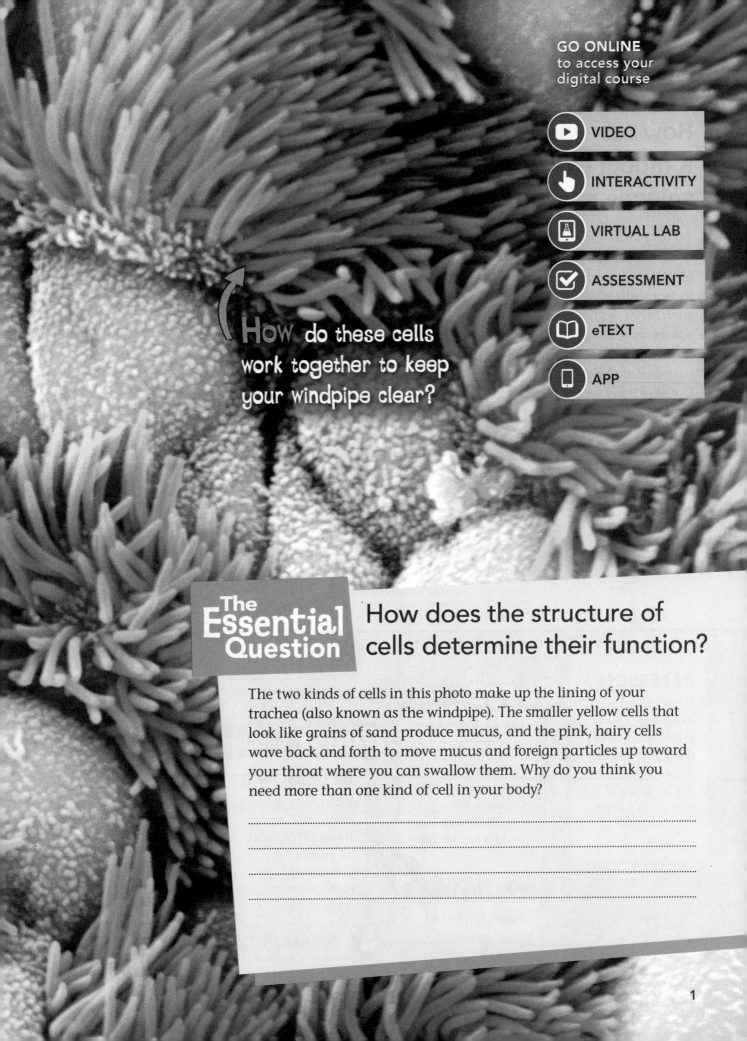

GO ONLINE
to access your
digital course

▶ VIDEO

👆 INTERACTIVITY

🎛 VIRTUAL LAB

☑ ASSESSMENT

📖 eTEXT

📱 APP

How do these cells work together to keep your windpipe clear?

The Essential Question

How does the structure of cells determine their function?

The two kinds of cells in this photo make up the lining of your trachea (also known as the windpipe). The smaller yellow cells that look like grains of sand produce mucus, and the pink, hairy cells wave back and forth to move mucus and foreign particles up toward your throat where you can swallow them. Why do you think you need more than one kind of cell in your body?

....

....

....

....

Quest KICKOFF

How can you design a model exhibit for a science museum?

Phenomenon Cells are often called "the building blocks of life." But that makes us think of wooden or plastic blocks that simply sit next to each other or stack neatly. In fact, cells have moving parts. And they interact with each other. To help people understand impossible-to-see processes such as these, museum staff—both scientists and engineers—try to engage and educate visitors with easy-to-see and hands-on models. In this problem-based Quest activity, you will plan and design a science exhibit on cells. By applying what you learn in each lesson, digital activity, and hands-on lab, you will gather information that will assist you in creating your exhibit. Then, in the Findings activity, you assemble, organize, and present your exhibit.

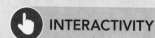
INTERACTIVITY

Cells on Display

MS-LS1-1 Conduct an investigation to provide evidence that living things are made of cells; either one cell or many different numbers and types of cells.
MS-LS1-2 Develop and use a model to describe the function of a cell as a whole and ways parts of cells contribute to the function.
MS-LS1-3 Use argument supported by evidence for how the body is a system of interacting subsystems composed of groups of cells.

NBC LEARN ▶ VIDEO

After watching the Quest Kickoff video on how museum models are planned and built, think about the qualities of a good science museum display. Record your thoughts in the graphic organizer.

Qualities of a Science Museum Display	
Good Qualities	**Bad Qualities**

IN LESSON 1
What will your exhibit teach the public about cell theory? Consider the challenges of explaining and modeling things that are hard to observe.

Quest CHECK-IN

IN LESSON 2
What do cells look like? How can you represent different cell parts? Design and build a model cell.

HANDS-ON LAB

Make a Cell Model

Quest CHECK-IN

IN LESSON 3
What cell parts are involved in cellular transport? Create an animation that shows how materials enter and leave the cell.

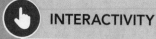
INTERACTIVITY

Put Your Cells in Motion

IN LESSON 4
Why is cell division important? Think about how to incorporate information about cell division into your exhibit.

The Body Fantastic exhibit at the Odyssium, a science museum in Edmonton, Alberta, Canada.

Quest CHECK-INS

IN LESSON 6

What factors affect cellular respiration? Research a disease and its impact on cell function. Consider how cell function affect the body at the atomic level.

HANDS-ON LAB

Accounting for Atoms

INTERACTIVITY

The Importance of Cells

IN LESSON 5

What is necessary for photosynthesis to take place? Explore the components necessary for photosynthesis.

Quest FINDINGS

Complete the Quest!

Determine the best way to present your museum exhibit. Then share your exhibit with museum guests. Evaluate and compare the different exhibits.

INTERACTIVITY

Reflect on Your Museum Exhibit

Structure and Function of Cells

Guiding Questions

- What evidence is there that cells make up all living things?
- How do cells determine the structure of living things?

Connections

Literacy Determine Central Ideas

Math Represent Quantitative Relationships

MS-LS1-1, MS-LS1-2

Vocabulary

cell
microscope
cell theory

Academic Vocabulary

distinguish

 VOCABULARY APP

Practice vocabulary on a mobile device.

Quest CONNECTION

Think about the different methods you can use to communicate information to people about something they cannot see.

Connect It!

🖊 **Circle the different structures you observe in the photograph.**

Cause and Effect With microscopes, we can see the cells inside us and around us. What reactions do you think people had when they first learned that they were surrounded by tiny living organisms?

....

....

....

Cells

What do a whale, a rose, bacteria, a ladybug, and you have in common? You are all living things, or organisms. All are made of **cells**, the basic unit of structure and function in living things. Cells form the parts of an organism and carry out its functions. The smallest organisms, such as the bacteria in **Figure 1,** are made of one cell, while the largest organisms may have trillions of cells.

Cell Structure The structure of an object refers to what it is made of and how its parts are put together. For example, the structure of a car depends on how materials such as plastic, metal, and rubber are arranged. The structure of a living thing is determined by the amazing variety of ways its cells are put together.

Cell Function A single cell has the same needs as an entire organism. For a cell to stay alive, it must perform biological functions. Those functions include obtaining energy, bringing in nutrients and water, and getting rid of wastes. Most organisms have bodies with many different cells that work together to help the organism to stay alive, grow, and reproduce. For example, cells in your circulatory system move blood around your body. This blood provides you with fresh oxygen and removes the waste product carbon dioxide. Cells in your heart pump blood to every part of you. Your body's cells work together to keep you alive.

✓ READING CHECK **Determine Central Ideas** How is a single cell similar to an elephant?

....

....

....

👆 **INTERACTIVITY**

Explore the function of different cell types in unicellular and multicellular organisms.

Cells Are Everywhere
Figure 1 Suppose you take a swab from someone's tongue. This is what you might see under the microscope. These cells are all bacteria of different shapes and sizes and with different functions.

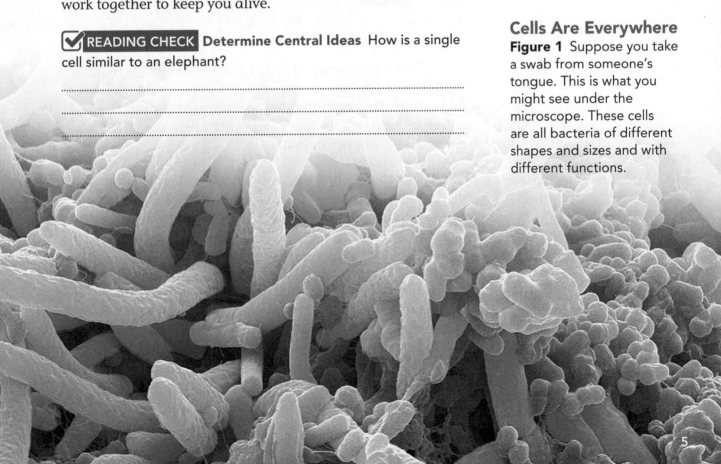

VIDEO

Learn more about the scientists who helped to develop the cell theory.

Cell Theory

It wasn't until the 1600s that scientists realized living organisms are made of cells. The invention of the **microscope**, an instrument that makes small objects look larger, made this discovery possible. The technology of the microscope led to new knowledge of how life is organized. As this technology improved over time, scientists were able to gather new information about cells and how they function. Scientists put all these discoveries together to develop a theory about cells.

Observing Cells
In the mid-1600s, English scientist Robert Hooke built his own microscopes to learn about nature. He made drawings of what he saw when he looked at the bark of cork oak trees (**Figure 2**). Hooke thought that the empty spaces he observed in the tree bark looked like tiny rooms, so he named them "cells." Tree bark, however, contains only dead cells.

Early Cell Observations
Figure 2 🖉 Hooke drew what he saw through his microscope in great detail. Draw a circle around one of Hooke's "cells."

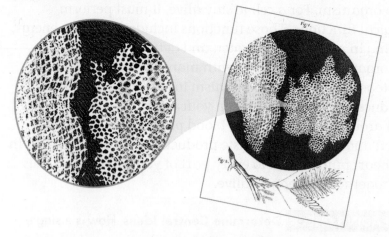

In 1674, Dutch businessman Anton van Leeuwenhoek (LAY von hook) was the first person to observe living cells through a microscope. He saw many tiny organisms swimming and hopping around in a drop of pond water. He named them "animalcules," or little animals.

By 1838, Matthias Schleiden, a scientist working with plants, noticed that all plants are made of cells. A year later, Theodor Schwann came to the conclusion that animals are made of animal cells. The timeline in **Figure 3** shows how the improvement of the microscope furthered the study of cells.

Before Schleiden and Schwann's suggestion that organisms are made up of cells, not much was known about the structure of organisms. These two scientists are credited with the development of the cell theory. Each scientist proposed a hypothesis (plural: hypotheses), a possible answer to a scientific question. Their hypotheses, supported through the observations and experiments of other scientists, led to a theory about cells and all living things.

Literacy Connection

Determine Central Ideas
How did early modern scientists learn about cells without performing experiments?

....

....

....

....

....

Microscopes & Cell Theory

Anton van Leeuwenhoek observes living microorganisms under the microscope.

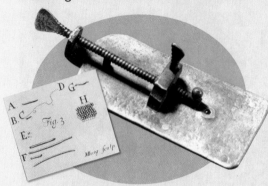

Robert Hooke studies bark and fossils with microscopes and coins the term "cells".

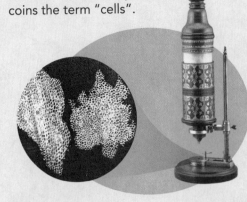

1650

1663

1674

1675

1825

Matthias Schleiden concludes that all plants are made of cells.

1838

1839

Theodor Schwann reaches the conclusion that all animals are made of cells.

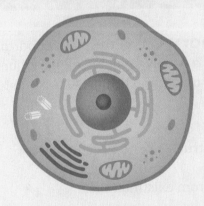

1850

1855

Rudolf Virchow proposes that cells are only made from other cells.

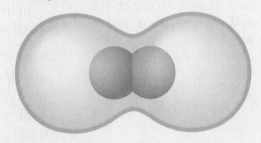

Scientists developed several types of electron microscopes that are 5,000 times more powerful than light microscopes.

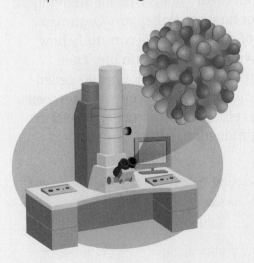

1875

1925

1930s

Magnifying the Power of Discovery

Figure 3 This timeline shows how technology and science advance together.

Infer Why didn't Robert Hooke recognize that cells are alive?

....

....

....

1950

7

Giant Cells

Figure 4 Bubble algae, or sea pearls, look like rubber balls. The bubble shown in this life-sized photo is a single cell! Some scientists consider eggs to be single cells as well. An ostrich egg is 15 cm long and a human egg is about the size of the period at the end of this sentence.

HANDS-ON LAB

Investigate Observe objects using a microscope.

Principles of Cell Theory One of the most important ideas in biology, **cell theory** is a widely accepted explanation of the relationship between cells and living things. According to this theory:

- All living things are made of cells.
- Cells are the basic units of structure and function in living things.
- All new cells are produced from existing cells.

Even though living things differ greatly from one another, they are all made of one or more cells. Cells are the basic unit of life. Most cells are tiny. But some, like those shown in **Figure 4**, can be surprisingly large. The cell theory holds true for all living things, no matter how big or how small they are. Organisms can be made of one cell or of many cells. We can study how one-celled organisms remove wastes to sustain life. Then we can use this information to understand how multi-celled organisms carry out the same task. And, because all new cells are produced from existing cells, scientists can study cells to learn about growth and reproduction.

☑ READING CHECK **Cite Textual Evidence** According to cell theory, how are bubble algae, or sea pearls, made?

....

....

Microscopes The cell theory could not have been developed without microscopes. The microscopes we use today have the same function as those used 200 years ago—to view tiny specimens. The advanced technology in the modern microscope, however, provides far greater detail for much closer observations. Light microscopes focus light through lenses to produce a magnified image. Electron microscopes are more complex. To create an image, electron microscopes use beams of electrons that scan the surface of the specimen. Look at the two different images of the same cells in **Figure 5**. Both types of microscopes do the same job in different ways, and both rely on two important properties—magnification and resolution.

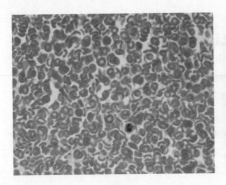 

Different Views

Figure 5 Red blood cells look very different when viewed using a light microscope (left) and an electron microscope (right).

Apply Concepts How could scientists today use current technologies to further support the cell theory?

....
....
....
....
....
....
....

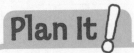

Plastic or Wood?

Two students in a science classroom are debating about whether the tables are made of wood or plastic. As the teacher passes by, she suggests, "Use cell theory to find the truth!"

Plan an Investigation Propose a scientific investigation to determine whether the tables are wooden or plastic. Include your hypothesis, what steps the students should take, and any materials they might need to carry out the procedure.

....
....
....
....
....
....
....
....

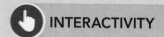
Explore how to use a microscope to observe specimens under different magnifications.

Magnification The compound light microscope you see in **Figure 6** magnifies an image using two lenses at once. One lens is fixed in the eyepiece. A second lens, called the objective, is located on the revolving nosepiece. A compound microscope usually has more than one objective lens. Each objective lens has a different magnifying power. By turning the nosepiece, you select the lens with the magnifying power you need. A glass rectangle called a slide holds a thin sample to be viewed. A light shines up and passes through the slide and the sample. The light then passes through the lens in the nosepiece and the eyepiece lens. Each lens magnifies the sample. Finally, the light reaches your eye and you get to see the sample in detail!

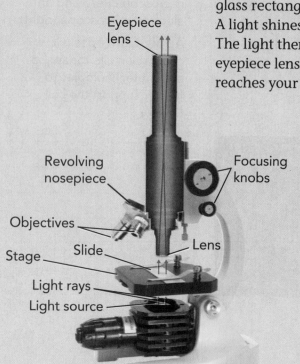

Eyepiece lens

Revolving nosepiece

Focusing knobs

Objectives

Slide

Stage

Lens

Light rays

Light source

Compound Light Microscope

Figure 6 This microscope has a 10× lens in the eyepiece. The revolving nosepiece holds three different objective lenses: 4×, 10×, and 40×.

Apply Which magnification would you select to look at a penny? Which would you select to look at a sample of pond water?

....

Academic Vocabulary

The verb *distinguish* has more than one meaning: "to manage to recognize something you can barely see" or "to point out a difference." What distinguishes technology from science?

....
....
....
....

Resolution A microscope image is useful when it helps you to see the details of an object clearly. The higher the resolution of an image, the better you can **distinguish** two separate structures that are close together, for example. Better resolution shows more details. In general, for light microscopes, resolution improves as magnification increases. Electron microscopes provide images with great resolution and high magnification. As you can see in **Figure 7**, greater resolution and higher magnification makes it relatively easy to study tiny objects.

☑ READING CHECK **Summarize Text** How does the resolution of a microscope help you to observe different structures of the cell?

....
....
....

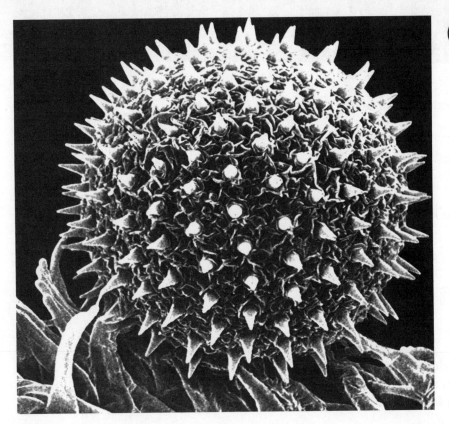

INTERACTIVITY

Investigate a sample to determine if it is living.

Extreme Close-Up

Figure 7 These plant pollen grains are magnified thousands of times.

Observe Look closely at the image. Describe some of the details you can distinguish at this very high resolution.

....

....

....

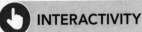

Math Toolbox

Getting the Right Magnification

The total magnification of the image from a microscope equals the magnifications of the two lenses multiplied together. If the objective lens magnifies the object 10 times, and the eyepiece lens also magnifies the object 10 times, the total magnification of the microscope is 10 x 10, or 100 times (expressed as "100×"). The image you see will be 100 times larger than the actual sample.

1. **Write an Expression** Calculate the total magnification of a microscope with eyepiece lens 10× and objective lens 4×.

....

2. **Evaluate Scale** If you use that microscope to view a human hair that is 0.1 mm across, how large will the hair appear in the image?

....

3. **Represent Quantitative Relationships** ✏ Draw a human hair at actual size, and at the size that it would appear in the the microscope image.

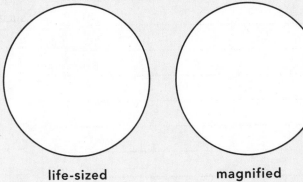

life-sized   magnified

MS-LS1-1, MS-LS1-2

1. Identify What are three functions of all cells?

....

....

....

2. Describe What are the three key points of cell theory?

....

....

....

....

3. Apply Concepts Scientists discover new kinds of life in the deep ocean every year. What does the cell theory tell them must be true about every new organism?

....

....

....

4. Construct Explanations Use evidence to explain how advancements in technology influenced cell theory.

....

....

....

5. Relate Structure and Function Compare and contrast the structure and function of a unicellular organism to that of a multicellular organism.

....

....

....

....

....

....

6. Use Models ✏ In the first circle, draw a small, simple picture of something that is big enough to see without magnification. In the second circle, draw it again under 5x magnification. If it is too big to fit in the circle, draw only the part of the object that fits inside.

7. Apply Scientific Reasoning Hooke and Van Leeuwenhoek made their discoveries around the same time. More than 150 years later, Schleiden, Schwann, and Virchow all made breakthroughs within a few years of each other. What are some possible reasons for the sudden development of the cell theory after such a long break?

....

....

....

....

....

MS-LS1-2

Viewing cells through a

"Thermal Lens"

This T-cell attacks cancer cells.

Cells have complex functions. Researchers have been trying to figure out how to target cells as a way to deliver drugs and medicines. The mid-infrared photothermal microscope is a new technology that lets scientists peer directly into living cells.

Until now, research into how cells use chemicals has been limited. Infrared imaging techniques could only use samples of dried tissue, a group of similar cells with a specific function. Because the water in live cells kept the infrared signals from passing all the way through the sample, scientists could not get detailed images. The new imaging technology works by shining a laser onto the surface of the tissue. This creates heat and a phenomenon called a 'thermal lens' effect, much like a mirage seen over a road on a hot day. The result is a detailed three-dimensional image of the cell.

Using the photothermal microscope will be essential for understanding how cancer treatment drugs get to and affect cancer cells. Now scientists can learn more about the chemistry of living systems and find better ways to treat many diseases.

New technologies like the mid-infrared photothermal microscope lets researchers see how various drug treatments affect cancer cells such as the one shown here on the left.

MY DISCOVERY

Investigate other conditions and diseases that could be better understood or treated using the new photothermal microscope.

Guiding Questions

- What are some special structures within a cell?
- How do the different parts of a cell help it function?
- How are animal cells different from plant cells?

Connection

Literacy Integrate with Visuals

MS-LS1-2

Vocabulary

organelle
cell wall
cell membrane
cytoplasm
nucleus
mitochondria
chloroplast
vacuole

Academic Vocabulary

structure
function

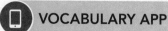
VOCABULARY APP

Practice vocabulary on a mobile device.

Quest CONNECTION

Think about how you can incorporate and represent the different cell structures in your exhibit.

Connect It !

✏️ **Circle three different structures inside this plant cell.**

Describe This plant cell has been sliced in half and you are looking into one of the halves. How would you describe the structure of the cell?

....

....

....

....

Parts of a Cell

Humans, mushrooms, and plants are all made of many parts. If you've ever taken apart a flower, a leaf, or a nut, you've seen that it also contains smaller parts. You could keep dividing the plant up into parts until you got all the way down to the individual cells. As you learned in your study of the cell theory, cells are the smallest functional units of living organisms. But within each cell there are working structures that help the cell function like an entire organism. Each **organelle** is a tiny cell structure that carries out a specific function within the cell. You can see that the cell in **Figure 1** may have many of the same organelles, but different organelles have a different **structure**. This is because each of the different organelles has a different **function**. Also, some organelles are found only in plant cells, some only in animal cells, and some are found in both plant and animal cells. Bacteria are unicellular organisms that do not contain as many different types of organelles as plant or animals cells. Together, the set of organelles in a cell keeps the cell functioning and contributing to the whole organism.

HANDS-ON LAB

Investigate the size of a single-celled organism.

Academic Vocabulary

Have you heard the terms *structure* and *function* used before? Using what you already know, identify two structures in your classroom and state their function.

....

....

....

Working as a Team

Figure 1 Many structures, or organelles, in this plant cell work together to help the cell survive. The cells, in turn, work together to help the plant survive and grow.

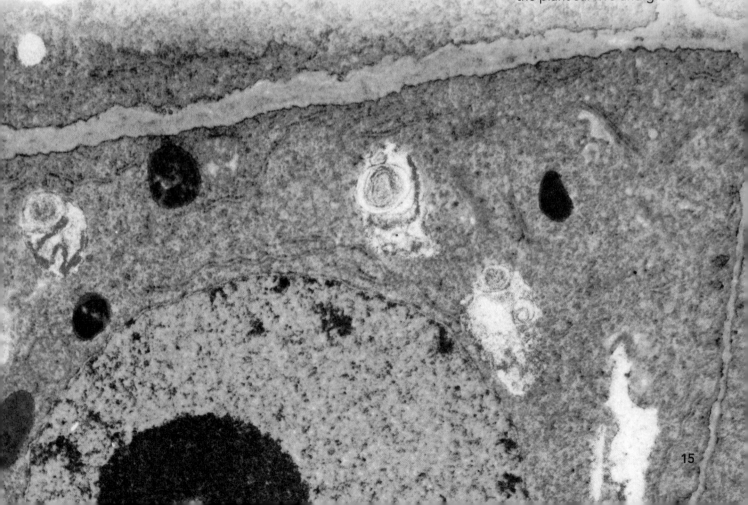

15

Plant and Animal Cell Differences

Figure 2 These illustrations show typical structures found in plant and animal cells. The functions of some organelles are also included.

1. **Develop Models** 🖊 Fill in the functions of the cell wall and the cell membrane in the boxes provided.

2. **Identify** 🖊 Draw a circle around the structure *inside* the plant cell that is not inside the animal cell.

3. **Use an Analogy** How would you describe the shape of the plant cell compared to the shape of the animal cell?

....

Plant Cell

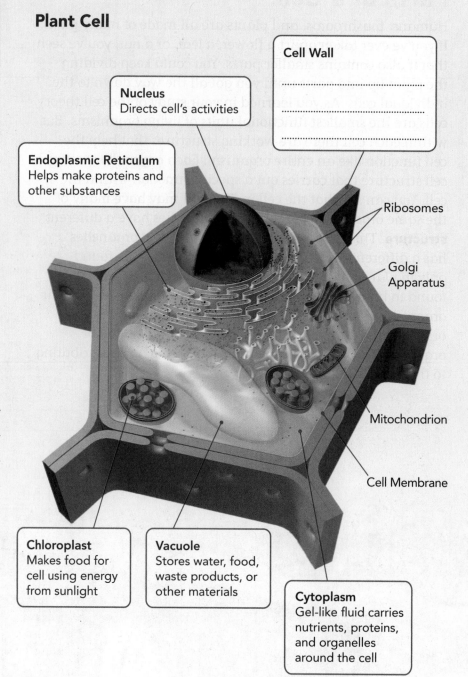

Cell Wall
....
....
....

Nucleus Directs cell's activities

Endoplasmic Reticulum Helps make proteins and other substances

Ribosomes

Golgi Apparatus

Mitochondrion

Cell Membrane

Chloroplast Makes food for cell using energy from sunlight

Vacuole Stores water, food, waste products, or other materials

Cytoplasm Gel-like fluid carries nutrients, proteins, and organelles around the cell

Cell Wall The rigid supporting layer that surrounds the cells of plants and some other organisms is the **cell wall**. While plants, protists, fungi, and some bacteria have cell walls, the cells of animals do not have cell walls. One function of the cell wall is to help protect and support the cell. The cell walls of plant cells are made mostly of a strong material called cellulose. The cell walls of fungi are made of chitin, the same material that forms the hard, outer skeleton of insects. Observe in **Figure 2** that there are small holes, or pores, in the plant cell wall. Pores allow materials such as water and oxygen to pass through the cell wall.

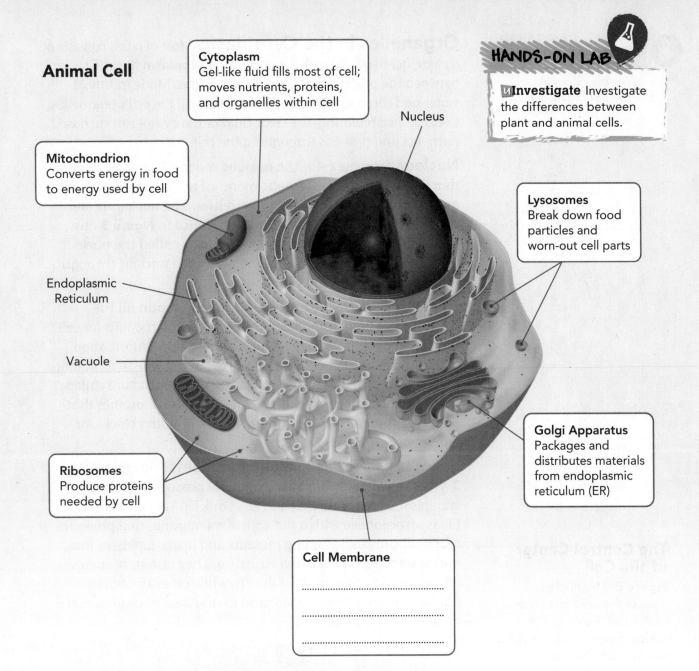

Animal Cell

Cytoplasm
Gel-like fluid fills most of cell; moves nutrients, proteins, and organelles within cell

Nucleus

Mitochondrion
Converts energy in food to energy used by cell

Lysosomes
Break down food particles and worn-out cell parts

Endoplasmic Reticulum

Lysosomes
Break down food particles and worn-out cell parts

Vacuole

Golgi Apparatus
Packages and distributes materials from endoplasmic reticulum (ER)

Ribosomes
Produce proteins needed by cell

Cell Membrane
....
....
....

HANDS-ON LAB

и**Investigate** Investigate the differences between plant and animal cells.

Cell Membrane The **cell membrane** is a thin, flexible barrier that surrounds a cell and controls which substances pass into and out of a cell. All cells have a cell membrane. In plant cells, the cell membrane is a fluid-like layer between the cell and the cell wall. As you can see in **Figure 2**, animal cells do not have a cell wall, so the cell membrane is the outermost layer. For all cells without a cell wall, the cell membrane forms the border between the cell and its environment. Think about how a dust mask allows you to breathe, but keeps harmful particles outside your body. One of the functions of the cell membrane is similar to that of a dust mask—it prevents harmful materials from entering the cell. Everything a cell needs, such as food particles, water, and oxygen, enters through the cell membrane. Waste products leave the same way.

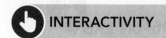

INTERACTIVITY

Explore the different functions of organelles.

The Control Center of the Cell

Figure 3 The nucleus acts as the control center of the cell. Folds of the endoplasmic reticulum (ER) surround the nucleus.

1. **Identify** 🖊 On the electron microscopy photo, label the nucleus, nuclear envelope, and ER.

2. **Apply Concepts** Why is the nucleus called the cell's "control center"?

....

....

....

....

....

....

....

Organelles in the Cytoplasm Most of a cell consists of a clear, gel-like fluid called cytoplasm. **Cytoplasm** fills the region between the cell membrane and the nucleus. Made mostly of water and some salt, the cytoplasm holds all the cell's organelles. Constantly circulating, the clear fluid of the cytoplasm carries nutrients and proteins throughout the cell.

Nucleus In some cells, the **nucleus** is a large oval organelle that contains the cell's genetic material in the form of DNA and controls many of the cell's activities. The nucleus is one of the largest of the cell's organelles. Notice in **Figure 3** that the nucleus is surrounded by a membrane called the nuclear envelope. Materials pass into and out of the nucleus through pores in the nuclear envelope.

Thin strands of genetic material called chromatin fill the nucleus. This genetic material contains the instructions for cell function. For example, chromatin helps to store information that will later make sure leaf cells grow and divide to form more leaf cells. Also in the nucleus is a dark, round structure called the nucleolus. The nucleolus produces dot-like ribosomes that produce proteins. Proteins are important building blocks for many parts of the body.

Endoplasmic Reticulum and Ribosomes In **Figure 3**, you can see a structure like a maze of passageways. The endoplasmic reticulum (en doh PLAZ mik rih TIK yuh lum), or ER, is an organelle with a network of membranes that processes many substances, including proteins and lipids. Lipids, or fats, are an important part of cell structure. They also store energy. Ribosomes dot some parts of the ER, while other ribosomes float in the cytoplasm. The ER and its attached ribosomes make proteins for use in the cell.

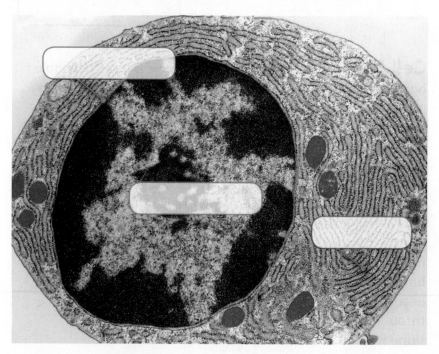

Golgi Apparatus As proteins leave the ER, they move to the Golgi apparatus, a structure that looks like flattened sacs and tubes. Considered the cell's warehouse, the Golgi apparatus receives proteins and other newly formed materials from the ER, packages them, and distributes them to other parts of the cell or to the outside of the cell.

Mitochondria Floating in the cytoplasm are rod-shaped structures. Look again at **Figure 2**. **Mitochondria** (myt oh KAHN dree uh; singular: mitochondrion) convert energy stored in food to energy the cell can use to live and function. They are the "powerhouses" of the cell.

Chloroplasts The **chloroplast** is an organelle in the cells of plants and some other organisms that captures energy from sunlight and changes it to an energy form that cells can use in making food. The function of the chloroplast is to make food, in the form of sugar, for the cell. Cells on the leaves of plants typically contain many green chloroplasts. Animal cells do not have chloroplasts because animals eat food instead of making their own food from sunlight.

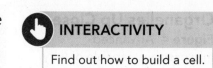

INTERACTIVITY

Find out how to build a cell.

✓ READING CHECK **Determine Conclusions** Suppose there is a drought and a plant cannot get enough water. What happens to the cytoplasm and the organelles in the plant cells?

....

....

Model It !

The Substance of Life

Earth is often called the water planet because water covers 75 percent of its surface. Cytoplasm, a jel-like fluid, is about 80 percent water. Cytoplasm has three important functions: it gives the cell form, it houses the other organelles in the cell, and it stores chemicals that the cell needs.

Develop Models What could you use to model cytoplasm? What would you use to represent each organelle? List the items you would use.

....

....

....

....

Organelles Up Close

Figure 4 Advanced microscopes capable of very high magnification allow scientists to see organelles in very fine detail. The actual images are not colored. All of these images have been colorized to help you see details.

1. Interpret Diagrams Fill in the blank under each image with the name of the organelle.

2. Classify For each organelle, fill in the small circle with A if it is found only in animal cells, P if it is found only in plant cells, or B if it is found in both kinds of cells.

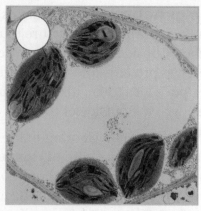

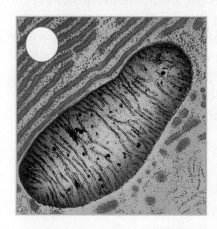

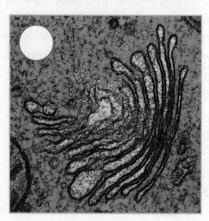

▶ **VIDEO**

Take a tour of the major structures of a cell.

Lysosomes You can think of lysosomes as a cell's recycling centers. Refer to the animal cell in **Figure 2**. Notice the small, round organelles? These are called lysosomes (LY suh sohmz). Lysosomes contain substances that break down large food particles into smaller ones. Lysosomes also break down old cell parts and release the materials so they can be used again.

Vacuoles Plant cells often have one or more large, water-filled sacs floating in the cytoplasm along with the other organelles shown in **Figure 4**. In some animals cells these sacs are much smaller. This structure is a **vacuole** (VAK yoo ohl), a sac-like organelle that stores water, food, or other materials needed by the cell. In addition, vacuoles store waste products until the wastes are removed. In some plants, vacuoles also perform the function of digestion that lysosomes perform in animal cells.

☑ READING CHECK **Integrate with Visuals** Use **Figure 2** to describe the main differences between lysosomes and vacuoles.

Cells Working Together

A unicellular organism must perform every function for the survival, growth, and reproduction of the organism. A bacterium is one example of a unicellular organism that performs all the functions that sustain life. When the only cell that makes up the bacterium dies, the entire organism dies. In a multicellular organism, there are many different types of cells with different functions, and they often look quite different from one another.

Specialized Cells Multicellular organisms are more complex than unicellular organisms. Because they are more complex, they are composed of different types of cells that perform different functions. One type of cell does one kind of job, while other types of cells do other jobs. For example, red blood cells are specialized to deliver oxygen to cells throughout your body. However, they would not travel through your body without the specialized cells of the heart, which send them to other cells needing oxygen. Just as specialized cells differ in function, they also differ in structure. **Figure 5** shows specialized cells from plants and animals. Each type of cell has a distinct shape. For example, a nerve cell has thin, thread-like extensions that reach toward other cells. These structures help nerve cells transmit information from one part of your body to another. The nerve cell's shape would not help a red blood cell fulfill its function.

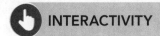

INTERACTIVITY

Investigate the functions of different specialized cells.

Literacy Connection

Integrate with Visuals
Which image in **Figure 5** shows you evidence that the cells are relaying information to each other? What does it remind you of?

....

....

....

....

Functions of Specialized Cells			
1. Animal cells that bend and squeeze easily through narrow spaces	**2.** Animal cells that relay information to other cells	**3.** Plant root cells that absorb water and minerals from the soil	**4.** Plant cells that make food

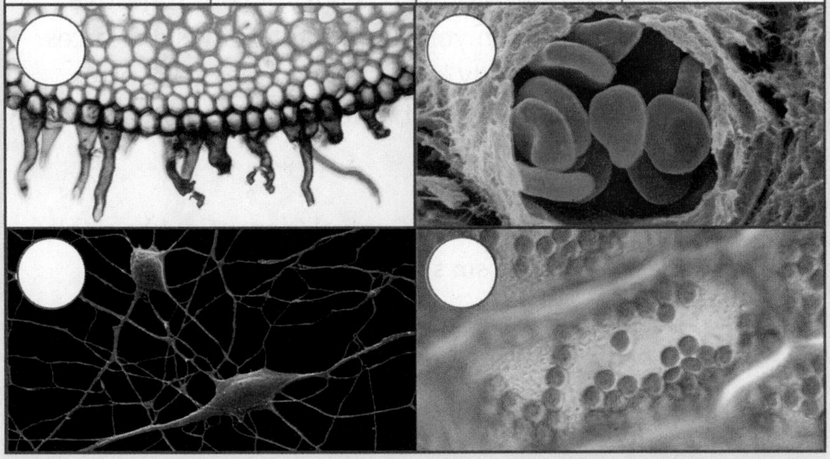

The Right Cell for the Job

Figure 5 Different cells carry out different functions.

1. **Draw Conclusions** ✏️ Match each function to a cell. Write the number of the function in the corresponding image.

2. **Consider Limitations** Recall the animal cell in **Figure 2**. Why is that model not a true representation of different types of animal cells?

....

....

....

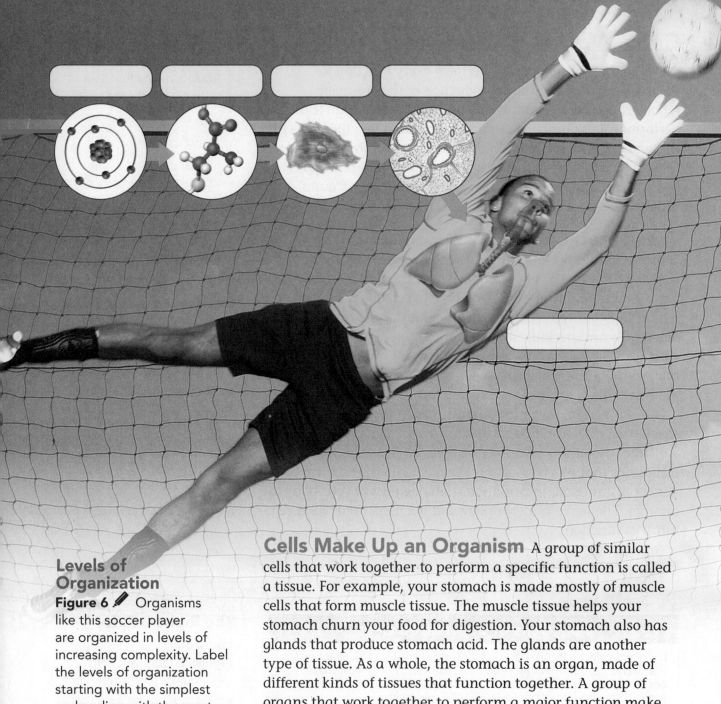

Levels of Organization

Figure 6 ✏ Organisms like this soccer player are organized in levels of increasing complexity. Label the levels of organization starting with the simplest and ending with the most complex. Then circle the organ system.

📓 **Make Meaning**
Consider a time when you worked on a team. In your science notebook, describe how members of your team had special skills that helped you to work together to solve a problem or overcome a challenge.

Cells Make Up an Organism A group of similar cells that work together to perform a specific function is called a tissue. For example, your stomach is made mostly of muscle cells that form muscle tissue. The muscle tissue helps your stomach churn your food for digestion. Your stomach also has glands that produce stomach acid. The glands are another type of tissue. As a whole, the stomach is an organ, made of different kinds of tissues that function together. A group of organs that work together to perform a major function make up an organ system. Your stomach is part of your digestive system, which breaks down your food into useful substances. **Figure 6** shows how the body builds up complex structures from atom to molecule to cell to tissue to organ to organ system.

✅ **READING CHECK** **Determine Central Ideas** Could a single part of a multicellular organism survive on its own? Explain.

....

....

....

MS-LS1-2

1. Interpret Photos What is the yellow structure, and what role does it play in a cell?

....

....

....

2. Explain Phenomena Why do cells have so many different organelles and structures?

....

....

....

....

3. Compare and Contrast What are the main differences between cell walls and cell membranes?

....

....

....

....

....

4. Apply Concepts Are there more tissues or more organs in your body? Explain your reasoning.

....

....

....

5. Determine Differences What are three differences between plant cells and animal cells?

....

....

....

....

Quest CHECK-IN

In this lesson, you learned about the different structures of plant and animal cells and how they function.

Develop Models How can a model help visitors to the exhibit better understand cell structures and their functions?

....

....

....

....

HANDS-ON LAB

Make a Cell Model

Go online for a downloadable worksheet of this lab. Design and build a model of a plant cell.

Guiding Question

- What is the primary role of the cell membrane in cell function?

Connections

Literacy Integrate with Visuals

Math Analyze Proportional Relationships

MS-LS1-2

Vocabulary

selectively
    permeable
diffusion
osmosis
endocytosis
exocytosis

Academic Vocabulary

maintain

 VOCABULARY APP

Practice vocabulary on a mobile device.

Quest CONNECTION

Consider how your exhibit can illustrate the processes that bring materials into the cell and take other materials out of the cell.

Connect It!

🖊 **Circle the area on the photo where you think the skunk spray odor will be strongest.**

Hypothesize How do you think it's possible for you to detect skunk spray from inside your house or from inside a moving car?

....

....

....

Moving Materials Into and Out of Cells

INTERACTIVITY

Discuss how objects move in and out of an area.

One evening you are out walking near your home. You spy something moving around on the ground. Look at **Figure 1**. Is it a black and white cat? As you move closer to get a better look, the animal fluffs up and raises its tail. It's a skunk! You hurriedly turn around and go in the other direction. You know that if you get sprayed by a skunk, people will be able to smell the stink from far away. Odor molecules will travel through the air to be inhaled by everyone around you.

Cells rely on the movement of surrounding gases, liquids, and particles to supply them with nutrients and materials. In order to live and function, cells must let certain materials enter and leave. Oxygen and water and particles of food must be able to move into a cell, while waste materials must move out. The same mechanism that lets materials in and out of a cell also lets those skunk spray molecules—the chemical makeup of odor—seep into the specialized cells in your nose that perceive smell.

Stinky Defense

Figure 1 When a skunk starts to feel threatened, you better watch out! Being sprayed is a miserable experience, and the smell travels fast through the air through the process of diffusion. Diffusion also carries useful molecules to the cells of every living organism.

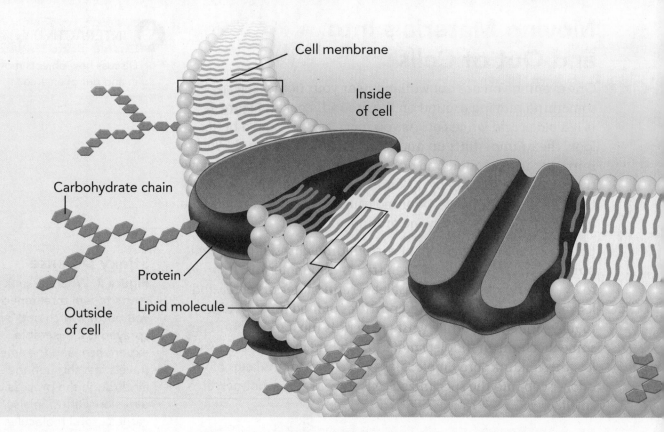

Cell membrane

Inside of cell

Carbohydrate chain

Protein

Lipid molecule

Outside of cell

A Selective Barrier

Figure 2 Carbohydrates, proteins, and lipids are important molecules that make up the structure of the cell membrane. They help move materials into and out of the cell through the cell membrane.

Use Models In what way is the cell membrane like a security guard?

....

....

....

....

....

....

....

Function of the Cell Membrane Every cell is surrounded by a cell membrane that lets substances in and out. This movement allows the cell to maintain homeostasis (a stable internal environment) and get all the chemicals needed to support life. The cell membrane is not rigid, but flexible. In **Figure 2**, you can see that different types of molecules play important roles in helping materials move across the cell membrane.

A permeable membrane allows liquids and gases to pass through it. Some materials move freely across the cell membrane. Others move less freely or not at all. The cell membrane is **selectively permeable**, which means some substances can cross the membrane, while others cannot. Substances that move into and out of a cell do so by means of one of two processes: passive transport or active transport.

Passive Transport

Moving materials across the cell membrane sometimes requires no energy. At other times, the cell has to use its own energy. Consider this analogy: If you pour a bucket of water down a slide, the water flows down easily with no effort on your part. Your role is passive. Now, suppose you have to push that same water back up the slide. You would have to use your own energy to move the water. The movement of dissolved materials across a cell membrane without using the cell's energy is called passive transport.

Diffusion Molecules are always moving. As they move, they bump into one another. Crowded, or concentrated, molecules collide more often. Collisions cause molecules to push away from one another. Over time, as molecules continue colliding and moving apart, they spread evenly throughout the space and become less concentrated. **Diffusion** (dih FYOO zhun) is the process by which molecules move from an area of higher concentration to an area of lower concentration. Consider a cell in the lining of your lungs. The cell is in contact with the air that you breathe. The air outside the cell has a higher concentration of oxygen. What happens? Oxygen moves easily into the cell. The diffusion of oxygen into the cell does not require the cell to use any of its energy. Diffusion is a form of passive transport. **Figure 3** shows how insects use spiracles instead of lungs to diffuse oxygen into their cells.

☑ READING CHECK **Write Informative Text** Why is it important for a cell membrane to be selectively permeable?

....

....

....

....

....

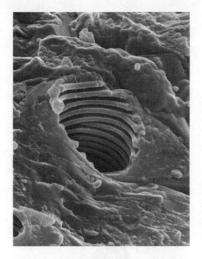

No Lungs Necessary
Figure 3 Spiracles are holes in the exoskeleton, or outer shell, of insects, that allow oxygen to enter and diffuse into the cells of the insect. Spiracles connect to air passages that lead into all parts of the insect.

Relate Function and Structure ✏ Circle the area where air can enter the insect's body.

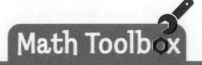
Math Toolbox

Breathing Without Lungs

The largest insects ever discovered were giant dragonflies that lived 300 million years ago. These dragonflies had a wingspan of 67 cm! Today the largest dragonfly has a wingspan of about 20 cm. The giant dragonflies existed at a time when the oxygen level in the atmosphere was about 35 percent, compared to 21 percent today. Use this information to answer the following questions.

1. **Analyze Proportional Relationships** What is the percentage size difference between the giant dragonfly and the modern dragonfly?

....

2. **Infer** Refer back to the spiracles in **Figure 3**. What do you think the relationship is between the spiracles, insect size, and air oxygen levels?

....

....

....

....

Model It

Raisins No More

Figure 4 Raisins are simply dried grapes—most of the water is removed. The cells of raisins are dead but still very high in sugar. If you soak raisins in water, the cells will take up water by the process of diffusion.

Develop Models ✏ Use the grape cell shown below as a reference. In the empty circles, first draw a raisin cell and then draw what the cell looks like after soaking the raisin in water overnight.

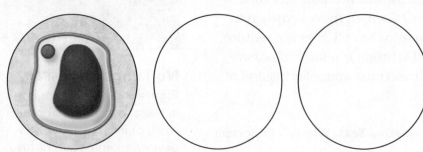

Osmosis Like oxygen, water passes easily into and out of a cell across the cell membrane. **Osmosis** is the diffusion of water molecules across a selectively permeable membrane. Many cellular processes depend on osmosis to bring them the water they need to function. Without enough water, most cells will die. Because it requires no energy from the cell, osmosis is a form of passive transport.

Osmosis can have important effects on cells and entire organisms. The soaked raisins in **Figure 4** are lighter in color and appear plumper due to a healthy flow of water both into and out of their cells. Under certain conditions, osmosis can cause water to move out of the cells more quickly than it moves in. When that happens, the cytoplasm shrinks and the cell membrane pulls away from the cell wall. If conditions do not change, the cells can die.

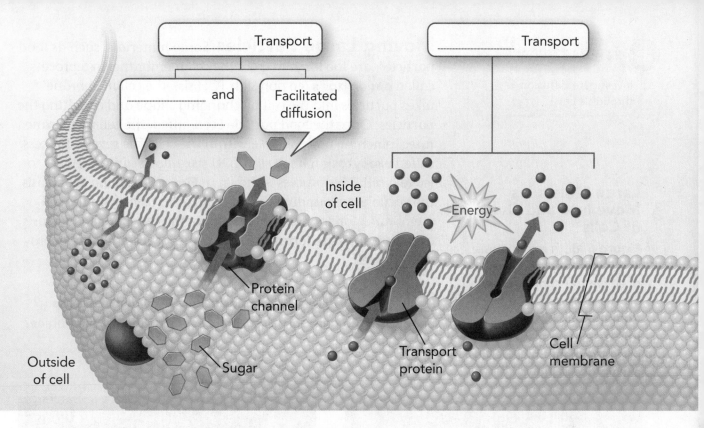

Facilitated diffusion

Transport

and

Transport

Inside of cell

Energy

Protein channel

Transport protein

Sugar

Cell membrane

Outside of cell

Facilitated Diffusion

Facilitated Diffusion Oxygen, carbon dioxide, and water freely diffuse across the cell membrane. Some molecules, such as sugar, cannot easily cross the cell membrane. In a process called facilitated diffusion, proteins in the cell membrane form channels through which the sugars can pass. The word *facilitate* means "to make easier." As shown in **Figure 5**, these proteins provide a pathway for the sugars to diffuse. The proteins function much the way downspouts guide water that flows from the roof of a house to the ground. Facilitated diffusion uses no cell energy and is a form of passive transport.

Active Transport

Active Transport During diffusion, molecules move randomly in all directions. A few molecules move by chance from areas of low concentration to areas of high concentration, but most molecules move toward areas of lower concentration. In many cases, cells need the concentration of a molecule inside the cell to be higher than the concentration outside the cell. In order to **maintain** this difference in the concentration of molecules, cells use active transport. Cells supply the energy to do this work—just as you would supply the energy to pedal your bike uphill. Active transport is the movement of materials across a cell membrane using cellular energy. As in facilitated diffusion, proteins within the cell membrane play a key role in active transport. Using the cell's energy, transport proteins "pick up" specific molecules passing by the cell and carry them across the membrane. Calcium, potassium, and sodium are some substances that are carried into and out of cells by active transport.

Crossing the Cell Membrane

Figure 5 Molecules move into and out of a cell by means of passive or active transport.

Interpret Diagrams ✏️
Complete the labels. Fill in the missing words.

Academic Vocabulary

To maintain means to keep in an existing state. When have you had to maintain something?

....

....

....

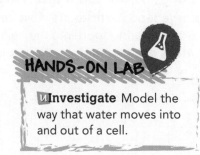

HANDS-ON LAB

и**Investigate** Model the way that water moves into and out of a cell.

29

Large Molecules Move Into and Out of Cells

Figure 6 Both endocytosis and exocytosis are forms of active transport. These processes require energy from the cell.

Interpret Diagrams
Fill in the blanks by labeling each process shown below.

Moving Large Particles

Some materials, such as food particles, are too large to cross the cell membrane. In a process called **endocytosis** (en doh sigh TOH sis), the cell membrane takes particles into the cell by changing shape and engulfing the particles. Once the food particle is engulfed, the cell membrane fuses, pinching off a vacuole within the cell. The reverse process, called **exocytosis** (ek soh sigh TOH sis), allows large particles to leave a cell. This process is shown in **Figure 6**. During exocytosis, the vacuole surrounding the food particles fuses with the cell membrane, forcing the contents out of the cell. Both endocytosis and exocytosis are forms of active transport that require energy from the cell.

READING CHECK **Draw Conclusions** Why don't cells use endocytosis to transport all substances across the cell membrane?

....

....

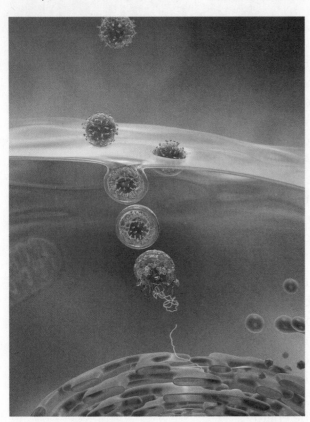

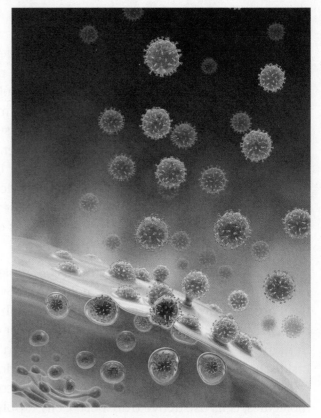

Large Molecules Entering the Cell
Large food particles are close to the cell. In order to bring food into the cell, the membrane wraps itself around a particle and draws it into the cytoplasm.

Large Molecules Leaving the Cell
Vacuoles carrying large particles of waste move toward the cell membrane. The vacuoles fuse with the membrane in order to push the waste particles out of the cell.

MS-LS1-2

1. Explain Phenomena Why do cells need to maintain homeostasis?

....

....

....

2. Determine Differences How is facilitated diffusion different from diffusion?

....

....

....

....

....

3. Construct Explanations What would happen to a cell placed in extremely salty water?

....

....

....

....

....

4. Compare and Contrast ✏ Fill in the Venn diagram below with the following terms: exocytosis, diffusion, endocytosis, osmosis

Into Cell   Out of Cell

5. Apply Scientific Reasoning How could disease-causing bacteria get inside a cell without damaging the cell membrane?

....

....

....

....

....

Quest CHECK-IN

In this lesson, you learned about the cell membrane and how cells take in the substances they need in order to function. You also learned how cells remove waste products through cellular processes.

Relate Structure and Function Consider which structures of the cell membrane function to help materials move into and out of the cell. How can you best model this information in your animation?

....

....

....

INTERACTIVITY

Put Your Cells in Motion

Go online to plan an animation that shows the ways materials enter and leave the cell. Then create your animation for the exhibit.

4 Cell Division

Guiding Questions

- What are the four functions of cell division?
- Which structures in a cell help it to reproduce?

Connections

Literacy Summarize Text

Math Analyze Quantitative Relationships

MS-LS1-2

Vocabulary

cell cycle
interphase
replication
mitosis
cytokinesis

Academic Vocabulary

sequence

 VOCABULARY APP

Practice vocabulary on a mobile device.

Quest CONNECTION

Think about the role that cell division plays in a healthy, functioning cell, and consider how you can incorporate this information into your exhibit.

Connect It !

✏️ **Using the x-ray image as a guide, place a circle on the biker to show where the broken bone is.**

Construct Explanations Where will the bike rider's body get new cells to repair the broken bones?

....

....

The Functions of Cell Division

The bike rider in **Figure 1** really took a tumble! Thankfully, he was wearing a helmet and only suffered a broken arm and a scraped elbow. His body will immediately begin to repair the bones, muscles, and skin. Where will his body get so many new cells to repair the damage? Recall that cells can only be produced by other cells. The new cells will come from older cells that divide in two, over and over again, until there are enough healthy cells to restore full function. Similarly, cell division can replace aging cells and those that die from disease.

Cell division also allows an organism to grow larger. A tiny fertilized egg cell splits into two, two into four, and so on, until a single cell becomes a multicellular organism. Another function of cell division is reproduction. Many single-celled organisms, such as yeasts, reproduce simply through cell division. Other organisms reproduce when cell division leads to the growth of new structures. For example, a strawberry plant can grow new stems and roots. These structures then break away from the parent plant and become a separate plant. Most organisms reproduce when specialized cells from two different parents combine, forming a new cell. This cell then undergoes many divisions and grows into a new organism.

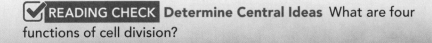

READING CHECK **Determine Central Ideas** What are four functions of cell division?

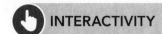
INTERACTIVITY

Reflect on where you think cell division is occurring in your body.

Reflect Think of a time when you injured yourself. In your Science Notebook, describe the appearance and feeling of the injury when it first happened and then how the injured area changed as your body healed.

Cell Division to the Rescue

Figure 1 As soon as you break a bone, your body sets to work repairing it. Many new cells are produced to clean up the mess and produce new tissues.

Phases of the Cell Cycle

Figure 2 The series of diagrams represents an entire cell cycle.

Interpret Diagrams What happens to the cell's genetic information during the cell cycle?

....

....

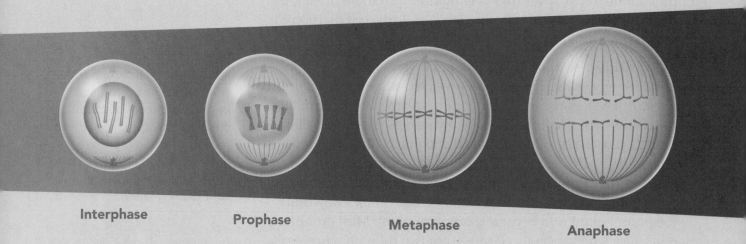

Interphase   Prophase   Metaphase   Anaphase

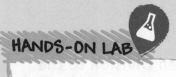

HANDS-ON LAB

Investigate Model how a cell divides.

Academic Vocabulary

Cell division follows a careful sequence of events. Describe the sequence of events on one of your typical school days.

....

....

....

....

....

The Cell Cycle

Most of the time, cells carry out their regular functions, but everything changes when a cell gets the signal to divide. At that point, the cell must accomplish several tasks to be ready for the big division into two "daughter cells." **Figure 2** summarizes those tasks.

First, the cell must grow in size and double its contents. This phase is called interphase. Next, the cell must divide up its contents so that the two daughter cells will have roughly equal contents. This second phase is called mitosis, and it has several stages.

Finally, the cell's cytoplasm physically divides in two in a phase called cytokinesis. The regular **sequence** of events in which the cell grows, prepares for division, and divides to form two daughter cells is known as the **cell cycle**. After the division is complete, each of the daughter cells begins the cycle again.

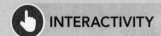
INTERACTIVITY

Explore the cell cycle and learn why living things go through the cell cycle.

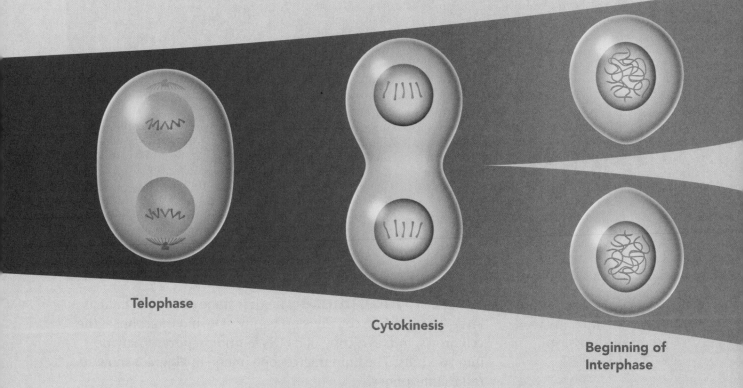

Telophase

Cytokinesis

Beginning of Interphase

Math Toolbox

Dividing Cells

Every cell division produces two daughter cells. You can see in the diagram that after one division, the single cell has become two cells.

🖊 Fill in the last two squares to show the results from two more cell divisions.

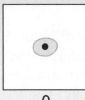

0
Divisions

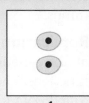

1
Division

2
Divisions

3
Divisions

1. **Analyze Quantitative Relationships** How does the number of cells increase with each new division of the cells?

....

2. **Calculate** How many cells would there be after five divisions?

....

3. **Hypothesize** Do you think all human cells divide at the same rate throughout life? Explain your reasoning.

....

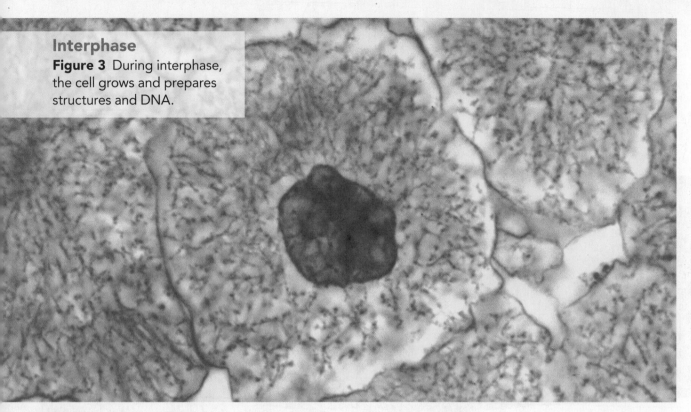

Interphase

Figure 3 During interphase, the cell grows and prepares structures and DNA.

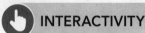
INTERACTIVITY

Discover how bones heal after they are broken.

VIDEO

Find out more about how cell division allows living things to grow.

Stage 1: Interphase

The first stage of the cell cycle is **interphase**, before cell division begins. During interphase, the cell grows, makes a copy of its DNA, and prepares to divide into two cells. The light microscope image in **Figure 3** shows a cell in interphase.

Growing Early in interphase, a cell grows to its full size and produces the organelles that both daughter cells will need. For example, plant cells make more chloroplasts. All kinds of cells make more ribosomes and mitochondria. Cells also make more enzymes, substances that speed up chemical reactions in living things.

Replication Recall that chromatin in the nucleus holds all the genetic information that a cell needs to carry out its functions. That information is in a complex chemical substance called DNA (deoxyribonucleic acid). In a process called **replication**, the cell makes a copy of the DNA in its nucleus before cell division. DNA replication results in the formation of threadlike structures called chromosomes. Each chromosome inside the nucleus of the cell contains two identical sets of DNA, called chromatids.

Preparing for Division Once the DNA has replicated, preparation for cell division begins. The cell produces structures that will help it to divide into two new cells. In animal cells, but not plant cells, a pair of centrioles is duplicated. The centrioles help later with dividing the DNA between the daughter cells. At the end of interphase, the cell is ready to divide.

Stage 2: Mitosis Once interphase ends, the second stage of the cell cycle begins. During **mitosis** (my TOH sis), the cell's nucleus divides into two new nuclei and one set of DNA is distributed into each daughter cell. Scientists divide mitosis into four parts, or phases: prophase, metaphase, anaphase, and telophase.

During prophase, DNA condenses into separate chromosomes. Recall that during replication, chromosomes formed. The two chromatids that make-up the chromosome are exact copies of identical DNA. The nuclear membrane that surrounds the DNA begins to break apart. In metaphase, the chromosomes line up along the center of the cell. The chromatids that will go to each daughter cell are lined up on that side of the cell. Next, in anaphase, fibers connected to the centrioles pull the chromatids apart into each side of the cell. The final phase of mitosis is telophase. During telophase, the chromatids are pulled to opposite ends of the cell. The nuclear membrane reforms around the DNA to create two new nuclei. Each nucleus contains a complete, identical copy of DNA. Test your knowledge of the phases of mitosis in **Figure 4**.

☑ READING CHECK **Summarize Text** What are the three things that a cell has to complete in order to be ready for cell division?

....

....

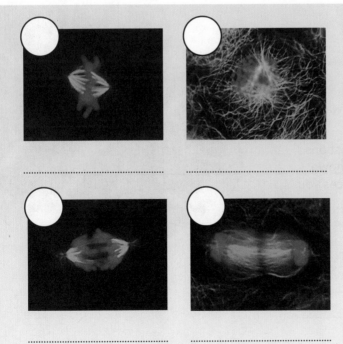

Scrambled Mitosis

Figure 4 These dividing cells have been marked with a dye that glows under fluorescent light. The dye makes it easy to see the DNA, stained blue, and fibers, stained green. The pictures are in the wrong order.

Identify ✏ Label each phase of mitosis in the space provided. Then, write the numbers 1 to 4 in the circles to show the correct order of the phases in mitosis.

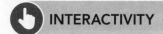
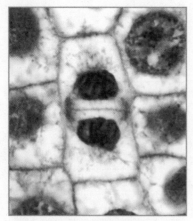

Plant Cytokinesis

Figure 5 One of these plant cells is dividing.

Identify 🖉 Find the cell that is dividing. Place an X on each daughter cell and trace the cell plate.

Stage 3: Cytokinesis

The final stage of the cell cycle is called **cytokinesis** (sy toh kih NEE sis). This stage completes the process of cell division. During cytokinesis, the cell's cytoplasm divides, distributing the organelles into each of the two new daughter cells. Cytokinesis usually starts at about the same time as telophase. When cytokinesis is complete, each daughter cell has the same number of chromosomes as the parent cell. Next, each cell enters interphase and the cell cycle begins again.

Cytokinesis in Animal Cells During cytokinesis in animal cells, the cell membrane squeezes together around the middle of the cell. The cytoplasm pinches into two cells. Each daughter cell gets about half of the organelles of the parent cell.

Cytokinesis in Plant Cells Cytokinesis is somewhat different in plant cells. A plant cell's rigid cell wall cannot squeeze together in the same way that a cell membrane can. Instead, a structure called a cell plate forms across the middle of the cell, as shown in **Figure 5**. The cell plate begins to form new cell membranes between the two daughter cells. New cell walls then form around the cell membranes.

☑ **READING CHECK** **Determine Conclusions** What would happen if cytokinesis did not occur?

....

....

Question It❗

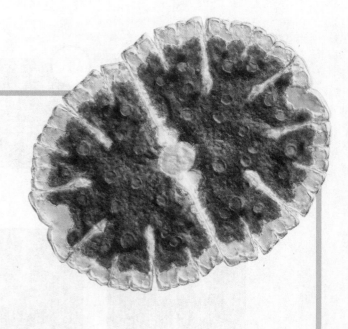

A Two-Celled Organism?

Two students examining a sample of lake water find an unusual-looking organism.

Develop Questions What kinds of questions would you have if you saw the organism shown here? List three questions and two resources you could use to help you to answer them.

....

....

....

....

☑ LESSON 4 Check

1. **Explain** Why is it important for the cells in your body to go through the cell cycle?

....

....

....

....

2. **Construct Explanations** How does a plant cell accomplish cytokinesis?

....

....

....

....

....

....

3. **Apply Concepts** When you look at cells under a microscope, how can you recognize cells that are dividing?

....

....

....

....

....

4. **Explain Phenomena** Why does the cell need to replicate its DNA during interphase?

....

....

....

....

5. **Draw Conclusions** If a single-celled organism is unable to undergo cell division, what will happen to that organism?

....

....

....

6. **Interpret Photos** What is happening during this part of the cell cycle?

....

....

....

7. **Form a Hypothesis** What would happen to a cell that didn't replicate its DNA before cell division?

....

....

....

8. **Develop Models** ✏ What happens during cytokinesis? Use the space below to sketch and label a diagram of an animal cell undergoing cytokinesis.

⑤ Photosynthesis

Guiding Questions

- How do plants and other organisms use photosynthesis to make food?
- What are the roles of light, carbon dioxide, water, and chlorophyll in photosynthesis?
- What role does photosynthesis play in cycling materials and energy through ecosystems?

Connections

Literacy Summarize Text

Math Represent Relationships

MS-LS1-6, MS-LS1-7, MS-LS2-3

Vocabulary

photosynthesis
autotroph
heterotroph
chlorophyll

Academic Vocabulary

equation

 VOCABULARY APP

Practice vocabulary on a mobile device.

Quest CONNECTION

Think about the factors that affect photosynthesis and what might be occurring in the greenhouse.

Connect It !

✎ **In the boxes, write the direct source of energy for each organism.**

Make an Inference Which of the organisms shown does not eat another organism for food?

....

Apply Scientific Reasoning What do you think would happen to each species if the water became too cloudy for sunlight to penetrate?

....

....

....

....

Living Things and Energy

Off the coast of Alaska, sea urchins graze on kelp beds under water. A sea otter begins the hunt for lunch. The otter will bring urchins up to the surface to feed on them.

Both the sea urchins and the otter in **Figure 1** use the food they eat to obtain energy. Every living thing needs energy. All the cells in every organism need energy to carry out their functions, such as making proteins and transporting substances into and out of the cell. Energy used by living things comes from their environment, similar to the raw materials cells use to function. Meat from the sea urchin provides the otter's cells with energy, while kelp provides energy for the cells of the sea urchin. Where does the energy in the kelp come from? Plants and certain other organisms, such as algae and some bacteria, obtain their energy in a different way. These organisms use the energy from sunlight to make their own food.

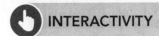

INTERACTIVITY

Identify what items are considered food.

Energy for Life
Figure 1 All living things need energy to survive.

kelp

otter

sea urchins

Summarize Text In your own words, summarize the main idea of the passage on this page.

....

....

....

....

....

....

....

....

Energy From the Sun

Cells capture energy in sunlight and use it to make food in a process called **photosynthesis.** The term *photosynthesis* comes from the Greek words *photos*, which means "light," and *syntithenai*, which means "putting together." Plants and other photosynthetic organisms link molecules together into useful forms using photosynthesis.

Nearly all living things obtain energy directly or indirectly from the sun's energy. This energy is captured from the sunlight during photosynthesis. In **Figure 2,** the leaf obtains energy directly from sunlight because plants use sunlight to make their own food during photosynthesis. When you eat an apple, you get energy from the sun that has been stored in the apple. You get the sun's energy indirectly from the energy that the apple tree gained through photosynthesis.

An Energy Chain

Figure 2 The energy of sunlight passes from one organism to another.

Explain Phenomena ✏ Draw arrows showing the flow of energy from the sun.

Making and Obtaining Food

Plants make their own food through the process of photosynthesis. **Autotrophs**, or producers, are able to create their own food in the form of glucose, an energy-giving sugar. Plants and algae, as well as some bacteria, are autotrophs. An organism that cannot make its own food, such as the sea urchin or otter, is a consumer, or a **heterotroph.** Many heterotrophs, like the fox in **Figure 3**, obtain food by eating other organisms. Some heterotrophs, such as fungi, absorb their food from other organisms.

✓ READING CHECK **Summarize Text** What is the difference between heterotrophs and autotrophs?

....

....

....

Reflect How is sunlight important in your life? In your science notebook, describe some of the positive and negative effects of sunlight.

Model It

Trace Energy to the Source

Figure 3 A fox catches and eats a rabbit that depends on plants for food.

Develop Models ✏ Draw a diagram that tracks how the sun's energy gets to the fox. In your diagram, label each organism as a heterotroph or an autotroph.

43

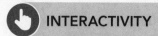
INTERACTIVITY

Describe the cycling of matter and energy that occurs during photosynthesis.

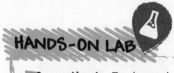

Investigate Explore why one stage of photosynthesis can take place in the dark.

Photosynthesis

Specific structures enable green plants and algae to use the sun's energy. Photosynthesis is a chemical reaction in plants that takes place mostly in chloroplasts, as shown in **Figure 4.** When plants use the sun's energy during photosynthesis to convert carbon dioxide and water into sugar, oxygen is a by-product. Because photosynthesis is a chemical reaction, several different factors affect the rate of chemical change. The availability of sunlight, water, and carbon dioxide are all factors required for photosynthesis.

Stage 1: Trapping the Sun's Energy

Chloroplasts, the green organelles in plant cells, use chlorophyll to absorb sunlight during the first stage of photosynthesis. The green color comes from pigments, which are colored chemical compounds that absorb light. The green photosynthetic pigment found in the chloroplasts of plants, algae, and some bacteria is **chlorophyll**.

Picture solar cells in a solar-powered calculator. Chlorophyll functions in a similar way. Solar cells take in light energy and convert it to a usable form so that it can power the calculator. Chlorophyll captures light energy that the chloroplast uses to create oxygen gas and sugar (**Figure 4**).

During Stage 1, sunlight splits water molecules in the chloroplasts into hydrogen and oxygen. The hydrogen combines with other atoms during Stage 2 and the oxygen is released into the environment as a waste product. A product is the substance formed after a reaction takes place. Some oxygen gas exits a leaf through openings on the leaf's underside. Almost all the oxygen in Earth's atmosphere is produced by living things through the process of photosynthesis.

Photosynthesis of Sugar

Figure 4 Photosynthesis takes place in the chloroplasts as shown in the diagram. Specialized structures in each chloroplast contain the chlorophyll.

Translate Information ✏
Add labels to the arrows in the diagram to indicate whether water, carbon dioxide, sugar, or oxygen is entering or leaving.

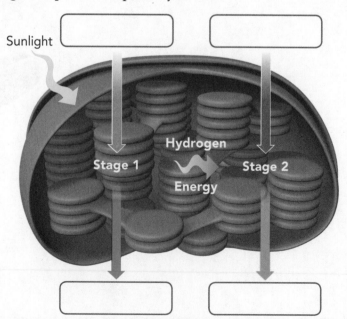

Sunlight

Stage 2: Making Food

Stage 2: Making Food In Stage 2 of photosynthesis, cells produce sugar. Sugars are carbohydrates that are useful for storing chemical energy or for building larger molecules. Glucose, which has the chemical formula $C_6H_{12}O_6$, is one of the most important sugars produced in photosynthesis. The energy stored in the chemical bonds of glucose allows cells to carry out vital functions.

The production of glucose is shown in **Figure 5.** Hydrogen (H) that came from splitting water molecules in Stage 1 is one reactant, the substance undergoing a change during a reaction. The other reactant is carbon dioxide (CO_2) from the air. Carbon dioxide enters the plant through the small openings on the underside of each leaf and moves into the chloroplasts. Powered by the energy captured in Stage 1, hydrogen and carbon dioxide undergo a series of reactions to produce glucose.

☑ READING CHECK Integrate with Visuals
🖉 On the picture, write R in the circles for the three raw materials, or reactants, of photosynthesis, and P in the circles of the two products.

Light energy

Oxygen

Carbon dioxide

Glucose

The Big Picture of Photosynthesis
Figure 5 This view of photosynthesis is from outside the plant. Plant cells also break down glucose to release the energy they need to grow and reproduce.

Water

45

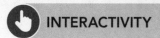
INTERACTIVITY

Determine what factors influence photosynthesis in modern and ancient plants.

Expressing Photosynthesis

The events of photosynthesis that lead to the production of glucose can be expressed as the following chemical **equation**:

$$\text{light energy} + 6\,CO_2 \text{ carbon dioxide} + 6\,H_2O \text{ water} \longrightarrow C_6H_{12}O_6 \text{ glucose} + 6\,O_2 \text{ oxygen}$$

Notice that six molecules of carbon dioxide and six molecules of water are in the equation to the left of the arrow. These compounds are raw materials, or reactants. One molecule of glucose and six molecules of oxygen are on the right side of the arrow. These compounds are products. An arrow, which means "yields," points from the raw materials to the products. Energy is not a raw material, but it is written on the left side of the equation to show that it is used in the reaction.

Plant cells use some of glucose produced in photosynthesis for food. The cells break down sugar molecules in a process called cellular respiration. The energy released from glucose can be used to carry out a plant's functions (**Figure 6**), such as growing and making seeds. Some glucose molecules are made into other compounds, such as cellulose for cell walls. Other glucose molecules are stored in the cells for later use. When you eat food from plants, such as potatoes or carrots, you are eating the plant's stored energy.

☑ READING CHECK **Determine Central Ideas** What happens to glucose and oxygen that is produced by plants during photosynthesis?

....

....

....

Academic Vocabulary

How is a chemical equation similar to a mathematical equation, and how do they model a natural phenomenon?

....

....

....

....

....

....

....

Photosynthesis is the Key

Figure 6 Green plants use the sugars produced in photosynthesis in many ways.

Interpret Diagrams 🖊 Label the leaves, roots, and seeds in the diagram. Then fill in the boxes with some of the ways plants use the products of photosynthesis.

Importance of Plant Cells

Plant cells were the first type of cells to be discovered with a microscope. Their cell walls appeared like small boxes. Because their cell walls are rigid, plant cells will not burst like a balloon filled with too much water. The ability to hold excess water is one reason that marsh plants are so important (**Figure 7**). During storms with heavy rainfall, such as hurricanes, marsh plants soak up water like a sponge. For this reason, marshland is considered a natural flood control.

Plants and algae that live in the water absorb about one sixth of all the sun's energy that falls on Earth. While you may not consider ocean plants when you hear the word "plant," they play a significant role in recycling oxygen on Earth. In fact, 85 percent of the oxygen in Earth's atmosphere—the air that we breathe—comes not from the trees around us, but from ocean plants.

Marsh Plants

Figure 7 Marshes, like the one pictured, are considered a natural flood control.

Apply Scientific Reasoning How do marshes control flooding?

....

....

....

Math Toolbox

All in the Balance

The photosynthesis equation states that 6 CO_2 and 6 H_2O molecules combine to form 1 $C_6H_{12}O_6$ molecule and 6 O_2 molecules. For every 6 carbon dioxide molecules, the reaction produces 1 glucose molecule.

1. **Represent Relationships** Write an equation using two variables to model how many glucose molecules are produced by 6 CO_2 molecules. Use x for the number of glucose molecules and y for the number of CO_2 molecules.

....

2. **Analyze Relationships** Calculate how many glucose molecules are produced by 6, 12, 18, and 24 CO_2 molecules. Plot these points on the graph. What is the relationship between the two variables?

....

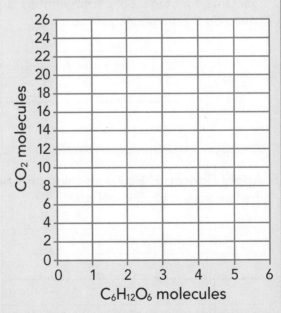

Proportion Relationship

y-axis: CO_2 molecules (0 to 26)
x-axis: $C_6H_{12}O_6$ molecules (0 to 6)

☑ LESSON 5 Check

MS-LS1-6, MS-LS1-7, MS-LS2-3

1. Analyze Systems Where does a plant get the energy necessary to drive the chemical reaction in photosynthesis?

....

....

....

2. Make Generalizations How do you know an organism is a heterotroph? Name three heterotrophs.

....

....

....

....

3. Construct Explanations Why are most plants green?

....

....

....

....

4. Identify What are the raw materials, or reactants, for Stage 2 of photosynthesis, and where do these materials come from?

....

....

....

....

5. Apply Concepts How does chlorophyll help the functioning of chloroplasts?

....

....

....

....

6. Predict The concentration of carbon dioxide in the atmosphere has been gradually increasing for many years. How might this increase affect photosynthesis?

....

....

....

....

7. Explain Phenomena What are the roles of light, carbon dioxide, and water in the production of food and oxygen?

....

....

....

....

....

....

....

....

8. Apply Scientific Reasoning Would you expect a plant to produce less oxygen on a sunny day or a cloudy day? Explain.

....

....

....

....

....

....

....

....

....

VIDEO

Examine how the different parts of an artificial leaf work.

AN ARTIFICIAL Leaf

How do you make photosynthesis more efficient? You engineer it! Professors Daniel Nocera and Pamela Silver from Harvard University show us how.

The Challenge: To create a more efficient way to cycle carbon through photosynthesis.

Plants carry out photosynthesis and remove carbon dioxide from the air. In the presence of light energy, they convert it into sugars for food or storage. This process helps cycle carbon through an ecosystem. However, photosynthesis isn't very efficient. Only 1 percent of the sunlight that hits a leaf is used during the process of photosynthesis.

Artificial photosynthesis uses the same process as plants, using solar energy, water, and carbon dioxide. The difference is including bioengineered bacteria. After water is split into oxygen and hydrogen, the bacteria feed on hydrogen and carbon dioxide and convert them into liquid fuels. This fuel-making process is ten times more efficient than photosynthesis.

An added bonus is that the process uses pure carbon dioxide from the air, producing no extra greenhouse gases. Researchers are currently exploring fuel production using "artificial leaves." This fuel may one day be an alternative to fossil fuels!

Light

This "artificial leaf" captures solar energy, producing fuel 10 times more efficiently than plant photosynthesis.

DESIGN CHALLENGE

Can you build a model of a tree that uses artificial leaves and artificial photosynthesis? Go to the Engineering Design Notebook to find out!

LESSON 6 Cellular Respiration

Guiding Questions

- How does cellular respiration break down food to produce energy and carbon dioxide?
- How can cells release energy without using oxygen?
- How are matter and energy conserved during cellular respiration?

Connections

Literacy Translate Information

Math Analyze Quantitative Relationships

MS-LS1-7

Vocabulary

cellular respiration
fermentation

Academic Vocabulary

produce
source

 VOCABULARY APP

Practice vocabulary on a mobile device.

Quest CONNECTION

Think about how understanding the process of cellular respiration can help explain what is occurring in the greenhouse.

Connect It!

✏️ **Draw arrows on Figure 1 to show the flow of energy from the food into the bikers, and then out into the environment as heat and motion.**

Construct a Graph ✏️ Sketch on the graph to show how the bikers' energy level may change over time as they start biking, stop for a snack, start biking again, and finish their ride.

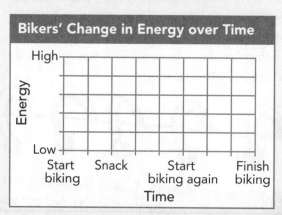

Bikers' Change in Energy over Time

Energy and Cellular Respiration

You and your friend have been biking all morning. The steepest part of the road is ahead. You'll need a lot of energy to get to the top! The food shown in **Figure 1** will provide some of that energy.

Plants and animals break down food into small, usable molecules, such as glucose. Energy stored in these molecules is released so the cell can carry out functions. **Cellular respiration** is the process in which oxygen and glucose undergo a complex series of chemical reactions inside cells, releasing energy. All living things need energy. Therefore, all living things carry out cellular respiration.

Using Energy A hot water heater stores hot water. To wash your hands, you turn on the faucet and draw out the needed hot water. Your body stores and uses energy in a similar way. When you eat, you add to your body's energy account by storing glucose, fat, and other substances. When cells need energy, they "draw it out" by breaking down the energy-rich compounds through cellular respiration.

Respiration People often use the word *respiration* when they mean *breathing*, the physical movement of air in and out of your lungs. In the study of the life sciences, however, respiration and breathing are not interchangeable. Breathing brings oxygen into your lungs. Cells use oxygen in cellular respiration. Exhaling removes the waste products of that process from your body.

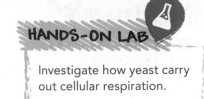

HANDS-ON LAB

Investigate how yeast carry out cellular respiration.

Food for Energy
Figure 1 Biking takes a lot of energy! Your body uses cellular respiration to get energy from the food you eat, such as trail mix.

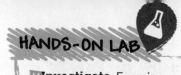
Cellular Respiration Process

Like photosynthesis, cellular respiration is a two-stage process. **Figure 2** shows both stages of cellular respiration. Stage 1 occurs in the cell's cytoplasm, where glucose is broken down into smaller molecules. Oxygen is not involved in this stage, and only a small amount of energy is released. Stage 2 occurs in a mitochondrion and uses oxygen. The smaller molecules produced in Stage 1 are broken down even more. Stage 2 releases a great deal of energy that the cell can use for all its activities.

Academic Vocabulary

How can the terms *produce* and *source* be used to describe a nation's economy?

....

....

....

....

Cellular Respiration Equation

The raw materials for cellular respiration are glucose and oxygen. Heterotrophs get glucose from consuming food. Autotrophs carry out photosynthesis to **produce** their own glucose. Air is the **source** of oxygen. The products of cellular respiration are carbon dioxide and water. Although respiration occurs in a series of complex steps, the overall process can be summarized in the equation:

$$\underset{\text{glucose}}{C_6H_{12}O_6} + \underset{\text{oxygen}}{6\,O_2} \longrightarrow \underset{\text{carbon dioxide}}{6\,CO_2} + \underset{\text{water}}{6\,H_2O} + \text{energy}$$

Releasing Energy

Figure 2 Cellular respiration takes place in two stages.

Integrate Information ✎ Fill in the missing terms in the spaces provided.

Stage 1 In the cytoplasm, ... is broken down into smaller molecules, releasing a small amount of ....

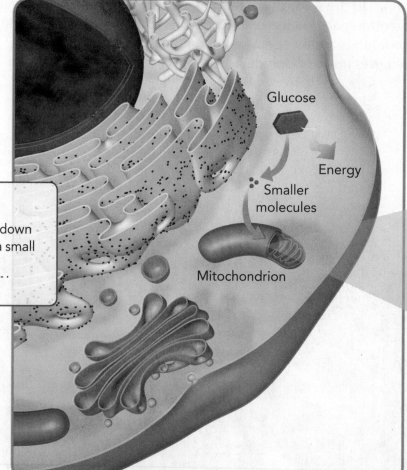

Glucose

Energy

Smaller molecules

Mitochondrion

Role of Mitochondria

It may be a small organelle, but the mitochondrion (plural, mitochondria) is well known as the cell's powerhouse. The function of the mitochondrion is to create large amounts of energy. In **Figure 2**, notice how the mitochondrion is structured. The folds inside the organelle create more surface area. Chemical reactions occur on these folds. Because of this increased surface area, many more chemical reactions can occur. In turn, more energy is created. Cells that need a great deal of energy may have thousands of mitochondria. If a cell needs more energy to survive, it can create more mitochondria.

Not all organisms use glucose and oxygen to carry out cellular respiration. Some organisms rely on a form of cellular respiration that uses fructose instead of glucose to create energy. For this chemical reaction, they do not need oxygen to break down the fructose.

✔️ READING CHECK **Determine Conclusions** Think about the job of the mitochondria. Which cells in your body would you expect to have the most mitochondria? Explain your reasoning.

....

....

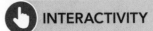

INTERACTIVITY

Explore what happens when the body breaks down glucose.

Literacy Connection

Translate Information ✏️
In **Figure 2**, circle the folds in the mitochondrion that increase the organelle's surface area.

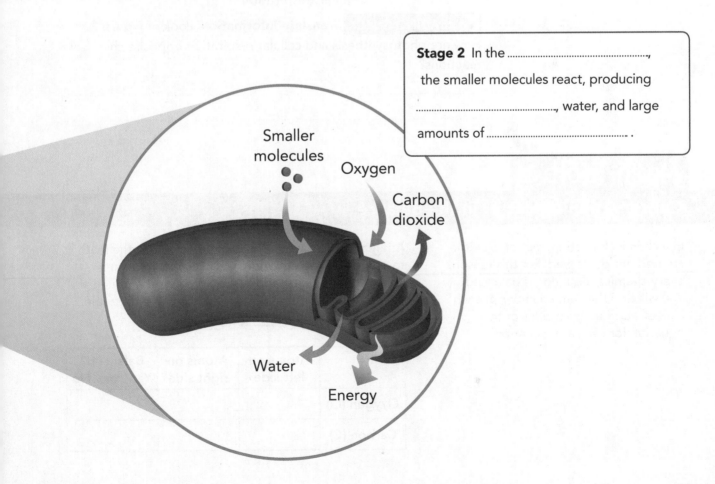

Stage 2 In the ...., the smaller molecules react, producing ...., water, and large amounts of ....

Smaller molecules

Oxygen

Carbon dioxide

Water

Energy

Related Processes

Figure 3 Carbon dioxide and oxygen cycle through cellular respiration and photosynthesis.

Relate Structure and Function ✎ Label the diagram to complete each of the processes.

Comparing Two Energy Processes

If you think the equation for cellular respiration is the opposite of the one for photosynthesis, you're right! Photosynthesis and cellular respiration can be thought of as opposite processes. The two processes form a cycle, keeping the levels of oxygen and carbon dioxide molecules relatively stable in Earth's atmosphere. As shown in **Figure 3**, living things cycle both gases repeatedly. The energy released through cellular respiration is used or lost as heat. Matter and energy is neither created or destroyed in this cycle.

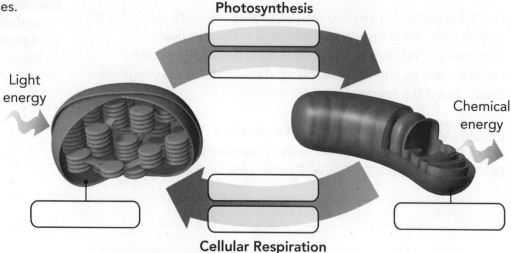

Photosynthesis

Light energy

Chemical energy

Cellular Respiration

✓ **READING CHECK** **Translate Information** Look at **Figure 3.** How are photosynthesis and cellular respiration opposite chemical reactions?

....

....

Math Toolbox

Conservation of Matter in the Balance

In a chemical reaction, matter is neither created nor destroyed. For this reason, every chemical equation is balanced. You will find the same number of each kind of atom on both sides of the equation for cellular respiration.

Analyze Quantitative Relationships ✎ Do the math to prove that the equation for cellular respiration is balanced for oxygen and carbon. Review the equation for cellular respiration below and complete the table.

$$C_6H_{12}O_6 + 6\,O_2 \longrightarrow 6\,CO_2 + 6\,H_2O$$

	Atoms on left side	Atoms on right side	Balanced? Yes or No
Oxygen (O)			
Carbon (C)			

Fermentation

Yeast, bacteria, and your own muscle cells can release energy from food without oxygen. The release of energy from food without using oxygen is called **fermentation**. Fermentation is very useful in environments with limited oxygen, such as in the intestines. However, fermentation releases much less energy than cellular respiration with oxygen.

Alcoholic Fermentation When you eat a slice of bread, you are eating a product of fermentation. Alcoholic fermentation takes place in live yeast cells—unicellular fungi—and in other single-celled organisms. This type of fermentation produces alcohol, carbon dioxide, and a small amount of energy. Bakers use these products of fermentation. Carbon dioxide creates gas pockets in bread dough. This causes the dough to rise.

Lactic Acid Fermentation Have you ever run as fast and hard as you could, like the sprinter in **Figure 4**? Although you started to breathe faster, your muscle cells used up oxygen faster than it could be replaced. Without enough oxygen, fermentation takes place. Your body supplies energy to your muscle cells by breaking down glucose without using oxygen. A compound called lactic acid is a product of fermentation in muscles. One popular misconception is that lactic acid "builds up in the muscles" and causes "muscle burn" as well as any lingering soreness. However, lactic acid actually fuels your muscles and goes away shortly after the workout. During exercise and intense physical activity, your body needs ATP—a substance the cells use as an energy source to meet high demands for energy. When the cells use ATP, it produces a proton. As protons pile up, the immediate area becomes acidic. The nerves near the muscles sense this acidity as muscle burn. But that sensation has nothing to do with lactic acid.

☑ READING CHECK **Determine Central Ideas** How does fermentation that causes dough to rise differ from fermentation in muscles?

....

....

standing

jogging

sprinting

Running Out of Oxygen
Figure 4 Your breathing and blood circulation can supply enough oxygen for cellular respiration when you exercise gently. During a sprint, your cells run low on oxygen and switch to lactic acid fermentation for energy.

Interpret Diagrams 🖊 For each activity, label the source of energy for the muscle cells. Is it oxygen or lactic acid?

55

Respiration and Fermentation in Bacteria

Figure 5 There are bacteria adapted to eat almost anything and live anywhere. Bacteria use every available process for getting energy from food.

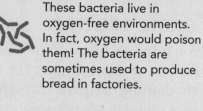

These bacteria live in oxygen-free environments. In fact, oxygen would poison them! The bacteria are sometimes used to produce bread in factories.

----

1. Synthesize Information
🖊 Read each image caption. In the circles provided, label each photo "LAF" for lactic acid fermentation, "AF" for alcoholic fermentation, or "CR" for cellular respiration.

2. Construct Arguments
Under each description, use evidence to justify how you classified the process.

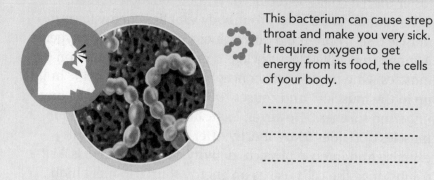

Yogurt is made from milk sugar by bacteria. The lactic acid produced in this reaction gives yogurt its sharp taste.

This bacterium can cause strep throat and make you very sick. It requires oxygen to get energy from its food, the cells of your body.

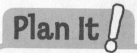

Plan It !

Long-Distance Space Travel

Many scientists and engineers are working toward the goal of sending astronauts to Mars. The trip is estimated to take about 9 months each way. It is very expensive to take enough oxygen to last the whole trip. The astronauts also need enough food, and there has to be a way to get rid of excess carbon dioxide created by their cellular respiration.

Implement a Solution Present a plan for the astronauts. Explain how growing food during space flight will help regulate carbon dioxide and oxygen levels. List the supplies the astronauts would need.

....

....

....

....

1. Identify Where does cellular respiration take place in the cell?

....

....

2. Define What are two examples of useful products made by fermentation?

....

....

3. Translate Information ✏ In the space below, sketch and label a diagram showing the relationship between photosynthesis and cellular respiration.

4. Construct Explanations Do plants and animals both use cellular respiration? Explain.

....

....

....

....

5. Apply Concepts How do heterotrophs get energy? Explain.

....

....

....

....

6. Explain Phenomena A classmate states that both energy and matter can be created during photosynthesis and cellular respiration. Is this true? Explain.

....

....

....

....

Quest CHECK-INS

In this lesson, you learned about the process of cellular respiration, in which the cells of an organism use sugar and oxygen to produce energy, carbon dioxide, and water.

Analyze Systems Why is cellular respiration necessary for the functioning of a healthy cell?

....

....

....

HANDS-ON LAB

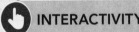

Accounting for Atoms

👆 **INTERACTIVITY**

The Importance of Cells

Go online to explore the importance of cell structure and healthy cell function.

Do the hands-on lab to investigate how matter is conserved in the processes of photosynthesis and cellular respiration.

MS-LS1-7

THE MIGHTY MOLE-RAT

What lives underground in a desert, is as small as a mouse, furless, and able to last for 18 minutes with no oxygen? It's the African naked mole-rat, of course!

To understand what's special about the naked mole-rat's feat, you have to understand a little about how animals process energy. The combination of chemical reactions through which an organism builds up or breaks down materials is called metabolism. Most mammals have a similar metabolism. They break down the sugar glucose and change it into energy their bodies can use. Most animals need oxygen to accomplish this. Without oxygen, animals cannot turn food into energy, so their cells will die. There are times when oxygen levels drop. At this point, their metabolism can usually switch to a form of fermentation. This is a temporary solution. As soon as oxygen levels are back up, the animals' metabolism will return to normal.

A Remarkable Animal

The naked mole-rat is the exception to the rule. Naked mole-rats survive because they use a different method to create energy. This method does not need oxygen or glucose.

When oxygen is plentiful, the Naked mole-rat's metabolism uses glucose to make energy. However, they live in cramped underground colonies with little oxygen. They thrive in these conditions, because they can switch their metabolism. Their blood contains more fructose than other mammals. When oxygen levels are low, they switch their metabolism to use fructose to make energy.

While closely related to mice, naked mole-rats are not so different from humans either. In the human liver, fructose gets changed into other molecules that our bodies use as energy. Think of what you could do if the entire human body could adapt to a fructose-based metabolism, similar to the mole-rats'! In addition to a fructose-based metabolism, the naked mole-rat has developed other remarkable traits, or characteristics. Read the table to learn more.

Use the chart to answer the questions.

1. **Infer** What is one advantage of the naked mole-rat's long life span?

2. **Predict** What do you think would happen if the naked mole-rats' burrows were exposed to extreme temperatures? Explain.

Remarkable Characteristics of the African Naked Mole-Rat

Characteristic	Explanation
Cold-blooded	Doesn't need to change body temperature because its habitat of underground burrows remains at a constant temperature
Cancer Resistant	Produces a "super sugar" that keeps cells from forming tumors
High Tolerance for Pain	Nerve receptors are less sensitive to pain
Long Life Span	Lives for up to 32 years

3. **Design Experiments** Scientists determined that naked mole-rats could undergo cellular respiration without oxygen. What sort of investigation do you think they used?

4. **Connect to Society** How might the naked mole-rat's ability to undergo cellular respiration without oxygen be applied to human medicine?

☑TOPIC 1 Review and Assess

1 Structure and Function of Cells

MS-LS1-1, MS-LS1-2

1. Which of the following is *not* stated in the cell theory?
   A. Cells are the basic unit of structure and function in all living things.
   B. Animal cells are generally more complex than plant cells.
   C. All living things are composed of cells.
   D. All cells are produced from other cells.

2. Reproduction is the function of both .... and organisms.

3. **Apply Concepts** How did technology impact the development of the cell theory?

....

....

....

....

2 Cell Structures

MS-LS1-2

4. Which of these structures breaks down sugars to provide energy for cell activities?
   A. vacuole   B. endoplasmic reticulum
   C. nucleus   D. mitochondrion

5. Name one structure found in an animal cell that is not found in a plant cell.

....

6. **Construct Explanations** Plant cells have a cell wall and cell membranes, but animal cells have only cell membranes. What is a possible reason for this difference?

....

....

....

3 Obtaining and Removing Materials

MS-LS1-2

7. A cell can bring in a large particle of food using the process of
   A. endocytosis.
   B. facilitated diffusion.
   C. osmosis.
   D. exocytosis.

8. Osmosis is the diffusion of ....

9. **Relate Structure and Function** Why is the cell membrane selectively permeable?

....

....

....

....

4 Cell Division

MS-LS1-2

10. What happens when a cell reproduces?
    A. Two similar daughter cells are created.
    B. One mother cell and one daughter cell are created.
    C. One mother and two similar daughter cells are created.
    D. One father and one mother cell are created.

11. **Construct Explanations** What is the purpose of cell division?

....

....

12. **Apply Concepts** At what point during the cell division process does one cell become two?

....

....

....

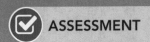
5 Photosynthesis

MS-LS1-6, MS-LS1-7, MS-L2-3

13. What provides the energy for the photosynthesis process?
- **A.** glucose
- **B.** sunlight
- **C.** carbon dioxide
- **D.** oxygen

14. Which organism is NOT a heterotroph?
- **A.** rabbit
- **B.** yeast
- **C.** tomato plant
- **D.** fungus

15. .... is a chemical that captures energy for photosynthesis.
- **A.** glucose
- **B.** lactic acid
- **C.** carbon dioxide
- **D.** chlorophyll

16. Describe What are two ways that plants use the carbohydrates produced in photosynthesis?

....

....

17. Draw Conclusions Explain why heterotrophs couldn't survive without autotrophs?

....

....

....

....

18. Determine Meaning. What is the relationship between the raw materials and the products in photosynthesis?

....

....

....

....

6 Cellular Respiration

MS-LS1-7

19. The second stage of cellular respiration takes place in the
- **A.** mitochondria.
- **B.** root nodules.
- **C.** chloroplast.
- **D.** atmosphere.

20. .... and .... can be considered opposite processes.
- **A.** fermentation, cellular respiration
- **B.** photosynthesis, nitrogen fixation
- **C.** evaporation, fermentation
- **D.** photosynthesis, cellular respiration

21. Apply Scientific Reasoning Why do you think plants hold on to a small amount of the oxygen produced during photosynthesis for use during cellular respiration?

$$C_6 H_{12} O_6 + 6 O_2 \longrightarrow 6 CO_2 + 6 H_2 O + \text{energy}$$
glucose + oxygen → carbon dioxide + water + energy

....

....

....

22. Determine Similarities How do the raw materials of photosynthesis compare to the products of cellular respiration?

....

....

....

....

....

....

MS-LS1-1, MS-LS1-2

Evidence-Based Assessment

Students in a life science class completed an investigation to see what cells really look like. They were given different samples of cells to observe under a microscope. Some cell samples came from animals, while others came from plants. The students were required to draw what they observed and label the organelles and other cell structures. The students found that not all cells look alike, but that they all share common features.

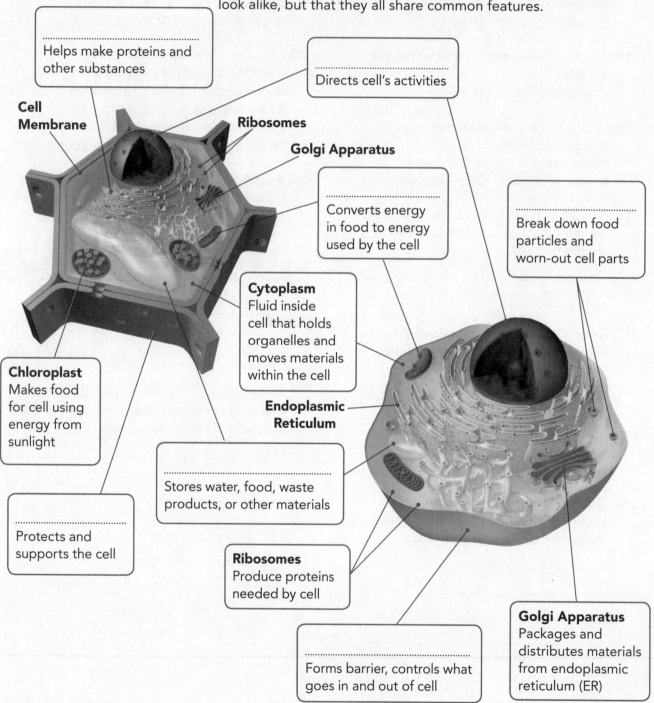

Helps make proteins and other substances

Directs cell's activities

Cell Membrane

Ribosomes

Golgi Apparatus

Converts energy in food to energy used by the cell

Break down food particles and worn-out cell parts

Cytoplasm
Fluid inside cell that holds organelles and moves materials within the cell

Endoplasmic Reticulum

Chloroplast
Makes food for cell using energy from sunlight

Stores water, food, waste products, or other materials

Protects and supports the cell

Ribosomes
Produce proteins needed by cell

Golgi Apparatus
Packages and distributes materials from endoplasmic reticulum (ER)

Forms barrier, controls what goes in and out of cell

1. **Develop Models** 🖊 Use each term to complete the missing labels in the diagrams of the animal cell and the plant cell: Cell Membrane, Cell Wall, Endoplasmic Reticulum, Lysosomes, Mitochondrion, Nucleus, and Vacuole. Then, circle the animal cell.

2. **Relate Structure and Function** What is the mitochondrion's function in the cell?
   A. store genetic information
   B. produce energy
   C. conduct photosynthesis
   D. synthesize proteins

3. **Determine Differences** Observe and compare the two types of cells. What are the features that make animal and plant cells different from each other?

   ....

   ....

   ....

   ....

4. **Distinguish Relationships** Why does the plant cell need both a cell wall and a cell membrane?

   ....

   ....

   ....

   ....

   ....

5. **Describe Patterns** Plant and animal cells, like these, undergo asexual reproduction. During the phase of the cell cycle known as interphase, a cell grows in size and doubles its contents. Why does the cell do this?

   ....

   ....

   ....

   ....

   ....

6. **Explain Phenomenon** Locate the chloroplast in the plant cell. What would happen to a plant if a disease somehow damaged the chloroplasts so that they could not function correctly? Explain.

   ....

   ....

   ....

   ....

   ....

   ....

   ....

   ....

Quest FINDINGS

Complete the Quest!

Phenomenon Take the time to evaluate your exhibit and add some finishing touches.

Optimize Performance Consider how you want to present your information. What sorts of changes could you make to your exhibit so that it is accessible to people with all sorts of information processing styles.

....

....

....

....

👆 **INTERACTIVITY**

Reflect on Your Museum Exhibit

MS-LS1-1

Design and Build a Microscope

Can you **design** and build your own **microscope** to **examine** small objects?

Background

Phenomenon Have you ever used a magnifying glass to read the date on a small coin more easily? What do you think would happen if you used a second magnifying glass to look through the first magnifying glass?

That's the basic idea behind a compound microscope—using one lens to look through a second lens to get a better view of small objects. This view often gives scientists the ability to understand how the structure of an organism helps with its function. In this activity, you will design and build your own microscope to examine small objects.

Materials

(per pair)

- book
- 2 hand lenses; one low-power and one high-power
- metric ruler
- cardboard tubes
- tape
- scissors
- rubber bands
- other common materials for building your microscope

Safety

Be sure to follow all safety guidelines provided by your teacher. The Safety Appendix of your textbook provides more details about the safety icons.

Herald Moth The wings on this Herald moth allow it to fly. Viewing the moth's wings up close could explain how the wing's structure enables the moth to fly.

Procedure

Part 1: Define the Problem

HANDS-ON LAB

ıDemonstrate Go online for a downloadable worksheet of this lab.

☐ **1.** Work with a partner to explore how lenses can be used to magnify objects. Using only your eyes, examine words in a book. Then use the high-power lens to examine the same words. Draw your observations in the space provided.

☐ **2.** Hold the high-power lens 5 to 6 cm above the words in the book. Keep the high-power lens about the same height above the words. Hold the low-power lens above the high power lens.

☐ **3.** Move the high-power lens up and down until the image is in focus and upside down. Once the image is in focus, experiment with raising and lowering both lenses. Your goal is to produce the highest magnification while keeping the image in clear focus.

☐ **4.** Measure and record the distance between the book and the high-power lens, and between the two lenses. Draw your observations through both lenses together.

Part 2: Design a Solution

☐ **5.** Using this information, design your own compound microscope. Think of creative ways to use the available materials. Your microscope should meet all the criteria shown.

☐ **6.** Sketch your design. Obtain your teacher's approval for your design. Then construct your microscope.

Part 3: Test and Evaluate Your Solution

☐ **7.** Test your microscope by examining printed words or a printed photograph. Then, examine other objects such as a leaf or onion skin. Record your observations. Did your microscope meet the criteria listed in Step 5?

☐ **8.** Examine microscopes made by other students. Based on your tests and your examination of other microscopes, identify ways you could improve your microscope.

Your microscope should:

- contain one low-power lens and one high-power lens
- allow the distance between the two lenses to be easily adjusted
- focus to produce a clear, enlarged, and upside-down image of the object

Part 1: Research and Investigate

Sketch what you observed:

eyes only   high-powered lens   both lenses

Measurements:

....

....

Part 2: Design and Build

Sketch of proposed microscope design:

Part 3: Evaluate and Redesign

Observations: Ideas to improve microscope:

....

....

....

....

....

....

....

Analyze and Interpret Data

1. **Evaluate Your Solution** When you used two lenses, how did moving the top lens up and down affect the image? What was the effect of moving the bottom lens up and down?

....

....

....

2. **Make Observations** Compare the images you observed using one lens with the image from two lenses. What do you think accounts for these differences?

....

....

....

3. **Apply Scientific Reasoning** How do you think that the compound microscope contributed to the development of the cell theory? Use evidence from your investigation.

....

....

....

4. **Use Models** How did modeling a microscope with the two lenses in Part 1 help you determine the design and function of your microscope? What types of limitations did you encounter as you designed and built your prototype?

....

....

....

....

5. **Engage in Argument** Imagine you are living in the year 1675. Write a letter to a scientific magazine that will convince scientists to use your new microscope rather than the single-lens variety used by Van Leeuwenhoek. Support your points with evidence from your investigation.

....

....

....

....

TOPIC
2

Human Body Systems

NGSS PERFORMANCE EXPECTATIONS

MS-LS1-3 Use argument supported by evidence for
how the body is a system of interacting subsystems
composed of groups of cells.

MS-LS1-8 Gather and synthesize information that
sensory receptors respond to stimuli by sending
messages to the brain for immediate behavior or
storage as memories.

HANDS-ON LAB

u**Connect** Use a model to explore
how the human body is organized.

How does this person maintain his balance on the slackline?

GO ONLINE
to access your digital course

▶ VIDEO

☝ INTERACTIVITY

🧪 VIRTUAL LAB

☑ ASSESSMENT

📖 eTEXT

📱 APP

The Essential Question

How do systems interact in the human body?

Walking on a slackline requires good balance and coordination. What different actions are taking place in the the body of the person on the slackline?

....

....

....

....

....

Quest KICKOFF

How do your body systems interact when you train for your favorite sport?

Phenomenon Nutritionists and physical trainers study human body systems and how they interact to help athletes maintain peak performance. In this Quest activity, you will develop a training plan for an athlete. In digital activities and labs, you will investigate how body systems interact to supply energy, manage materials, and control processes in order to develop a well-rounded plan. By applying what you have learned, you will produce a training and nutrition presentation for the athlete.

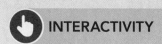

INTERACTIVITY

Peak Performance Plan

MS-LS1-3 Use argument supported by evidence for how the body is a system of interacting subsystems composed of groups of cells.

MS-LS1-8 Gather and synthesize information that sensory receptors respond to stimuli by sending messages to the brain for immediate behavior or storage as memories.

NBC LEARN ▶ VIDEO

After watching the video, which explores a typical day in the life of a teen athlete, think about the requirements of playing a physically demanding sport. List the following in order of importance, with the first being the most important: strength, endurance, flexibility.

1 ....

2 ....

3 ....

IN LESSON 1
What are the functions of body systems? Think about the body systems that are most important to the athlete's performance.

Quest CHECK-IN

IN LESSON 2
What skills, movements, and processes are involved in the athlete playing the sport? Identify the system interactions that are required by the sport.

INTERACTIVITY

Training Systems

Quest CHECK-IN

IN LESSON 3
What are the athlete's nutritional needs? Design a nutrition plan for your athlete that maximizes his or her performance.

INTERACTIVITY

Training Table

A training program designed for this athlete prepared his body to accomplish his personal goal of running through a desert.

Quest CHECK-IN

IN LESSON 4

What effect does the body's demand for more energy have on the circulatory and respiratory systems? Determine how different activities affect heart and respiration rates.

HANDS-ON LAB

Heart Beat, Health Beat

Quest CHECK-IN

IN LESSON 5

What is muscle memory? Consider how training the nervous system can improve the athlete's performance.

INTERACTIVITY

Why Practice Makes Perfect

Quest FINDINGS

Complete the Quest!

Organize your findings about system interactions and nutrition to develop a presentation for your athlete.

 INTERACTIVITY

Reflect on Peak Performance Plan

(1) Body Organization

Guiding Questions

- How do groups of cells form interacting subsystems in the body?
- How do the structures of specialized organs relate to their functions in the body?

Connections

Literacy Support Author's Claim

Math Identify Equivalent Expressions

MS-LS1-3

Vocabulary

tissue
organ
organ system

Academic Vocabulary

organized

 VOCABULARY APP

Practice vocabulary on a mobile device.

Quest CONNECTION

Consider the importance of cells and how they contribute to the proper functioning of organs and organ systems.

Connect It!

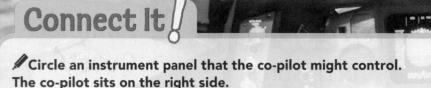

✏️ **Circle an instrument panel that the co-pilot might control. The co-pilot sits on the right side.**

Use an Analogy If an airplane has parts that function like a person's parts, then what part of the body does the pilot represent? Explain your reasoning.

....

....

....

Organization of the Body

Driving a car safely requires constant attention, even in the best road conditions. Controlling an airplane is even more demanding. For a plane to fly safely to its destination, all of its systems must be in good working order. The plane's steering system, brake system, lights, tires, and jet engines are all vital to a safe flight. The pilot and the co-pilot must be skilled at operating the instrument panels shown in **Figure 1**. They have to be able to steer the plane safely through all sorts of conditions. At times, they must fly the plane while relying on the instruments and screens in the cockpit, because they cannot see where the plane is headed.

Like an airplane, your body is **organized** into systems that work together. For example, your digestive and circulatory systems work together to help the cells in your body get the energy they need to function. When you walk up the stairs or ride a bike, your nervous, skeletal, and muscular systems are working together to move your body. Each system is made up of smaller parts, with the smallest being the cells that form the basic units of every living thing. Just as an airplane cannot function properly without its landing gear or its electrical system, the same is true for your body: You need each of your systems so that you can survive and grow.

✔ READING CHECK **Support Author's Claim** How is the human body similar to an airplane?

....

....

Academic Vocabulary

What steps do you take to get organized for an upcoming project?

....

....

....

....

All Systems Go

Figure 1 All systems in an airplane, including the pilot and co-pilot, must function properly in order to operate the plane.

Levels of Organization

The smooth functioning of your body depends on its organization. Recall that the levels of organization in the human body are cells, tissues, organs, and organ systems. All tissues are made up of cells. Organs are made of different kinds of tissues. And organ systems are made from organs that work together to perform bodily functions.

Cells and Tissues You are alive because specialized cells are performing their functions throughout your body. When similar cells that perform the same function are grouped together they form a **tissue.** Muscle tissue, for example, contracts, or shortens, to make parts of your body move. Nerve tissue carries electrical signals from the brain all over the body and back again. Connective tissue, such as bone and fat, provides support for your body and attaches all of its parts together. Skin, the largest organ in the human body, has epithelial (ep uh THEE lee ul) tissue that protects your insides from damage. Epithelial tissue covers the inner and outer surfaces of your body.

Math Toolbox

Counting Cells in the Body

Scientists and mathematicians have wondered about the number of cells in the human body for centuries. Estimates of the number of cells have ranged from 100 billion to 1 quadrillion, or a 1 followed by 15 zeros! It's easier to write one quadrillion using exponents: 1×10^{15} where the exponent 15 is the number of zeros.

A team of European scientists recently completed a new estimate of the human cells in an average person. Their estimate is about 37 trillion cells per person.

Name	Number	Written with Power of Ten Exponent
million	1,000,000	1×10^6
billion	1,000,000,000	1×10^9
trillion	1,000,000,000,000	1×10^{12}
quadrillion	1,000,000,000,000,000	1×10^{15}

1. **Identify Equivalent Expressions** How do you write 37 trillion as a number and using the power of ten exponent?

....

2. **Analyze Quantitative Relationships** How does the new European estimate compare to the smallest and largest estimates of other research groups?

....

....

Organs and Systems

Organs and Systems Your kidneys, heart, brain, and skin are all organs. An **organ** is a body structure composed of different kinds of tissues that work together. Each organ has a specific function in the body. Because its structure is more complex, the job of an organ is usually more complex than that of a tissue. For example, kidneys remove waste from your blood and form urine. Each kidney contains muscle, connective, and epithelial tissues. In addition, nervous tissue connects to the kidney and helps to control its function. Look at **Figure 2** to see where the different kinds of tissue are found in the kidney. Each tissue contributes in a different way to the kidney's job of filtering blood.

Every organ is part of an **organ system**, which is a group of organs that work together, performing major functions. For example, your kidneys are part of your excretory system. The excretory system also includes the skin, lungs, and liver.

✓ **READING CHECK Summarize Text** What type of cells work together to make a tissue?

....

....

Many Tissues Make an Organ

Figure 2 Kidneys filter blood to remove waste and excess water.

Explain Phenomena What might happen to a kidney if the muscle tissue does not function properly?

....

....

....

....

Epithelial tissue in the renal cortex gives the kidney structure and protects the nephrons that filter the blood.

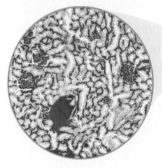

Nerve cells help the kidney pump and filter blood.

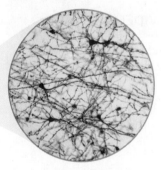

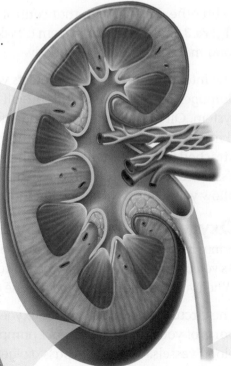

Renal capsule covering connective and fat tissues also protects the kidney.

Muscle cells in the ureter drain urine to the bladder.

75

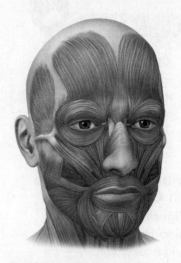

Make a Face

Figure 3 A multitude of facial muscles allows for a variety of expressions.

Interpret Diagrams
✏ Draw an X on the muscles involved in blinking your eyes.

▶ VIDEO

Find out how your body is like an orchestra.

Human Organ Systems

Eleven major organ systems keep the human body running smoothly. All of the systems work together to support proper functioning.

Control Systems To function properly, each part of your body must be able to communicate with other parts of your body. Your body communicates using the nervous system, which is made up of the brain, spinal cord, and nerves. The nervous system sends information through nerve cells to control your actions.

Many body functions are controlled through the endocrine system, a collection of glands that produces important chemicals. The chemicals in turn affect your energy level, body temperature, digestion, and even your moods!

Structural Systems Three organ systems work to shape, move, and protect your body. The skeletal system includes your bones and connective tissues. The main functions of the skeletal system support your body, protect your organs, make blood cells, and store minerals. Connective tissues cushion the bones and attach bones to muscles.

The muscular system includes 650 muscles that control your movements, help you to stand up straight, and allow you to breathe. The muscles that control your face are shown in **Figure 3**. The muscular system also keeps your blood and your food moving through your body.

The integumentary system protects your body from outside damage. Skin, hair, and nails are all parts of the integumentary system. Oil and sweat glands under the skin help to keep your skin waterproof and your temperature comfortable. Your skin is attached to muscles, which are anchored to bones by connective tissue. Together, these three systems provide your shape and allow you to move your body in many ways.

Oxygen and Transport Systems The respiratory system brings in oxygen and moves out carbon dioxide by way of the lungs. As you breathe in fresh air, oxygen diffuses into the red blood cells. When you breathe out, carbon dioxide diffuses back into the air.

The circulatory system carries oxygen-rich blood to all the parts of your body. Your heart pumps the blood through your blood vessels. Blood cells pass oxygen to your cells and pick up carbon dioxide. Your veins then bring the blood back to your heart and lungs. The circulatory system also transports nutrients, wastes, and disease-fighting cells all over your body through your bloodstream.

Food and Waste Processing Systems

Food you put into your mouth begins a journey through your digestive system. Your esophagus squeezes the food down into the stomach, where the food is crushed and broken down by acids. Next, the food travels into the intestines. Useful substances pass through the intestinal walls into the blood. The liver and pancreas produce substances that help to break down food. So do trillions of bacteria that live in your intestines. Some parts of the food cannot be digested. Those parts pass out of your body as waste. You can think of the digestive system as a long tube that runs through your body. Food passes through the tube and back out into the world without ever entering the tissues of your body.

The excretory system gets rid of waste products and toxic substances in your body. Kidneys produce urine, sweat glands in your skin make sweat, and lungs release wastes from the body into the air. Meanwhile, the liver breaks down toxic chemicals into substances that the kidneys can pull out of your blood.

☑ READING CHECK **Determine Conclusions** What would happen if your organ systems stopped functioning properly?

....

....

Literacy Connection

Support Author's Claim
Is it true that the human body can make its own chemicals? Cite evidence from the text.

....

....

....

....

Model It!

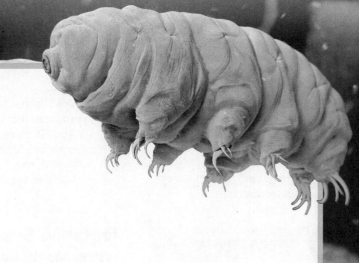

What? No Bones?

Figure 4 Most of the known animals on Earth are invertebrates. These organisms lack the backbone found in humans, birds, reptiles, and other vertebrates.

Develop Models ✎ Choose a kind of invertebrate— snail, insect, worm, octopus, water bear (shown here), and spider are just a few. Consider how an animal maintains its structure with no bones. Then sketch a diagram to explain how your animal moves with no bones connected to its muscles.

Organ Systems in the Human Body

Figure 5 The structures of different body systems all work together to allow you to grow, obtain energy, move, stay healthy, and reproduce.

Analyze Systems ✏ Use the key on the right to label each body system. There may be more than one function for each system.

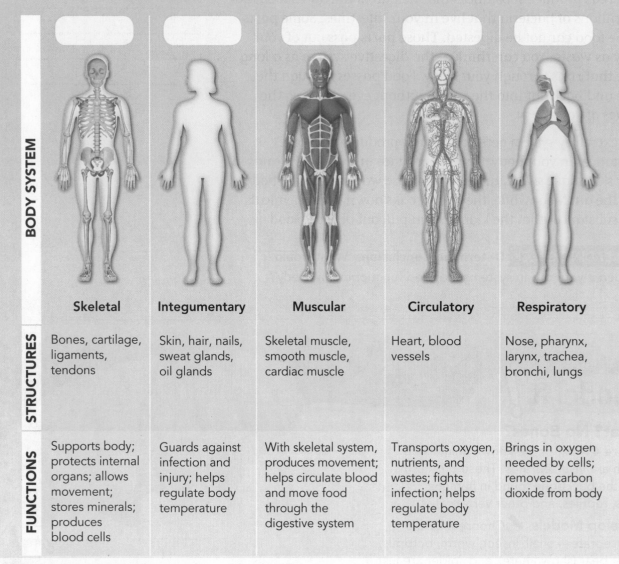

	Skeletal	**Integumentary**	**Muscular**	**Circulatory**	**Respiratory**
STRUCTURES	Bones, cartilage, ligaments, tendons	Skin, hair, nails, sweat glands, oil glands	Skeletal muscle, smooth muscle, cardiac muscle	Heart, blood vessels	Nose, pharynx, larynx, trachea, bronchi, lungs
FUNCTIONS	Supports body; protects internal organs; allows movement; stores minerals; produces blood cells	Guards against infection and injury; helps regulate body temperature	With skeletal system, produces movement; helps circulate blood and move food through the digestive system	Transports oxygen, nutrients, and wastes; fights infection; helps regulate body temperature	Brings in oxygen needed by cells; removes carbon dioxide from body

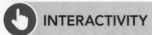

INTERACTIVITY

Explore the structures and functions of different body systems.

Defense System The immune system is your defense system against infections. Lymph nodes and lymph vessels trap bacteria and viruses. "Swollen glands" are lymph nodes that have grown larger to fight off an infection. White blood cells produced inside your bones also attack and destroy bacteria and other causes of disease. As shown in **Figure 5** above, many different organs work together to help to fight off invading disease organisms.

KEY
A Structural Support System
B Oxygen and Transport System
C Food and Waste Processing System
D Defense System
E Reproductive System
F Control System

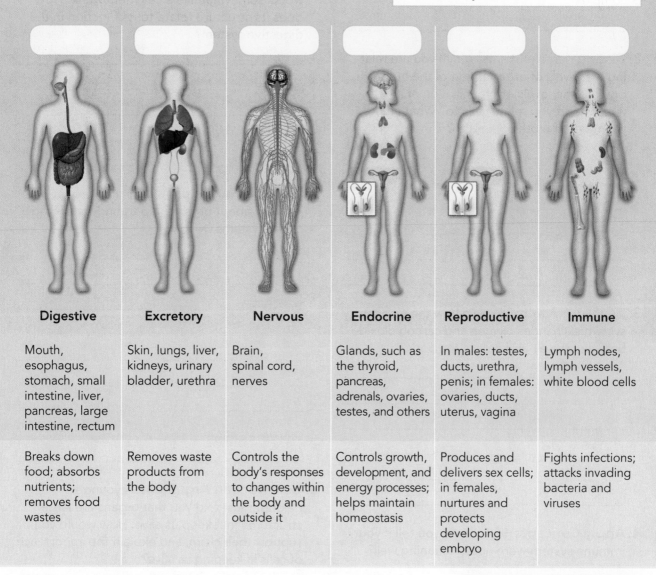

Digestive	Excretory	Nervous	Endocrine	Reproductive	Immune
Mouth, esophagus, stomach, small intestine, liver, pancreas, large intestine, rectum	Skin, lungs, liver, kidneys, urinary bladder, urethra	Brain, spinal cord, nerves	Glands, such as the thyroid, pancreas, adrenals, ovaries, testes, and others	In males: testes, ducts, urethra, penis; in females: ovaries, ducts, uterus, vagina	Lymph nodes, lymph vessels, white blood cells
Breaks down food; absorbs nutrients; removes food wastes	Removes waste products from the body	Controls the body's responses to changes within the body and outside it	Controls growth, development, and energy processes; helps maintain homeostasis	Produces and delivers sex cells; in females, nurtures and protects developing embryo	Fights infections; attacks invading bacteria and viruses

Reproductive System

The reproductive system is responsible for producing sperm and eggs and (in females) for nurturing the fetus until birth. Male reproductive organs include the testes (also known as testicles) and the penis. Female reproductive organs include the ovaries, uterus, and vagina. A cell can reproduce itself to make a new cell, but it takes a whole organ system to create a new human.

READING CHECK **Cite Textual Evidence** Identify an example of how multiple body systems work together to perform a specific function.

....

....

INTERACTIVITY

Explain how the human body is organized and how different body systems work together.

MS-LS1-3

1. **Patterns** What is the level of organization in the human body from the least to the most complex?

2. **Distinguish Relationships** If you are relating the levels of organization of the human body to the levels of organization of a city, what would you relate cells to? What would you relate the other levels to?

3. **Analyze Systems** Explain how the respiratory system exchanges oxygen and carbon dioxide between the air and cells in the body?

4. **Apply Concepts** How could you tell if your immune system were not functioning well?

5. **Construct Explanations** If the brain is the control center of the body, why does it have nerves connected to your organs?

6. **Relate Structure and Function** The thin layer of epithelial tissue in the small intestines works somewhat like a cell membrane. How does its structure relate to its function in the digestive system?

7. **Support Your Explanation** How does learning about organs help us understand how organ systems work?

8. **Construct an Argument** A younger neighbor just told you that organs are large structures that keep us alive. How would you support their claim, and explain the importance of cells in keeping us alive?

Artificial SKiN

👆 **INTERACTIVITY**

Identify criteria, constraints, and materials that need to be considered when building an artificial limb.

How do you help people who suffer due to severely damaged skin? You engineer new skin for them! Bioengineers may have solved a big problem.

The Challenge: To grow artificial skin that functions like the real thing.

Phenomenon Until recently, using artificial skin presented doctors with challenges and risks. Without hair follicles and oil glands, the skin could not function properly to help maintain homeostasis, the process that keeps internal conditions in the body stable. But new developments in cell research and bioengineering may have overcome this obstacle.

To make the artificial skin, bioengineers took cells from the mouths of mice. After treating the cells with chemicals, the scientists were able to form random clumps of a mix of cell types that you might find in a newly fertilized egg.

When researchers placed these cells into other mice, the cells gradually changed into specialized tissue. Once this happened, the scientists transplanted them out of those mice and into the skin tissue of other mice. Here the tissues developed normally as integumentary tissue, with hair follicles and oil glands. They also discovered that the implanted tissues made normal connections with the surrounding nerve and muscle tissues, allowing the different body systems to interact normally.

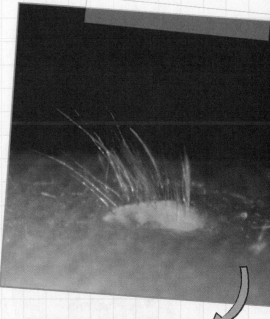

This artificial skin (genetically modified to "glow" green) is able to function just like real skin. It can grow hair and is able to sweat.

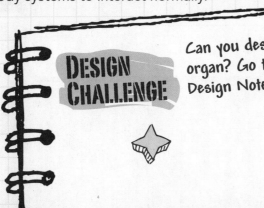

DESIGN CHALLENGE

Can you design an artificial organ? Go to the Engineering Design Notebook to find out!

Guiding Questions

- How do organ systems interact to carry out all the necessary functions for an organism's growth and survival?
- How do organ systems interact to maintain homeostasis?

Connection

Literacy Cite Textual Evidence

MS-LS1-3

Vocabulary

stimulus
response
gland
hormone
stress

Academic Vocabulary

interactions
stable

 VOCABULARY APP

Practice vocabulary on a mobile device.

Quest CONNECTION

Think about how systems interact and why one body system is dependent on the functioning of healthy cells in other body systems.

Connect It !

In the space provided on the image, list the body systems that you think are involved in skateboarding.

Predict If one of these body systems were to stop interacting with the other systems, would this activity still be possible? Explain.

....

....

....

Systems Working Together

All the systems in the human body work together to perform all the necessary functions for life. Cells need oxygen provided by the respiratory system and carried by the circulatory system. Organs carry out commands from the nervous system. And every part of the body changes its activities based on signals from the endocrine system.

Movement How is the skateboarder in **Figure 1** able to do what she does? **Interactions** between the skeletal, muscular, and nervous systems make it possible. Skeletal muscles are attached to the bones of the skeleton and provide the force that moves bones. Muscles contract and relax. When a muscle contracts, it shortens and pulls on the bones to which it is attached.

Try standing on one leg and bending the other leg at the knee. Hold that position. You can feel that you are using the muscles at the back of your thigh. Your nervous system controls when and how your muscles act on your bones.

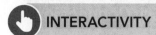

INTERACTIVITY

Explore how joints function in the human body.

Academic Vocabulary

What kinds of interactions are there between people in your neighborhood?

....

....

....

....

Poetry in Motion
Figure 1 We can accomplish impressive feats when all the body's systems are working together properly.

83

Literacy Connection

Cite Textual Evidence
The central idea of this text is that the body is organized into systems that interact with each other. As you read, underline evidence that organ systems interact with each other.

Controlling Body Functions The nervous system has two ways of controlling body functions: electrical signals from nerves and chemical signals from the endocrine system. Both methods help you to respond to your environment.

Transporting Materials All cells need oxygen and nutrients, and they need to get rid of carbon dioxide and other wastes. But most cells are locked into position with no way to move in search of food. So how can they stay alive? The answer is that blood vessels from the circulatory system carry nutrients to and waste from the cells in the body. Blood vessels divide into smaller and smaller branches until the tiniest, called capillaries, are only as wide as one blood cell. Capillaries, visible in **Figure 2**, pass near every cell in the body.

Blood picks up oxygen from the lungs and food molecules from the intestines and delivers them to needy cells. At the same time, blood collects carbon dioxide and waste from the cells. The carbon dioxide is returned to the lungs to be released into the air. Waste products are filtered from the blood by the kidneys in the excretory system and passed out of the body in urine.

✓ **READING CHECK** **Determine Meaning** Why do the capillaries have to be so small?

....

....

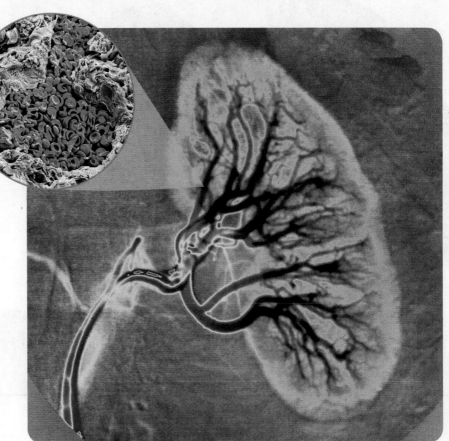

Special Delivery
Figure 2 Blood cells, like those shown in the inset, travel through a network of blood vessels to transport materials to and from every part of the body.

Predict How do you think a blocked blood vessel would affect an organism?

....

....

....

....

....

....

Stimulus and Response

Your eyes, ears, skin, nose, and taste buds all send information about your environment to your nervous system. Your senses let you react to loud noises, hot objects, and the odor of your favorite food. Any change or signal in the environment that can make an organism react in some way is called a **stimulus** (plural: stimuli). A **response** is an action or change in behavior that occurs as a result of a stimulus. Responses are directed by your nervous system but often involve other body systems as well. Your muscular and skeletal systems help you reach for food, and your digestive system releases saliva before the food even reaches your mouth. **Figure 3** shows an example of stimulus and response used in an American Sign Language expression.

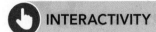

INTERACTIVITY

Investigate how different body systems work together.

Plan It !

Reaction Time

The time that passes between a stimulus and a response is the reaction time. A short reaction time could save you from a fall or a burn, and it might help you beat video games.

Plan Your Investigation Plan an investigation to measure reaction times under different conditions. Choose two or three factors that you suspect may influence reaction time, such as time of day, type of stimulus, environmental conditions, or state of mental alertness. How could you display your results?

....

....

....

....

....

....

....

....

....

....

....

....

....

....

Don't Burn Your Mouth

Figure 3 The American Sign Language expression for *hot* shows a reaction to hot food.

Apply Concepts Use the terms *stimulus* and *response* to explain what the sign is expressing.

....

....

....

....

HANDS-ON LAB

⚗ **Investigate** Identify the body systems used to perform specific actions.

Hormonal Control The endocrine system uses chemical signals instead of nerves to control body functions. The endocrine system is made up of many **glands**, organs that produce and release chemicals either through tiny tubes called ducts or directly into the bloodstream. For example, when something startles you, your adrenal glands send signals that prepare you to fight or run away. Your heart pumps faster, your lungs let in more air, and your ability to feel pain decreases. The pupils of your eyes even grow larger and allow in more light. You are ready for action.

The chemical produced by an endocrine gland is called a **hormone**. Hormones are carried through your body by the circulatory system. These chemicals affect many body processes. One hormone interacts with the excretory system and the circulatory system to control the amount of water in the bloodstream. Another hormone interacts with the digestive system and the circulatory system to control the amount of sugar in the bloodstream. Hormones also affect the reproductive systems of both males and females. **Figure 4** shows some of the effects of hormones on boys during puberty.

☑ **READING CHECK** **Cite Textual Evidence** What text on this page supports the idea that the endocrine system functions differently from the nervous system?

....

....

....

Hormones and Puberty

Figure 4 Hormones can have dramatic and long-lasting effects.

Make Observations Identify some of the changes you see between the before-puberty and after-puberty pictures.

....

....

....

Interacting Systems

Figure 5 This swimmer's body systems work together as she pushes herself to excel.

Apply Concepts Read the descriptions of functions happening in the swimmer's body. Then identify the main systems involved.

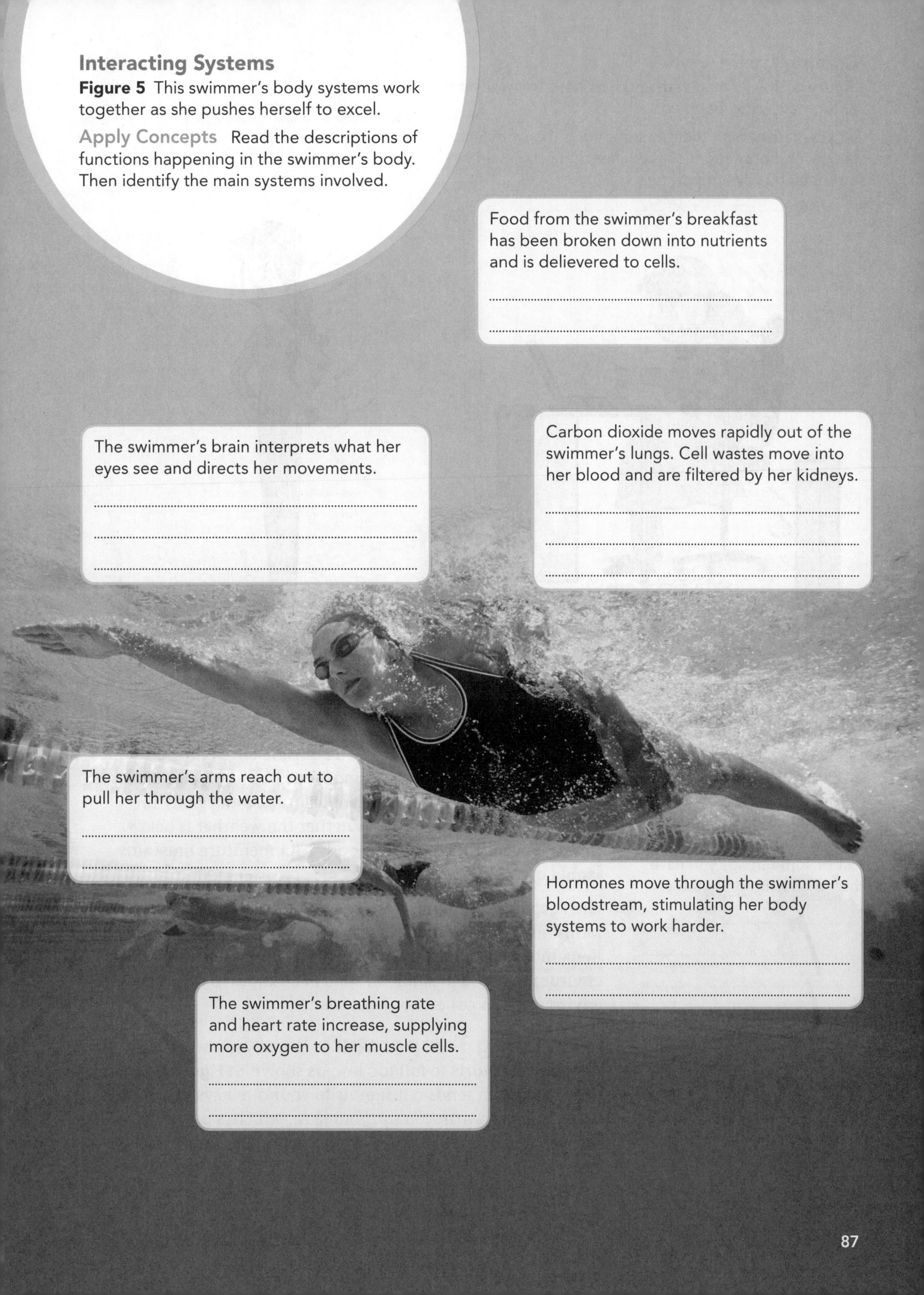

Food from the swimmer's breakfast has been broken down into nutrients and is delievered to cells.

....

....

The swimmer's brain interprets what her eyes see and directs her movements.

....

....

....

Carbon dioxide moves rapidly out of the swimmer's lungs. Cell wastes move into her blood and are filtered by her kidneys.

....

....

....

The swimmer's arms reach out to pull her through the water.

....

....

Hormones move through the swimmer's bloodstream, stimulating her body systems to work harder.

....

....

The swimmer's breathing rate and heart rate increase, supplying more oxygen to her muscle cells.

....

....

Cooling Down

Figure 6 The woman in the first image is using several different ways to warm up.

Apply Concepts Identify some ways the woman in the second drawing might cool her body and maintain a constant body temperature.

....

....

....

Homeostasis

Academic Vocabulary

Stable is a common word to describe something that hasn't changed much and isn't expected to change much in the future. Make a list of some things you have heard described as stable.

....

....

....

....

What happens when you go outside in the cold? Does your body temperature fall to meet the outside temperature? It does not, and that's a very good thing! Your body only functions well around 37°C. It is vitally important for your body to maintain that temperature. Whether the weather is below freezing or roasting hot, your body's temperature must stay **stable** and remain close to 37°C.

Each organism requires specific conditions to function. Maintaining those conditions is necessary for life to continue. Remember that the condition in which an organism's internal environment is kept stable in spite of changes in the outside environment is called homeostasis.

Regulating Temperature When your body temperature starts to fall too low, as shown in **Figure 6**, your nervous system sends out signals to your other systems to take action to warm you up. Your skin, which is part of the integumentary system, develops goosebumps. Your muscles cause you to shiver. You tend to move your large muscles to generate heat. All of these actions help to raise your temperature back to normal.

▶ **VIDEO**

Find out how a house's heating system is like your body.

Keeping Balance Structures in your inner ear sense the position of your head. They send this information to your brain, which interprets the signals. If your brain senses that you are losing your balance, then it sends messages to your muscles to move in ways that help you stay steady. **Figure 7** shows the cycle of how your body keeps its balance.

Meeting Energy Needs When the cells in your body need more energy, hormones from the endocrine system signal the nervous system to make you feel hungry. After you eat, other hormones signal your brain to make you feel full.

Maintaining Water Balance All the chemical reactions that keep you alive take place within the watery environment of your cells. If your body needs more water, then your nervous system causes you to feel thirsty. Your senses, muscles, and skeleton take you to a source of water. After you have had enough water, your nervous system causes your thirst to end. Soon after, the water passes through your digestive system to your circulatory system and from there into your cells. Water balance is restored!

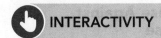

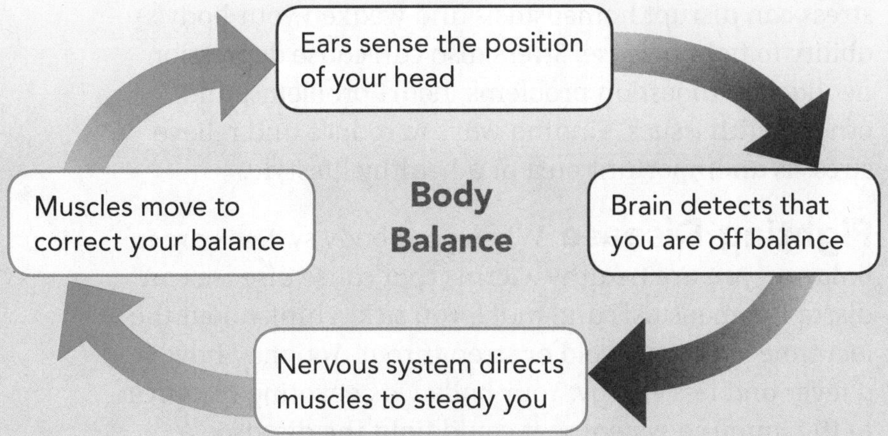

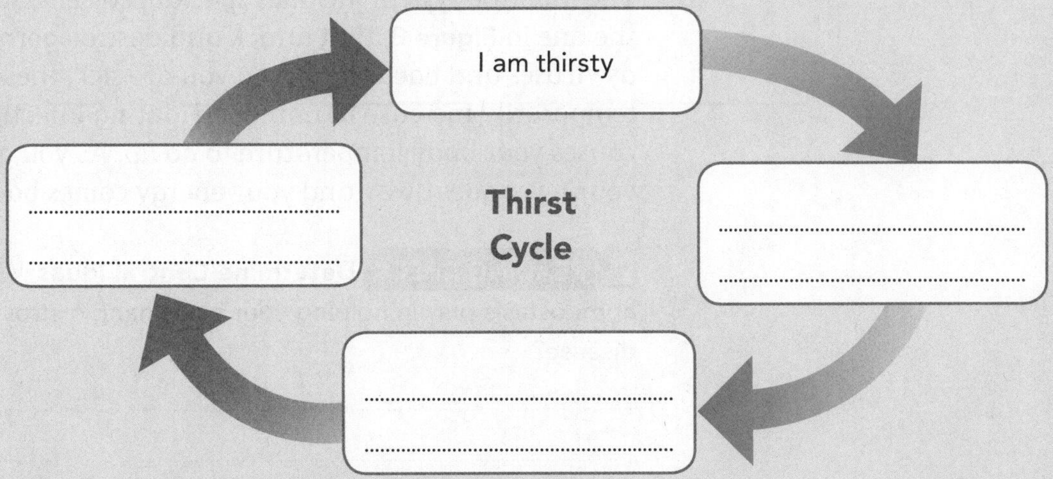

INTERACTIVITY

Explain how body systems interact to maintain homeostasis.

Maintaining Homeostasis
Figure 7 Interactions among your ears, brain, and muscular system make up the balance cycle.

Sequence ✏️ Fill in the missing steps to create a diagram of the thirst cycle.

☑ READING CHECK
Translate Information What role does the nervous system play in maintaining homeostasis? Explain.

....

....

....

....

....

....

....

Body Balance

Ears sense the position of your head

Brain detects that you are off balance

Nervous system directs muscles to steady you

Muscles move to correct your balance

Thirst Cycle

I am thirsty

[blank box]

[blank box]

[blank box]

Defense Against Disease

Figure 8 The green cell is an immune cell. It engulfs the orange and blue bacteria cells, and destroys them.

Apply Concepts How do you think the immune system is affected by stress?

....

....

....

....

....

....

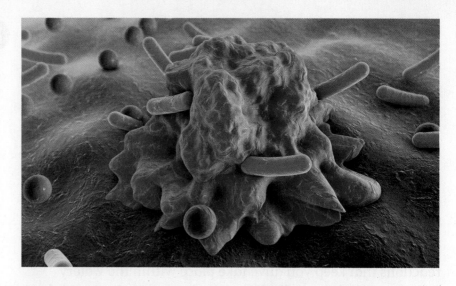

INTERACTIVITY

Analyze symptoms to see what body systems are affected by an illness.

VIDEO

Go inside the world of a medical illustrator.

Managing Stress In general, **stress** is the reaction of a person's body to potentially threatening, challenging, or disturbing events. Each person experiences stress differently. One person may enjoy taking on the challenge of a math test, while someone else might freeze with fear.

Some stress is unavoidable. If stress is over quickly, then the body returns to its normal, healthy condition. However, too much stress for too long a time can be unhealthy. Ongoing stress can disrupt homeostasis and weaken your body's ability to fight disease. Stress also can cause depression, headaches, digestion problems, heart problems, and other health issues. Finding ways to reduce and relieve stress is an important part of a healthy lifestyle.

Fighting Disease When your body systems are in balance, you are healthy. Germs that cause disease can disrupt homeostasis and make you sick. Think about the last time you had a cold or strep throat. You may have had a fever and less energy. Your body was devoting resources to the immune system so it could fight the disease.

The immune system includes specialized cells, such as the one in **Figure 8**, that attack and destroy germs, such as viruses and bacteria. When you are sick, these cells temporarily increase in number. Fighting infection sometimes causes your body temperature to go up. As you get well, your fever goes away and your energy comes back.

☑ READING CHECK **Determine Central Ideas** What role does homeostasis play in helping your body handle stress and fight disease?

....

....

....

MS-LS1-3

1. Define What is a hormone?

....

....

2. Analyze Systems What are four conditions in the body related to maintaining homeostasis?

....

....

3. Compare and Contrast How are chemical signals and electrical signals alike? How are they different?

....

....

....

....

4. Cause and Effect Explain how getting sick can affect the body's ability to maintain homeostasis.

....

....

....

....

5. Apply Concepts Pick one material that is moved within the body by the organ systems. Describe which systems are involved and how they work together.

....

....

....

....

....

....

6. Draw Conclusions Explain how the circulatory system interacts with other body systems to maintain homeostasis.

....

....

....

....

....

....

7. Develop Models ✎ Start with the sentence "I feel hungry." In the space below, draw a cycle diagram to show how your body would respond to this situation.

Quest CHECK-IN

In this lesson, you learned about how body systems interact with one another to carry out functions necessary for growth and survival. You also explored how body systems interact to maintain homeostasis.

Apply Concepts Why is it important to understand how different body systems interact when developing a training plan?

....

....

....

INTERACTIVITY

Training Systems

Go online to identify body systems with their functions and use that information to begin a training plan.

MS-LS1-3

AGENTS OF
Infection

Your immune system is constantly working to fight off infections. Most of the time, the lymph nodes, lymph vessels, and white blood cells that are part of your immune system are able to attack invading viruses and bacteria to fight off infection. But some agents of infection are harder to conquer than others...

There are thousands of living and nonliving things that cause infections. The living ones include bacteria, fungi, worms, and single-celled organisms called protists. A bacterium is responsible for strep throat. Ringworm is caused by a fungus. Dysentery can result from a bacterial infection as well as amoebas. The good news about being infected with one of these organisms is that, for the most part, the infections they cause can be cured with medical treatment. There are also a number of ways that you can protect yourself from infections. For example, you can reduce your chances of getting or spreading an infection by washing your hands and by avoiding touching your face if your hands are not clean.

Nonliving viruses also cause infections. Viruses can cause diseases such as HIV, the common cold, and chicken pox. Only a few medications can treat them. A virus is hard to treat because it uses living cells to make copies of itself. These cells are damaged or destroyed when the new virus particles are released. The virus particles then infect other cells. Depending on the type of infection, people may get better over time. Sometimes a viral infection is so severe that symptoms never go away and conditions worsen.

You may have heard of the Zika virus or the flesh-eating bacterium *Vibrio vulnificus*. Each of these causes serious symptoms in people, often requiring hospitalization. Read about some of these infections in the table.

Medical professionals and patients need to take safety precautions, such as hand washing, to prevent the spread of infection.

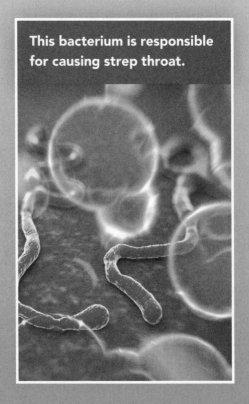

This bacterium is responsible for causing strep throat.

Infectious Agent	Type of Organism	Cause/Transmission	Symptoms	Treatment
Zika	Virus	Mosquito bites or transmission from infected person	Fever, rash, joint pain	There is no specific medicine or vaccine for Zika virus.
Brain-eating *Naegleria fowleri*	Amoeba	Infection occurs most often from diving, water skiing, or other water sports when water is forced into the nose.	Headache, fever, stiff neck, loss of appetite, seizures, coma	A number of drugs kill *N. fowleri* amoebas in the test tube. But even when treated with these drugs, very few patients survive.
Flesh-eating *Vibrio vulnificus*	Bacterium	It releases a toxin that causes the immune system to release white blood cells that destroy the individual's flesh.	Sweats, fever, and chills with red, swollen, blister-like patches on the body	Either the affected tissue has to be amputated, or antibiotics have to be administered.

Use the text and the table to answer the following questions.

1. **Determine Differences** How are viruses different from other infectious agents, such as bacteria and fungi?

....

....

....

2. **Construct an Argument** Do you think science and medicine will ever be able to discover a cure for Zika? Explain.

....

....

....

....

3. **Solve Problems** What are some steps you can take to protect yourself against an infectious disease?

....

....

....

....

③ Supplying Energy

Guiding Questions

- What are the important nutrients your body needs to carry out its processes?
- How does food become the materials your body can use?
- How do your body's systems process the food you eat?

Connections

| Literacy | Write Arguments |
| Math | Analyze Proportional Relationships |

MS-LS1-3

Vocabulary

digestion
nutrients
carbohydrates
peristalsis
saliva
enzyme

Academic Vocabulary

absorption
elimination

📱 **VOCABULARY APP**

Practice vocabulary on a mobile device.

Quest CONNECTION

Consider how the foods you eat can help you reach your peak health.

Connect It!

✏️ **Circle the food choice the runner should make to get the most energy for the race.**

Make Observations Consider your daily activities. Which require the most energy? What would happen if you did not eat enough food?

....

....

Make Generalizations Why are your food choices important?

....

....

....

Food and Energy

What have you done so far today? You woke up, got dressed, ate breakfast, and came to school. Later today, you may have karate, dance, or basketball. You may be running in a race like the people in **Figure 1**. All of these activities require energy. In fact, your cells require energy for all the processes that go on inside your body, including breathing, thinking, and growing.

Living things get energy from food. Plants make their own food. Animals and decomposers get their food by eating other organisms and breaking it down into its component parts. **Digestion** is the process by which your body breaks down food into small nutrient molecules.

Nutrients are the substances in food that provide the raw materials the body's cells need to carry out all their essential processes. Some nutrients are broken down and used for energy. Other nutrients are used to repair damaged cells or to help you grow. Your body needs nutrients to perform every function. Therefore, you constantly need nutrients from food to keep up with the body's demand.

INTERACTIVITY

Learn how our bodies get energized.

Literacy Connection

Write Arguments A classmate claims that an apple and cupcake, both about the same size, give you the same amount of energy. Do you agree or disagree with this statement? Explain.

....

....

....

....

Running Takes Energy
Figure 1 Everything you do in a day takes energy. The cells in your body need a steady supply of energy to keep functioning.

95

How Sweet It Is

Figure 2 Our bodies can digest simple carbohydrates very quickly so they can give a quick burst of energy.

Form an Opinion ✏ Circle a simple carbohydrate that you think makes a healthy snack. Then, explain why you think that's a better choice than some others.

....
....
....
....
....
....

Academic Vocabulary

The base word of *absorption* is *absorb*. What else can absorb materials? How does this help you understand the term *absorption*?

....
....
....
....

HANDS-ON LAB

Investigate Discover how Calories in different foods are measured.

Main Nutrients

Main Nutrients The purpose of digestion is the **absorption** of six important nutrients you get from food: carbohydrates, proteins, fats, vitamins, minerals, and water.

Carbohydrates An energy-rich organic compound, such as sugar or a starch, that is made of the elements carbon, hydrogen, and oxygen, is called a **carbohydrate**. They can be quickly broken down and the body can use the energy released in this process. This energy is measured in Calories. High Calorie foods can give you more energy than low Calorie foods.

A carbohydrate can be simple or complex, depending on the size of its molecules. Simple carbohydrates, such as the ones shown in **Figure 2**, are smaller molecules and taste sweet. Complex carbohydrates, such as fiber, are larger molecules. Whole grains, such as brown rice, are considered healthy sources of complex carbohydrates. They are high in fiber and nutrients.

Proteins Your body needs protein for growth and body repair. Proteins are made of smaller components called amino acids. Beans, beef, chicken, eggs, fish, and nuts are all protein sources.

Fats While carbohydrates provide quick energy, fats provide a concentrated energy source and the body also uses fats for long-term energy storage. There are two main types— saturated fat and unsaturated fat. Saturated fats usually come from animal products, such as lard. They are solid at room temperature. Unsaturated fats usually come from plant products and are oils, such as olive oil. They are liquid at room temperature. People should limit saturated fat intake because they are linked to heart disease and other illnesses.

Vitamins Vitamins are nutrients that help your body with chemical reactions. They do not provide any energy or building materials, but without them, you would not be able to function. Your body can make small amounts of some vitamins, such as vitamins D and K, but most have to be taken in through your diet. Vitamins can be fat-soluble or water-soluble. Fat-soluble vitamins, such as A and K, are stored in the fatty tissues of the body and released when needed. Water-soluble vitamins, such as vitamin C, dissolve in water and are not stored in large amounts by the body. Citrus fruit, such as oranges, are high in vitamin C.

Minerals Minerals are nutrients that are not made by the body, but are needed to carry out chemical processes. Calcium for bones and iron for blood are two examples of minerals that are taken in through the diet. Calcium is common in dairy products, such as milk and cheese. Iron is found in meat and leafy green vegetables, such as spinach.

Water Of the six nutrients you need, water is the most important. While the human body can go a few weeks without eating food, it could only survive a few days without water. Survival time without water hinges on both environmental conditions and level of activity. For example, someone hiking in the desert under a blazing sun needs more water than someone in cooler conditions. You get water from much of the food you eat, but you still need to drink water every day.

INTERACTIVITY

Discover how food is broken down into bits and pieces in the digestive system.

Reflect Consider the different types of food you eat every day. Are they all equally nutritious?

☑ READING CHECK **Cite Textual Evidence** Underline some recommended sources of each of the main nutrients your body needs.

Plan It !

Nutritionist recommend that people eat a diet that balances the main nutrients while limiting simple carbohydrates, saturated fats, and foods high in salt.

Apply Concepts Describe a dinner you would like to eat that includes all of the main nutrients, but is low in the nutrients that you should limit.

....

....

....

....

....

The Digestive Process

Digestion can be classified into two main types—mechanical and chemical. Mechanical digestion involves the physical breakdown and movement of food. Chemical digestion, as the name suggests, involves the chemical breakdown of food.

Mechanical Digestion The mouth and stomach are the main places where mechanical digestion happens. The movement of the food through the esophagus and the intestines is also part of mechanical digestion. Waves of smooth muscle contractions that move food through the esophagus toward the stomach are called **peristalsis**.

Math Toolbox

Monitoring Sodium Intake

Sodium is a mineral that our bodies need to function. It helps our muscular and nervous systems work and it helps us stay hydrated. However, in certain people too much salt may lead to high blood pressure, which puts people at risk for heart disease, stroke, and other illnesses.

1. **Analyze Proportional Relationships** According to the nutrition facts for these potato chips, a serving has 170 mg of sodium, or 7% of the daily recommended value for an average adult. Based on this information, how many milligrams of sodium should an average adult consume in a day? Show your work.

2. **Calculate** How many servings of potato chips would it take for you reach the maximum amount of sodium you should consume in a day? Show your work.

3. **Apply Mathematical Concepts** The American Heart Association recommends that adults consume no more than 1500 mg of sodium a day for optimal heart health. How would this change the percentage of the daily recommended value? How many servings of chips would it take to reach this adjusted maximum daily value?

Nutrition Facts

Serving Size 1 oz (28g/About 15 chips)

Amount Per Serving	
Calories 160	Calories from Fat 90

	% Daily Value*
Total Fat 10g	**16%**
Saturated Fat 1.5g	**8%**
Trans Fat 0g	
Cholesterol 0mg	**0%**
Sodium 170mg	**7%**
Potassium 350mg	**10%**
Total Carbohydrate 15g	**5%**
Dietary Fiber 1g	**5%**
Sugars less than 1g	
Protein 2g	

Vitamin A 0%	•	Vitamin C 10%
Calcium 0%	•	Iron 2%
Vitamin E 6%	•	Thiamin 4%
Niacin 6%	•	Vitamin B₆ 10%

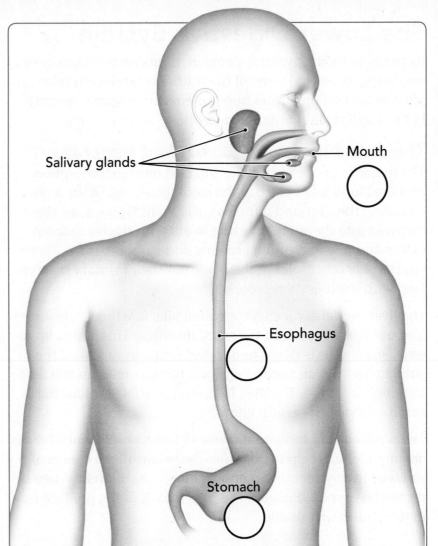

Salivary glands

Mouth

Esophagus

Stomach

Upper Digestive System

Figure 3 The upper digestive system includes the mouth, esophagus, and the stomach.

Synthesize Information

✎ For each part of the digestive system, write M if mechanical digestion takes place and write C if chemical digestion occurs.

Chemical Digestion As shown in **Figure 3**, chemical digestion begins in the mouth. Fluid called **saliva** is released from glands in the mouth and plays an important role in both mechanical and chemical digestion. Your saliva contains chemicals. Some of these chemicals are called enzymes. **Enzymes** are proteins that speed up chemical reactions in the body. Enzymes cause the food to break down faster. Chemical digestion starts in the mouth, which is shown in **Figure 3**, with an enzyme found in saliva. This acts specifically on the carbohydrate starch. Saliva also moistens the food so it can be easily swallowed. Chemical digestion continues in the stomach, where other enzymes and hydrochloric acid further break down food. The partially-digested material then passes into the small intestine, where most chemical digestion takes place.

✓ READING CHECK **Determine Central Ideas** What role do enzymes play on the process of digestion? Explain.

....

....

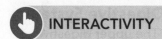
The Lower Digestive System

By the time food leaves the stomach, it has been broken into very small parts and some of the nutrients have been released. Most of the carbohydrates and proteins have been digested, but fats still remain as large molecules.

The Small Intestine, Liver, and Pancreas

The majority of chemical digestion and nutrient absorption into the blood takes place in the small intestine. Other organs, including the liver and pancreas, shown in **Figure 5**, secrete enzymes into the small intestine to aid with the breakdown of fats and any remaining proteins and carbohydrates. These organs play other roles in the body, but their primary role is to help with the digestion process.

The liver produces an enzyme called bile. Bile breaks down fat into small fat droplets in the small intestine. This allows fat to be digested. Bile is stored in another small organ called the gall bladder. When needed, the gall bladder releases bile into the small intestine. The liver is also responsible for filtering blood and storing certain vitamins.

The pancreas produces an enzyme called trypsin, which breaks down proteins. The pancreas also makes insulin, a chemical involved in a system that monitors blood sugar levels. When a person has Type 1 diabetes, the pancreas does not produce as much insulin as it should.

Got Greens?

Figure 4 Fiber is an important part of a healthy diet. Vegetables are an excellent source of fiber. Because the human body cannot break down fiber, it passes through the digestive system virtually unchanged.

Apply Concepts Why is it important to get plenty of fiber in your diet?

....

....

....

Lower Digestive System

Figure 5 Most chemical digestion takes place in the small intestine.

Interpret Diagrams Why does the gall bladder need to be close to the liver?

....

....

....

....

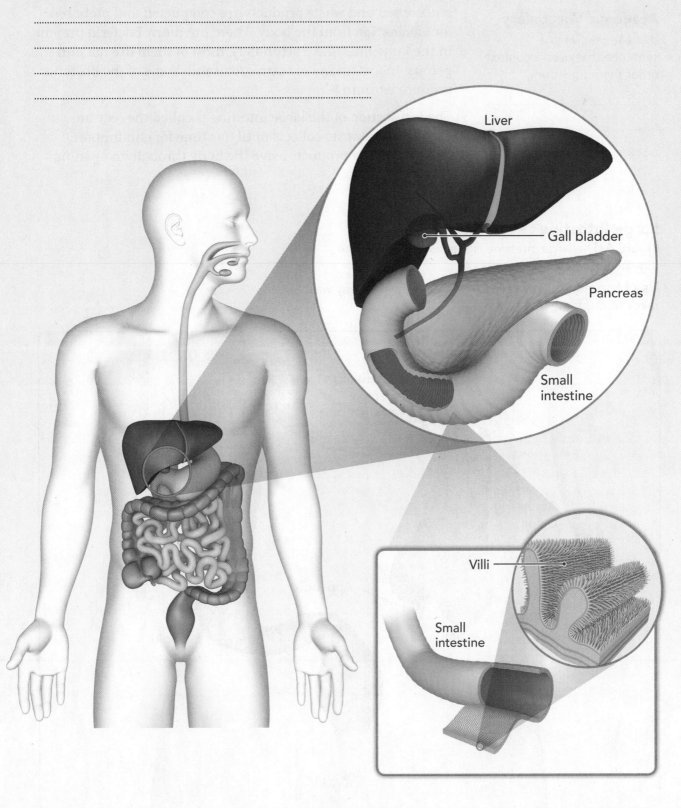

Liver

Gall bladder

Pancreas

Small intestine

Villi

Small intestine

The Large Intestine

The Large Intestine As shown in **Figure 6**, the last stage of digestion occurs in the large intestine. The large intestine is actually shorter than the small intestine—1.5 m versus 6–8 m. It is in the large intestine that water from food is reabsorbed and waste products are compacted and prepared for **elimination** from the body. There are many bacteria present in the large intestine. Fortunately, most of them are not dangerous. In fact, many of them are useful. Some of the bacteria produce vitamin K.

The last section of the large intestine is called the rectum. This is where waste collects until it is time for elimination. The solid waste products leave the body through an opening called the anus.

Academic Vocabulary

Use *elimination* in a sentence that uses a context other than digestion.

....

....

....

....

Large Intestine

Figure 6 The large intestine is the last section of the digestive system.

Use Models ✎ Draw a line that shows the pathway waste takes through the large intestine.

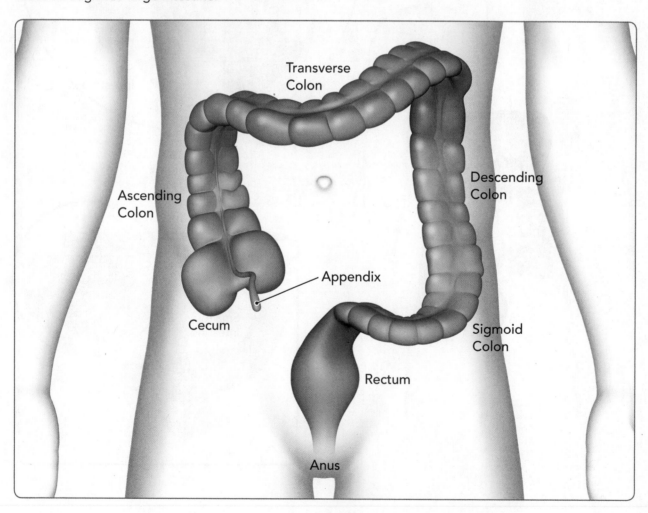

Human Digestive System

Figure 7 Like all body systems, the digestive system relies on many organs working together.

Analyze Systems ✏ Circle the names of the organs that provide chemicals for your body to perform chemical digestion. Then, place the pathway of food through the body in sequential order from 1 through 6.

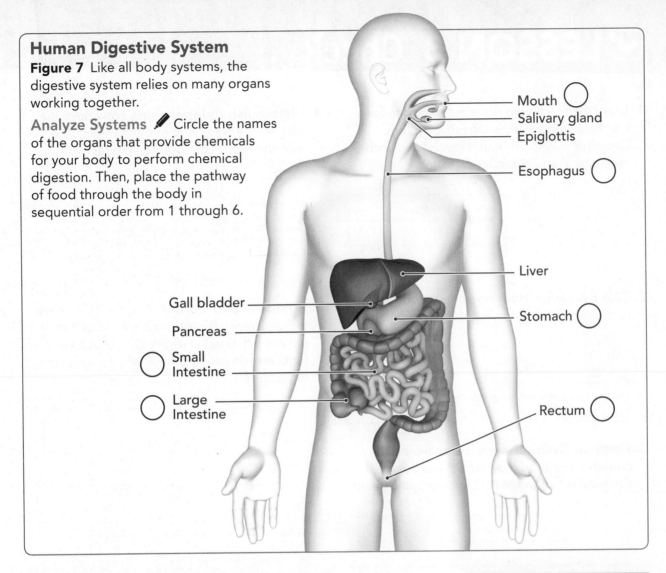

Mouth ◯
Salivary gland
Epiglottis
Esophagus ◯
Liver
Gall bladder
Pancreas
Small Intestine ◯
Large Intestine ◯
Stomach ◯
Rectum ◯

The Digestive System as a Whole

You have read about the functions of the different organs that make up the digestive system, which are shown in **Figure 7**. It is important to realize that the digestive system is related to many other systems in the human body. For example, after nutrients are absorbed in the small intestine, they are transported around the body in the blood. The pumping of the heart and the rest of the circulatory system make sure all of your cells get the nutrients they need.

INTERACTIVITY

Find out what a day in the life of a cell is like.

✅ READING CHECK **Write Arguments** Your sister claims that the digestive system works by itself to give your body energy. She states that small branches from the stomach get food to the cells throughout your body. Do you agree with this statement? Why?

....

....

....

....

....

☑ LESSON 3 Check

MS-LS1-3

1. **Identify** Starting in the mouth, food follows a pathway through the digestive system. Describe how the mouth is involved in both mechanical and chemical digestion.

....

....

....

....

2. **Cite Evidence** How can you use food labels to determine how rich in nutrients a food is?

....

....

....

....

3. **Form an Opinion** If you are analyzing the nutrients in a food, how would you decide if the food is healthy or not? Support your claim.

....

....

....

....

....

4. **Distinguish Relationships** How does the release of energy and nutrients from digestion help the rest of the body's systems?

....

....

....

....

....

5. **Compare and Contrast** Both the liver and the pancreas are responsible for producing enzymes that aid in digestion. What other functions do each perform when carrying out digestion?

....

....

....

....

....

....

....

Quest CHECK-IN

In this lesson, you learned about nutrients that are important for maintaining a healthy body. You also learned about the digestive system and how it supports other systems in the body.

Evaluate Consider how your dietary needs might differ from someone else's and how you might need to modify your diet based on a day's activities. Why is it important to eat a variety of different foods?

....

....

....

....

👆 INTERACTIVITY

Training Table

Go online to investigate the ideal nutrients for different athletes.

You Can't Order OUT IN SPACE

Nutritionists and dieticians promote healthy eating habits and develop nutrition plans tailored to an individual's dietary or medical needs. But what if your client is an astronaut?

Space is a microgravity environment, which means astronauts experience near-weightlessness. While floating around seems like fun, it has serious consequences for the human body. Microgravity affects muscle mass, bone density, and cardiovascular health. It also impacts how the body digests food and processes essential vitamins and minerals.

At NASA, nutritionists work with food scientists to develop meals that counteract the harmful effects of living in space. Nutrients such as iron are added to meals to help deal with bone and muscle loss. The challenge for the nutritionists is creating meals that can be prepared and consumed in microgravity!

 VIDEO

Find out how a nutritionist helps people make healthy diet choices.

MY CAREER

Type "nutritionist" or "dietician" into an online search engine to learn more about these careers.

Space food is often packaged in individual meal pouches, similar to the chicken the astronaut is eating.

LESSON

4 Managing Materials

Guiding Questions

- How are materials transported in the body?
- How does the respiratory system interact with other systems to exchange gases?
- How does the excretory system interact with other systems to remove wastes from the body?

Connections

Literacy Draw Evidence

Math Represent Quantitative Relationships

MS-LS1-3

Vocabulary

circulatory system
artery
capillary
vein
lymph
bronchi
alveoli
excretion
nephron

Academic Vocabulary

contract

 VOCABULARY APP

Practice vocabulary on a mobile device.

Quest CONNECTION

Think about how the circulatory and excretory systems are needed to keep a body in peak performance shape.

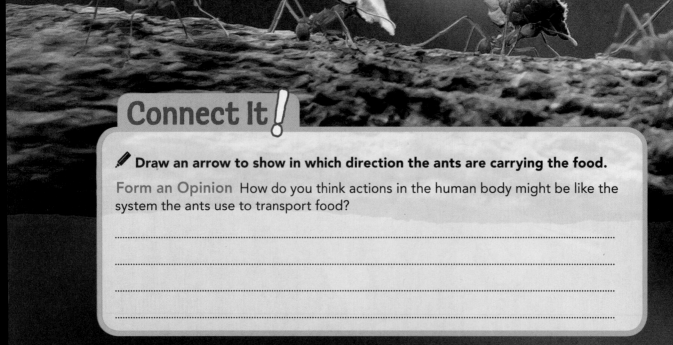

Connect It!

✏️ **Draw an arrow to show in which direction the ants are carrying the food.**

Form an Opinion How do you think actions in the human body might be like the system the ants use to transport food?

....

....

....

....

The Circulatory System

Ants, such as the ones in **Figure 1**, are known for cooperating to transport food to their colonies. Your body has a similar system that transports nutrients and other life-sustaining resources. It is called the **circulatory system**, and it includes the cardiovascular system and the lymphatic system. In addition to bringing nutrients and oxygen to the cells, the circulatory system also removes waste products and helps to fight off diseases and infections.

The main structure of the circulatory system is the heart. This fist-sized organ has the never-ending job of pumping blood around the body. The heart is a muscle that **contracts** and relaxes constantly in order to do its job. Your heart beats around 100,000 times every day. Blood moves from the heart to the lungs and then back to the heart again before it is transported out to the body. Blood moving through the vessels allows for the exchange of gases and brings nutrients to all the cells. For this reason, blood is often called the "river of life."

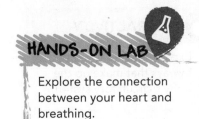

HANDS-ON LAB

Explore the connection between your heart and breathing.

Academic Vocabulary

What are some other words you can think of that are synonyms for *contracts*?

Transporting Materials
Figure 1. Just as the circulatory system moves materials in your body, these ants transport food to their colony

INTERACTIVITY

Explore the highways and byways that make up the body's circulatory system.

Write About It Trace the journey of a molecule of oxygen from the time it enters your body until it reaches a muscle in your fingertip. Describe each step of the process.

The Cardiovascular System
The part of the circulatory system that pumps blood throughout the body is the cardiovascular system. In this system, the heart pumps blood through the body using the various blood vessels. Start on the right side of **Figure 2**.

Blood travels from the lungs to the left atrium down to the left ventricle. It then takes nutrients and oxygen to the cells of the body, where it picks up waste products, such as carbon dioxide. The blood returns through the right atrium. It goes down to the right ventricle, and out to the lungs where gas is exchanged. Then, the process starts all over again.

This continuous process of pumping blood is a double loop system, as shown in **Figure 3**. In loop one, the blood travels from the heart to the lungs and then back to the heart. In loop two, the oxygenated blood moves from the heart out to the body and deoxygenated blood is returned to the heart.

Special cells called red blood cells play a key role in transporting oxygen throughout the body. They take up oxygen in the lungs and deliver it to cells throughout the body. Red blood cells also absorb carbon dioxide in the body and transport it to the lungs, where it is released from the body.

Structure of the Heart

Figure 2 🖊 The human heart has four main chambers. Each upper chamber is called an atrium and each lower chamber is called a ventricle. The right ventricle has a special collection of cells called the pacemaker that keeps the heart beating in a regular rhythm. Label the four chambers of the heart.

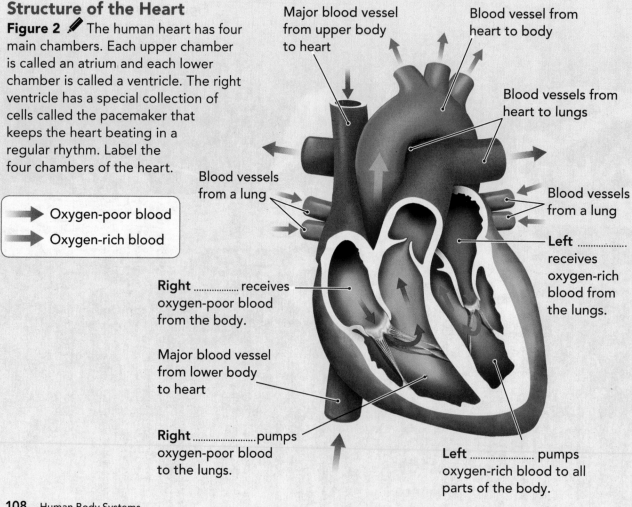

➡ Oxygen-poor blood

➡ Oxygen-rich blood

Major blood vessel from upper body to heart

Blood vessel from heart to body

Blood vessels from heart to lungs

Blood vessels from a lung

Blood vessels from a lung

Left .... receives oxygen-rich blood from the lungs.

Right .... receives oxygen-poor blood from the body.

Major blood vessel from lower body to heart

Right .... pumps oxygen-poor blood to the lungs.

Left .... pumps oxygen-rich blood to all parts of the body.

Double Loop System

Figure 3 ✏ Blood flows from the right atrium to the right ventricle and then to the lungs through a special artery called the pulmonary artery. Here it gets oxygenated and then is pumped back to the heart by way of the pulmonary vein. Draw arrows to show the direction of the blood flow.

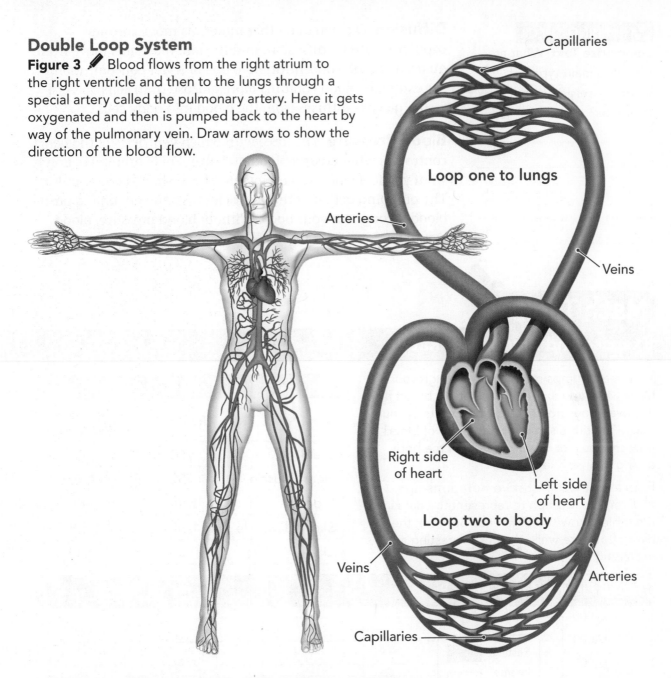

Capillaries

Loop one to lungs

Arteries

Veins

Right side of heart

Left side of heart

Loop two to body

Veins

Arteries

Capillaries

Transport Through the Circulatory System

You know that the main function of the circulatory system is to move materials, such as nutrients and oxygen, to all of the cells of the body. A series of vessels makes this process possible.

Blood Vessels Your heart is connected to the rest of your body through a system of vessels, which are illustrated in **Figure 3**. Not all vessels in the body are the same. Different vessels have different structures and functions. An **artery** carries blood away from the heart. It is a thick-walled and muscular vessel. On the other hand, a **vein** carries blood back to the heart. It has thinner walls than arteries. A **capillary** is a tiny vessel where substances are exchanged between the blood and body cells. Capillaries can be thought of as connecting arteries and veins.

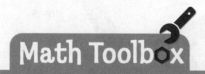
Summarize Text What are the three main types of blood vessels and what are their jobs?

....

....

....

....

....

Diffusion Oxygen and other materials move through capillary walls by diffusion. In diffusion, materials move from an area of high concentration to one of lower concentration. For example, blood contains more glucose than cells do. As a result, glucose diffuses from the blood into body cells

Blood Pressure The force with which ventricles of the heart contract is what creates blood pressure. This pumping action is what you feel when you are aware of your heartbeat or pulse. The pumping action of the ventricles is strong enough to push blood throughout your body. Without blood pressure, blood would not be able to reach all parts of your body.

Math Toolbox

Exercise and Blood Flow Rate

Your heart pumps more blood through your body when you exercise. The rate of blood flow, however, does not increase in all parts of your body. The table shows how the rate of blood flow changes for different parts of the body during intense exercise.

Represent Quantitative Relationships

Draw a bar graph to represent the data in the table. Show the difference between the blood flow rate while the body is resting and exercising intensely.

Body Part	Blood Flow Rate, cm³/min	
	Resting	**Intense Exercise**
Brain	750	750
Heart Muscle	250	750
Kidneys	1,100	600
Skeletal Muscle	1,200	12,500
Skin	500	1,800

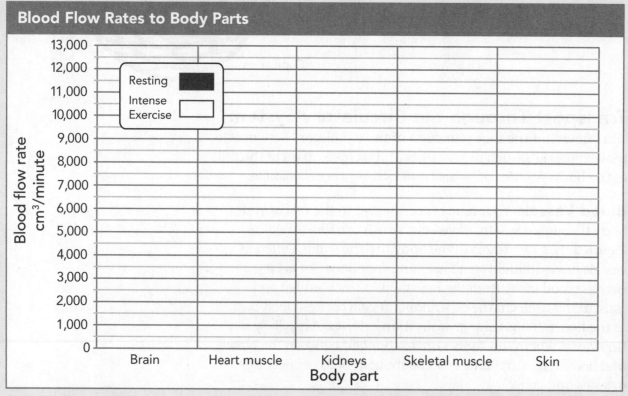

Blood Flow Rates to Body Parts

The Lymphatic System

Figure 4 ✏ The lymphatic system is part of the circulatory system. Its main function is to transport components of blood back into the circulatory system. On the diagram, label the lymph nodes and the lymph vessels.

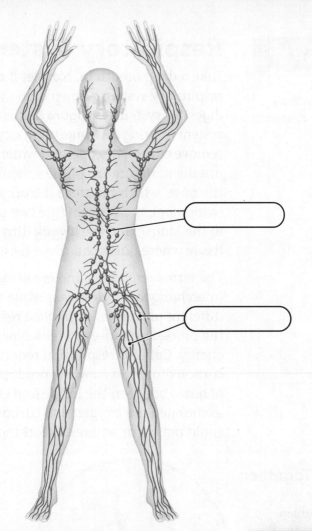

The Lymphatic System

In addition to red blood cells, blood also contains white blood cells, platelets, and plasma. White blood cells fight off diseases. Platelets help clot wounds. Plasma is the liquid part of the blood. As these components of blood move through the cardiovascular system, the fluid moves into the surrounding tissues. From here it needs to move back into the bloodstream. This job is done by the other component of the circulatory system—the lymphatic system. As shown in **Figure 4**, the lymphatic system is a network of vessels that returns fluid to the bloodstream.

Once the fluid is inside the lymphatic system, it is called **lymph** and consists of water, white blood cells, and dissolved materials such as glucose. Lymph flows through vessels called lymph vessels. The vessels connect to small knobs of tissue called lymph nodes, which filter lymph, trapping bacteria and other disease-causing microorganisms in the fluid.

☑ **READING CHECK** **Determine Central Ideas** The lymphatic system helps to remove bacteria and other microorganisms from the body. Why would this be important for you?

....

....

Literacy Connection

Draw Evidence Summarize the evidence on this page that supports the statement that the systems of the body work together to keep the body healthy.

....

....

....

....

....

....

....

....

....

INTERACTIVITY

Investigate how the circulatory and respiratory systems respond to changes in the environment.

Respiratory System

Take a deep breath in. Now let it out. You have just used your respiratory system, shown along with the circulatory and digestive systems in **Figure 5**. It is the job of the respiratory system to bring air containing oxygen into your body and remove carbon dioxide and water from your body. The lungs are the main organs of the system. Other structures include the nose, which moistens the air you breathe, the trachea (windpipe), the **bronchi** (the two passages that direct air into to the lungs), and the **alveoli** (tiny thin-walled sacs of lung tissue where gases can move between air and blood).

The terms *respiration* and *breathing* are often used interchangeably. However, while they are related, they are different processes. *Respiration* refers to cellular respiration, the process cells use to break down glucose in order to produce energy. Cellular respiration requires oxygen and produces carbon dioxide as a waste product. Breathing is the exchange of gases between the inside and outside of the body. The gases exchanged are oxygen and carbon dioxide. Cellular respiration could not occur without breathing.

Systems Work Together

Figure 5 🖊 Cellular respiration and breathing both require body systems working together. Circle the body system responsible for the exchange of gases. Complete the labels.

Form an Opinion How do you think having a strong respiratory system helps the circulatory system?

....

....

....

....

....

....

....

....

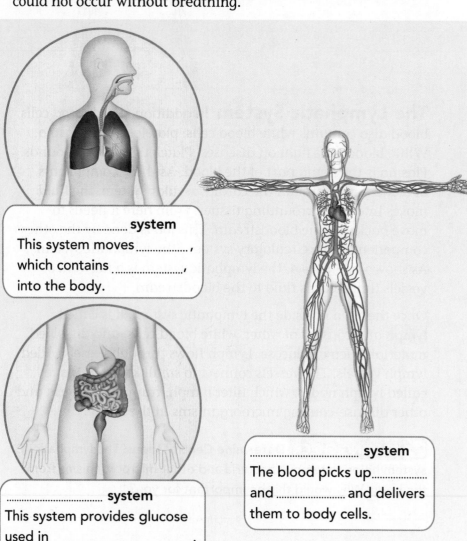

.... **system**
This system moves ....,
which contains ....,
into the body.

.... **system**
This system provides glucose
used in ....

.... **system**
The blood picks up...................
and .... and delivers
them to body cells.

Breathing and Gas Exchange

Figure 6 ✏ Complete the diagram labels on the right. In each diagram below, draw an arrow below the diaphragm to show the direction the lungs and diaphragm move when we breathe.

Apply Concepts Pneumonia is an infection people can get in their lungs. It causes the alveoli in your lungs to fill with fluid. How do you think this disease affects breathing?

....
....
....
....

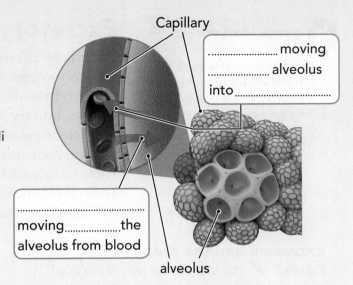

Capillary

.... moving
.... alveolus
into ....

....
moving.................the
alveolus from blood

alveolus

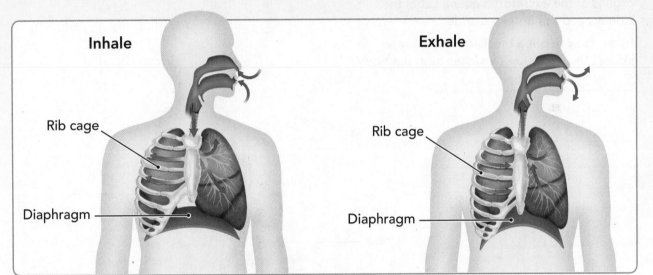

Inhale

Rib cage

Diaphragm

Exhale

Rib cage

Diaphragm

The Breathing Process
When you inhale, your rib muscles and diaphragm contract as shown in **Figure 6**. The chest moves upward and outward as it expands. The air pressure within the lungs lowers, so air moves in. When you exhale, the opposite happens. The muscles relax and the chest lowers. The pressure within the lungs is increased, so air is forced out.

Process of Gas Exchange
Gases move between the alveoli and the blood. After air enters the alveoli, oxygen passes through the capillary walls into the blood. At the same time, carbon dioxide and water pass from the blood into the alveoli. This continual exchange maintains the correct concentrations of gases within the blood.

☑ **READING CHECK** **Draw Evidence** How is the respiratory system interconnected with other systems of the body?

....
....
....

INTERACTIVITY

Investigate how human body systems work together to maintain homeostasis during long-term physical activity.

Excretory System

The process of removing wastes is called **excretion**. The excretory system, which is illustrated in **Figure 7**, removes waste products from the body. The main organs of this system are the kidneys, urinary bladder, urethra, lungs, skin, and liver. All of these organs work together to rid the body of waste. As your cells perform their various functions, they produce waste products. These include carbon dioxide, excess water, and other materials. These wastes need to be removed from the body in order to maintain homeostasis.

Excretion and the Kidneys

Figure 7 🖊 The kidneys are two of the main organs of the excretory system. Label the kidneys and the urinary bladder.

Infer How might a blockage in the ureter impact the excretion of wastes from the body?

....

....

....

....

....

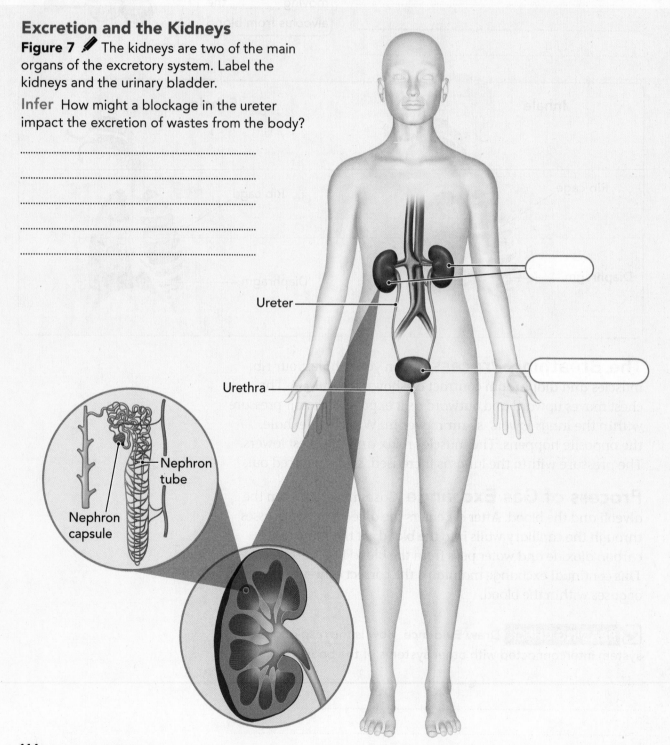

Ureter

Urethra

Nephron tube

Nephron capsule

Kidneys The kidneys are two bean-shaped organs that filter blood and regulate the amount of water in the body. The kidneys remove water and urea, a chemical produced from the breakdown of proteins. While the lungs remove some water, most water is excreted from the body in the form of urine, which includes water and urea. Liquid waste collects in the urinary bladder and is expelled through the urethra.

Each kidney is composed of millions of tiny tubes called nephrons. A **nephron** is a small filtering structure in the kidneys that removes wastes from blood and produces urine. This filtration process happens in two stages. First, the nephrons filter both the wastes and the needed materials from the blood. Next, the needed materials are returned to the blood and wastes are excreted.

The Lungs, Skin, and Liver The respiratory system, digestive system, and integumentary system work with the excretory system to remove wastes from the body. When you exhale, you are not only removing carbon dioxide from the body, but some water as well. Your integumentary system, which includes your skin (**Figure 8**), also removes waste. Sweat glands in your skin release water from your cells to help cool your body. Sweat also contains a small amount of urea. The liver produces urea from proteins and other wastes, including pieces of old red blood cells. Removing waste products from the body helps maintain homeostasis. However, if a disease or some blockage prevents these products from being removed, the body's internal environment can become toxic.

READING CHECK **Read and Comprehend** What are three ways your body excretes waste?

....

....

....

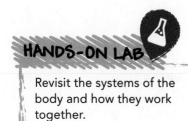

HANDS-ON LAB

🧪**Investigate** Find out how your body's systems work together.

HANDS-ON LAB

Revisit the systems of the body and how they work together.

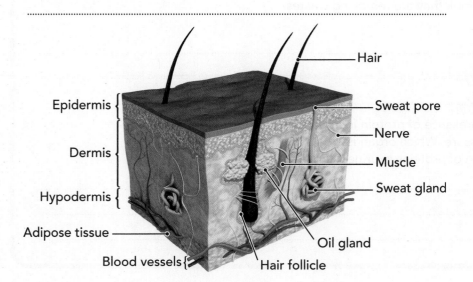

Epidermis
Dermis
Hypodermis
Adipose tissue
Blood vessels
Hair follicle
Oil gland
Hair
Sweat pore
Nerve
Muscle
Sweat gland

Skin and Excretion
Figure 8 🖉 As your body temperature rises, your sweat glands release water to help cool you off. Sweat is a form of excretion. Circle where a bead of sweat would form on the surface of the skin.

Model It!

Body's Waste Disposal System

✏️ Complete the table.

Organ	System to which it belongs	How it works in excretion
Lungs		
Skin		
Liver		
Kidneys		

1. **Interpret Photos** How does the photo of the people, who have exercised, demonstrate excretion?

....

....

2. **Explain** How else do you think they are removing wastes from their bodies?

....

....

....

3. **Evaluate Evidence** The presence of protein in urine can indicate diabetes or high blood pressure. Which organ is most likely contributing to the presence of proteins in urine? Explain.

....

....

....

☑ LESSON 4 Check

MS-LS1-3

1. **Identify** What are the major organs of the circulatory system?

....

....

....

....

....

2. **Summarize** Where does diffusion occur in the circulatory and respiratory systems?

....

....

....

....

....

....

....

....

3. **Analyze Structures** How do the circulatory and respiratory systems work together to transport gases to all parts of the body?

....

....

....

....

....

....

....

....

....

4. **Analyze Systems** How does the excretory system remove wastes from the blood of the circulatory system?

....

....

....

....

Quest CHECK-IN

In this lesson, you learned about the structures and functions of the circulatory, respiratory, and excretory systems. You also learned how these systems work together to manage materials that go into and out of your body.

Analyze Systems Consider how your body systems interact when you train for your favorite sport. How does physical exertion impact your heart, lungs, and kidneys?

....

....

....

....

....

HANDS-ON LAB

Heart Beat, Health Beat

Go online and download the lab to explore how physical activity affects heart and perspiration rates.

Controlling Processes

Guiding Questions

- Which systems control processes in the human body?
- How does the body sense and respond to stimuli in the environment?
- How do the cells that make up the nervous system respond to stimuli?

Connection

Literacy Integrate with Visuals

MS-LS1-8

Vocabulary

neuron
synapse
brain
spinal cord
gland
negative
  feedback
reflex

Academic Vocabulary

impulse

 VOCABULARY APP

Practice vocabulary on a mobile device.

Quest CONNECTION

Consider how your nervous and endocrine systems are involved in athletic challenges.

Connect It!

✏ **Circle the stimulus in the image that may cause the diver to respond.**

Construct Explanations   What senses is the diver using to receive information about this encounter? Explain.

....

....

Cause and Effect   Why would the diver know to respond to the stimulus? Explain.

....

....

....

Nervous System

The Internet allows us to communicate quickly with friends near and far. The nervous system is your body's communication network. Your nervous system receives information about what is happening both inside and outside your body. Then it directs how your body responds to this information. For example, in **Figure 1**, the diver's nervous system responds to the information it receives about the sharks. Your nervous system also helps maintain homeostasis, which keeps your internal environment stable. Your nervous system consists of your brain, spinal cord, and nerves.

Like any system, the human nervous system is made up of organs and tissues. A cell that carries information through the nervous system is called a nerve cell, or **neuron**. The structure of a neuron helps it function. Neurons are made up of dendrites and axons. A dendrite is the branched structure that picks up information. The axon receives information from the dendrite and sends it away from the cell.

The nervous system is divided into two systems: the central nervous system (CNS) and the peripheral nervous system (PNS). The brain and spinal cord make up the CNS. The job of the CNS is to control most of the functions of the body and mind. The PNS is a network of nerves that branches out from the CNS and connects to the rest of the body.

HANDS-ON LAB

Test how your knee responds to an external stimulus.

Reflect In your notebook, describe three instances in which your body seems to react to something in the environment, without any thought or conscious decision on your part.

Reacting to the Environment

Figure 1 The diver's encounter with sharks provides stimuli that will result in both immediate reactions and lasting memories.

Neurons The nervous system is made up of three kinds of neurons. A sensory neuron picks up a stimulus from the internal or external environment and converts the stimulus into a message. An interneuron carries this message from one neuron to another. A motor neuron sends the message to a muscle or gland, which reacts accordingly.

Nerve Impulses The function of a neuron is to transmit information. When the dendrite receives information, the neuron sends the information along the cell through the long axon. The message carried by the neuron is called a nerve impulse. The axon transmits the **impulse** to nearby cells.

Synapse As shown in **Figure 2**, the junction where one neuron can transfer an impulse to another neuron is called a **synapse**. At the axon tips, electrical signals change to chemical signals. This allows the signal to bridge the gap and continue to the next neuron. The impulse is converted to an electrical signal again, and travels through the neuron to another neighboring one.

☑ READING CHECK **Interpret Visuals** Identify the path that the nerve impulse will take, starting and ending with the dendrite.

....

....

Academic Vocabulary

Many people say, 'that was an impulse purchase.' Use your understanding of the word *impulse* to explain the context in which the author is using the term in the paragraph.

....

....

....

Signal and Synapse

Figure 2 🖊 Synapses are gaps between neurons where the impulse changes from electrical to chemical and back again. Draw an arrow on the diagram to indicate the direction the nerve impulse is traveling.

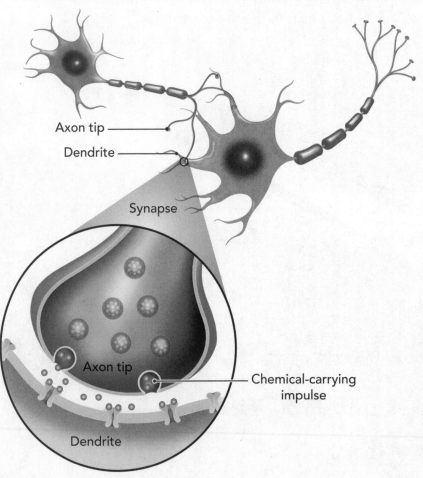

Axon tip

Dendrite

Synapse

Axon tip

Chemical-carrying impulse

Dendrite

Parts of the Nervous System

Figure 3 The brain sits atop the human nervous system, with bundled neurons branching out from the spinal cord.

Cause and Effect What could happen if the brain stem were damaged?

....

....

....

....

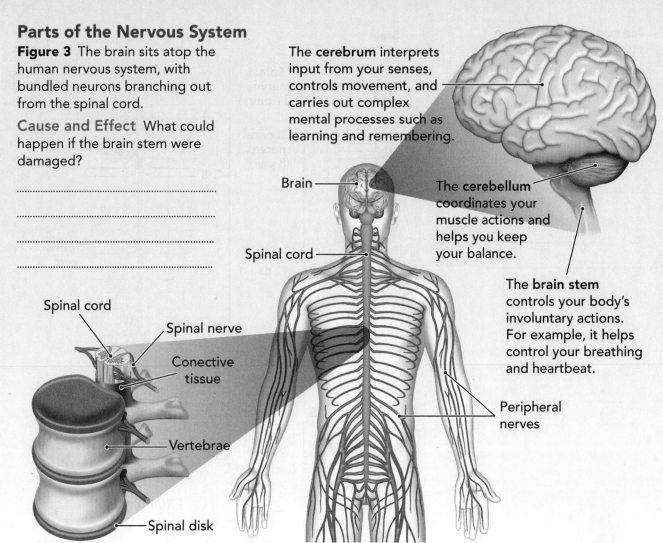

The **cerebrum** interprets input from your senses, controls movement, and carries out complex mental processes such as learning and remembering.

Brain

The **cerebellum** coordinates your muscle actions and helps you keep your balance.

Spinal cord

The **brain stem** controls your body's involuntary actions. For example, it helps control your breathing and heartbeat.

Spinal cord

Spinal nerve

Conective tissue

Vertebrae

Peripheral nerves

Spinal disk

Central Nervous System

The central nervous system, which is shown in **Figure 3**, controls the functions of the body. The **brain** is the part of the CNS that is located in the skull and controls most functions of the body. The **spinal cord** is a thick column of nervous tissue that links the brain to most of the nerves that branch out through the body. Most stimuli travel through the spinal cord to the brain. The brain then directs a response, usually back out through the spinal cord.

The Brain The human brain has about 100 billion neurons, all of which are interneurons. These interneurons handle thousands of messages each day. The brain is covered by layers of connective tissue and fluid that help protect the brain from injury. The brain itself has three main components. These control voluntary and involuntary actions such as heart rate, memory, and muscular coordination.

The Spinal Cord The vertebral column that you can feel with your fingers down the length of your neck and back contains the spinal cord. Like the brain, layers of connective tissue surround the spinal cord, along with a layer of fluid.

HANDS-ON LAB

Investigate Explore the different parts of the nervous system.

121

Nerve Pairs

Figure 4 Each nerve pair is connected to specific parts of the body.

Interpret Visuals Which parts of the body do you think the thoracic nerve pairs communicate with?

....

....

....

....

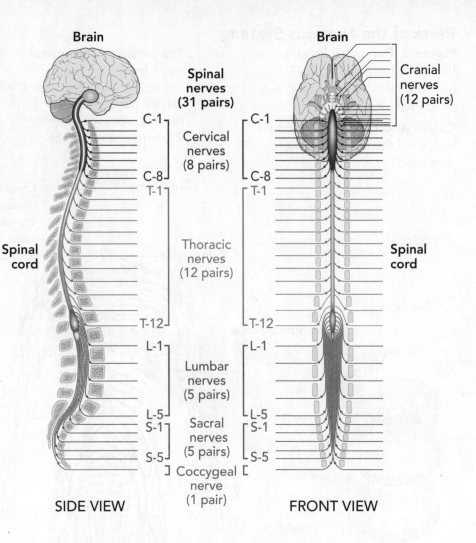

Brain

Spinal nerves (31 pairs)

C-1

Cervical nerves (8 pairs)

C-8

T-1

Thoracic nerves (12 pairs)

Spinal cord

T-12

L-1

Lumbar nerves (5 pairs)

L-5

S-1

Sacral nerves (5 pairs)

S-5

Coccygeal nerve (1 pair)

SIDE VIEW

Brain

Cranial nerves (12 pairs)

C-1

C-8

T-1

Spinal cord

T-12

L-1

L-5

S-1

S-5

FRONT VIEW

Autonomic Response

Figure 5 ✏ One of these pupils is responding to darkness, while the other is responding to light. Circle the eye that is responding bright light.

Contraction of round muscles of the iris constricts pupil.

Contraction of radial muscles of the iris dilates pupil.

Peripheral Nervous System

The network of nerves that connects the central nervous system to the rest of the body is called the peripheral nervous system. It has 43 pairs of nerves, as shown in **Figure 4**, and controls both involuntary and voluntary actions. Twelve pairs of nerves begin in the brain and branch out to parts of the head, while the other pairs begin in the spinal cord and branch out through the torso from the spine. In each nerve pair, one nerve goes to the left side of the body and the other goes to the right. Each spinal nerve has axons of sensory and motor neurons. Sensory neurons bring impulses to the central nervous system. Motor neurons carry impulses from the central nervous system out to the body.

Somatic and Autonomic Systems

The peripheral nervous system has two groups of nerves. The somatic nervous system controls voluntary actions, like typing a text message or throwing a ball. The autonomic nervous system controls involuntary actions, such as digestion or pupil dilation (**Figure 5**).

Reflexes The involuntary reaction of jumping when you hear a loud noise is called a **reflex**. It is an automatic response that occurs without conscious control. While skeletal muscles are largely within your conscious control through the somatic nervous system, some skeletal muscle contractions occur without the brain's involvement.

Pain is one type of stimulus that can trigger what is known as a reflex arc. Sensory neurons detect a pain stimulus, such as sticking your finger on a sharp object (**Figure 6**), and send impulses to the spinal cord. Interneurons in the spinal cord carry the impulses directly to motor neurons in the arm and hand. These motor neurons trigger muscle contractions in the hand to bring the fingertip away from the painful stimulus. At the same time, pain impulses travel to the brain, where they can be interpreted and stored as memories. This is how we learn to not press our fingertips against things like cactus spines and fishhooks.

✓ **READING CHECK** **Sequence** What is the sequence of neurons involved in a reflex arc?

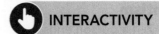
INTERACTIVITY

Find out how the human brain stacks up against a computer.

Model It

Learning from Experience

Figure 6 The hooks on this fishing lure would cause pain if you accidentally snagged them on your fingertip.

Develop Models 🖊 In the space, draw a diagram of a brain, spine, arm, and hand. Use arrows and labels to model a reflex arc showing how a person would react to getting snagged by a hook. Also show how pain impulses would reach the brain and result in learning something from the experience.

Figure 7 If a person ends up with too much or too little growth hormone, his or her height will be affected.

Identify Unknowns What do you think are some possible health problems of someone with gigantism? Explain.

....

....

....

....

Endocrine System

The human body has two systems that maintain homeostasis: the nervous system and the endocrine system. The nervous system maintains homeostasis by sending nerve impulses throughout the body. The endocrine system regulates the body by releasing chemicals called hormones, such as those that regulate height (**Figure 7**). The endocrine system is made up of different glands. A **gland** is an organ that produces and releases chemicals through ducts or into the bloodstream. The hormones of the endocrine system and the glands that regulate them are shown in **Figure 8**.

Regulators One of the links between the nervous system and the endocrine system is the hypothalamus. This gland is located deep inside the brain, just above the spinal cord. Its function is to send out nerve and chemical signals. Its nerve signals control sleep, hunger, and other basic body processes. It produces hormones—chemicals signals that regulate other glands and organs of the endocrine system.

Below the hypothalamus is the pituitary gland. This pea-sized gland receives signals from the hypothalamus and releases hormones. Some of these hormones are signals to other endocrine glands. Others, such as growth hormone, go to work directly on different body tissues.

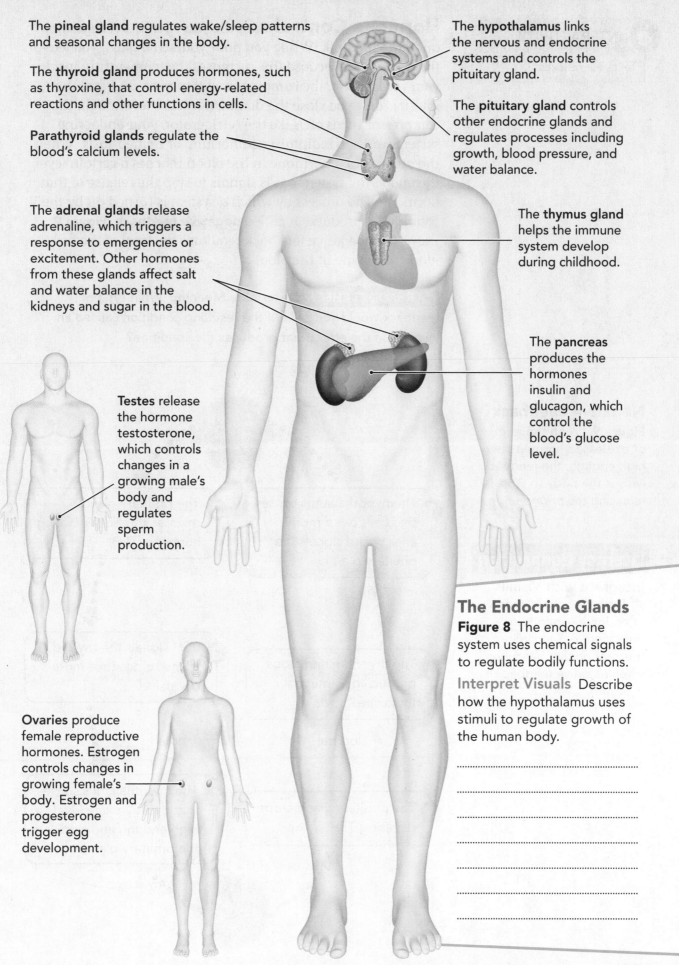

The **pineal gland** regulates wake/sleep patterns and seasonal changes in the body.

The **thyroid gland** produces hormones, such as thyroxine, that control energy-related reactions and other functions in cells.

Parathyroid glands regulate the blood's calcium levels.

The **adrenal glands** release adrenaline, which triggers a response to emergencies or excitement. Other hormones from these glands affect salt and water balance in the kidneys and sugar in the blood.

Testes release the hormone testosterone, which controls changes in a growing male's body and regulates sperm production.

Ovaries produce female reproductive hormones. Estrogen controls changes in growing female's body. Estrogen and progesterone trigger egg development.

The **hypothalamus** links the nervous and endocrine systems and controls the pituitary gland.

The **pituitary gland** controls other endocrine glands and regulates processes including growth, blood pressure, and water balance.

The **thymus gland** helps the immune system develop during childhood.

The **pancreas** produces the hormones insulin and glucagon, which control the blood's glucose level.

The Endocrine Glands

Figure 8 The endocrine system uses chemical signals to regulate bodily functions.

Interpret Visuals Describe how the hypothalamus uses stimuli to regulate growth of the human body.

....

....

....

....

....

....

....

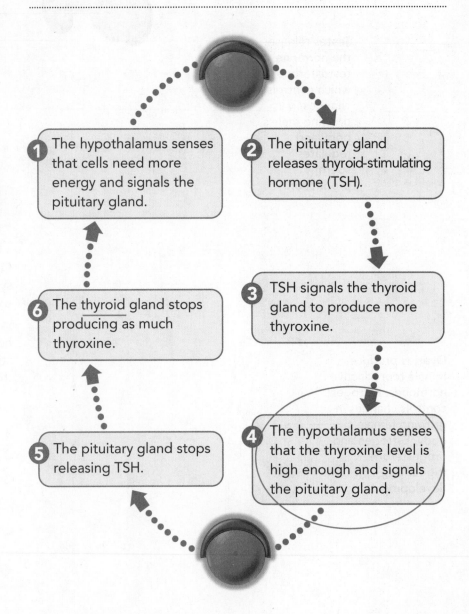

INTERACTIVITY

Test your reflexes.

Hormone Control

Hormone Control Suppose you open the refrigerator and grab the milk. While you pour yourself a glass, you leave the door open. Because this increases the temperature inside your refrigerator, the compressor will turn on and cool the interior after you close the door. Once it is cool enough, the compressor turns off. Like the refrigerator, your endocrine system works to maintain equilibrium, or homeostasis. When the amount of a hormone in the blood reaches a certain level, the endocrine system sends signals to stop the release of that hormone. The process by which a system is turned off by the condition it produces is called **negative feedback**. **Figure 9** shows how negative feedback regulates the level of the hormone thyroxine in the blood.

☑ READING CHECK **Determine Meaning** What type of feedback would you call it if the resulting condition caused an increase in the effect that produces the condition?

Negative Feedback

Figure 9 When the level of a released hormone is high enough, the feedback causes the body to stop releasing the hormone.

Literacy Connection

Integrate with Visuals
✏ Underline the names of endocrine glands in the diagram, and circle the caption that describes when negative feedback is provided.

1 The hypothalamus senses that cells need more energy and signals the pituitary gland.

2 The pituitary gland releases thyroid-stimulating hormone (TSH).

3 TSH signals the thyroid gland to produce more thyroxine.

4 The hypothalamus senses that the thyroxine level is high enough and signals the pituitary gland.

5 The pituitary gland stops releasing TSH.

6 The thyroid gland stops producing as much thyroxine.

MS-LS1-8

1. **Identify** What is the name for the division of the nervous system that handles involuntary actions and processes of the body?

....

2. **Analyze Systems** What are the two main physical components of the central nervous system?

....

3. **Cause and Effect** Describe the two signals and pathways that are activated when you touch something and experience pain.

....

....

....

....

....

....

....

....

....

....

4. **Patterns** Describe the role chemical signals play a role in both the nervous system and the endocrine system.

....

....

....

....

....

....

5. **Construct Explanations** Why would it be advantageous to have two separate pathways to react to and learn from pain?

....

....

....

....

....

....

....

....

Quest CHECK-IN

In this lesson, you learned how the nervous system and endocrine system regulate the body and respond to stimuli from the environment.

Evaluate Why are coordination between motor neurons and the brain's ability to learn and make memories essential to improving at a physical activity?

....

....

....

....

👆 INTERACTIVITY

Why Practice Makes Perfect

Go online to explore how athletes develop muscle memory.

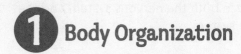# ☑ TOPIC 2 Review and Assess

1 Body Organization

MS-LS1-3

1. Because its structure is more complex,
   A. a tissue has a more complex function than an organ.
   B. a cell has a more complex function than a tissue.
   C. an organ has a more complex function than a tissue.
   D. a cell has a more complex function than an organ.

2. **Patterns** What is the relationship among organs, cells, and tissues?

....

....

....

....

2 Systems Interacting

MS-LS1-3

3. The main purpose of homeostasis is to
   A. fight disease-causing organisms.
   B. keep internal conditions stable.
   C. produce offspring.
   D. replicate DNA.

4. **Explain Phenomena** Suppose you sit in the same position so long that your leg starts to hurt. How do the body's different parts interact to stop the pain?

....

....

....

....

....

....

3 Supplying Energy

MS-LS1-3

5. The liver helps the circulatory system by
   A. filtering blood of harmful substances.
   B. helping blood vessels to absorb nutrients.
   C. storing bile that is released into the bloodstream.
   D. releasing chemicals that begin to break down food in the mouth.

6. .... in the stomach are responsible for the mechanical digestion that takes place there.

7. **Develop Models** ✏ Draw a flow chart to show how the digestive, circulatory, and excretory systems work together to process food and supply nutrients to the body.

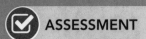
 Managing Materials

MS-LS1-3

8. Which of the following organs function as both a respiratory organ and an excretory organ?
   A. liver   B. skin
   C. kidneys   D. lungs

9. Organs such as the kidneys, lungs, skin, and liver work together to
   A. remove carbon dioxide.
   B. eliminate excess water.
   C. help maintain homeostasis.
   D. filter out urea.

10. One role of rib bones in the .... system is to protect the heart from physical injury.

11. **Relate Structure and Function** How does the structure of the alveoli in the lungs help with their function in the respiratory system?

   ....

   ....

   ....

   ....

   ....

12. **Construct Explanations** Explain how the respiratory and circulatory systems work together to manage materials in the body.

   ....

   ....

   ....

   ....

   ....

   ....

   ....

5 **Controlling Processes**

MS-LS1-8

13. The spinal cord is a thick column of
    A. blood vessels that helps to support and hold up the body.
    B. bony discs that protects nervous tissue.
    C. muscle tissue that connects nerve cells in the brain with nerve cells in the body.
    D. nervous tissue that connects the brain to the body's nerves.

14. The .... system releases hormones that .... processes in the body.

15. **Analyze Systems** How does the nervous system regulate basic body processes?

   ....

   ....

   ....

   ....

   ....

   ....

16. **Apply Scientific Reasoning** Suppose a child reaches for a hot pan on the stove and burns himself. Explain how the child's brain functions to protect his body from injury both at that moment as well as in the future.

   ....

   ....

   ....

   ....

   ....

   ....

   ....

MS-LS1-3, MS-LS1-8

Evidence-Based Assessment

Crigler-Najjar syndrome is a rare inherited disorder with about 100 confirmed cases worldwide. Children born with the syndrome do not produce a certain liver enzyme. As a result, a toxic substance builds up in the body, which causes damage to other body systems.

The diagram below details some of the major effects of this disorder.

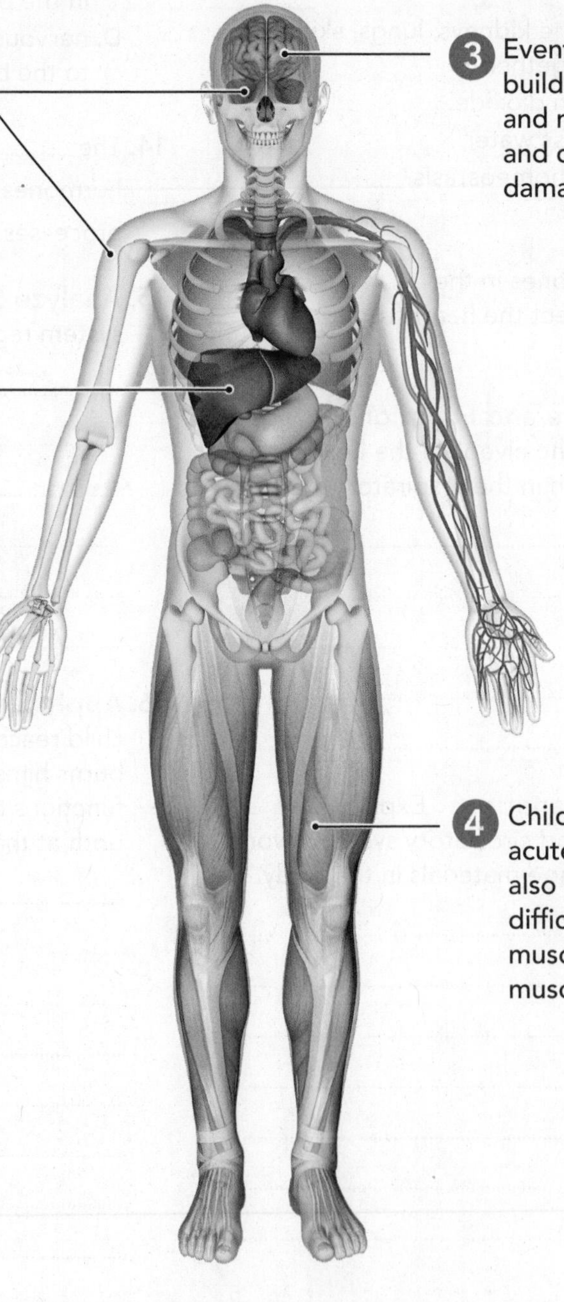

2 As the bilirubin level increases, it enters the bloodstream and builds up in the eyes and skin. This causes them to become yellow, a condition known as jaundice.

1 After about 115 days in the bloodstream, red blood cells are broken down in the liver. This produces a toxic substance called bilirubin. Without the enzyme, the liver cannot convert the bilirubin into a form that can be safely removed from the body.

3 Eventually, bilirubin builds up in the brain and nervous tissue and causes neurological damage.

4 Children with acute cases can also suffer from difficulty in coordination, muscle weakness, and muscle spasms.

1. **Cause and Effect** Which of the following body systems does not seem to be directly affected by the syndrome?
   A. circulatory system   B. nervous system
   C. skeletal system   D. muscular system

2. **Use Models** Why would a child with Crigler-Najjar syndrome suffer from muscle weakness and spasms?
   A. Red blood cells attack the liver, causing it to release bilirubin, which attacks the muscular system.
   B. The brain does not function properly, so it signals the body to produce excess bilirubin, which damages muscle tissue.
   C. Red blood cells die and build up in muscle tissue, which interferes with their proper functioning.
   D. Bilirubin builds up in the body and causes damage to the nervous system, which affects the muscular system.

3. **Apply Concepts** How are cells and tissue in the liver affected by Crigler-Najjar syndrome?

....
....
....
....
....
....
....

4. **Analyze Systems** How does Crigler-Najjar syndrome affect the circulatory system?

....
....
....
....
....
....
....

5. **Construct Arguments** How does Crigler-Najjar syndrome demonstrate that the body depends on many interactions among different body systems in order to function properly?

....
....
....
....
....
....
....
....

Quest FINDINGS

Complete the Quest!

Phenomenon Organize your data and determine the best way to present your training and nutrition plan.

Cause and Effect Why is it important to consider how one body system impacts other body systems when designing a successful training plan?

....
....
....
....
....
....

👆 **INTERACTIVITY**

Reflect on Peak Performance Plan

131

Reaction Research

How can you design and conduct an investigation about reaction times?

Background

Phenomenon You've been hired by a video game company to do some research and gather data on reaction times. Reaction time refers to the amount of time it takes for a person to recognize a stimulus and then direct the body to respond with an action. The developers are working on a new rhythm game in which the player presses buttons on the controller in time with visuals and music. They want to know how quickly a player might react to different stimuli, such as a shape changing color on the screen, a musical beat, or a vibration or rumble in the controller.

You will design and conduct an investigation to explore how different factors affect reaction times. Then you will analyze the data you have collected and draw some conclusions to share with the game developers.

Materials

(per pair)
- meter stick (with centimeters marked)
- calculator

Safety

Be sure to follow all safety guidelines provided by your teacher. The Safety Appendix of your textbook provides more details about the safety icons.

Design Your Investigation

1. You and your partner can test reaction times with the meter stick. The subject sits at a table with a hand extended beyond the edge of the table as shown. The researcher holds up the meter stick so that the 0 lines up with the top of the subject's hand. The meter stick is dropped and the subject grabs it as quickly as possible. Measure the distance the meter stick falls by recording the centimeter mark closest to the top of the subject's hand.

2. You can use an equation to calculate how long it takes an object to fall based on how far an object falls. In the following equation, t is time, d is distance, and a is acceleration. To calculate the reaction time, use a calculator to solve the equation. (Note: A falling object accelerates due to gravity at a rate of 980 cm/s^2.)

$$t = \sqrt{(2d/a)}$$

3. Based on the data that the developers want, identify the three types of stimuli that you will test in your investigation.

- ....
- ....
- ....

4. Develop a procedure for your investigation based on the three stimuli you identified.
Write your procedure in the space provided.
As you plan your investigation, consider these questions.

- How will you use the meter stick to determine reaction times?
- What tests will you perform to collect data about reaction times for each type of stimulus?
- How many trials of each test will you perform?
- What data will you record?

5. After getting your teacher's approval, carry out the investigation. Make a table in the space provided to record your data.

Procedure

_____

_____

_____

_____

_____

_____

_____

_____

_____

_____

_____

_____

Data Table

Analyze and Interpret Data

1. **Cause and Effect** What trends or patterns do you notice in the data? What might explain these trends or patterns?

   ....

   ....

   ....

   ....

2. **Analyze Systems** Choose one stimulus that you tested in the investigation. Identify the body systems that are involved in responding to that stimulus. Then, draw a flow chart to diagram the process and explain how the systems interact.

   ....

3. **Communicate** What conclusions would you share with the game developers? Which types of cues in the game would likely increase the chances of a player doing better? Explain.

   ....

   ....

   ....

   ....

   ....

4. **Construct Arguments** Aside from the three different stimuli, what other variables could you test to see how reaction time is affected? What other fields or industries might find data about reaction times useful? Explain.

   ....

   ....

   ....

   ....

Reproduction and Growth

NGSS PERFORMANCE EXPECTATIONS

MS-LS1-4 Use argument based on empirical
evidence and scientific reasoning to support an
explanation for how characteristic animal behaviors
and specialized plant structures affect the
probability of successful reproduction of animals
and plants respectively.

MS-LS1-5 Construct a scientific explanation based
on evidence for how environmental and genetic
factors influence the growth of organisms.

MS-LS3-2 Develop and use a model to describe
why asexual reproduction results in offspring
with identical genetic information and sexual
reproduction results in offspring with genetic
variation.

HANDS-ON LAB

uConnect Use a model to investigate
how parental care can influence the
survival of offspring.

Why does this tree have such a strange shape?

GO ONLINE
to access your
digital course

▶ VIDEO

👆 INTERACTIVITY

🧪 VIRTUAL LAB

☑ ASSESSMENT

📖 eTEXT

📱 APP

The Essential Question

What factors influence the growth of organisms and their ability to reproduce?

Only found on Socotra Island, off the coast of Yemen, the cucumber tree grows in a hot and dry climate. How do you think the tree's shape helps it to survive?

....

....

....

....

Quest KICKOFF

How can we reduce the impact of construction on plants and animals?

STEM **Phenomenon** Environmental scientists study habitats and the organisms that live there. They investigate how the availability of resources—such as water, food, and space—affects the ability of plants and animals to survive and reproduce. In this Quest activity, you will consider how to build a basketball court on school grounds, with minimal impact on local plants and animals. In digital activities, you will explore the factors that affect plant and animal growth and reproduction. By applying what you have learned, you will develop a construction proposal for the basketball court.

 INTERACTIVITY

Construction Without Destruction

MS-LS1-5 Construct a scientific explanation based on evidence for how environmental and genetic factors influence the growth of organisms.

NBC LEARN ▶ VIDEO

After watching the video, which explores how construction impacts habitats and organisms, consider the issue on a local level. Choose a plant or animal, and then explain how human activity in your town or city affects the organism.

....

....

....

....

....

....

....

....

....

IN LESSON 1

How do different organisms reproduce? Think about how the court's impact on the habitat might affect the ability of organisms to survive and reproduce there.

Quest CHECK-IN

IN LESSON 2

What effect might tree removal and construction work have on plants in the area? Assess the environmental impact on the ability of the plants to survive and reproduce.

 INTERACTIVITY

Protect the Plants

Quest CHECK-IN

IN LESSON 3

How does construction work impact animals? Think about how construction noise might interfere with the ability of an organism to reproduce successfully.

 INTERACTIVITY

The Mating Game

Before construction begins for a facility, such as a basketball court, professionals complete a construction proposal. It often outlines how organisms may be impacted once the construction is complete.

Quest CHECK-IN

IN LESSON 4

STEM How can the impact of the court's location and construction be minimized? Develop a plan that ensures the successful survival and reproduction of plants and animals.

👆 INTERACTIVITY

Make Your Construction Case

Quest FINDINGS

Complete the Quest!

Present your construction plan using the information and data that you have collected as evidence to support your recommendations.

👆 INTERACTIVITY

Reflect on Your Basketball Court Plans

Patterns of Reproduction

Guiding Questions

- How do organisms reproduce and transfer genes to their offspring?
- How do offspring produced by asexual reproduction and sexual reproduction compare?
- Why do different offspring of the same parent usually look different?

Connections

Literacy Cite Textual Evidence

Math Summarize Distributions

MS-LS3-2

Vocabulary

asexual reproduction
sexual reproduction
fertilization
trait
gene
inheritance
allele

Academic Vocabulary

dominant

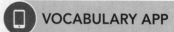 **VOCABULARY APP**

Practice vocabulary on a mobile device.

Quest CONNECTION

Think about how fruit-bearing plants reproduce to form offspring.

Connect It!

✏️ **The pictures show offspring with their mothers. Circle the offspring you think might look like the father.**

Construct Explanations Summarize what you already know about how the three kinds of animals in the picture produce offspring.

....

....

....

....

....

....

Asexual and Sexual Reproduction

INTERACTIVITY

Consider the traits that make you unique.

Living things reproduce. Giraffes make more giraffes, hermit crabs make more hermit crabs, and bald eagles make more bald eagles. Some animals produce offspring that look exactly like the parent. Others, such as humans and the animals in **Figure 1,** produce offspring that look different from the parents.

Animals use one of two main methods—asexual or sexual reproduction—to produce offspring. Reproduction guarantees that a species' genes are passed on to the next generation.

Asexual Reproduction A reproductive process that involves only one parent and produces offspring that are genetically identical to the parent is called **asexual reproduction**. It is the simplest form of reproduction. Animals such as sponges, corals, and certain jellyfish reproduce asexually.

One form of asexual reproduction is fragmentation. During fragmentation, a new organism forms from a piece of the original. For example, a whole new sea star can develop from a single arm that breaks off (see **Figure 2**). Another method of asexual reproduction is called budding. In this process, a new animal grows out from the parent until it fully matures and breaks off. Sponges and some sea anemones reproduce in this way.

Reflect What do you think is the benefit of reproducing asexually? In your science notebook, explain how asexual reproduction could give some animals an advantage.

Reproduction Results in Offspring
Figure 1 All living things have the ability to reproduce.

141

Sexual vs. Asexual Reproduction

Figure 2 (top) A new sea star, identical to its parent, is developing from a single arm. (bottom) The fur patterns of the African wild-dog pups are different from their mother's.

Classify Which offspring resulted from sexual reproduction?

....

Sexual Reproduction

Consider the variety of trees, birds, fish, and plants in the world around you. Clearly, many life forms are unique. When organisms reproduce sexually, their offspring display a variety of traits. Even members of the same species are not exact copies of each other. Sexual reproduction is responsible for the variety of life you see.

In **sexual reproduction**, two parents combine their genetic material to produce a new organism which differs from both parents. Sexual reproduction involves an egg cell and a sperm cell joining to form a new cell in a process called **fertilization**. Sperm cells are from the father and contain half of the father's chromosomes. Egg cells are from the mother and contain half the mother's chromosomes. When fertilization occurs, a full set of chromosomes is present in the new cell.

Because offspring receive roughly half their genetic information from each parent, they receive a combination of specific characteristics. A specific characteristic that an organism can pass to its offspring through its genes is called a **trait**. A **gene** is a sequence of DNA that determines a trait and is passed from parent to offspring. As a result, offspring may look very similar to their parents, or they may look very different, like the wild dogs in **Figure 2**. These differences are known as variations, and they are what make you different from your siblings. Individual variations depend on which genes were passed on from each parent.

Model It

Develop Models ✏ Suppose two neighborhood dogs produce offspring. Draw a picture of the mother and the father. Draw one offspring that might result from the parents. Label the traits the father passed on to the offspring and the traits the mother passed on to the offspring.

Comparing Types of Reproduction Both methods of reproduction have advantages and disadvantages. Organisms that reproduce asexually do not have to find a mate. They can also produce many offspring fairly quickly. The downside is that all of the offspring have exactly the same genetic makeup as the parent. This can be a problem if the environment changes. If one individual organism is unable to tolerate the change, then chances are the rest of the identical offspring will not be able to handle it either.

Organisms that reproduce sexually pass on genes with greater genetic variation. This variation may increase their chances of surviving in a changing environment. It is possible that they received a gene from a parent that helps them adapt to the changing environment. One potential downside of sexual reproduction is that the organism needs to find a mate. This can sometimes be a problem for animals, such as polar bears, that live in remote areas.

 VIDEO

Compare asexual reproduction and sexual reproduction.

✓ READING CHECK **Cite Textual Evidence** What are some advantages of wild dogs reproducing sexually?

....

....

....

Math Toolbox

Sexual Reproduction

Gestation is the time period between fertilization and birth. The data in the table are based on recorded observations from hundreds of pregnant individuals in each species.

Animal	Gestation Range (days)	Median Gestation Time (days)	Bottom Quartile Median (days)	Top Quartile Median (days)
Hamster	16–23	20	17	22
Red Fox	49–55	52	50	53
Gerbil	22–26	24	23	25
Leopard	91–95	93	92	94

1. **Distinguish Relationships** What is the relationship between the size of the animal and how long it takes for its offspring to develop?

....

....

2. **Summarize Distributions** 🖊 Choose two species from the table and construct a box plot for each one.

Inheritance of Traits

Figure 3 Fur color, like human hair color, depends on which genes are inherited from the parents.

▶ **VIDEO**

Explore the relationship between inheritance and alleles.

Academic Vocabulary

Describe a situation in which you have been dominant.

....

....

....

....

....

....

Inherited Traits

When sperm and egg cells come together, genetic information from the mother and father mix. **Inheritance** is the process by which an offspring receives genes from its parents. Genes are located on chromosomes and describe the factors that control a trait. Each trait is described by a pair of genes, with one gene from the mother and one from the father. Sometimes the pair of genes are the same. At other times, there are two different genes in the pair.

For example, imagine a mouse with white fur and a mouse with brown fur have offspring. The genes for fur color from each parent are different. As shown in **Figure 3,** some of the offspring produced may be brown, some may be white, and others may be combinations of more than one color. Each offspring's fur color depends on how its inherited genes combine.

An **allele** is a different form of the same gene. One allele is received from each parent, and the combination of alleles determines which traits the offspring will have. In the simplest case, alleles are either dominant or recessive. If an offspring inherits a **dominant** allele from either parent, that trait will always show up in the offspring. But, if the offspring inherits recessive alleles from each parent, a recessive trait will show. This relationship allows parents with two dominant alleles to pass on recessive alleles to their offspring. For example, two brown-eyed people may have a blue-eyed child. However, most genetic traits do not follow these simple patterns of dominant and recessive inheritance.

Incomplete Dominance

Sometimes intermediate forms of a dominant trait appear. This means that mixing of colors or sizes occurs. Incomplete dominance may occur when a dominant allele and recessive allele are inherited. The offspring will have a mixture of these two alleles. For example, in some species of sheep, gray fleece results from a dominant white-fleece allele and a recessive black allele. Incomplete dominance also occurs in petal color in some species of plants. **Figure 4** shows how petal color can result in the blending of two colors.

Codominance

Unlike incomplete dominance, which shows blending of traits, codominance results in both alleles being expressed at the same time. In cattle, horses, and dogs, there is a color pattern called roan. This color pattern appears when a dominant white-hair allele and a dominant solid-color allele is inherited. The offspring has hairs of each color intermixed, giving the solid-color a more muted or mottled look.

Incomplete Dominance
Figure 4 ✏ Circle the flowers that demonstrate incomplete dominance in petal color.

Model It

Apply Concepts ✏ Draw the parents of this flower in the box. Assume that the flower's color is determined by codominance.

		Father's blood type				
		A	**B**	**AB**	**O**	
Mother's blood type	**A**	A or O	A, B, AB, or O	A, B, or AB	A or O	**Child's blood type must be**
	B	A, B, AB, or O	B or O	A, B, or AB	B or O	
	AB	A, B, or AB	A, B, or AB	A, B, or AB	A or B	
	O	A or O	B or O	A or B	O	

Human Blood Types

Figure 5 A gene with multiple alleles is expressed as one of four blood types: A, B, AB, and O.

Multiple Alleles

Every offspring inherits one allele from each parent for a total of two alleles. However, sometimes one trait has more than two alleles. For example, there are three alleles for blood type—A, B, and O. The A and B blood types are codominant and O is recessive. As you see in **Figure 5**, you receive two of the multiple alleles from each parent, but each possible combination of alleles results in one of four different blood types. Multiple alleles are not found only in blood types. **Figure 6** shows how fur color in some rabbits is the result of multiple alleles.

Multiple Alleles

Figure 6 These rabbits all came from the same litter.

Cite Evidence What evidence from the picture demonstrates that the fur color of these rabbits results from multiple alleles?

....

....

....

....

Polygenic Inheritance

Some traits are controlled by more than one gene. In polygenetic inheritance, these different genes are expressed together to produce the trait. Human height is an example of this. If the mother is 5 feet 2 inches tall and the father is 6 feet tall, then you might think that all of the offspring would be 5 feet 7 inches. However, there can be a large variation among the heights of the children. This fact is due to multiple genes working together to produce the trait.

☑ **READING CHECK** **Determine Central Ideas** How do alleles influence inherited traits? Explain with an example of incomplete dominance.

....

....

....

Genes and the Environment

What kinds of things have you learned in your life? Maybe you know how to paint. Maybe you can ride a unicycle. Or maybe you know how to solve very complicated math problems. Whatever your abilities, they are acquired traits that are the result of learned behaviors.

Acquired Traits The traits you inherited can be affected by your experience. For example, humans are born with teeth, vocal cords, and tongues—all of which enable us to speak. The language you learn to use depends on your environment. You were not born speaking a particular language, but you were born with the capacity to learn languages, whether a spoken language or sign language. The ability for language is an inherited trait. The language or languages you use, however, are acquired traits.

The combination of inherited traits and acquired traits helps many organisms to survive in their environment. The fox squirrel in **Figure 7** has inherited traits from its parents that help it survive in its environment. The squirrel also acquired traits that help it survive, by learning behaviors from its parents and by interacting with its environment.

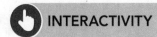

INTERACTIVITY

Find out how we learn about genes and traits from studying twins.

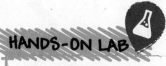

HANDS-ON LAB

☑**Investigate** Explore traits in an imaginary organism.

Acquired Traits

Figure 7 This fox squirrel has traits that were inherited as well as traits that were acquired through learning.

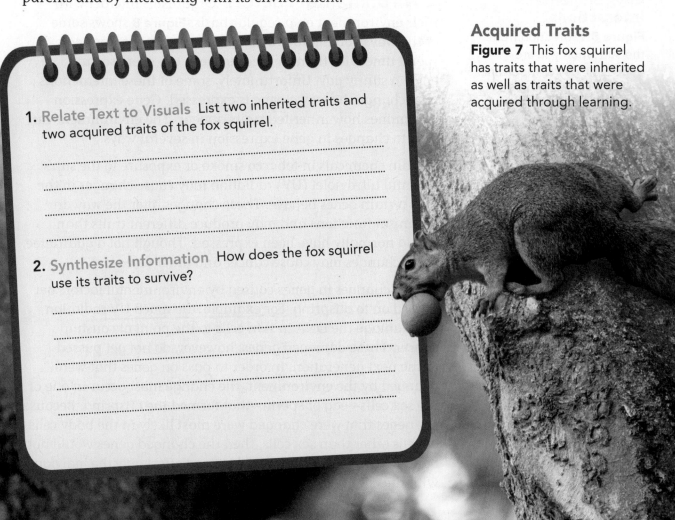

1. **Relate Text to Visuals** List two inherited traits and two acquired traits of the fox squirrel.

....

....

....

....

2. **Synthesize Information** How does the fox squirrel use its traits to survive?

....

....

....

....

....

Environmental Interactions

Figure 8 Protection from the sun when you are outside all day is important.

Implement a Solution List three acquired behaviors that people have learned to protect themselves from ultraviolet light.

....

....

....

....

....

Environmental Factors Organisms interact with their environment on a regular basis. **Figure 8** shows some of the ways you interact with your environment. You may spend time with friends, breathe fresh air, exercise, and enjoy a sunny day. Unfortunately, some of these interactions may change the way a gene is expressed. Gene expression determines how inherited traits appear. The environment can lead to changes in gene expression in several ways.

Certain chemicals in tobacco smoke or exposure to the sun's harmful ultraviolet (UV) radiation may cause changes in the way certain genes behave. These changes alter the way an organism functions and may produce different traits than would normally have been expressed. Though not a guarantee, these changes may cause cancer and other diseases.

Not all changes in genes caused by environmental factors get passed on to offspring. For example, too much UV radiation can damage the DNA in skin cells to the point of causing cancer. These damaged genes, however, do not get passed to the next generation. In order to pass on genes that were changed by the environment, the change must occur in one of the sex cells—egg or sperm—that formed the offspring. Because the genes that were changed were most likely in the body cells, or cells other than sex cells, then the changed genes would not be passed on to you, and would instead affect only the individual with the changed genes.

1. **Distinguish Relationships** What does inheritance mean in terms of reproduction?

....

....

....

2. **Determine Differences** 🖊 Indicate whether each of the listed traits is acquired from the environment or has been inherited.

Trait	Acquired	Inherited
Brown fur in rabbits		
Length of an elephant's trunk		
Having a spiked haircut		
An overweight horse		
Feather patterns of a parrot		

3. **Explain Phenomena** What happens if an offspring inherits a dominant allele from one of its parents?

....

....

....

4. **Construct Explanations** What is a possible benefit to an organism expressing codominant or incomplete dominant traits?

....

....

....

....

....

....

5. **Support Your Explanation** How does sexual reproduction differ from asexual reproduction?

....

....

....

....

....

....

....

6. **Apply Concepts** A species of butterfly has alleles for wing color that are either blue or orange. But, when a blue butterfly and an orange butterfly mated, the wings of the offspring were blue and orange. Explain the process through which wing color was expressed.

....

....

....

....

7. **Synthesize Information** Human hair color is a trait with very broad variation. Which pattern of inheritance could account for human hair color? Explain your answer.

....

....

....

....

....

....

② Plant Structures for Reproduction

Guiding Questions

- How do plants reproduce?
- How do seeds become new plants?
- Which specialized plant structures affect the probability of successful reproduction?

Connection

Literacy Cite Textual Evidence

MS-LS1-4

Vocabulary

zygote
pollination
cones
ovule
fruit
germination

Academic Vocabulary

disperse

 VOCABULARY APP

Practice vocabulary on a mobile device.

Quest CONNECTION

Consider how building a basketball court could impact local plants.

Connect It !

🖊 **Circle the fruits shown here.**

Explain Where in the fruit are seeds found and what is their purpose?

....

....

Plant Reproduction

Have you ever run from a bee buzzing around a garden? Have you taken the time to appreciate the pleasant scent and beautiful colors of a rose? Have you challenged a friend to see who could spit a watermelon seed the farthest? If you have done any of these things, you are already familiar with some of the methods plants use to reproduce.

When a seed, like ones from the fruits and vegetables in **Figure 1**, is planted in healthy soil and gets plenty of water and sunlight, it can grow into an adult plant. But this is just one part in the process of how plants reproduce. A lot must first happen in a plant's life before it can produce a seed that can grow into a plant. Surprisingly to some, plants are like animals in that reproduction requires a sperm cell fertilizing an egg cell for a new organism to begin.

To ensure successful reproduction, plants have evolved specialized structures over time. Different types of plants have different structures and methods that help them reproduce. But the goal is the same: to produce new generations of life.

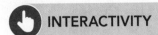

INTERACTIVITY

Explore the relationship between seeds and the food we eat.

Find the Fruit
Figure 1 Fruits may not look alike, but they function just the same. Inside a seed is a partially developed plant.

Plant Life Cycles

Figure 2 ✐ Complete the diagrams. Identify the sporophyte and gametophyte stage in each diagram.

The Life Cycle of a Moss Plant

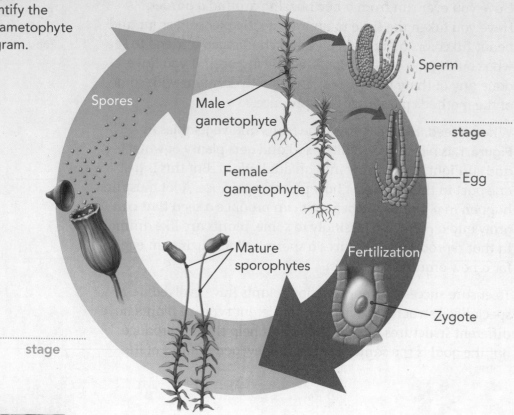

Spores

Male gametophyte

Female gametophyte

Mature sporophytes

Sperm

.... stage

Egg

Fertilization

Zygote

.... stage

Spore Production

Figure 3 Fern sporophytes are the recognizable parts of the plant.

Identify What is the purpose of the sporophyte stage?

....

....

....

....

Plant Life Cycles

Plants have complex life cycles that include two different stages: the sporophyte (SPOH ruh fyt) and gametophyte (guh MEE tuh fyt) stages. During the sporophyte stage, a plant produces the spores that will eventually develop into gametophytes. During the gametophyte stage, male and female gametophytes produce sex cells that will eventually be involved in the process of fertilization, which occurs when a sperm cell unites with an egg cell to produce a new organism.

Nonvascular and Seedless Vascular Plants

Mosses and other nonvascular plants produce sporophytes that resemble small trees or flowers. The sporophytes release spores that grow into male and female gametophytes. These gametophytes produce the sperm and egg cells that are needed for a **zygote**, or fertilized egg, to form and develop into a new sporophyte as is shown in **Figure 2**.

The life stages of seedless vascular plants, such as ferns, are similar to nonvascular plants in some ways. Sporophytes produce spores that develop into gametophytes. But fern gametophytes have both male and female structures that produce sex cells. When a sperm cell fertilizes an egg cell, a new sporophyte begins to develop.

The Life Cycle of an Angiosperm

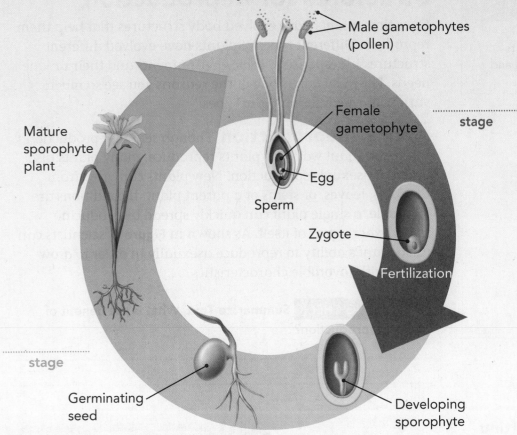

Male gametophytes (pollen)

Female gametophyte

stage

Egg

Sperm

Mature sporophyte plant

Zygote

Fertilization

Germinating seed

Developing sporophyte

stage

Other Vascular Plants The two other types of vascular plants are gymnosperms and angiosperms. Unlike both ferns and mosses, gymnosperm and angiosperm gametophytes actually develop inside structures within a larger sporophyte. In gymnosperms, they develop inside cones, and in an angiosperm like the one shown in **Figure 2**, they develop inside flowers.

The male gametophyte in these types of plants is called pollen. Pollen contains cells that will mature into sperm cells. For reproduction to occur, pollen must travel to the female gametophyte so it can fertilize egg cells. This process of transferring pollen from male reproductive structures to female reproductive structures in plants is called **pollination**. Pollination must occur in these plants before fertilization can occur.

✅**READING CHECK** **Determine Central Ideas** How do the sporophyte stage and gametophyte stage make a cycle?

....

....

....

....

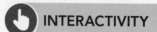
INTERACTIVITY

Explore how plant structures help plants reproduce asexually and sexually.

Structures for Reproduction

Over time, plants have evolved body structures that help them reproduce. Different types of plants have evolved different structures in response to their environments and their unique needs. Reproduction is one of the reasons you see so much variety in the different plant types.

Asexual Reproduction Though sexual reproduction is the dominant way that plants reproduce, many plants also undergo asexual reproduction. New plants can grow from the roots, leaves, or stems of a parent plant. If conditions are favorable, a single plant can quickly spread by producing many exact copies of itself. As shown in **Figure 4**, scientists can use a plant's ability to reproduce asexually in order to grow plants with favorable characteristics.

☑ READING CHECK **Summarize Text** What is the benefit of asexual reproduction?

....

....

Apple Tree Grafting

Figure 4 Grafting is one way that humans can reproduce plants. Part of a plant's stem is cut and then attached to another plant. These apple trees have been grafted in order to ensure that the desired characteristics from the original tree are maintained in future trees.

Apply Concepts Is grafting a form of sexual or asexual reproduction?

....

Male and Female Cones

Figure 5 Male cones, such as the ones to the right, hold pollen. Female cones, such as the two shown below, open when the weather is warm and dry. They close when conditions are cold and wet.

Apply Scientific Reasoning How do you think the cone's ability to open and close helps with reproduction?

....

....

....

....

....

Gymnosperms Trees such as pines, redwoods, firs, cedars, and hemlocks are all classified as gymnosperms. Many gymnosperms have needle-like leaves and deep roots. However, all have cones and unprotected seeds. These two characteristics set them apart from other vascular plants.

The structures in **Figure 5** are **cones**, which are the reproductive structures of gymnosperms. Male cones hold pollen, whereas the female cone has an **ovule**, the structure holding the egg. The female cone also makes a sticky substance on the outside of the cone, needed for pollination. Pollen from the male cone is light enough to be carried by the wind. When the wind blows, pollen may land on the sticky female cone. When this happens, the egg may become fertilized. The ovule seals off and the zygote develops into a plant embryo in the seed. Seeds can remain in the female cone for a few years, until they mature.

The seeds of gymnosperms are "naked," meaning they are unprotected. Once the female cone matures, the scales open, exposing the seeds. As wind blows, the exposed seeds are blown out of the cone and spread by the wind.

Literacy Connection

Cite Textual Evidence Which detail in the text helped you understand what gymnosperms are?

....

....

....

....

....

....

....

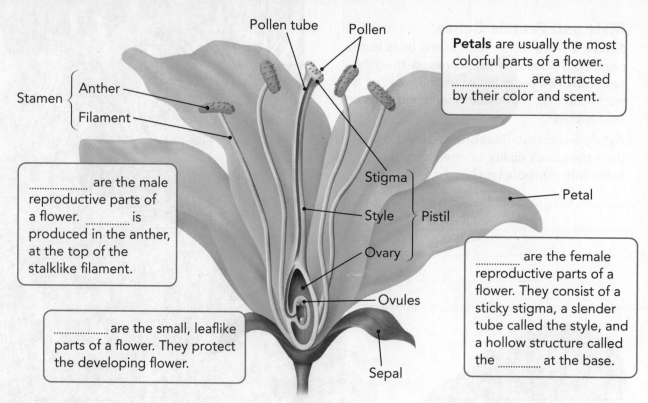

Pollen tube

Pollen

Petals are usually the most colorful parts of a flower. .... are attracted by their color and scent.

Stamen { Anther
Filament

.... are the male reproductive parts of a flower. .... is produced in the anther, at the top of the stalklike filament.

Stigma

Style } Pistil

Ovary

Petal

.... are the female reproductive parts of a flower. They consist of a sticky stigma, a slender tube called the style, and a hollow structure called the .... at the base.

.... are the small, leaflike parts of a flower. They protect the developing flower.

Ovules

Sepal

Flower Parts and Their Jobs

Figure 6 ✏ Flowers contain the reproductive structures of angiosperms. Complete the diagram by filling in the missing words.

Relate Structure and Function What is the purpose of the flower's petals? Why is their function important?

....
....
....
....
....

HANDS-ON LAB

☑**Investigate**
Demonstrate how flower structures relate to successful reproduction.

Angiosperms All angiosperms share two important characteristics. They all produce flowers and fruits that contain seeds. The angiosperm life cycle begins when pollen forms in the flower's anthers. These structures are found at the end of the stamens, which are the male reproductive structure. The female reproductive structure is the pistil and has three parts: the stigma, style, and ovary. When pollen falls on the stigma, pollination may occur, which can lead to fertilization.

Some angiosperms are pollinated by the wind, but most rely on animals called pollinators, such as bees and hummingbirds. When an organism enters a flower to obtain food, it becomes coated with pollen. Some of the pollen can drop onto the flower's stigma as the animal leaves. The pollen can also be brushed onto the stigma of the next flower the animal visits. If the pollen falls on the stigma of a similar plant, fertilization can occur. A sperm cell joins with an egg cell inside an ovule within the ovary at the base of the flower. The zygote then begins to develop into the seed's embryo. Other parts of the ovule develop into the rest of the seed.

Additional structures help a flowering plant to reproduce successfully. Colorful, often pleasantly-scented petals surround the plant's reproductive organs and attract pollinators. Green sepals protect the growing flower. The flower is what develops the **fruit**—the ripened ovary and other structures of an angiosperm enclosing one or more seeds.

Seed Dispersal Fruits are the means by which angiosperm seeds are **dispersed**. Often the scent and color of fruit attracts animals to the plant. Animals eat the fruit and then the seeds in it pass through the animal's digestive system. As the animal moves around, seeds are deposited in different areas in the animal's dung, or droppings. The droppings have an added benefit of providing nutrients and moisture for the seed.

In other cases, seeds disperse by falling into water or being carried by the wind. Seeds with barbs attach to fur or clothing and are carried away. Others are ejected by the seed pods and scattered in different directions. Seeds dispersed far from the parent plant have a better chance of surviving. Distance keeps the new plant from competing with the parent plant for light, water, and nutrients. When a seed lands in a spot with suitable conditions, germination may occur. **Germination** occurs when the embryo sprouts out of the seed.

READING CHECK Cite Textual Evidence How do the examples of seed dispersal given in the text help you understand the role of seed dispersal in plant reproduction?

....

....

....

Academic Vocabulary

Use *dispersed* in another sentence that uses a context other than seeds and plants.

....

....

....

....

INTERACTIVITY

Explore the relationship between plants and pollinators.

Model It

Flower to Fruit
The male and female flower parts enable reproduction to take place. They contain structures to form the egg and sperm that will join to create the zygote.

Use a Model ✏ Draw a sequence of pictures to show the steps that must take place for a flowering plant to reproduce and form a new seedling.

MS-LS1-4

1. Define What is a fruit?

....
....
....

2. Draw Conclusions Why do flowers have brightly-colored petals and attractive scents?

....
....
....
....
....

3. Determine Differences How does seed dispersal in angiosperms differ from seed dispersal in gymnosperms?

....
....
....
....
....
....
....

4. Compare and Contrast In what ways are sexual and asexual production in plants similar, and in what ways do they differ?

....
....
....
....
....
....
....
....
....

5. Explain Tell how seeds are produced and spread in gymnosperms.

....
....
....
....
....
....
....
....

Quest CHECK-IN

In this lesson, you learned about plant structures that help them reproduce successfully.

Apply Concepts How might knowing about the ways the local plants reproduce help in the planning and design of the basketball court?

....
....
....
....
....

INTERACTIVITY

Protect the Plants

Go online to assess the impact of the construction project on plants.

GARDENING in Space

▶ VIDEO

Learn more about growing plants in space.

Do you know how to grow plants in space? You engineer it! NASA engineers and astronauts show us how.

This is not a picture taken from above. These plants are growing sideways!

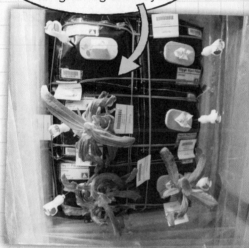

The Challenge: To grow plants on long space flights.

Phenomenon Future space-flight missions will take months, years, and eventually multiple lifetimes, to reach their distant destinations. These missions will rely on growing plants in space as a source of food for astronauts, a method for recycling carbon dioxide into breathable oxygen, and potentially as part of the process that recycles, filters, and purifies water.

Plant structures and their functions are adapted to life on Earth. Leaves grow toward sunlight and roots grow down, due to gravity. In space, with no sunlight and very little gravity, plants do not grow easily. Because water floats away without gravity, watering plants in space is also tricky. Astronauts grow some plants directly in water. Other plants grow in a spongy clay-like material that allows water to reach all the roots.

NASA engineers have designed plant growth chambers used on the International Space Station (ISS) to investigate the effects of space on plant growth. The systems use LED lights and have multiple sensors to track data on temperature, moisture, and oxygen levels.

The Veggie System was installed in 2014. It allows the astronauts to grow their own food aboard the ISS.

DESIGN CHALLENGE
Can you design and build a model of a lunar growth chamber for plants? Go to the Engineering Design Notebook to find out!

Animal Behaviors for Reproduction

Guiding Questions

- What causes animals to behave in certain ways?
- What are some different ways in which animals reproduce?
- How can the behavior of animals increase their chances of reproducing?

Connections

Literacy Summarize Text

Math Draw Comparative Inferences

MS-LS1-4

Vocabulary

behavior
instinct
pheromone
mating system
migration

Academic Vocabulary

typically

 VOCABULARY APP

Practice vocabulary on a mobile device.

Quest CONNECTION

Think about how construction of your basketball court may impact animal breeding areas.

Connect It!

✏ **Circle the most vulnerable member of this elephant herd.**

Make Observations What do you notice about where the young elephants are in relation to the older ones?

....

....

Construct Explanations Why do you think the elephants travel this way?

....

....

Animal Behavior

Have you ever noticed how busy animals are? Most are constantly looking for food or trying to avoid other animals that think of them as food. Many also spend a lot of time looking for mates and caring for their young. All of these actions are examples of an animal's behavior. The way an organism reacts to changes in its internal conditions or external environment is **behavior**. Like body structures, the behaviors of animals are adaptations that have evolved over long periods of time.

Some behaviors are learned while others are known without being taught. An **instinct** is a response to a stimulus that is inborn and that an animal performs correctly the first time. For example, when sea turtles hatch from their eggs, they know by instinct to travel to the ocean. Other behaviors are learned. Learning is the process that leads to changes in behavior based on practice or experience.

The goal of most animal behaviors is to help them survive or reproduce (**Figure 1**). When an animal looks for food or hides from a predator, it is doing something that helps it stay alive. When animals search for mates and build nests for their young, they are behaving in ways that help them reproduce.

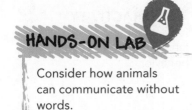

HANDS-ON LAB

Consider how animals can communicate without words.

Elephant Behavior

Figure 1 The adult elephants stay close to the baby for its protection. Many animals instinctively risk their own safety to protect their young from danger.

INTERACTIVITY

Find out more about animal behavior.

Literacy Connection

Summarize Text After reading each section of text, briefly summarize the key ideas from that section to a family member or classmate or make an audio recording of yourself. Later, go back and listen to the recording or play it for someone else. Clarify any ideas that may be confusing.

Mating Behaviors When animals mate, a male animal fertilizes a female animal's egg cells with his sperm cells. The fertilized egg will eventually develop into a new organism. This process is an important part of ensuring the continued survival of the species. Scientists believe that the drive to reproduce evolved in animals over time as a way to ensure the success of their species and their own individual genes.

The behavior patterns related to how animals mate are called **mating systems**, and they vary from species to species. Some species of animals are monogamous. That means that they only mate with one other organism for a period of time, which can range from just a season or to their entire lives. In other animal species, such as baboons, a male has multiple female mates at one time. There are other species in which females have multiple male mates. Honeybees use this mating system. In still other species, males and females both have multiple mates during any one period of time. Scientists believe that these different mating systems evolved over time to best meet the needs of each particular species.

Model It !

The terms defined below are used to describe the different mating systems that are observed in animal species.

monogamy: one female mates with one male
polygyny: one male mates with multiple females
polyandry: one female mates with multiple males
polygynandry: females mate with multiple males and males mate with multiple females

Develop Models 🖊 Use the information above and the symbols for male and female, which are shown to the right, to model the four types of mating systems in the space provided. Monogamy has been completed for you.

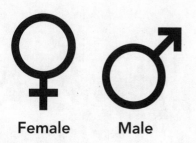

Female   **Male**

Monogamy

Courtship Behaviors
Figure 2 This male peacock shows off his elaborate feathers to attract females that he hopes to mate with.

Predict How do you think this peacock's feathers help him to attract mates?

....

....

....

....

....

....

....

....

Imagine a male walrus swimming in the icy water making a series of whistling and clacking sounds. A group of females looks on from the floating ice pack. One joins the male in the water and they dive together in a dance-like ritual. This courtship behavior is an activity that prepares males and females of the same species for mating. These behaviors are ways for animals to attract the attention of potential mates.

Communication Animals communicate in many ways, using sounds, scents, and body movements. Often, the goal of communication is reproduction.

One way animals communicate is with sound. You have probably heard birds singing outside. Birds sing for many reasons, but one of the reasons they sing is to attract mates. Many animals also use chemical scents to send messages. A chemical released by one animal that affects the behavior of another animal of the same species is called a **pheromone** (fehr uh mohn). In many species of moths, for example, females release a pheromone into the air that is a signal to males that she is ready to mate.

Competition Animals compete for resources, such as food and water. They also compete for access to mates, which may involve displays of aggression. Aggression is a threatening behavior that one animal uses to intimidate or dominate another animal. Another competitive behavior that is often observed in animals is establishing and maintaining a territory. A territory is an area that is occupied and defended by an animal or group of animals. An animal that is defending its territory will drive away other animals that may compete with it for mates.

Reflect As you learn about animal behaviors related to reproduction, spend some time observing animals in the area around your neighborhood and school. Record notes and observations in your science notebook. Explain what type of behavior you think you were observing and why.

Reproductive Strategies

Different animal species have different ways of caring for their young. Some species have no contact with their offspring, while others spend many years caring for them. For example, most amphibian larvae, or tadpoles, develop into adults without parental help. Similarly, the offspring of most reptiles, such as snakes, are independent from the time they hatch. Offspring that do not receive parental care must be able to care for themselves from the time of birth. Generally, animals that provide no parental care release many eggs at a time. Although many will not survive, the sheer number of potential offspring ensures that at least some will make it.

Parental Investment The offspring of most birds and all mammals **typically** spend weeks to years under the care and protection of a parent. Most bird species lay eggs in nests that one or both parents build. Then one or both parents sit on the eggs, keeping them warm until they hatch. After hatching, one or both parents will feed and protect their young until they are able to care for themselves. Young mammals, such as the infant chimpanzee in **Figure 3**, are usually quite helpless for a long time after they are born. After birth, mammals are fed with milk from the mother's body. One or both parents may continue caring for their offspring until the young animals are independent. Typically, animals that provide parental care have only a few offspring at a time. Many only have one. Scientists believe that these animals work harder to care for their young because they have fewer or no other offspring to take their place.

Parenting Behavior

Figure 3 This female chimpanzee carries her infant on her back until it is old enough to better care for itself.

Distinguish Relationships What are the benefits and drawbacks of this behavior for the mother chimpanzee?

....

....

....

....

....

....

....

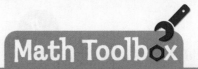

Survivorship Curves

To show how the probability of death changes with age for different species, scientists use graphs called survivorship curves. In a Type I survivorship curve, individuals are most likely to live a full life. In a Type III survivorship curve, individuals are most likely to die when they are young. In a Type II survivorship curve, an individual's chance of dying remains constant.

Draw Comparative Inferences What can you infer about the role of parental care for the three species represented in the graph?

....

....

....

....

....

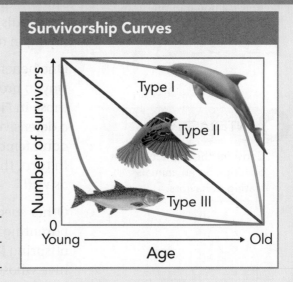

Survivorship Curves

Type I

Type II

Type III

Number of survivors

0

Young ⟶ Old

Age

Fertilization Strategies

For animals that reproduce sexually, a new organism begins when a sperm cell and an egg cell are joined in the process of fertilization. Fertilization may occur in one of two ways: externally or internally. **External fertilization** occurs when eggs are fertilized outside of a female's body, and **internal fertilization** occurs when eggs are fertilized inside a female's body.

The male fish in **Figure 4** are fertilizing the females' eggs by releasing their sperm into a cloud of eggs the female just released. The fertilized eggs will develop outside the female's body. Not all the eggs will become fertilized but the huge number of potential offspring means that many will.

When fertilization occurs internally, a male animal releases sperm directly into a female's body where the eggs are located. The fertilized eggs may develop inside or outside the mother's body. Many animals, such as reptiles and birds, lay eggs in which offspring develop until they hatch. For others, including most mammals, offspring develop inside the mother's body until they are ready to be born.

✓ READING CHECK **Determine Central Ideas** How are internal and external fertilization alike and different?

....

....

....

External Fertilization
Figure 4 Male fish release sperm in a cloud over the eggs.

Make Observations What makes the image an example of external fertilization?

....

....

165

HANDS-ON LAB

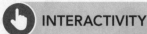

Investigate Explore how salmon migrate from the ocean back to their home river.

INTERACTIVITY

Consider the impact of light pollution on an animals' mating behaviors.

Cooperative Behaviors

In some cases, animals increase their chances for surviving and reproducing when they live and work together. For example, some fish form schools, and some insects live in large groups. Hoofed mammals, such as bison and wild horses, often form herds. Living in a group helps these animals stay alive.

One benefit of living in a large group is that it is an effective way to protect young animals from predators. Elephants like those in **Figure 1** protect the offspring of the group by forming a defensive circle around them. By working together, each adult female helps to protect the offspring of the other females. In turn, the other members of the group protect her offspring as well.

Other species of animals that live in groups may take on parenting responsibilities of animals that are not their offspring (**Figure 5**). For example, there are worker bees in a hive whose sole job is providing food and protection for the bee larvae. They may not be the parents of the offspring, but they still work hard to care for the hive's young.

☑ **READING CHECK** **Summarize Text** How can cooperative behaviors help animals that are raising offspring?

....

....

....

....

Working Together

Figure 5 Orcas live in a pod. All adult members of the pod help parent any offspring in the pod. Likewise, some spiders live in a nest and work together to raise their young.

Integrate Information What is the benefit of shared responsibility when raising young? Explain.

....

....

....

....

....

....

....

....

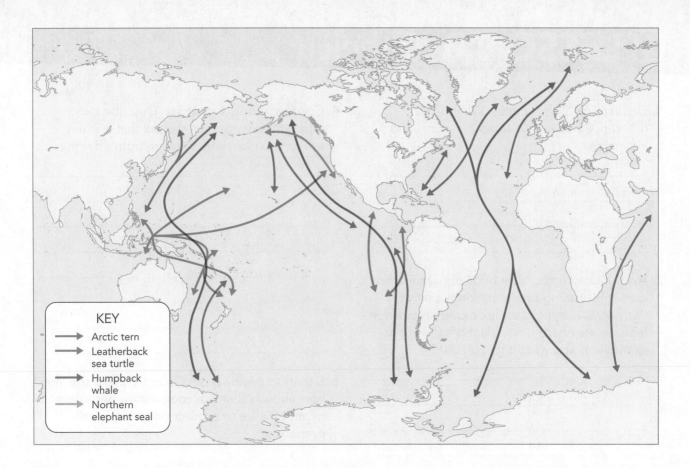

KEY
→ Arctic tern
→ Leatherback sea turtle
→ Humpback whale
→ Northern elephant seal

Migratory Behaviors

Many animals spend their entire lives in a relatively small area. But there are many others that migrate. **Migration** is the regular, seasonal journey of an animal from one place to another and back again. Animals have different reasons for migration. Some migrate to an area that provides plenty of food or a more comfortable climate during a harsh season. Others, such as the animals whose migratory routes are shown in **Figure 6**, migrate to a better environment for reproduction. In some cases, large groups of animals of the same species gather together in the same place at the same time so they can mate. They may also stay there to begin the process of raising their young. By migrating every year, these animals increase their chances of finding a mate and producing offspring in conditions that will be favorable to their survival.

Animal behaviors related to mating and raising offspring are often tied to Earth's cycles. Polar bears, for example, mate in the spring and give birth in the winter. Other animals reproduce with more or less frequency, but almost all follow some kind of predictable cycle. Following these patterns ensures that offspring are born when they have the best chances of survival.

Migratory Routes

Figure 6 Many animals travel thousands of miles every year to mate and raise their young.

Use Models ✏ A friend took a road trip across the United States from the west coast to the east coast. Draw an arrow on the map showing the trip. How does your friend's trip compare to the animal trips represented in the map?

....

....

....

....

MS-LS-4

1. Determine Differences What is the difference between learned behaviors and instincts?

....

....

....

....

2. Apply Concepts Male birds of paradise are known for having bright markings that they flash while making complex movements when females are nearby. What is this behavior an example of and what is its purpose?

....

....

....

....

3. Explain Phenomena Describe how animals use pheromones to attract potential mates.

....

....

....

....

4. Compare and Contrast Describe two different parenting strategies that animals use and explain why they are both effective.

....

....

....

....

....

....

....

....

5. Develop Models ✏ Draw a picture showing how animals that use cooperative behaviors might be able to protect offspring from predators.

Quest CHECK-IN

In this lesson, you learned how animal behaviors can help individuals find mates. You also learned how animal parenting behaviors can affect how likely their offspring are to survive.

Explain Phenomena Consider various ways a male bird might attract a female mate. Suppose the male bird is of a species that does not display colorful feathers, the way peacocks do. What sort of behaviors could the male birds use to attract female birds?

....

....

....

👆 INTERACTIVITY

The Mating Game

Go online to explore different techniques and behaviors that animals use to increase their odds of reproductive success.

MS-LS1-4

Avian Artists

As male birds go, the Vogelkop bowerbird is rather plain. It doesn't have the bright feathers of a cardinal or the fancy plumage of a peacock. But what the bowerbird lacks in color, it makes up for in engineering and decorating skills.

The Vogelkop bowerbird displays some of the most complex courtship behavior observed in birds. To attract a mate, the male builds an elaborate structure out of twigs, called a bower. After completing the bower, the male bowerbird collects brightly colored flowers and berries to decorate the bower. Males compete to build the most magnificent bowers and amass the most beautiful collections in the hopes of impressing female bowerbirds.

When a female comes by to inspect the bower and collection, the male will strut and sing inside the bower. If the female likes the male's decorating expertise, then they will mate. The female will leave to build a nest and raise the young on her own.

MY DISCOVERY

What other animal species display extraordinary behavior when it comes to courtship? Do some research to find out more.

Male Vogelkop bowerbirds spend years making their bowers.

The Vogelkop bowerbird lives on the island of New Guinea in the Pacific Ocean.

4 Factors Influencing Growth

Guiding Questions

- How do environmental and genetic factors influence an organism's growth?
- What stimulates plant growth?
- Which factors control plant and animal growth?

Connections

Literacy Analyze Text Structure

Math Represent Quantitative Relationships

MS-LS1-5

Vocabulary

hormone
auxin
tropism
photoperiodism
dormancy
metamorphosis

Academic Vocabulary

stimuli
essential

 VOCABULARY APP

Practice vocabulary on a mobile device.

Quest CONNECTION

Practice communicating how to present your construction plans to the school board.

Connect It !

✏ **Vines are plants that can use other structures, such as trees, for support. Circle a vine in the picture and draw an arrow to show the direction of its growth.**

Analyze Properties How do you think the vine was able to grow up the tree?

....

....

Construct Explanations Why do you think the vine used the tree to grow?

....

....

Growth and Development of Organisms

Living things on Earth grow and develop from the beginning of their lives. But the way organisms grow and develop, and the size they reach, varies from species to species.

Several factors influence how organisms grow. Some of these factors are determined by their genetic characteristics and are part of their normal life cycle. Other factors occur outside of the organism and can be related to their access to needed resources, the conditions in their environment, and their responses to other **stimuli**.

To increase their odds for survival, plants and animals have changed over time. These changes are a result of adapting to stimuli in the environment. The vines in **Figure 1**, for example, grow in response to their environment. Vines have evolved to grow around larger trees and other structures as a means of accessing sunlight and gaining space for further growth.

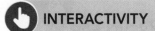

INTERACTIVITY

Explore the conditions required for living things to grow and thrive.

Academic Vocabulary

Often, a dog barks when someone rings the doorbell and knocks on the door. What are the stimuli in this situation?

....

....

....

Plant Growth

Figure 1 These vines have evolved the adaptation of growing up and around other trees.

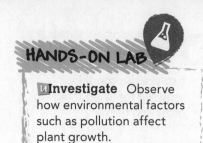

HANDS-ON LAB

Investigate Observe how environmental factors such as pollution affect plant growth.

Plant Responses and Growth

If you've ever grown a garden, you've probably witnessed how plants grow over time. As with all living things, plant growth is controlled by responses to stimuli. For plants, these responses are controlled by **hormones**, chemicals that affect growth and development. One important plant hormone is called **auxin** (AWK sin). It speeds up the rate at which plant cells grow and controls a plant's response to light.

Tropisms

In animals, a typical response to a stimulus is to move toward or away from it. But plants cannot move in the same way that animals do, so they often respond by growing either toward or away from a stimulus. A plant's growth response toward or away from a stimulus is called a **tropism** (TROH piz um). Touch, gravity, and light are three stimuli that trigger tropisms in plants.

The stems of some plants, such as the vines in **Figure 1**, show a response to touch called thigmotropism. As a vine grows, it coils around any object it touches. This is an example of positive thigmotropism, because the vine grows toward the stimulus. Plants also know which direction to grow, because they respond to gravity. This response is called gravitropism. Roots show positive gravitropism if they grow downward. Stems, on the other hand, show negative gravitropism (**Figure 2**). Plants' response to light is called phototropism. The leaves, stems, and flowers of plants grow toward light.

How Plants Respond
Figure 2 Plants respond to stimuli from the environment in a variety of ways.

Negative Gravitropism The stems of plants respond to the stimulus of gravity by growing upward, away from gravity.

Positive Phototropism When stems and leaves grow toward sources of light, it shows positive phototropism.

Patterns 🖊 Place a circle where the sun would be in the picture above.

Seasonal Change Depending on where you live, you may have noticed flowers blooming in the spring and the leaves of trees changing color in autumn. These changes are caused by changing conditions brought on by the seasons.

In many plants, the amount of darkness it experiences determines when it blooms. A plant's response to seasonal changes in the length of night and day is called **photoperiodism**. As shown in **Figure 2**, plants respond differently to the length of nights. Other plants are not affected at all by the lengths of days and nights.

Have you ever wondered why some trees lose their leaves in the fall? As winter draws near, many plants prepare to go into a state of **dormancy**. Dormancy is a period when an organism's growth or activity stops. Dormancy helps plants survive freezing temperatures and the lack of liquid water. With many trees, the first visible change is that the leaves begin to turn color. Cooler weather and shorter days cause the leaves to stop making chlorophyll. As chlorophyll breaks down, yellow and orange pigments become visible. This causes the brilliant colors of autumn leaves like the ones shown in **Figure 2**. Over the next few weeks, sugar and water are transported out of the tree's leaves. When the leaves fall to the ground, the tree is ready for winter.

Literacy Connection

Analyze Text Structure
Text structure describes how a text is organized. Section headings can give you clues about how a text is organized. What do you notice about the text structure on this page?

....

....

....

....

....

....

....

....

Photoperiodism Irises, left, bloom when days are getting longer and nights are getting shorter. Chrysanthemums, above, bloom when the lengths of the day and night reaches a certain ratio.

Dormancy Some species of trees go into a state or dormancy every winter.

Analyze Benefits Why do you think some trees evolved to go into a state of dormancy during the winter months?

....

....

....

173

Plant Diseases

Figure 3 Insects, worms, and other pests can cause disease in plants and have an impact on their growth.

Make Observations ✏️ Circle the diseased parts of the plant.

📓**Write About It** Locate two plants in or around your home, school, or neighborhood: one that appears healthy and one that does not. Explain which factors you think are helping the healthy plant grow and which factors are keeping the unhealthy one from growing to its full size.

Environmental Conditions
In ideal conditions, a plant will reach a certain maximum size that is normal for its species. However, in some cases, plants do not get enough of the resources they need, so they do not grow as large as they normally would. A lack of sunlight, for instance, may keep a plant from growing to full size or weaken its structure.

In addition to sunlight, plants need nutrient-rich soil and water to grow. Soil contains the nutrients a plant needs to carry out its life processes. Nutrient-poor soil may result from an area being overly crowded with plants. Competition for the nutrients in the soil may mean that few plants get the nutrients they need. Similarly, if a plant does not receive enough water, it will not grow to a healthy size. Diseases like the one shown in **Figure 3** can impact plant growth as well.

Plan It!

Water Needs and Plant Growth

Plan Your Investigation You want to find out how the amount of water you give plants affects their growth. In the space below, describe a plan for an investigation that can help you answer this question.

....

....

....

....

....

....

....

Animal Growth

Like plants, animals grow and develop starting at the beginning of their lives. Also like plants, their growth is affected by both internal and external stimuli to which they are constantly responding.

Embryo Development After fertilization, the offspring of animals develop in different ways. The growing offspring, or embryo, may develop outside or inside the mother's body.

One way animal embryos develop is inside an egg that is laid outside the parent's body. Most invertebrates lay eggs. Many fish, reptiles, and birds do, too. The contents of the egg provide the nutrients a developing embryo needs. The eggs of land vertebrates, such as reptiles and birds, are called amniotic eggs. When inside the parent's body, amniotic eggs are covered with membranes and a leathery shell.

In other cases, an embryo develops inside an egg that is kept, or retained, within the parent's body. The developing embryo gets its nutrients from the egg's yolk, just like the offspring of egg-laying animals. The egg hatches either before or after being released from the parent's body. This type of development is found in some species of fish, amphibians, and reptiles.

In placental mammals, which include elephants, wolves, and humans, the embryo develops inside the mother's body. The mother provides the embryo with everything it needs during development. As is shown in **Figure 4**, essential nutrients and gases are exchanged between the embryo and the mother through an organ called the placenta. The embryo develops inside its mother's body until its body systems can function on their own.

INTERACTIVITY

Observe how animals grow and develop over time.

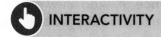

INTERACTIVITY

Find out how cows are being bred to be bigger and bigger.

Academic Vocabulary

What does it mean when someone describes something as being essential? Use *essential* in a sentence.

....

....

....

....

....

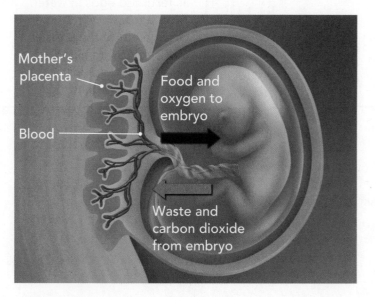

Mother's placenta

Food and oxygen to embryo

Blood

Waste and carbon dioxide from embryo

Placental Mammal Development

Figure 4 The embryos of placental mammals develop inside their mothers' bodies.

Draw Conclusions What would be some of the advantages of this type of embryo development compared to an amniotic egg laid outside the mother's body?

....

....

....

....

....

175

Life Cycles

Figure 5 Different animals go through different life cycles. Unlike you, both of these animals go through metamorphosis.

Sequence ✏️ Add arrows to the diagram to show the order in which these stages occur.

Egg

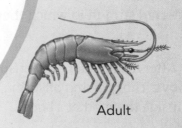

Adult

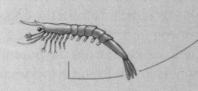

Postlarval stage

Larval stages

Crayfish and other crustaceans, such as crabs and shrimp, begin their lives as tiny, swimming larvae. The bodies of these larvae do not resemble those of adults. Eventually, crustacean larvae develop into adults.

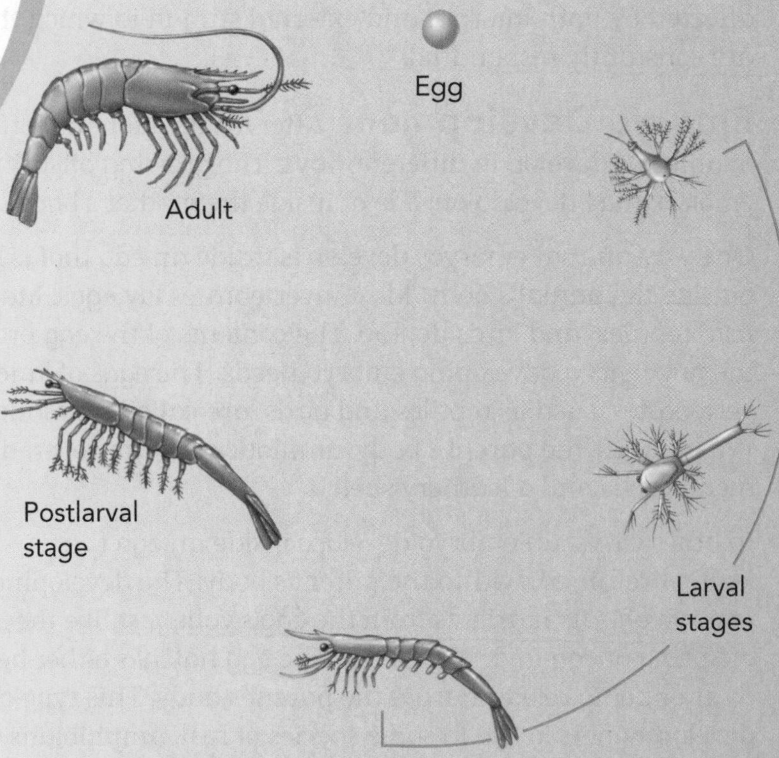

Adult frogs reproduce sexually.

Eggs are fertilized outside the female's body.

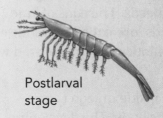

Frogs begin their life cycle as fertilized eggs in water. After a few days, tadpoles wriggle out of the eggs and begin swimming. Over time, tadpoles develop into adult frogs.

Front legs develop and the tail is absorbed.

A tadpole hatches from an egg.

Hind legs develop.

Comparing Life Cycles Many young animals, including most vertebrates, look like small versions of adults from the time they are born. Other animals go through the process of **metamorphosis**, or major body changes, as they grow and develop into adults (**Figure 5**).

External and Internal Factors Animal growth and development are affected by both internal and external factors. Internal factors include genetic and hormonal characteristics that are part of an organism's life processes. External factors, on the other hand, are the environmental conditions that an animal may or may not have any control over.

Environmental Conditions Access to resources and exposure to diseases and parasites can also affect the growth and development of animals. If animals do not receive the nutrition they need during development or if they become sick, they may not reach their full adult size. Space is another resource that can affect animal growth. For example, the growth of some species of fish, such as goldfish like the one in **Figure 6**, is affected by how large a body of water they live in. If its living space is not large enough, it will not reach its full adult size.

☑ READING CHECK **Determine Meaning** How is your life cycle different from animals that undergo metamorphosis?

....

....

....

INTERACTIVITY

Construct an explanation with evidence for how environmental and genetic factors influence the growth of organisms.

Figure 6 If a goldfish's tank is too small, its growth may be restricted.

Draw Conclusions In ideal conditions, a goldfish will grow to be about 10 to 20 cm long. But most people think of goldfish as very small fish that only grow to be a few centimeters long. What conclusion can you draw from this information?

....

....

....

....

....

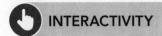
Genes The genes an offspring inherits from its parents are a major factor in how it develops and grows. In your own classroom, you can probably observe how students' heights vary. Part of these differences is due to the genes your classmates inherited from their parents. Children usually grow up to be about the same height as their parents.

Hormones Another internal factor that influences growth and development are the hormones that are naturally produced by animals' bodies. For instance, male animals produce greater amounts of testosterone than female animals. In many animal species, the production of testosterone in male animals results in males growing to be larger than females.

Math Toolbox

Human Malnutrition and Height

In 1945, after World War II, the Korean Peninsula was divided into two nations: North Korea and South Korea. The two countries had different forms of government and economic systems. The data table shows the average heights in the two countries from 1930 to 1996.

1. **Represent Quantitative Relationships** Use the data in the table to make a bar graph in the space below.

2. **Synthesize Information** Are the height differences in these two countries likely the result of genetics, hormones, or environmental conditions? Explain why.

....
....
....
....
....
....
....
....
....
....

Years	Average height of North Koreans (cm)	Average height of South Koreans (cm)
1930–1939	159.4	158.9
1940–1949	160.6	161.1
1950–1959	161.8	163.1
1960–1969	162.7	165
1970–1979	163.5	166.7
1980–1989	164.5	167.8
1990–1996	165.2	168.4

Source: NCD Risk Factor Collaboration, 2017

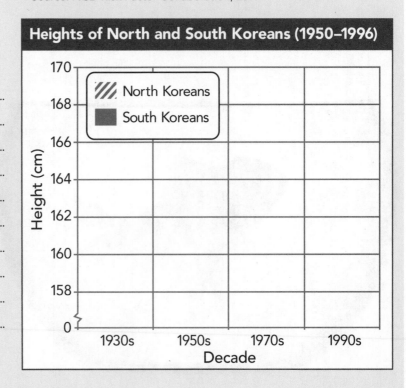

Heights of North and South Koreans (1950–1996)

Legend: North Koreans, South Koreans

Height (cm) — Decade: 1930s, 1950s, 1970s, 1990s

MS-LS1-5

1. **Distinguish Relationships** Describe three types of stimuli that cause plants to exhibit tropism.

....

....

....

....

....

....

2. **Cause and Effect** What causes plants to bloom in different seasons?

....

....

....

....

3. **Explain** Why might soil have an effect on plant growth?

....

....

....

4. **Distinguish Differences** How does offspring development in egg-laying animals and placental mammals differ?

....

....

....

....

....

5. **Develop Models** ✎ Draw diagrams showing three different ways that animal embryos develop. Include labels.

Quest CHECK-IN

In this lesson, you learned about some of the factors that affect the growth and development of plants and animals. You also learned about some of the different stages that animals go through as they develop.

Optimize Your Solution Consider the environmental impact of new construction near a wildlife habitat. At what point during the year do you think construction would have the least impact? Explain.

....

....

....

....

🖐 INTERACTIVITY

Make Your Construction Case

Go online to consider the criteria and constraints involved in your construction project.

Case Study

Warmer Waters, FEWER FISH

A temperature increase of a few degrees does not seem like much cause for concern. But it turns out that even small increases in water temperature are having a big impact.

The increased warmth of the water is affecting the growth of certain species of fish. Atlantic cod, which are used to very cold water, can adapt to higher temperatures. In fact, populations of cod exposed to warmer waters ranging from 12 to 15 degrees Celsius (53.6°F to 59.0°F) tend to benefit. The cod grow larger and reproduce more. But as soon as the water warms barely one degree Celsius beyond that high range, to 15.9°C (60.6°F), the growth and development of the fish suffers.

Temperature–Size Rule

In Norway, every fall for over a century, scientists have measured and recorded the size of Atlantic cod. These annual surveys have included well over 100,000 cod so far. Recently, scientists made a key observation. As soon as the temperature in the Atlantic cod's habitat rose above 15 degrees Celsius, the Atlantic cod suffered from stunted growth.

Water is a heat sink—it readily absorbs heat from everything around it. The researchers found that in years with very high summer temperatures, the ocean's surface waters were much warmer, too. And the juvenile cod raised in these warmer waters were smaller than usual. The young fish simply did not grow as large as they could. This small difference may not seem significant at first. But there is a consequence to consider: Size determines an individual's success at survival and reproduction. The smaller individuals tend to have fewer offspring.

An Atlantic cod can grow quite large, up to 1.2 meters, and weigh as much as 40 kilograms. The largest cod ever captured was a whopper, weighing over 96 kg (211 lb)!

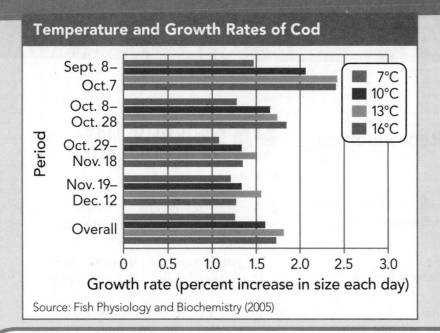

Temperature and Growth Rates of Cod

Source: Fish Physiology and Biochemistry (2005)

Answer the following questions.

1. **Analyze Data** Refer to the graph. At what temperature does the Atlantic cod grow most slowly? Which temperature seems to be ideal for growth? Explain.

2. **Cite Evidence** What is the evidence that warmer water temperature is an environmental factor influencing the growth of a species?

3. **Apply Scientific Reasoning** Why are some scientists concerned about the Atlantic cod population as the air temperature increases? Explain.

4. **Connect to Society** One out of seven people on Earth depends on fish as a protein source. What could happen if warming waters have a similar effect on other stocks of fish?

☑TOPIC 3 Review and Assess

1 Patterns of Reproduction

MS-LS3-2

1. Asexual reproduction is different from sexual reproduction in that the offspring of asexual reproduction
   A. are identical to the parent.
   B. contain half the chromosomes of the parent.
   C. have no genetic material.
   D. have more variety in their traits.

2. Different forms of a gene are called
   A. alleles.
   B. offspring.
   C. recessive.
   D. traits.

3. Which example best describes incomplete dominance?
   A. humans with blood type AB
   B. flowers with red petals
   C. horses with roan color pattern
   D. sheep with gray fleece

4. .... inheritance refers to any trait that is controlled by more than one gene.

5. **Patterns** Explain why sexual reproduction results in offspring with more genetic variation than asexual reproduction.

   ....
   ....
   ....
   ....
   ....
   ....
   ....
   ....

2 Plant Structures for Reproduction

MS-LS1-4

6. A maple tree produces male and female flowers. Which term best describes the maple?
   A. gymnosperm   B. angiosperm
   C. sporophyte   D. non-vascular

7. Both ferns and cedar trees rely on .... to successfully fertilize themselves.

8. **Relate Structure and Function** What are two specialized structures of an apple tree that increase the chances that it will reproduce and have offspring that survive? Explain.

   ....
   ....
   ....
   ....
   ....
   ....

9. **Construct Arguments** Coconut palms are tropical trees usually found growing on shorelines. The tree produces fruit in a hard shell that can float on water. How does this help ensure the tree's successful reproduction?

   ....
   ....
   ....
   ....
   ....
   ....
   ....

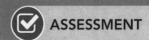
3 Animal Behaviors for Reproduction

MS-LS1-4

10. What are mating systems?

A. threatening behaviors that animals use to gain control over other animals

B. behavior patterns that are related to how animals reproduce

C. chemicals released by one animal that affect the behavior of another animal of the same species

D. behaviors related to the movement of animals from one place to another and back again

11. Which statement about fertilization strategies is true?

A. Internal fertilization mostly occurs in fish and amphibians.

B. Internal fertilization results in eggs that develop outside the female's body.

C. External fertilization is common for animals that live in water.

D. External fertilization occurs in all land animals.

12. Cooperative behaviors can .... (increase/decrease) an animal's chances of surviving to reproduce.

13. Apply Scientific Reasoning In general, how is the number of offspring produced by an animal related to the amount of time and energy it invests in caring for its young?

....

....

....

....

....

....

....

4 Factors Influencing Growth

MS-LS1-5

14. Which is *not* a stimulus that can trigger tropisms in plants?

A. light

B. gravity

C. touch

D. temperature

15. An insect such as the butterfly goes through the process of .... as it grows and develops into an adult.

16. Cause and Effect Oak trees go into a state of dormancy during the winter. Suppose that a forest of oaks grows in an area that begins to experience warmer winters due to climate change. What effect do you think this will have on the oak trees? Explain.

....

....

....

....

....

17. Construct Explanations How do environmental conditions affect the growth of an animal?

....

....

....

....

....

....

....

....

....

MS-LS1-4, MS-LS1-5

Evidence-Based Assessment

A team of researchers investigated how climate change and warming temperatures affected animals in the Colorado Rocky Mountains. One of the animals they studied was the yellow-bellied marmot. This large rodent lives in small colonies and survives the harsh winters by hibernating for eight months. The marmots forage for grasses and seeds, which only grow once the winter snow has melted.

Because the ground is bare of snow for such a brief time each year, the marmots have a very short breeding season. It begins as soon as they come out of hibernation. Not long after, the snow melts and more food becomes available to the marmots.

However, the researchers discovered that warming temperatures were disrupting marmot hibernation patterns. They compiled data about the first marmot sighted coming out of hibernation each year for over 20 years. The data is summarized in the graph.

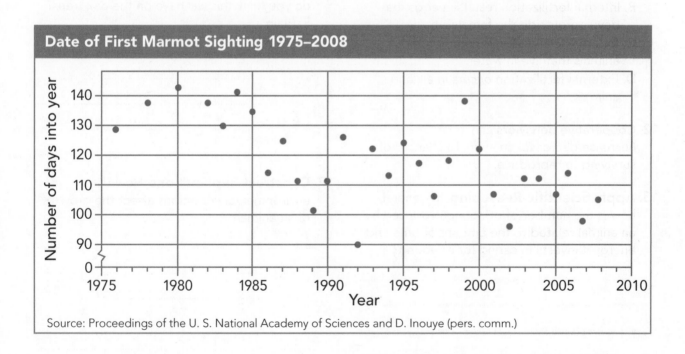

Date of First Marmot Sighting 1975–2008

Source: Proceedings of the U. S. National Academy of Sciences and D. Inouye (pers. comm.)

1. **Analyze Data** What trend is shown by the data in the graph?
   A. The first marmot coming out of hibernation tends to be sighted earlier and earlier.
   B. The first marmot coming out of hibernation was sighted later each year.
   C. The date the first marmot came out of hibernation fluctuated randomly.
   D. There was little or no change in the date the first marmot was sighted each year.

2. **Engage in Argument** What environmental factor do you think influences when marmots wake from hibernation? Support your response with details or data from the researchers' investigation.

....

....

....

....

....

....

....

....

....

3. **Cause and Effect** How does the marmot's behavior after coming out of hibernation help to ensure that it will successfully reproduce?

....

....

....

....

....

....

....

....

....

4. **Construct Explanations** The researchers found that while the air temperature was increasing earlier each year, the snow was not melting at a faster rate. Explain what effect an earlier breeding season will have on the growth of young marmots if the snow melts the same time year to year.

....

....

....

....

....

....

....

....

....

Quest FINDINGS

Complete the Quest!

Phenomenon Finalize and present your construction plan using the information you have gathered as evidence to support your recommendations.

Apply Concepts Is there a way your town or city could ensure that the wild plants and animals that live there have the resources they need to grow and reproduce?

....

....

....

....

....

INTERACTIVITY

Reflect on Your Basketball Court Plans

Clean and Green

How can you evaluate **claims** about laundry **detergents** that are marketed as **safe** for the environment?

Background

Phenomenon Many businesses promote products, such as soaps and detergents, that are environmentally friendly. Greenwashing, which is a combination of the terms *green* and *whitewashing*, is the practice of claiming that a product is more environmentally safe than it really is. You are a budding botanist working with an environmental watchdog group. You must evaluate the biological effects of "natural" detergents that claim to be safer for the environment than regular detergents.

In this investigation, you will design and conduct an experiment to determine the effects of "eco-friendly" laundry detergents on plant growth. It will probably take several days for the seeds to germinate. Keep in mind that the factors for healthy plant growth include height, color, and general appearance.

Materials

(per group)

- 3 plastic Petri dishes with lids
- potting soil
- graduated cylinder
- 30 radish seeds
- masking tape
- day-old tap water
- metric ruler
- wax pencil
- "regular" detergent solution
- "eco-friendly" detergent solution
- scale or balance

Be sure to follow all safety guidelines provided by your teacher. The Safety Appendix of your textbook provides more details about the safety icons.

Design Your Investigation

1. With your group, discuss how you will investigate the effects of the detergents on plant growth. Also, discuss the types of data you will need to collect in order to determine how environmental factors affect plant growth.

2. Work together to identify the factors you will control and the variables you will change. Think about what a plant normally needs from its environment in order to live and grow. Decide what measurements and observations you will need to make and how often you will need to make them. To make these decisions, consider the following questions:

   • How many different groups of seeds will you use?
   • How will you determine the number of seeds that germinate in each group?
   • How will you determine the health of the shoots in each group of seeds?
   • What qualitative observations will you make?

3. Write a detailed procedure for your experiment in the space provided. Make sure you describe the setup for your investigation, the variables you will measure, a description of the data you will collect, and how you will collect the data. Before proceeding, obtain your teacher's approval.

4. In the space provided, construct a data table to organize the data you will collect. When constructing your data table, consider the following questions:

   • How many seeds will you put in each petri dish?
   • How many times will you collect data?
   • Will you collect data at the same time each day, or at different times?
   • What qualitative observations will you record?

5. Carry out your procedure for investigating the effect of your pollutant on plant growth. You will need to make observations once a day over several days. Make your measurements each day and record the data you collect.

Procedure

....

....

....

....

....

....

....

....

....

....

....

....

Data Table and Observations

Analyze and Interpret Data

1. **Calculate** Identify the dependent variables you measured in this investigation. Calculate the percentage of seeds that had germinated each day in each dish. Then, calculate the mean length of the shoots for each day you collected data. Make this calculation for the seeds in each dish.

....

....

....

....

2. **Cause and Effect** Describe any patterns you see in the data for the seedlings grown under the three conditions in the Petri dishes. Summarize the data by writing a cause-and-effect statement about the effects of the detergents on the growth of the plants.

....

....

....

....

....

3. **Make Generalizations** Based on the results of your experiment, do you think the manufacturer's claim is valid? Is the product is safe for the environment? Explain.

....

....

....

....

4. **Compare Data** Share your results among the groups that tested the other "natural" detergents. Look for similarities and differences in the data. What do you think might account for any differences?

....

....

....

....

....

NGSS PERFORMANCE EXPECTATIONS

MS-LS2-1 Analyze and interpret data to provide evidence for the effects of resource availability on organisms and populations of organisms in an ecosystem.

MS-LS2-3 Develop a model to describe the cycling of matter and flow of energy among living and nonliving parts of an ecosystem.

HOW are these manatees well suited to their environment?

HANDS-ON LAB

uConnect Explore how you are part of a cycle on Earth.

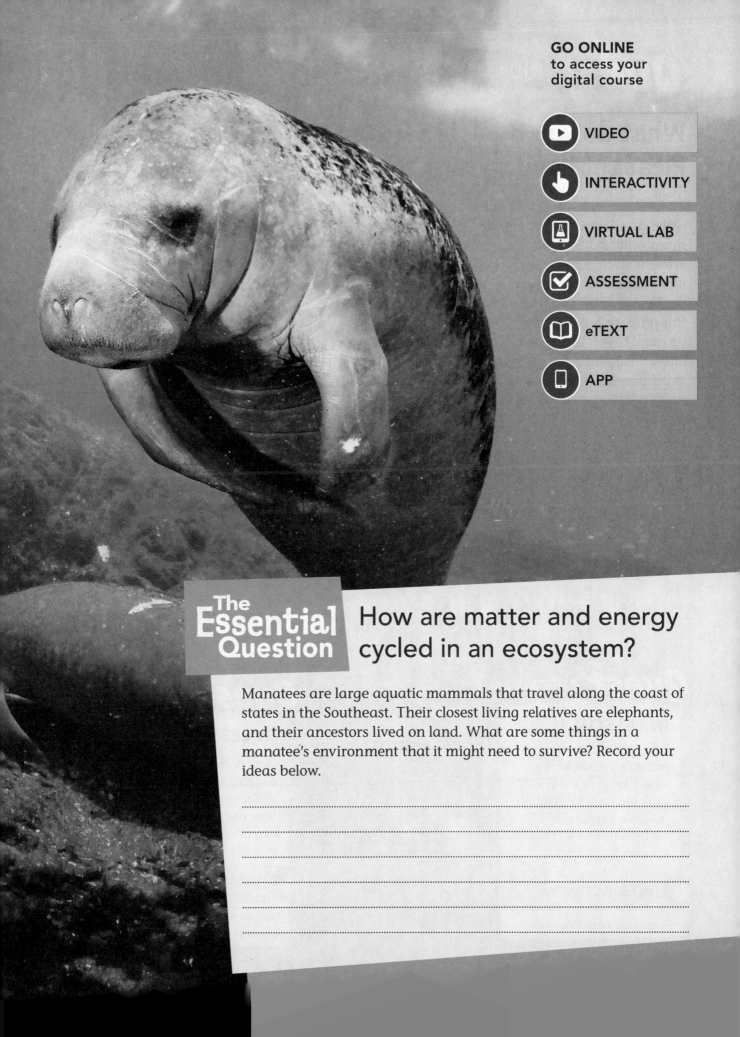

GO ONLINE
to access your
digital course

▶ VIDEO

👆 INTERACTIVITY

⚗ VIRTUAL LAB

☑ ASSESSMENT

📖 eTEXT

📱 APP

The **Essential Question**

How are matter and energy cycled in an ecosystem?

Manatees are large aquatic mammals that travel along the coast of states in the Southeast. Their closest living relatives are elephants, and their ancestors lived on land. What are some things in a manatee's environment that it might need to survive? Record your ideas below.

....

....

....

....

....

....

Quest KICKOFF

What do you think is causing Pleasant Pond to turn green?

Phenomenon In 2016, algal blooms turned bodies of water green and slimy in Florida, Utah, California, and many other states. These blooms put people and ecosystems in danger. Scientists that study lakes and other inland bodies of water, known as limnologists, are working to predict and prevent future algal blooms. In this problem-based Quest activity, you will investigate an algal bloom at a lake and determine its cause. In labs and digital activities, you will apply what you learn in each lesson to help you gather evidence to solve the mystery. With enough evidence, you will be able to identify what you believe is the cause of the algal bloom and present a solution in the Findings activity.

 INTERACTIVITY

Mystery at Pleasant Pond

MS-LS2-1 Analyze and interpret data to provide evidence for the effects of resource availability on organisms and populations of organisms in an ecosystem.
MS-LS2-3 Develop a model to describe the cycling of matter and flow of energy among living and nonliving parts of an ecosystem.

NBC LEARN ▶ VIDEO

After watching the above Quest Kickoff Video, which explores the effects of a toxic algal bloom in Lake Erie, think about the impact that shutting down the water supply might have on your community. Record your ideas below.

....
....
....
....
....
....
....
....
....
....

Quest CHECK-IN

IN LESSON 1

What are some possible causes of the algal bloom in the pond? Evaluate data to identify possible explanations for the problems at the pond.

 INTERACTIVITY

Suspicious Activities

Quest CHECK-IN

IN LESSON 2

How do nutrients affect organisms in an aquatic environment? Investigate how the nonliving factors can affect the organisms in a pond.

INTERACTIVITY

Nutrients and Aquatic Organisms

An algal bloom can seriously disrupt an ecosystem by interfering with an organism's ability to find food or function properly.

Quest CHECK-IN

IN LESSON 3

How are cycles of matter and energy affected by environmental change? Explore the cycling of matter and the flow of energy among organisms in a pond.

👆 **INTERACTIVITY**

Matter and Energy in a Pond

Quest FINDINGS

Complete the Quest!

Write a news story explaining what you think is the cause of the algal bloom in the pond. Tell how it has impacted the ecosystem and include a proposal for restoring the pond.

👆 **INTERACTIVITY**

Reflections on a Pond

193

Living Things and the Environment

Guiding Questions

- How are populations affected by changes to the amount and availability of resources?
- How are population size and resource availability related?

Connections

Literacy Cite Textual Evidence

Math Represent Relationships

MS-LS2-1

Vocabulary

organism
habitat
biotic factor
abiotic factor
population
community
ecosystem
limiting factor

Academic Vocabulary

resources
density

 Vocabulary App

Practice vocabulary on a mobile device.

Quest CONNECTION

Consider the many ways living and nonliving components of an ecosystem interact, and how changes to any of those components could affect an ecosystem such as a pond.

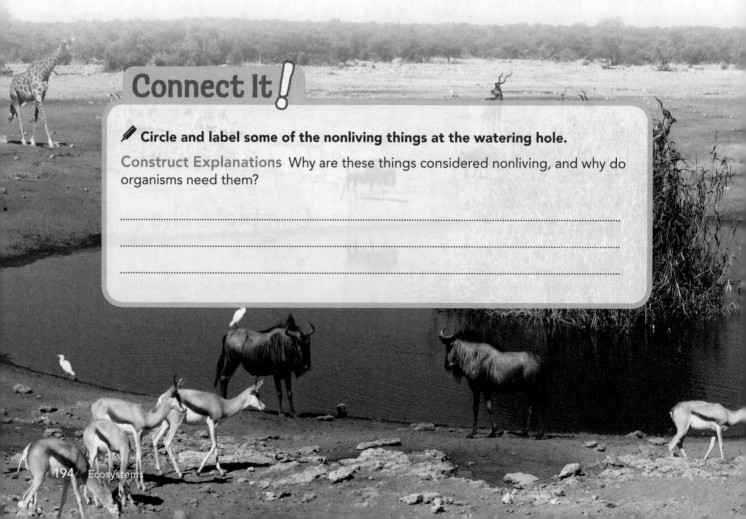

Connect It !

🖉 **Circle and label some of the nonliving things at the watering hole.**

Construct Explanations Why are these things considered nonliving, and why do organisms need them?

....

....

....

Organisms and Habitats

At the watering hole shown in **Figure 1**, animals such as giraffes stop to quench their thirst. A giraffe is an **organism**, or living thing. Different types of organisms live in different types of surroundings, or environments. An organism gets food, water, shelter, and other things from its environment that it needs to live, grow, and reproduce. These are called **resources**. An environment that provides the things a specific organism needs to live, grow, and reproduce is called a **habitat**.

In nature, every organism you see in a particular habitat is there because that habitat meets the organism's needs. Some organisms have the ability to move from one habitat to another as conditions change or as different needs arise, but many organisms stay in the same habitat for their entire lives. The living and nonliving things in a particular environment and the interactions among them define the habitat and its conditions.

HANDS-ON LAB

Explore the relationships among living and nonliving things in a local area.

Academic Vocabulary

Have you heard the term *resources* in other contexts? List some examples.

....

....

....

....

A Hangout in the Habitat

Figure 1 In any environment, like this watering hole in Etosha National Park in Namibia, Africa, living and nonliving things interact with each other.

INTERACTIVITY

Explore the factors in a habitat.

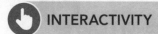

VIDEO

Explore biotic and abiotic factors in everyday life.

Reflect What are some of the biotic and abiotic factors in the ecosystem in which you live?

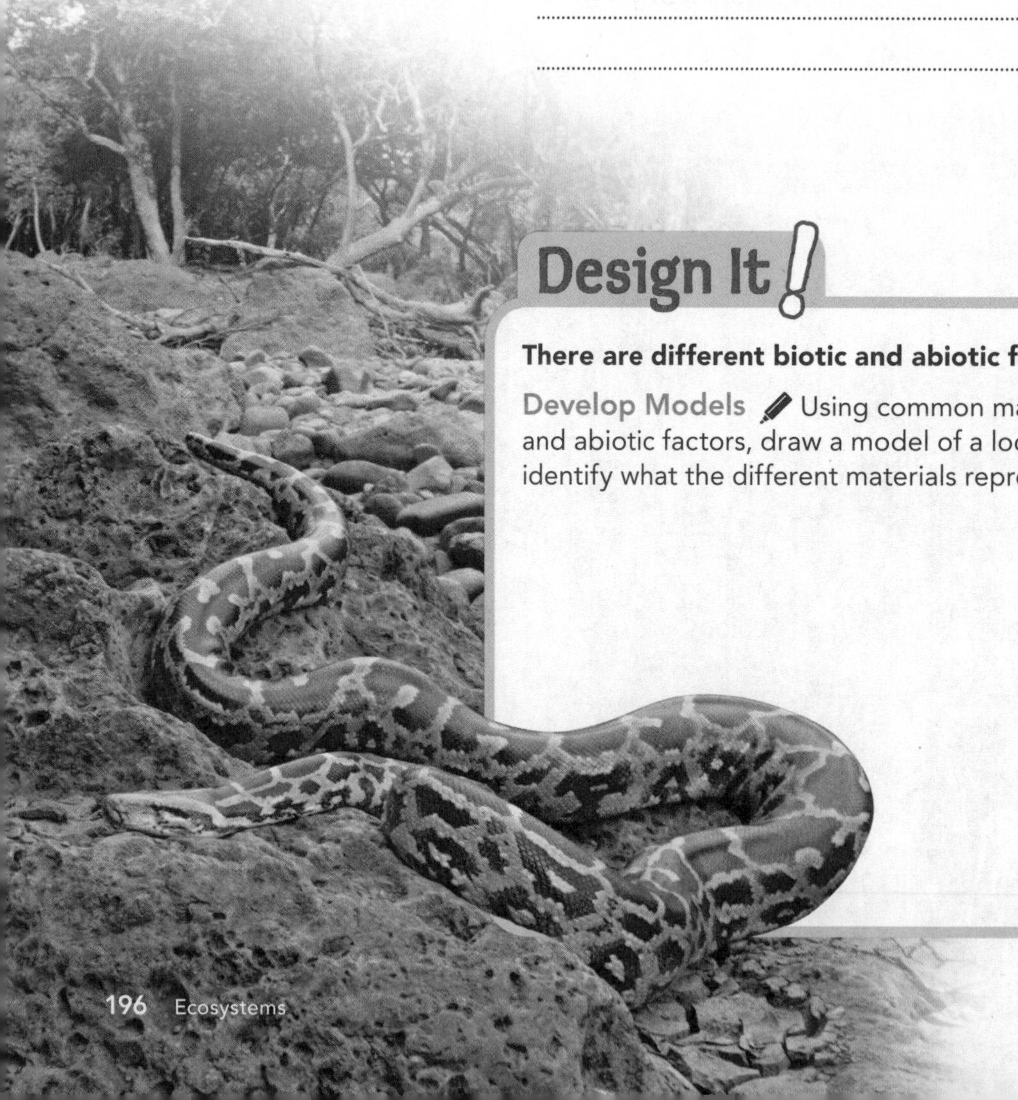

Biotic Factors

What types of living things are in the python's tropical rain forest habitat below (**Figure 2**)? The parts of a habitat that are or were once alive and that interact with an organism are called **biotic factors**. These biological components include the trees and plants. Animals that the python eats are biotic factors, as are the other snakes it encounters. Waste products made by these organisms and others are also considered biotic factors. Bacteria, mushrooms, and other small organisms are other types of biotic factors that play important roles in the habitat.

Abiotic Factors

Organisms also interact with nonliving things in the environment. **Abiotic factors** are the nonliving parts of an organism's habitat. These physical components include water, oxygen, space, rocks, light, temperature, and soil. The quality and condition of the abiotic factors can have a major effect on living things. For example, water in a habitat may contain pollutants. The poor quality of the water may result in sickness or death for the organisms that live there.

READING CHECK **Cite Textual Evidence** Why do you think snakes do not live in the Arctic tundra? Use evidence from the text to support your answer.

....

....

Python Habitat

Figure 2 A python interacts with many biotic and abiotic factors in its habitat.

Design It!

There are different biotic and abiotic factors in a habitat.

Develop Models Using common materials to model biotic and abiotic factors, draw a model of a local habitat. Include a key to identify what the different materials represent.

Organism

Population

Community

Ecosystem

Ecosystem Organization

Most organisms do not live all alone in their habitat. Instead, organisms live together in populations and communities that interact with abiotic factors in their ecosystems. Interactions can also occur among the various populations. **Figure 3** summarizes the levels of organization in an ecosystem.

Organisms All of the Indian pythons that live in South Asia are members of one species. A species (SPEE sheez) is a group of organisms that can mate with each other and produce offspring that can also mate and reproduce.

Populations All the members of one species living in a particular area are referred to as a **population**. The Indian pythons of India's Keoladeo Ghana National Park, for example, are one example of a population.

Communities A particular area usually contains more than one species of organism. The Keoladeo Park is home to hundreds of bird species, as well as mammals, plants, and other varieties of organisms. All the different populations that live together in an area make up a **community**.

The community of organisms that lives in a particular area, along with the nonliving environment, make up an **ecosystem**. The study of how organisms interact with each other and with their environment is called ecology.

☑ READING CHECK **Determine Meaning** What makes up a community in an ecosystem?

....

....

....

Levels of Organization

Figure 3 A single individual in an ecosystem is the organism, which forms a population with other members of its species. Different species form communities in a single ecosystem.

Apply Concepts Make a prediction about how a lack of resources in an ecosystem might impact the levels of organization.

....

....

....

....

....

....

....

....

....

Literacy Connection

Cite Textual Evidence Suppose farmers in an area spray insecticides on their crops. A population of birds that feeds on insects begins to decline. Underline the text that supports the idea that the insecticide may be responsible for the decline in the bird population.

Populations

Remember from your reading that a population consists of all of the organisms of the same species living in the same area at the same time. For example, all of the pythons living in the same rainforest would be a distinct population. There are several things that can change a population's size.

Births and Deaths New individuals generally join a population by being born into it. A population grows when more individuals are born into it than die in any period of time. So when the birth rate (the number of births per 1,000 individuals for a given time period) is greater than the death rate (the number of deaths per 1,000 individuals for a given time period) a population may increase. When the birth rate is the same as the death rate, then the population usually remains stable. In situations where the death rate is greater than the birth rate, the population will decrease.

Math Toolbox

Graphing Population Changes

Changes over time in a population such as white-tailed deer in Ohio can be displayed in a graph.

Deer Population Trends, 2000–2010			
Year	Population (estimated)	Year	Population (estimated)
2000	525,000	2006	770,000
2001	560,000	2007	725,000
2002	620,000	2008	745,000
2003	670,000	2009	750,000
2004	715,000	2010	710,000
2005	720,000		

1. **Represent Relationships** ✎ Use the data table to complete a graph of the changes in the deer population. Then describe the trend in the graph.

....

....

....

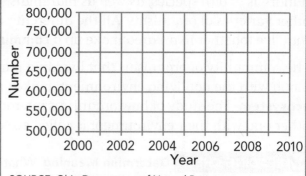

SOURCE: Ohio Department of Natural Resources

2. **Analyze and Interpret Data** What factors do you think might be responsible for the changes in the deer population?

....

....

Immigration and Emigration

A population's size also can increase or decrease when individuals move into or out of the population. Immigration (im ih GRAY shun) means moving into a population. Emigration (em ih GRAY shun) means leaving a population. For instance, if food is scarce, some members of the antelope herd in **Figure 4** may wander off in search of a better habitat. If they become permanently separated from the original herd, they will no longer be part of that population.

Population Density

If you are a scientist studying an ecosystem or population, it can be helpful to know the population **density** —the number of individuals in an area of a specific size. Population density can be represented as an equation:

$$Population\ density = \frac{Number\ of\ individuals}{Unit\ area}$$

For example, suppose an ecologist estimates there are 800 beetles living in a park measuring 400 square meters. The population density would be 800 beetles per 400 square meters, or 2 beetles per square meter.

☑ READING CHECK Summarize Text How do birth and death rates affect a population's size?

....

....

....

HANDS-ON LAB

☑**Investigate** Model how space can be a limiting factor.

Academic Vocabulary

Have you heard the term *density* before? What did it mean in that other context?

....

....

Emigration

Figure 4 Food scarcity is just one cause of emigration.
Cause and Effect What other factors might cause individuals in this antelope herd to emigrate?

....

....

....

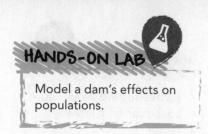
Limited Space

Figure 5 ✏️ In the image of the gannets, circle or shade the available space in the environment for nesting and raising young.

Cause and Effect How does the lack of space act as a limiting factor for these gannets?

....
....
....
....
....

Factors That Limit Population Growth

In general, a population grows if conditions are favorable. Eventually, however, some factor in the environment, such as the availability of food, will limit the size of a population. An environmental factor that causes a population to stop growing or to decrease in size, such as a fatal disease infecting organisms, organisms, is a **limiting factor**.

Food and Water Food and water can be limiting factors for virtually any population. An adult elephant eats an average of around 180 kilograms of vegetation each day to survive. Suppose the trees in its habitat can provide 1000 kilograms of vegetation daily. In this habitat, not more than 5 adult elephants could survive. The largest population that an area can support is called its carrying capacity.

Climate and Weather Changes in climate can limit population growth. Warmer weather in the early winter, for example, can cause some plants to continue growing. Natural disasters such as hurricanes and floods can have immediate and long-term effects on populations.

Space and Shelter Other limiting factors for populations are space and shelter, as illustrated by the nesting site in **Figure 5**. When individual organisms must compete for space to live or raise young, the population can decrease. Competition for suitable shelter also can limit the growth of a population.

☑️ **READING CHECK** **Summarize Text** How do limiting factors affect a population of organisms?

....
....

1. **Identify** Identify the levels of organization in an ecosystem from smallest to largest.

....

....

Answer questions 2 and 3 using the graph below.

Changes in Mouse Population

2. **Analyze Data** What trends do you observe in the mouse population for the four years?

....

....

....

3. **Interpret Data** Does the data support the idea that this population is relatively stable? Give evidence to support your answer.

....

....

....

4. **Construct Explanations** How can biotic and abiotic factors in an ecosystem affect populations? Give two examples of each.

....

....

....

....

....

....

5. **Analyze Systems** Why is climate considered to be a limiting factor for populations in an ecosystem?

....

....

....

Quest CHECK-IN

In this lesson, you learned how ecosystems are organized and how different factors affect populations.

Cause and Effect What effect might an algal bloom in a pond have on populations of organisms that make their home there?

....

....

....

....

....

....

☞ INTERACTIVITY

Suspicious Activities

Go online to research and explore explanations for the algal bloom. Then, using the information you have gathered, identify three possible causes for the bloom.

MS-LS2-1

THE CASE OF THE DISAPPEARING

Cerulean Warbler

The cerulean warbler is a small, migratory songbird named for its blue color. Cerulean warblers breed in eastern North America during the spring and summer. The warblers spend the winter months in the Andes Mountains of Colombia, Venezuela, Ecuador, and Peru in northern part of South America.

The population of cerulean warblers is decreasing very quickly. No other population of songbirds is decreasing more rapidly in eastern North America. Populations of warblers have been declining at a rate of about 3 percent a year. This means that there are 3 percent fewer warblers from one year to the next. Habitat loss, especially in the region where the birds spend the winter, is thought to be the main reason. Look at the Cerulean Warbler Range Map.

Habitat Loss in the Wintering Range

By 2025, there will be 100 million more people in South America than there were in 2002. As human population size increases, the demands on the land and local habitats also increase. Forests are cleared and habitats for native plants and animals are lost to make room for planting crops and for raising cattle. These crops and cattle are needed to feed the increased population of people in the area.

Cerulean warblers inhabit the dense, evergreen forests that grow at middle elevations in the Andes Mountains. Their preferred habitat is tall, mature trees where they can feed on insects.

Cerulean Warbler Range Map

EQUATOR

KEY

Breeding range (April–Spetember)

Wintering range (October–March)

Migration route

However, this habitat is also the preferred area to grow shade-coffee crops. The tall trees provide shade for the shorter coffee plants. Shade-coffee takes longer to grow and produces less coffee than sun-grown coffee crops. Forested areas are often cleared to make room for sun-grown coffee and other more profitable crops needing direct sunlight. This reduces the size of the warbler's habitat. As shown in the graph, the rate of clearing has decreased in recent years because the forests that are left are on steep slopes. These steep slopes and high elevations are not suitable for farming. Look at the bar graph below.

Use the graph to answer the following questions.

1. **Patterns** Describe any patterns you see in the graph.

....

....

....

....

2. **Predict** What do you think the data will look like for each country until 2020? Why?

....

....

....

....

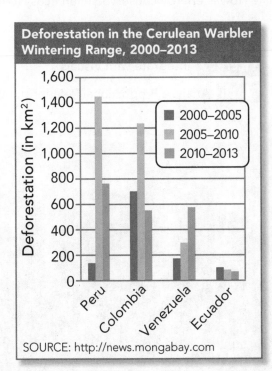

Deforestation in the Cerulean Warbler Wintering Range, 2000–2013

SOURCE: http://news.mongabay.com

3. **Construct Explanations** Explain how you think changing levels of deforestation in the wintering range affects the cerulean warbler population.

....

....

4. **Solve Problems** What are some strategies that you think can be used in northern South America to stabilize and protect the warbler populations?

....

....

....

Energy Flow in Ecosystems

Guiding Questions

- What are the energy roles in an ecosystem?
- How is energy transferred between living and nonliving parts of an ecosystem?
- How is energy conserved in an ecosystem?

Connections

Literacy Integrate with Visuals

Math Analyze Proportional Relationships

MS-LS2-3

Vocabulary

producer
consumer
decomposer
food chain
food web
energy pyramid

Academic Vocabulary

role

 Vocabulary App

Practice vocabulary on a mobile device.

Quest CONNECTION

Think about how the energy roles played by organisms in the pond ecosystem are important to the stability of the system.

Connect It !

✎ **Shade in one of the arrows to indicate the direction in which energy flows between the frog and the fly.**

Analyze Systems Where do you think the plants in the image get the energy they need to grow and survive?

....

....

....

Energy Roles in an Ecosystem

In gym class, have you ever been assigned to play a position like catcher or goalie for your class team? If so, you know what it's like to have a specific **role** in a system. Similar to positions in sports, every organism has a role in the movement of energy through its ecosystem.

Energy roles are based on the way organisms obtain food and interact with other organisms. In an ecosystem, organisms play the energy role of either a producer, consumer, or decomposer.

Producers
Energy enters most ecosystems as sunlight. Some organisms, such as the plants shown in **Figure 1** and some types of bacteria, capture the energy of sunlight. These organisms use the sun's energy to recombine atoms from molecules of water and carbon dioxide into food molecules in a process called photosynthesis.

An organism that can make its own food is a **producer**. Producers become the source of food for other organisms in an ecosystem. In a few ecosystems, producers obtain energy from a source other than sunlight. Deep in the ocean, some bacteria convert chemical energy into food from hydrothermal vents in the ocean floor. They are the producers in these ecosystems that include worms, clams, and crabs.

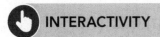

INTERACTIVITY

Identify the sources of your dinner.

Academic Vocabulary

Have you heard the term *role* in other contexts? List some examples.

....

....

....

Obtaining Energy

Figure 1 Many small pond organisms, like the fly, obtain energy from green plants. They, in turn, serve to provide energy for larger organisms, like the frog.

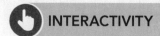

INTERACTIVITY

Model energy roles and energy flow in ecosystems.

INTERACTIVITY

Explore the roles living things play in ecosystems.

Write About It What are some producers, consumers, scavengers, and decomposers you have seen in your neighborhood?

Life and Death in an Alaskan Stream

Figure 2 Salmon migrate upstream to this forest environment after spending most of their lives at sea. As they travel, many of them become food for the ecosystem's carnivores.

Develop Models Label the producers, consumers, decomposers, and scavengers in the image.

Consumers Organisms like the animals in **Figure 2** cannot produce their own food. A **consumer** obtains energy by feeding on other organisms.

Scientists classify consumers according to what they eat. As consumers eat, the food is broken down into molecules that help supply them energy.

Consumers that eat only animals are carnivores. Great white sharks, owls, and tigers are examples of carnivores. Some carnivores are scavengers. A scavenger is a carnivore that feeds on the bodies of dead organisms. Scavengers include hagfish and condors. Some carnivores will scavenge if they cannot find live animals to prey upon.

Herbivores are consumers that eat only plants and other photosynthetic organisms. Grasshoppers, rabbits, and cows are herbivores.

Consumers that eat both plants and animals are omnivores. Raccoons, pigs, and humans are omnivores.

Decomposers If the only roles in an ecosystem were producer and consumer, then some of the matter that is essential for life, such as carbon and nitrogen, would remain in the waste products and remains of dead organisms. However, decomposers have a role in ecosystems to prevent this from happening. **Decomposers** break down biotic wastes and dead organisms, returning the raw materials to the ecosystem. For example, after adult salmon swim upstream and reproduce, they die. Their carcasses litter the riverbeds and banks. Bacteria in the soil help break down the carcasses, releasing their nutrients to trees, grasses, shrubs, and other producers that depend on them.

In a sense, decomposers are nature's recyclers. While obtaining energy for their own needs, decomposers also return matter in the form of simple molecules to the environment. These molecules can be used again by other organisms. Mushrooms, bacteria, and mold are common decomposers.

☑ **READING CHECK** **Integrate with Visuals** In terms of their energy roles, what similarities do the bear, salmon, and coyote in **Figure 2** share?

....

....

HANDS-ON LAB

ⓤ**Investigate** Observe how decomposers get energy.

Food chain

Grizzly bear

Salmon

Crustaceans

Zooplankton

Phytoplankton

Energy and Matter Transfer

Energy in most ecosystems comes from sunlight, and producers convert this energy into food through photosynthesis. The energy and matter are contained in atoms and molecules that are transferred to herbivores that eat the producers. Then they move on to carnivores feeding on the first, or primary, consumers. The energy and matter next move on through other meat-eating secondary consumers. This movement of energy and matter can be described through different models: food chains, food webs, and energy pyramids.

Food Chains A food chain is one way to show how energy and matter move through an ecosystem. A **food chain** is a series of events in which one organism eats another and obtains energy and nutrients. **Figure 3** illustrates one example of a food chain. The arrows indicate the movement of energy and matter as organisms are consumed up the food chain.

Food Webs Energy and matter move in one direction through a food chain, but they can also take different paths through the ecosystem. However, most producers and consumers are part of many overlapping food chains. For example, a salmon could be consumed by a shark in the ocean before it even has the chance to migrate upstream and encounter a bear. A more realistic way to show how energy and matter cycle through an ecosystem is with a food web. As shown in **Figure 4**, a **food web** consists of many overlapping food chains in an ecosystem.

Organisms may play more than one role in an ecosystem. Look at the crayfish in **Figure 4**. A crayfish is an omnivore that is a first-level consumer when it eats plants. However, when a crayfish eats a snail, it is a second-level consumer.

Food Chain

Figure 3 The food chain tracing a path from the phytoplankton to the grizzly bear is a simple way of showing how energy and matter flow from one organism to the next in the Alaskan stream ecosystem shown in **Figure 2**.

Identify Limitations What are some limitations of modeling the flow of energy and matter in an ecosystem with a food chain?

....

....

....

Model It!

Food Web

Figure 4 This food web depicts relationships among some of the organisms that live in a forest that has a small pond.

Develop Models Complete the food web by drawing and identifying the missing organisms listed below. Add arrows to the diagram to complete the web.

mushrooms   red fox   snail   garter snake

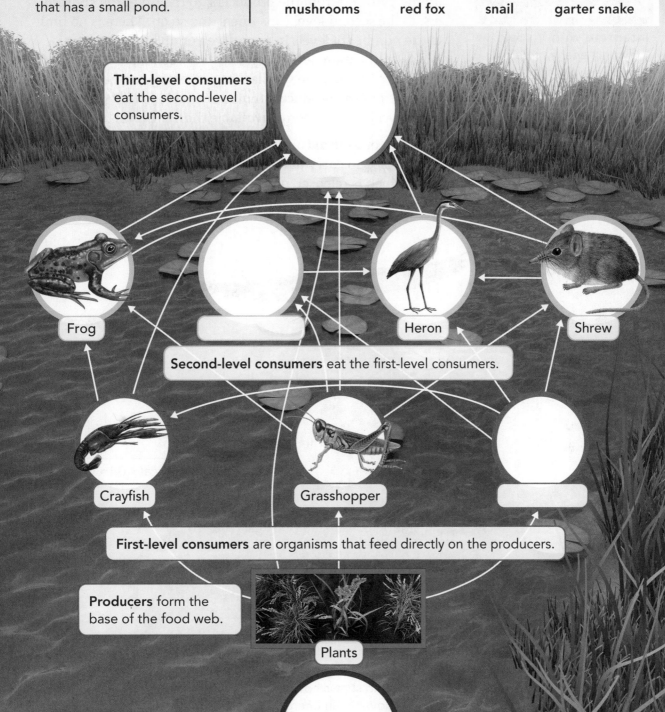

Third-level consumers eat the second-level consumers.

Frog

Heron

Shrew

Second-level consumers eat the first-level consumers.

Crayfish

Grasshopper

First-level consumers are organisms that feed directly on the producers.

Producers form the base of the food web.

Plants

Decomposers break down the wastes and remains of other organisms.

Literacy Connection

Integrate with Visuals

Why is an energy pyramid shaped like a triangle with the point on top?

....

....

....

Energy Pyramids

A diagram called an **energy pyramid** shows the amount of energy that moves from one feeding level to another in a food web. Each step in a food chain or food web is represented by a level within an energy pyramid, as shown in **Figure 5**. Producers have the most available energy so they make up the first level, or base, of the pyramid. Energy moves up the pyramid from the producers, to the first-level consumers, to the second-level consumers and so on. There is no limit to the number of levels in a food web or an energy pyramid. However, the more levels that exist between a producer and a given consumer, the smaller the percentage of the original energy from the producers that is available to that consumer. Each level has less energy available than the level below.

When an organism consumes food it obtains energy and matter used to carry out life activities. These activities produce heat, which is released and lost to the environment, reducing the amount of energy available to the next level.

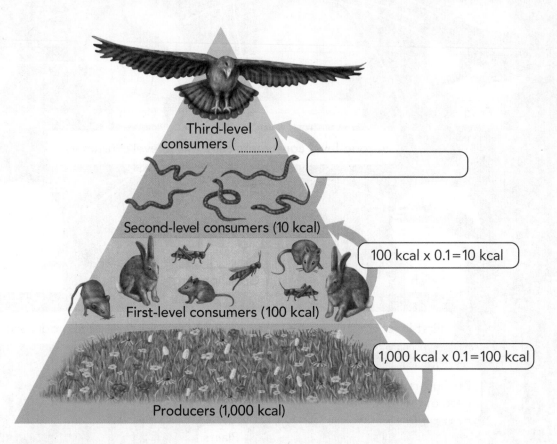

Third-level consumers (..........)

Second-level consumers (10 kcal)

100 kcal x 0.1 = 10 kcal

First-level consumers (100 kcal)

1,000 kcal x 0.1 = 100 kcal

Producers (1,000 kcal)

Energy Pyramid

Figure 5 This energy pyramid shows how the amount of available energy decreases as you move up an energy pyramid from the producers to the different levels of consumers. Only about 10 percent of the energy is transferred from level to level. Energy is measured in kilocalories, or kcal.

Calculate ✏ Write in the missing equation and fill in the energy that gets to the hawk at the top.

Energy Availability As you can see in **Figure 5**, only about 10 percent of the energy at one level of a food web is available to the next higher level. This greatly limits how many different levels a food chain can have, as well as the numbers of organisms that can be supported at higher levels. This is why it is typical for there to be fewer organisms as you move from one level of a pyramid or one "link" in a food chain up to the next level.

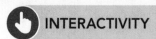 **INTERACTIVITY**

Model how altering a food web affects the flow of energy and matter in an ecosystem.

☑ READING CHECK **Summarize Text** Why is energy reduced at each level of the energy pyramid?

....

....

....

Math Toolbox

Relationships in an Energy Pyramid

In a small forest ecosystem, caterpillars eat plants. Carolina wrens eat the caterpillars, and black rat snakes eat the wrens. Suppose that the plants contain 550,000 kilocalories.

1. Calculate ✏ Complete the pyramid by calculating the energy available to each level.

2. **Analyze Proportional Relationships** How would the amount of energy in the pyramid change if the caterpillars ate only half of the available plants?

....

....

....

....

....

Third-level
consumers

Second-level
consumers

First-level consumers

550,000 kcal

Producers

☑ LESSON 2 Check

MS-LS2-3

1. **Analyze Systems** Which model best illustrates the flow of energy and matter in an ecosystem—a food chain or a food web? Explain.

....

....

....

....

....

2. **Evaluate Claims** A student says an organism that is both a first-level and second-level consumer is an omnivore. Is that student correct? Explain.

....

....

3. **Apply Concepts** Suppose a rancher wants to buy some grassland to raise cattle. What should she know about energy flow before she invests in the land or the cattle?

....

....

....

....

....

....

4. **Identify Patterns** In Massachusetts, a team of scientists studying great white sharks estimates that a population of 15,000 seals supports fewer than 100 sharks during the summer. Why are there so few top-level consumers in this system?

....

....

....

....

....

....

5. **Cause and Effect** Human activity can affect ecosystems by removing producers, consumers, and decomposers. What limiting factors may result from human actions, and what effects might they have on the flow of energy and matter in an ecosystem?

....

....

....

....

....

....

....

Quest CHECK-IN

In this lesson, you learned about the general roles that organisms can play in an ecosystem, as well as how relationships among those roles can be modeled through food chains, food webs, and energy pyramids.

Apply Concepts How might knowing about energy roles help you understand what's happening in the pond?

....

....

 INTERACTIVITY

Nutrients and Aquatic Organisms

Go online to analyze what might happen to a pond ecosystem when nutrient levels are altered. Then discuss how the results of your analysis could help you solve the mystery.

Eating Oil

Do you know how tiny organisms can clean up oil spills? You engineer it! Strategies used to deal with the Deepwater Horizon oil spill, the worst in U.S. history, show us how.

The Challenge: To clean up harmful oil from marine environments

Phenomenon On April 20, 2010, part of an oil rig in the Gulf of Mexico exploded. It leaked oil for 87 days. By the time the leak was fixed, about 200 million gallons of oil had spilled into the water. Oil destroys beaches, marshlands, and marine ecosystems. It coats birds, fish, and marine animals, such as dolphins and sea turtles. The oil makes it difficult for many animals to move and get food, and causes others to suffocate.

Ecologists engineered a solution that relied on nature to help with the cleanup. They poured chemicals into the water that helped break up the oil into smaller droplets. Then the bacteria and fungi in the water broke down the oil droplets.

Bioremediation uses natural living things to reduce contaminants in an environment. In the event of an oil spill, oil-eating populations of bacteria and fungi grow quickly. Now, scientists are working to engineer ways to increase the speed at which these decomposers work and to make sure the oceans can support optimal populations of these tiny oil eaters.

INTERACTIVITY

Design your own method to clean up an oil spill.

The oil-eating bacteria helped in the cleanup after the Deepwater Horizon oil spill.

DESIGN CHALLENGE

Can you put decomposers to work and build your own composter? Go to the Engineering Design Notebook to find out!

Guiding Questions

- How is matter transferred between the living and nonliving parts of an ecosystem?
- How is matter conserved in an ecosystem?

Connections

Literacy Determine Central Ideas

Math Analyze Relationships

MS-LS2-3

Vocabulary

Law of Conservation of Mass
Law of Conservation of Energy
evaporation
condensation
precipitation

Academic Vocabulary

system
components

 VOCABULARY APP

Practice vocabulary on a mobile device.

Quest CONNECTION

Consider how the cycling of matter among organisms might help explain what is wrong in the greenhouse.

Connect It !

✏️ **Draw arrows on Figure 1 and label them to show how energy enters or leaves the terrarium.**

Predict What would happen to the ecosystem in the terrarium if it were a closed system for energy?

....

....

Explain Phenomena Why is this ecosystem considered a closed system and how could that system be changed?

....

....

....

Conservation of Matter and Energy

During photosynthesis and cellular respiration, matter (mass) and energy can only change form. **The Law of Conservation of Mass** states that matter is neither created nor destroyed during any chemical or physical change. **The Law of Conservation of Energy** states that when one form of energy is transformed to another, no energy is lost in the process. Energy cannot be created or destroyed, but it can change from one form to another.

The terrarium in **Figure 1** is a closed **system** for matter. Matter cannot enter or exit. The plants, soil, rocks, water, microorganisms, animals, and air in the terrarium are all **components** of the system. The components may change over time, but their total mass will remain the same. All over Earth, mass and energy are cycling through different forms without being created or destroyed.

✅ READING CHECK **Distinguish Facts** What would you tell a classmate who claims that food is destroyed when you eat it?

....

....

INTERACTIVITY

Consider your role in the cycling of energy.

Academic Vocabulary

The schools in one area are often called a *school system*. What are some of the *components* of this system?

....

....

....

....

Ecosystem in a Jar
Figure 1 After it is sealed, a terrarium becomes a closed system for matter. But energy can still flow in and out through the glass.

Water Cycle

Recall that matter is made up of tiny particles called atoms and two or more atoms can join to make a molecule. Two hydrogen atoms combined with one oxygen atom forms a molecule of water.

Water is essential for life. Water cycles in a continuous process from Earth's surface to the atmosphere and back, in various forms, or states. The water cycle involves the processes of evaporation, condensation, and precipitation. Follow along on **Figure 3** as you read about each process to explore it in more detail.

Evaporation Water molecules move from Earth's surface up to the atmosphere by evaporation. **Evaporation** is the process by which molecules at the surface of liquid water absorb enough energy to change to a gas. This water vapor rises into the atmosphere. The energy needed for evaporation comes from sunlight. Water evaporates from oceans, lakes, fields, and other places. Smaller amounts of water also evaporate from living things. For example, plants release water vapor from their leaves. In addition, animals release liquid water in their wastes and water vapor when they exhale. You may recall that one of the products of cellular respiration is water.

Spring Water

Figure 2 The water at Yellow Springs is high in iron, which stains the rocks orange.

Model It!

Where does your water come from?

Yellow Springs, Ohio, shown in **Figure 2**, has been a source of refreshing water for animals and people for centuries. Geologists studying the Yellow Spring have determined that the spring is fed by rain that falls only a few miles north. After the rain soaks into the ground, it travels underground for 12 to 18 months before flowing out of the spring.

Develop Models ✐ Does your drinking water come from a central water supply, a well, or bottles? Identify the source of your water and trace its origin back as far as you can. Make a model of the path the water takes to get to your home.

Condensation Rising water vapor reaches a point in the atmosphere where it cools. As it cools, it turns back into small droplets of water in a liquid state. The process of a gas changing to a liquid is **condensation.** The water droplets collect around dust particles and eventually form clouds. Dew is water that has condensed on plants or other objects on a cool morning.

Precipitation Condensing water vapor collects as clouds, but as the drops continue to grow larger, they become heavier. Eventually the heavy drops fall in the form of **precipitation:** rain, snow, sleet, or hail. Precipitation can fall into oceans, lakes, or rivers. Precipitation falling on land may soak into the soil and become groundwater, or it may run off the land and flow into rivers or oceans.

HANDS-ON LAB

Investigate Model the water cycle.

Write About It Think how you interacted with water today. Where did that water come from? Where did it go next? Write a story that traces the water molecule's trip.

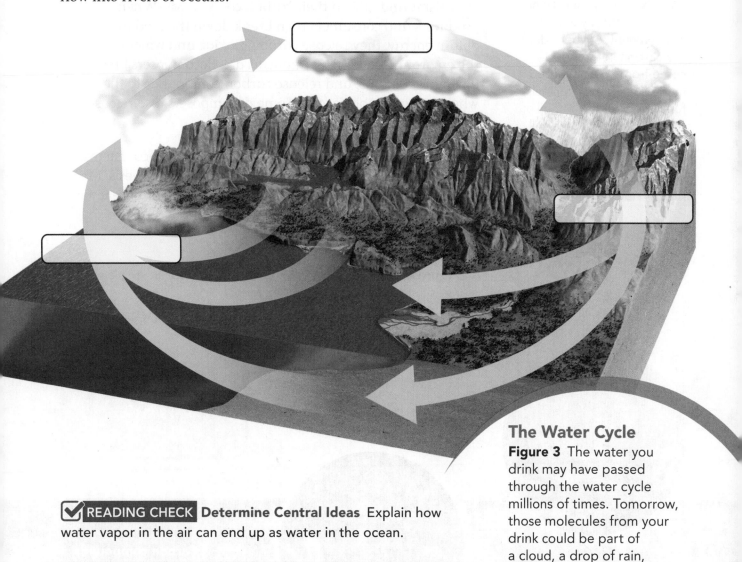

The Water Cycle

Figure 3 The water you drink may have passed through the water cycle millions of times. Tomorrow, those molecules from your drink could be part of a cloud, a drop of rain, a stream, or water vapor in the air.

Identify Label the three processes of the water cycle.

✔ READING CHECK **Determine Central Ideas** Explain how water vapor in the air can end up as water in the ocean.

....

....

....

Carbon and Oxygen Cycles

Carbon and oxygen are essential for life. Carbon is the building block of living things. For example, carbon is a major component of bones and the proteins that build muscles. Most organisms also use oxygen for their life processes. **Figure 4** shows how carbon and oxygen cycles in ecosystems are linked. Producers, consumers, and decomposers all play roles in recycling carbon and oxygen.

Carbon Cycle

Most producers take in carbon dioxide gas from the air during photosynthesis. Producers use the carbon to make food—carbon-containing molecules, such as sugars and starches. Carbon is also converted by plants to compounds that help plants grow. Consumers eat other organisms and take in their carbon compounds. When producers and consumers then break down the food to obtain energy, they release carbon dioxide and water into the environment. When organisms die, decomposers break down the remains, and release carbon compounds to the soil where it is available for use. Some decomposers also release carbon dioxide into the air.

Oxygen Cycle

Oxygen also cycles through ecosystems. Producers release oxygen as a product of photosynthesis. Most organisms take in oxygen from the air or water and use it to carry out cellular respiration.

Literacy Connection

Determine Central Ideas Work with a partner. Think about one food you have eaten recently. Where did the carbon in that food come from? Was the food made from plants, animals, fungi, or bacteria—or all of those sources? Where will the carbon go now that you have eaten the food? Share your response with another pair of students.

The Carbon and Oxygen Cycles

Figure 4 Producers, consumers, and decomposers all play roles in recycling carbon and oxygen.

Interpret Diagrams ✏ Draw arrows to show how carbon and oxygen move through the ecosystem.

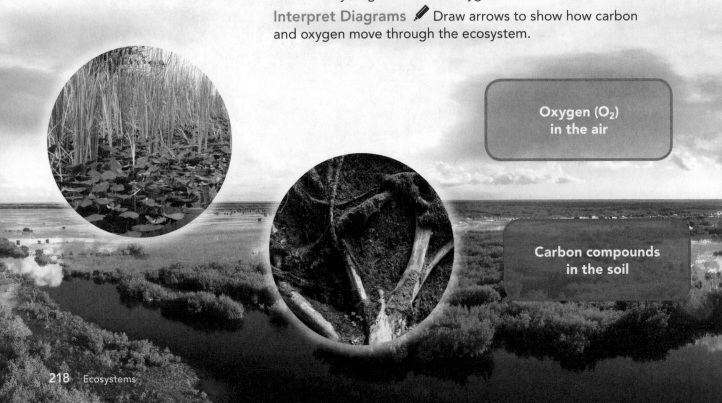

Oxygen (O_2) in the air

Carbon compounds in the soil

Law of Conservation On Earth, the number of carbon and oxygen atoms remains constant. Recall that atoms are not created or destroyed in chemical reactions. According to the Law of Conservation of Mass, atoms may appear in different chemical compounds as they get recycled through Earth's various systems, but they are never created or destroyed.

Human Impact Some human activities affect the levels of carbon and oxygen in the air. When humans burn gasoline, natural gas, and plant fuels, carbon dioxide is released into the atmosphere. Carbon dioxide levels also rise when humans clear forests to create farmland or to use the wood for lumber or fuel.

When trees are removed from an ecosystem, there are fewer producers to absorb carbon dioxide. If fallen trees are left on the ground, decomposers will break down their tissues through cellular respiration and release carbon dioxide into the air. Burning the trees has the same effect, because carbon dioxide is produced during combustion.

☑ READING CHECK **Summarize Text** Describe the roles of producers and consumers in the oxygen cycle.

....

....

....

👆 **INTERACTIVITY**

Investigate and identify the cycles of matter.

Carbon dioxide (CO_2) in the air

Nitrogen Cycle in Ecosystems

Like carbon, nitrogen is one of the necessary elements of life. Nitrogen is an important component for building proteins in animals and an essential nutrient for plants. In the nitrogen cycle, nitrogen moves from the air into the soil, into living things, and back into the air or soil. The air around you is about 78 percent nitrogen gas (N_2). However, most organisms cannot use nitrogen gas. Nitrogen gas is called "free" nitrogen because it is not combined with other kinds of atoms.

Nitrogen Fixation Most organisms can use nitrogen only after it has been "fixed," or combined with other elements to form nitrogen-containing compounds. Nitrogen fixation is the process of changing free nitrogen into a usable form of nitrogen, as shown in **Figure 5**. Certain bacteria perform most nitrogen fixation. These bacteria live in bumps called nodules on the roots of legume plants. Clover, beans, peas, alfalfa, peanuts, and trees such as mesquite and desert ironwood are all common legume plants. Nitrogen can also be "fixed" by lightning. About 10 percent of the nitrogen needed by plants is fixed by lightning.

Nitrogen Cycle

Figure 5 In the nitrogen cycle, free nitrogen from the air is fixed into compounds. Consumers can then use these nitrogen compounds to carry out their life processes.

Make Observations
✎ Circle the steps where free nitrogen is changed to a form plants and animals can use.

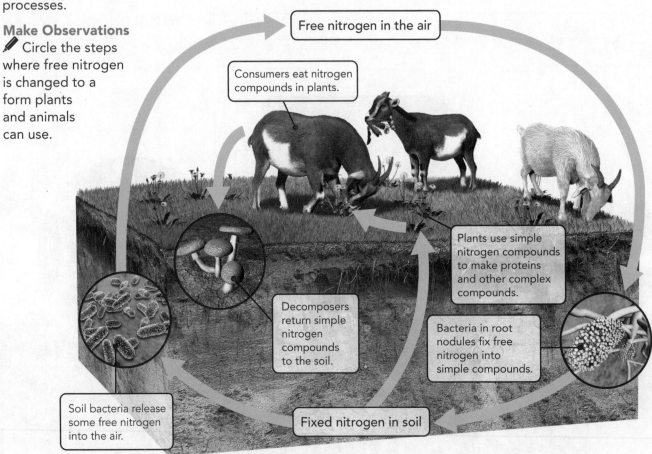

Free nitrogen in the air

Consumers eat nitrogen compounds in plants.

Plants use simple nitrogen compounds to make proteins and other complex compounds.

Decomposers return simple nitrogen compounds to the soil.

Bacteria in root nodules fix free nitrogen into simple compounds.

Soil bacteria release some free nitrogen into the air.

Fixed nitrogen in soil

Recycling Free Nitrogen Once nitrogen has been fixed, producers can use it to build proteins and other complex molecules. Nitrogen can cycle from the soil to producers and then to consumers many times. At some point, however, bacteria break down the nitrogen compounds into free nitrogen. The free nitrogen rises back into the air and the cycle begins again. This is also an example of the Law of Conservation of Mass. Throughout the cycling of nitrogen, the number of atoms remains constant. Nitrogen atoms may take the form of gas (free nitrogen) or they may take the form of nitrogen-containing compounds, but the atoms are never created or destroyed.

☑ READING CHECK **Summarize Text** Why is nitrogen fixation necessary?

....

....

....

Lightning and Nitrogen

Figure 6 The electrical energy of lightning splits apart N_2 molecules into nitrogen atoms. The nitrogen atoms combine with water to make nitrogen compounds that plants can use.

Math Toolbox

Dependent and Independent Variables

Soybean plants are legumes that host nitrogen-fixing bacteria in their root nodules. Researchers wanted to know whether the plants would produce more seeds if nitrogen-fixing bacteria called *Rhizobia* were added to the soil during planting. The graph below shows the results of the experiment.

1. **Analyze Relationships**
   ✏ Underline the independent variable and circle the dependent variable in the graph. Then explain their relationship.

   ....

   ....

   ....

2. **Interpret Graphs** Did the bacterial treatment have any effect? Use evidence from the graph to support your answer.

   ....

   ....

   ....

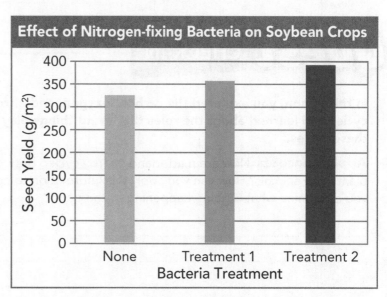

Effect of Nitrogen-fixing Bacteria on Soybean Crops

Seed Yield (g/m²) vs Bacteria Treatment: None, Treatment 1, Treatment 2

MS-LS2-3

1. Describe What are the two roles of bacteria in the nitrogen cycle?

....

....

....

....

2. Explain Phenomena How does water get up to the atmosphere, and how does it get back down to Earth's surface?

....

....

....

3. Develop Models ✎ Sketch and label a diagram in the space below showing how carbon cycles through an ecosystem.

4. Apply Concepts What is the Law of Conservation of Mass? Why is it important in Earth's recycling of water, oxygen, carbon, and nitrogen. Give one example.

....

....

....

....

....

....

5. Draw Conclusions How would the carbon and oxygen cycles be affected if there were plants but no consumers or decomposers on Earth?

....

....

....

....

....

....

....

....

Quest CHECK-IN

In this lesson, you explored the carbon, oxygen, and nitrogen cycles and learned about the roles that living things play in these cycles.

Apply Concepts How are matter and energy cycled between plants and animals? How can you apply this information to help you determine what is going happening to the pond?

....

....

....

....

👆 INTERACTIVITY

Matter and Energy in a Pond

Go online to to investigate how matter and energy are cycled in a pond ecosystem.

MS-LS2-1, MS-LS2-3

An Appetite for Plastic?!

Organic materials, such as bone and leaves, get cycled through ecosystems by decomposers. Materials like rock and metal break down more slowly. Plastics, however, are manufactured products that cannot be broken down easily. Additionally, they are problematic for the environment. Scientists have been trying for decades to discover a way to degrade plastic. Now, it seems they may have found an answer inside the guts of two tiny larvae.

Wax worms live in beehives where they feed off beeswax. What is bad for bees, may be good for people who are looking for a way to deal with Earth's plastic problem. Scientists have found out that wax worms can digest plastic bags! How they do this isn't clear yet. It may be that bacteria living in the wax worm's gut allow it to break down the plastic. Another possibility is that the wax worm produces an enzyme, a substance that speeds up reactions in an organism's body, that helps it degrade the plastic.

Wax worms aren't the only ones getting attention for their eating habits! Mealworms are the larvae of a species of beetle. They are fed to pet reptiles, fish, and birds. Scientists have observed that mealworms can break down plastic foam, such as the kind used in coffee cups and packing materials.

Scientists are trying to figure out how these larvae are able to degrade plastic. It may be a long time before we figure out how to use that knowledge on a scale large enough to reduce global plastic pollution.

MY DISCOVERY

Use the Internet or other sources to investigate how wax worms and mealworms are able to break down different types of plastics. Create a chart that shows what type of plastic each larva can eat and how its body is able to break down plastic.

Mealworms are able to break down plastic foam.

A wax worm can munch its way through through this plastic shopping bag.

☑ TOPIC 4 Review and Assess

1 Living Things and the Environment

MS-LS2-1

1. Which of the following describes a population?
   A. 85 great white sharks off Cape Cod
   B. thousands of dolphins and whales around Hawaii
   C. a mating pair of seagulls migrating to an island
   D. corals, sponges, algae, reef fish, lobsters, and giant clams

2. Which of the following is a biotic factor that might limit a population of mice?
   A. water for the mice to drink
   B. rainy weather that floods the mice's nests
   C. owls that prey on the mice
   D. rocks in which the mice can hide from predators

3. In terms of its effect on population, which factor is most similar to birth rate?
   A. immigration
   B. density
   C. emigration
   D. carrying capacity

4. **Apply Concepts** Name two biotic and two abiotic factors you might find in a desert ecosystem.

   ....

   ....

   ....

5. **Construct Explanations** Describe how the availability of water can limit the growth of a population that otherwise has unlimited resources.

   ....

   ....

   ....

   ....

   ....

2 Energy Flow in Ecosystems

MS-LS2-3

6. Which of the following terms describes a straight series of connections among organisms that feed on each other?
   A. food web
   B. ecosystem
   C. community
   D. food chain

7. Mushrooms and bacteria are important
   A. predators.
   B. decomposers.
   C. producers.
   D. herbivores.

8. **Construct Explanations** What does an energy pyramid show?

   ....

   ....

   ....

   ....

   ....

9. **Develop Models** 🖊 Draw a food web to illustrate the relationships among grass, a grasshopper, a mouse, a rabbit, a coyote, and hawk. Use the following information:
   - grass is a producer
   - a grasshopper is a first-level consumer
   - a mouse and a rabbit are first- and second-level consumers
   - a coyote is a second- and third-level consumer
   - a hawk is a third-level consumer

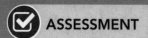
3 Cycles of Matter

MS-LS2-3

10. Distinguish Relationships What is different about how producers and consumers get energy?

_____

_____

_____

_____

_____

11. Determine Similarities In terms of how they get energy, are decomposers more like producers or consumers? Explain.

_____

_____

_____

_____

12. Consider Limitations In your opinion, is a food web or a food chain a more accurate representation of how energy and matter flow in an ecosystem? Explain.

_____

_____

_____

_____

_____

_____

_____

13. What do consumers release as they break down food to obtain energy?
A. sugar
B. carbon dioxide and water
C. free nitrogen
D. oxygen

14. Rain, hail, and snow are all examples of
A. condensation.   B. evaporation.
C. erosion.   D. precipitation.

15. In one form of nitrogen fixation, the .... energy of .... splits nitrogen molecules into atoms.
A. chemical, water vapor
B. mechanical, consumers
C. electrical, lightning
D. released, bacteria

16. Apply Scientific Reasoning Cite evidence to show that living systems follow the Laws of Conservation of Mass and Energy.

_____

_____

_____

_____

_____

17. Explain Phenomenon How is carbon cycled between organisms and the environment?

_____

_____

_____

_____

_____

MS-LS2-3

Evidence-Based Assessment

A team of field biologists is studying energy roles and relationships among organisms in a tropical rainforest habitat in Southeast Asia. One of the biologists diagrams some of these relationships in a food web.

Southeast Asian Rainforest Food Web

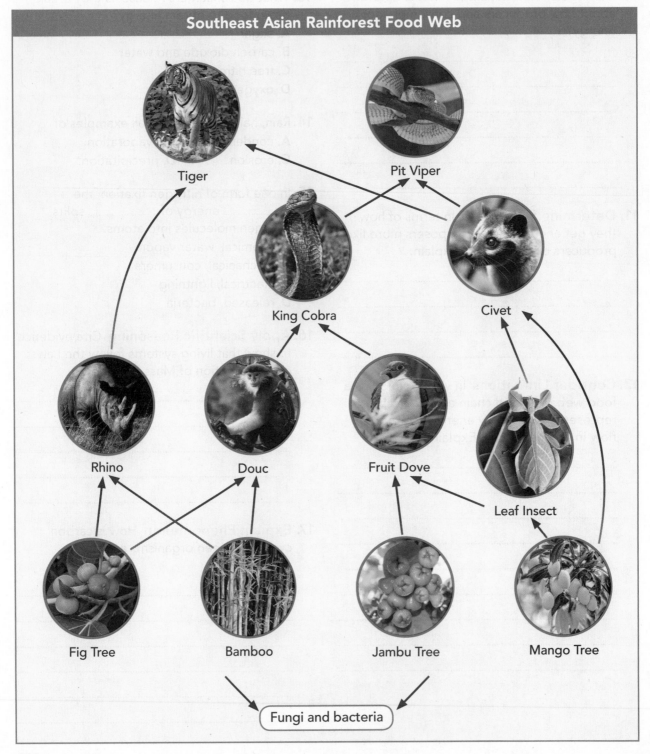

1. **Make Observations** Which organism from the food web is a producer?
   (A.) bamboo   B. civet
   C. douc   D. tiger

2. **Apply Concepts** Why are there only two organisms, the tiger and pit viper, at the top level of this food web?

   ....
   ....
   ....
   ....
   ....

3. **Analyze Systems** Explain the role of decomposers in cycling of matter between the living and nonliving parts of the Southeast Asian rainforest ecosystem.

   ....
   ....
   ....
   ....
   ....
   ....
   ....
   ....

4. **Evaluate Reasoning** If the fruit dove were removed from the food web, how would it impact the Southeast Asian rainforest ecosystem?

   ....
   ....
   ....
   ....
   ....
   ....

5. **Construct Arguments** As matter is cycled and energy flows through this system, how are both conserved? Use details from the food web to support your response.

   ....
   ....
   ....
   ....
   ....
   ....
   ....
   ....
   ....

Quest FINDINGS

Complete the Quest!

Phenomenon Identify what you believe is the cause of the algal bloom at Pleasant Pond, and describe the impact it has had on the organisms in this ecosystem. Include a proposal about restoring the pond using evidence from your investigation.

Cause and Effect What is the connection between the water in Pleasant Pond—an abiotic factor—and the biotic factors?

   ....
   ....
   ....

👆 **INTERACTIVITY**

Reflections on a Pond

MS-LS2-1, MS-LS2-3

Last Remains

How can you **confirm** an owl's role in a **food web**?

Background

Phenomenon Your community has a rodent problem! Squirrels and mice seem to be taking over. Some members of your community have suggested that introducing more barn owls into the neighborhood will bring the rodent population under control. But people want to be sure that barn owls do hunt and eat mice and squirrels before they go to the trouble of introducing these nocturnal birds to the community.

You will design and carry out an investigation by observing remains found in an owl pellet—undigested material an owl spits up. You will relate your findings to food webs and energy flow in the owl's ecosystem. Using the evidence you have collected, you will confirm whether or not the idea to introduce more barn owls into your community will help to bring the rodent population under control.

Materials

(per pair)
- goggles, 2 pair
- gloves, 2 pair
- owl pellet, 1 per pair
- probes, 2
- tweezers, 1 pair
- hand lens
- paper towels
- bone identification charts

Safety

Be sure to follow all safety guidelines provided by your teacher. The Safety Appendix of your textbook provides more details about the safety icons.

Barn owl

House mouse

Gray squirrel

Design Your Investigation

1. Your investigation will involve observing an owl pellet, which is regurgitated or "spit up" remains of food. Owls generally eat their prey whole and then get rid of the parts of the organisms that they cannot digest, such as bones and fur.

2. Develop a procedure for your investigation. Consider the following questions to help develop your plan:
   - How will you use the materials provided by your teacher?
   - What observations will you make?
   - How will you use the remains in the pellet to determine what the owl eats?
   - How can you use the bone identification charts to help you identify the remains of organisms?

3. Write the procedure for your investigation in the space provided.

4. Create a data table to record your observations. Include whether each organism you find inside the owl pellet is a herbivore, a carnivore, or an omnivore.

5. After receiving your teacher's approval for the procedure you developed, carry out your investigation.

HANDS-ON LAB

иDemonstrate Go online for a downloadable worksheet of this lab.

Procedure

Data Table and Observations

Analyze and Interpret Data

1. **Make Observations** What information did you find out by observing the remains in the owl pellet?

....

....

....

....

2. **Develop Models** Diagram the cycling of matter and energy in the barn owl's habitat. Begin by drawing a food chain. Then develop the food chain into a simple food web using additional organisms that you might find in the habitat. Include captions for your diagram that explain the cycling matter and flow of energy among the organisms.

3. **Construct Arguments** Do you think the introduction of more barn owls into your community will solve your mouse and squirrel problem? Use evidence from your investigation to support your response.

....

....

....

....

4. **Draw Conclusions** Owls hunt at night. Using your findings from the owl pellet, what conclusions can you draw about whether squirrels and mice are more active during the day or at night?

....

....

....

....

Populations, Communities, and Ecosystems

NGSS PERFORMANCE EXPECTATIONS

MS-LS2-1 Analyze and interpret data to provide evidence for the effects of resource availability on organisms and populations of organisms in an ecosystem.

MS-LS2-2 Construct an explanation that predicts patterns of interactions among organisms across multiple ecosystems.

MS-LS2-3 Develop a model to describe the cycling of matter and flow of energy among living and nonliving parts of an ecosystem.

MS-LS2-4 Construct an argument supported by empirical evidence that changes to physical or biological components of an ecosystem affect populations.

MS-LS2-5 Evaluate competing design solutions for maintaining biodiversity and ecosystem services.

HANDS-ON LAB

uConnect Explore how communities change in response to natural disasters.

VIDEO

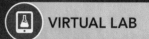 INTERACTIVITY

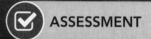 VIRTUAL LAB

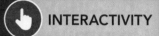 ASSESSMENT

 eTEXT

APP

Why would these deer risk crossing a busy road?

The Essential Question

How do living and nonliving things affect one another?

Crossing a road can be dangerous business. What might the deer be trying to get to on the other side of the road that makes it worth the risk? List some living and nonliving resources that the road makes it difficult for the deer to get to.

....

....

....

....

....

....

Quest KICKOFF

Should an Animal Crossing Be Constructed in My Community?

STEM **Phenomenon** A company wants to build a new factory nearby, but wants the state to build a new highway to the location. The highway would allow employees and products to access the site. However, the highway would pass through an area with endangered species. Before the state decides, they contact a wildlife biologist to study the impact the highway would have on the local ecosystem. In this problem-based Quest activity, you will investigate how the construction of highways can affect organisms. By applying what you learn in each lesson, in a digital activity or hands-on lab, you will gather key Quest information and evidence. With the information, you will propose a solution in the Findings activity.

 INTERACTIVITY

To Cross or Not to Cross

MS-LS2-5 Evaluate competing design solutions for maintaining biodiversity and ecosystem services.

NBC LEARN ▶ VIDEO

After watching the Quest kickoff video, where a wildlife biologist discusses animal crossings in Banff National Park, fill in the 3-2-1 activity.

3 organisms I think are at risk locally

....

....

2 ideas I have to help them

....

....

....

1 thing I learned from the wildlife biologist

....

....

Quest CHECK-IN

IN LESSON 1

How do animal crossings effect ecosystems? Analyze some effects then brainstorm ideas for your animal crossing and identify the criteria and constraints you need to consider.

 INTERACTIVITY

Research Animal Crossings

Quest CHECK-IN

IN LESSON 2

How does community stakeholder feedback impact your design ideas, criteria, and constraints? Evaluate your design.

 INTERACTIVITY

Community Opinions

Quest CHECK-IN

IN LESSON 3

STEM What are the criteria and constraints for the animal crossing? Evaluate competing design solutions.

HANDS-ON LAB

Design and Model a Crossing

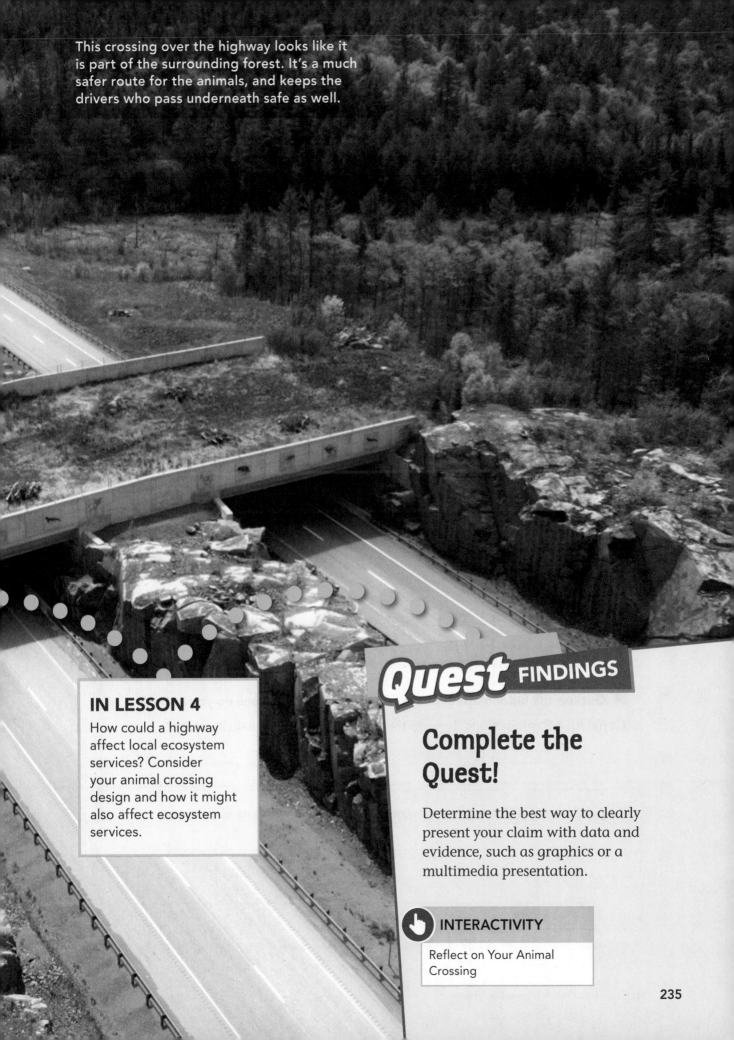

This crossing over the highway looks like it is part of the surrounding forest. It's a much safer route for the animals, and keeps the drivers who pass underneath safe as well.

Quest FINDINGS

IN LESSON 4

How could a highway affect local ecosystem services? Consider your animal crossing design and how it might also affect ecosystem services.

Complete the Quest!

Determine the best way to clearly present your claim with data and evidence, such as graphics or a multimedia presentation.

INTERACTIVITY

Reflect on Your Animal Crossing

① Interactions in Ecosystems

Guiding Questions

- How can resource availability affect interactions between organisms?
- How is population size affected by predation and symbiotic relationships?
- How are patterns of interactions between organisms similar in different ecosystems?

Connections

Literacy Determine Central Ideas

Math Construct Graphs

MS-LS2-1, MS-LS2-2

Vocabulary

niche
competition
predation
symbiosis
commensalism
mutualism
parasitism

Academic Vocabulary

interactions

 Vocabulary App

Practice vocabulary on a mobile device.

Quest CONNECTION

Think about how an algal bloom in a pond might affect organisms and their relationships.

Connect It !

✎ **Outline the hidden insect in the image. What adaptations do you notice?**

Construct Explanations How do the animal's adaptations help it survive?

....

....

Apply Scientific Reasoning How does your body adapt to its environment?

....

....

....

....

Adaptations and Survival

Each organism in an ecosystem has special characteristics. These characteristics influence whether an individual can survive and reproduce in its environment. A characteristic that makes an individual better suited to a specific environment may eventually become common in that species through a process called natural selection.

In this process, individuals with characteristics that are well-suited to a particular environment tend to survive and produce more offspring. Offspring inheriting these characteristics also are more likely to survive to reproduce. Natural selection results in adaptations—the behaviors and physical characteristics that allow organisms to live successfully in their environments. As an example, a great white shark's body is white along its underside, but dark across the top. The shark blends with the surroundings in the water whether being looked at from below or above. **Figure 1** shows another example of how a species adapts to its environment.

Individuals with characteristics that do not help them survive in their environments are less likely to reproduce. Over time, these unhelpful characteristics may affect the survival of a species. If individuals in a species cannot adapt successfully to changes in their environment, the species can become extinct.

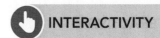

INTERACTIVITY

Identify competition in your daily life.

Reflect In what ways have organisms in your local area adapted to the environment? In your science notebook, describe characteristics that make the organism successful.

Adaptation and Survival
Figure 1 Different kinds of adaptations work together to aid survival.

237

INTERACTIVITY

Model what competition looks like in nature.

Niche

The organisms in any ecosystem have adaptations that help them fill specific roles or functions. The role of an organism in its habitat is called its niche. A **niche** includes how an organism obtains its food, the type of food the organism eats, and what other organisms eat it.

Remember that an organism's energy role in an ecosystem is determined by how it obtains food and how it interacts with other organisms. Adaptations by a species allow a population to live successfully on the available resources in its niche. Abiotic factors also influence a population's ability to survive in the niche it occupies. Lack of water or space, for example, may cause a population to decline and no longer fit well into that niche. Biotic factors, such as predators or a reduced food source, affect the populations in a niche and may change an organism's ability to survive.

A niche also includes when and how the organism reproduces and the physical conditions it requires to survive. Every organism has a variety of adaptations that suit it to specific living conditions and help it survive. Use **Figure 2** to describe characteristics of a giraffe's niche.

Niche Characteristics

Figure 2 This picture shows that organisms occupy many niches in an environment.

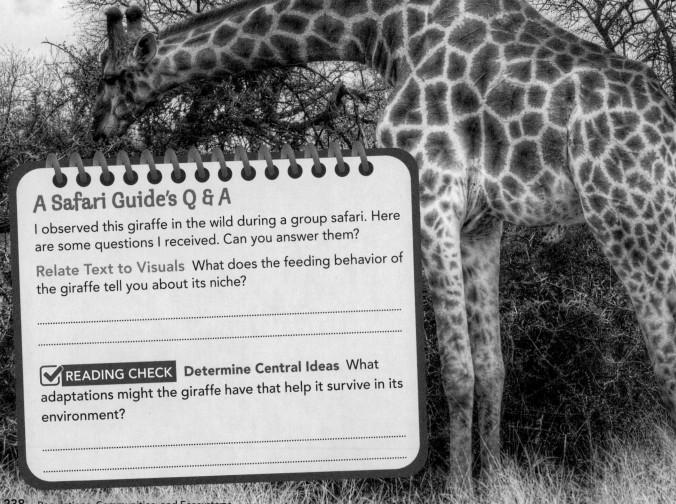

A Safari Guide's Q & A

I observed this giraffe in the wild during a group safari. Here are some questions I received. Can you answer them?

Relate Text to Visuals What does the feeding behavior of the giraffe tell you about its niche?

....

....

✓ **READING CHECK** **Determine Central Ideas** What adaptations might the giraffe have that help it survive in its environment?

....

....

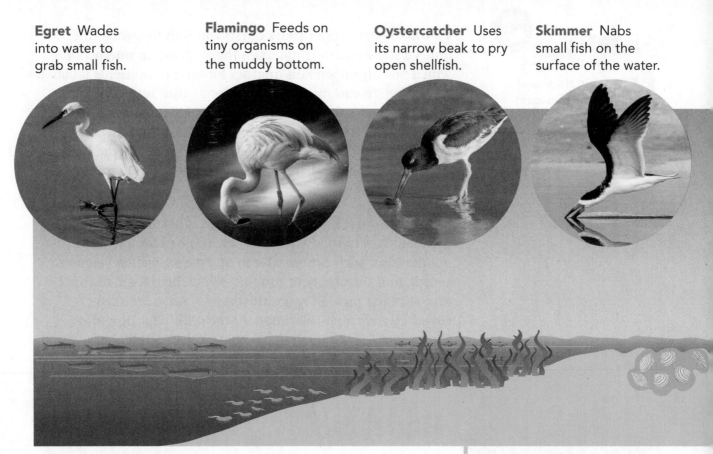

Egret Wades into water to grab small fish.

Flamingo Feeds on tiny organisms on the muddy bottom.

Oystercatcher Uses its narrow beak to pry open shellfish.

Skimmer Nabs small fish on the surface of the water.

Competition and Predation

In every type of ecosystem, a range of **interactions** takes place among organisms every day. Two major types of interactions among organisms are competition and predation.

Competition More than one species of organism can live in the same habitat and obtain the same food. For example, in a desert ecosystem, a flycatcher and an elf owl both live on the saguaro cactus and eat insects. However, these two species do not occupy exactly the same niche. The flycatcher is active during the day, while the owl is active mostly at night.

When two species share a niche, one of their populations might be affected. The reason for this is **competition**. The struggle between organisms to survive as they use the same limited resources is called competition. For example, different species of birds in a park compete for the same bugs and worms to eat. If one population of birds is more successful, it will increase while the other population decreases.

In any ecosystem, there are limited amounts of food, water, and shelter. Organisms that share the same habitat often have adaptations that enable them to reduce competition. Observe the shorebirds in **Figure 3** and discover how their niches vary in the shoreline habitat.

Shorebird Competition
Figure 3 ✏ Draw a line from each bird to the location where it feeds.

Academic Vocabulary
How have you heard the term *interactions* used in another subject and what does the word mean in that context?

....

....

....

....

....

Predation

A tiger shark bursts through the water and grabs a sea snake swimming on the surface. An interaction in which one organism kills another for food or nutrients is called **predation**. In this interaction, one organism is the predator and the other is the prey. The tiger shark, for example, is the predator and the sea snake is the prey. These interactions happen throughout nature. Predator and prey interactions may reduce the number of organisms or eliminate the populations.

Adaptations

All species have ways of supporting their survival in their environment. Some predators have adaptations, such as sharp teeth and claws, well-developed senses, and the ability to run fast, which help them to catch and kill their prey. Prey organisms may have protective coverings, warning coloration, or the ability to camouflage themselves to help them avoid being killed. Study the predator-prey interaction in **Figure 4**.

Model It

Predator and Prey Adaptations

Figure 4 In a rainforest ecosystem, a gecko finds out that the flexible snake can hold onto tree bark with its muscles and scales as it hunts.

Develop Models ✐ Consider a grassland ecosystem of tall, tan savanna grasses. Draw either a predator or a prey organism that might live there. Label the adaptations that will allow your organism to be successful.

Population Size Predation affects population size. Changes in population size occur when new members arrive or when members leave. Population size increases if more members enter than leave, and declines if more members leave than arrive. Too many predators in a area can decrease the prey population, leading to less food availability and possible predator population decline. In general, predator and prey populations rise and fall together in predictable patterns.

☑ READING CHECK **Summarize** What effect do competition and predation have on population size?

....

....

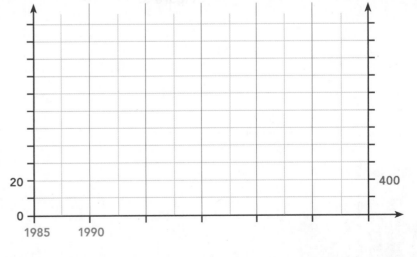

Math Toolbox

Predator-Prey Interactions

Moose and Wolf
Populations on Isle Royale

On Isle Royale, an island in Lake Superior, the populations of wolves (the predator) and moose (the prey) rise and fall in cycles.

Year	Wolves	Moose
1985	22	976
1990	15	1,315
1995	16	2,117
2000	29	2,007
2005	30	540
2010	19	510
2015	2	1,300

1. **Construct Graphs** ✎ Create a double line graph of the data above. Fill in the x-axis and both y-axes. Use a different color line for each animal and provide a key.

2. **Analyze and Interpret Data** Describe the relationship shown by your graph and suggest factors that impact it.

....

....

....

....

....

241

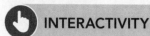
INTERACTIVITY

Classify symbiotic relationships.

VIDEO

Explore the three types of symbiotic relationships.

Literacy Connection

Determine Central Ideas As you read, determine the central idea of the text. Note how this idea is developed through examples. Underline examples that you think most clearly explain the central idea.

Symbiotic Relationships

Symbiosis is a third type of interaction among organisms. **Symbiosis** (sim bee OH sis) is any relationship in which two species live closely together. There are three types of symbiotic relationships: commensalism, mutualism, and parasitism.

Commensalism Birds build nests in trees to make a place to live. The tree is unharmed. This relationship is an example of **commensalism**. Commensalism (kuh MEN suh liz um) is a relationship in which one species benefits and the other species is neither helped nor harmed.

Mutualism In some interactions, two species may depend on one another. In Africa, oxpecker birds and zebras display this relationship. The oxpecker bird rides on the zebra's back, eating bugs that crawl on the animal. The bird gets a meal and the zebra has harmful pests removed. This relationship is an example of **mutualism** (MYOO choo uh liz um), which is a relationship in which both species benefit.

Commensalism is not very common in nature because two species are usually either helped or harmed a little by any interaction. Scientists may disagree on whether a particular relationship truly demonstrates commensalism.

For example, clownfish live among the poisonous and stinging tentacles of sea anemones to avoid being eaten by larger fish. Some scientists think that the relationship between clownfish and sea anemones is commensalism, while others think the sea anemones also benefit from this relationship, making it an example of mutualism. Identifying examples of commensalism can be difficult. See examples of some of these relationships in **Figure 5**.

Mutualism and Commensalism

Figure 5 Some relationships more clearly show benefits to one or both species than others.

1. **Synthesize Information** 🖊 Read each image caption. Label each photo "M" for mutualism or "C" for commensalism in the circle provided.

2. **Use Evidence** 🖊 Beneath each image, use evidence to justify how you classified the relationship.

Hummingbirds feed on nectar deep within a flower. While sipping, the flower's pollen rubs off on the hummingbird. The bird can carry it to another flower.

Evidence

....

....

The banded mongoose feeds on ticks and other tiny animals that nestle in the warthog's fur and feed off of the warthog.

Evidence

....

....

....

Barnacles feed by filtering tiny organisms from the water. They grow on objects below the surface, such as piers and rocks, and attach themselves to whales.

Evidence

....

....

....

Remora attach themselves to the underside of a manta ray with a suction-cup-like structure. Mantas are messy eaters and remora feed on the food scraps.

Evidence

....

....

....

Parasitism

Parasitism If you've ever seen a dog continually scratching itself, then it may have fleas. This interaction is an example of **parasitism** (PAHR uh sit iz um). Parasitism is a relationship that involves one organism living with, on, or inside another organism and harming it.

The organism that benefits is called a parasite. The host is the organism that the parasite lives in or on. The parasite is generally smaller than its host. The fleas, for example, are parasites that harm the dog by biting it to feed on its blood for nourishment. Pets can suffer from severe health problems as a result of these bites. Study the examples of parasitism in **Figure 6**.

Parasitic Relationships
Figure 6 Unlike a predator, a parasite does not usually kill the organism it feeds on. If the host dies, the parasite could lose its source of food or shelter.

✓ READING CHECK **Integrate with Visuals** 🖊 In each picture, label the host and the parasite shown.
Construct Explanations How does parasitism differ from other symbiotic relationships?

....

....

....

....

....

Fish lice feed on the blood and other internal fluids of the fish. Eventually the fish may quit eating and lose color from the stress caused by the lice.

A braconid wasp lays its eggs under the skin of the tomato hornworm. After the larvae emerge, they form cocoons on the hornworm. As the larvae develop inside the cocoons, they feed on the insides of the hornworm.

☑ LESSON 1 Check

MS-LS2-1, MS-LS2-2

1. Identify What are the five different types of interactions between organisms?

....
....
....
....
....
....
....
....

Use the graph you constructed on wolf and moose populations to help you answer Questions 2 and 3.

2. Patterns What patterns do scientists observe between predator-prey relationships like the wolves and moose on Isle Royale?

....
....
....
....
....
....
....

3. Interpret Data Use the data from your graph to provide evidence for the effects of resource availability on individuals and populations in an ecosystem.

....
....
....
....

4. Construct Explanations Do the patterns of interactions between organisms, such as competition and predation, change when they occur in different ecosystems?

....
....
....
....
....
....
....

5. Cause and Effect Predict the effects on a predator-prey relationship, such as the one between a frog and blue heron, in a wetland ecosystem in the midst of a drought.

....
....
....
....

Quest CHECK-IN

In this lesson, you learned how organisms in ecosystems interact with one another and how resource availability can affect these interactions. You also discovered that these interactions can influence population size.

Analyze Systems Why is it important to maintain existing organism interactions and availability of resources when building a new highway?

....
....
....

👆 **INTERACTIVITY**

Research Animal Crossings

Go online to investigate the effects of highways and animals crossings.

② Dynamic and Resilient Ecosystems

Guiding Questions

- How can changes to physical or biological components of an ecosystem affect organisms and populations?
- How do natural events impact the environment?
- How do human activities impact ecosystems?

Connection

Literacy Write Arguments

MS-LS2-1, MS-LS2-2, MS-LS2-4

Vocabulary

succession
pioneer species

Academic Vocabulary

colonize
dominate

 Vocabulary App

Practice vocabulary on a mobile device.

Quest CONNECTION

Consider how changes in a pond ecosystem over time might affect the organisms that live there.

Connect It !

✎ **Circle the living organisms in the photo. Think about why the number of living organisms is limited here.**

Predict How do you think this landscape will change in the future?

....

....

Succession

Ecosystems and their communities are always changing. Natural disasters, such as floods and tornadoes, can cause rapid change. Other changes occur over centuries or even longer. Humans can have a major impact on ecosystems as well. The series of predictable changes that occur in a community over time is called **succession**. As you can see in **Figure 1**, organisms can establish habitats in even the harshest environments.

Primary Succession Disruptions to the physical or biological components of an ecosystem can impact organism populations living there. For example, lava from a volcanic eruption is creating new land by the sea. When the lava cools and hardens, no organisms are present. Over time, living things will **colonize** these areas. Primary succession is the series of changes that occur in an area where no soil or organisms exist.

Pioneer Species The first species to populate an area are called **pioneer species.** These species are usually mosses and lichens, carried to the area by wind or water. Lichens are fungi and algae growing in a symbiotic relationship. They give off acidic compounds that help dissolve rock into soil. As pioneer species die, their remains add nutrients to the thin soil and help build it up.

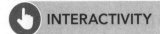

INTERACTIVITY

Consider what happens when an ecosystem is disturbed.

Academic Vocabulary

Where else have you heard the term *colonize*, or the related term *colony*? Provide an example.

....

....

....

....

Succession

Figure 1 Harsh landscapes like this hardened lava flow transform over time as lichens and plants establish themselves.

Mature Communities After lichens help to form a thin layer of soil, plants that produce seeds can establish themselves. Wind, water, and birds can bring seeds into the area. If the soil is adequate and there's enough rainfall, seedlings will emerge and may grow to adulthood. As the plants grow, they will shed leaves that will break down to make more soil. Plants will attract animals that will further enhance the soil by leaving waste and their own remains. Over time, the buildup of organic matter will improve the soil and allow for a more diverse community to establish itself in the area. Reaching this mature community can take centuries, but once it's established it can last for thousands of years or more if it is not disturbed or disrupted.

☑ **READING CHECK** **Write Arguments** Explain why disruptions to mature communities should be avoided if possible.

....

....

Model It

Pioneers

Figure 2 The images show how pioneer species begin the process of succession, which changes an area over time.

Integrate Information ✏ Draw pictures to represent the missing stages of primary succession.

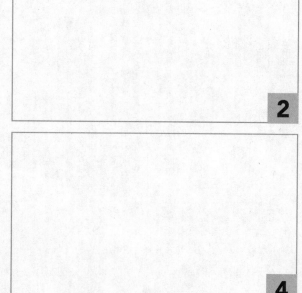

Secondary Succession

In 2016, wildfires raged in drought-stricken regions of the West, especially California. Fires lead to secondary succession. Secondary succession is the series of changes that occur in an area where the ecosystem has been disturbed, but where soil and organisms already exist. Natural disruptions that affect the physical and biological components of an ecosystem include fires, hurricanes, tsunamis, and tornadoes. Human activities, such as farming, logging, or mining, may also disturb an ecosystem and cause secondary succession to occur.

Unlike primary succession, secondary succession occurs in a place where an ecosystem and community exist. Secondary succession usually occurs more rapidly than primary succession because soil is already present and seeds from some plants may remain in the soil. **Figure 3** shows the changes by succession in an area. Over time, more and more organisms can live in the area and it starts to resemble places that were never disturbed in the first place.

Secondary Succession

Figure 3 When an area such as this amusement park is abandoned, the natural ecosystem begins to reestablish itself.

1. **Form a Hypothesis** Identify a place in your community where succession might occur if people abandoned the area.

   ....

2. **Apply Concepts** ✏ Sketch what the location would look like years later after being abandoned.

3. **Construct an Argument** Explain how changes to the physical and biological components of the ecosystem would affect the populations that make up the community.

   ....

   ....

   ....

   ....

HANDS-ON LAB

Investigate Identify examples of succession in a local ecosystem.

INTERACTIVITY

Propose causes for a changes in a population and predict future changes.

Academic Vocabulary

What does it mean when a sports team *dominates* its rival team?

....

....

....

Ecosystem Disruptions and Population Survival

When changes to physical and biological components occur rapidly or lastingly, most populations in the ecosystem do not survive. However, some organisms do survive the changes. Organisms surviving a fast-changing ecosystem often have adaptations that help them thrive in the new conditions.

Georgia, South Carolina, and Florida have an ecosystem of the longleaf pine forest, as shown in **Figure 4.** Longleaf pine trees **dominate** this ecosystem. These trees grow in a pattern that permits sunlight to reach the forest floor. Longleaf pine seeds need a soil free from undergrowth and germinate quickly in the soil. Longleaf pines are dependent on regular forest fires from lightning strikes to burn away grasses and invasive hardwood trees such as oak to remain healthy and reproduce. Mature trees' bark and early growth are fire-resistant.

Longleaf pines support a healthy ecosystem. Red-cockaded woodpeckers depend on mature trees for nesting sites. If fires don't burn the undergrowth, predators can reach the nests. Swallowed-tailed kites build nests high in the trees. Bachmann's sparrows favor mature pine forests where underbrush has been removed by fires. These bird populations have been reduced due to logging of the longleaf pines and previous fire suppression practices, which opened space for invasive oaks.

Most organisms reappear at some point after the fire because of adaptations such as heat-resistant seeds that may sprout or underground roots that can grow. Young longleaf pines develop a long taproot that enables them to grow after a fire.

Changes to Populations
Figure 4 In the longleaf pine ecosystem, some organisms are adapted to survive fire and others are not.

☑ READING CHECK **Determine Central Ideas** How does a wildfire impact a population of oak trees?

....

....

Apply Concepts How might a wildfire help the longleaf pine population survive a deadly fungal infection on the needles of seedlings?

....

....

☑ LESSON 2 Check

MS-LS2-1, MS-LS2-2, MS-LS2-4

1. Define What are pioneer species? How do they affect the variety of organisms in an ecosystem?

....

....

....

....

....

....

2. Construct an Argument Support the argument that a forest fire impacts a population of birds that nest in the trees.

....

....

....

....

....

....

....

3. Construct Explanations Explain how the physical and biological components of the ecosystem in the image are being disrupted.

....

....

....

....

....

....

....

....

Quest CHECK-IN

In this lesson you learned that changes to physical or biological components of an ecosystem can affect the populations of organisms that live there.

Apply Concepts How might mature communities of organisms be affected by the construction of a new highway? How does an animal crossing solve some of these problems?

....

....

....

....

☞ INTERACTIVITY

Community Opinions

Go online to learn about reactions to a proposed crossing from members of the community. Based on the feedback, consider the constraints the animal crossing should meet.

Field Biologist

Ecology in ACTION

Some biologists study the cells of living things. Others study living things as a whole. Field biologists study living things— along with their communities and ecosystems. Field biologists research the way all living things interact in an environment. Within this field, they may have a special focus on plants, animals, insects, soil, or many other subjects.

Some field biologists manage fisheries or work as pollution control technicians. Others might perform research on the environmental health of a specific plant, animal, or ecosystem. They might also be responsible for regulating and enforcing laws that protect the environment. Just as often, field biologists work for industries as environmentalists, monitoring the effects of an industry on its local environment. Field biologists may monitor any disruptions within parts of an ecosystem and determine how populations of organisms might be impacted.

To become a field biologist, you need to understand a wide range of sciences, including ecology, botany, zoology, marine biology, and ecosystem analysis. In the coming years, field biologists will study the long-term effects of certain industries on the environment. They will also analyze the effects of global warming on ecosystem interactions.

 VIDEO

Field Biologist

MY CAREER

Type "field biologist" into an online search engine to learn more about this career.

Polar bears feed on seals that gather on and around slabs of sea ice. As sea ice shrinks, field biologists monitor how these animals are trying to adapt and how their populations are changing as a result.

③ Biodiversity

GUIDING QUESTIONS

- What is the value of biodiversity?
- What factors affect biodiversity?
- How do human activities impact biodiversity?

Connections

Literacy Cite Textual Evidence

Math Use Ratio Reasoning

MS-LS2-4, MS-LS2-5, MS-LS4-1

Vocabulary

biodiversity
keystone species
extinction
invasive species

Academic Vocabulary

value
economic

📱 **VOCABULARY APP**

Practice vocabulary on a mobile device.

Quest CONNECTION

Consider how to build an animal crossing so that road construction does not negatively impact local biodiversity.

Connect It !

✎ **Circle the parts of the ecosystem shown here that you think are important to people.**

Identify Unknowns What do you think are two important ways that humans benefit from a healthy ecosystem? Explain.

....

....

The Value of Biodiversity

Earth is filled with many different ecosystems that provide habitats for each and every organism. Some organisms live in one ecosystem their entire lives. Other organisms are born in one ecosystem and migrate to another. Healthy ecosystems have biodiversity. **Biodiversity** is the number and variety of different species in an area. Healthy ecosystems also provide the opportunity for different species to interact. This is often essential for their survival, such as a predator finding prey.

Changes in an ecosystem affect the species in that ecosystem. They are usually linked to available resources. Biodiversity increases as more resources are available. It decreases when fewer resources are available. When biodiversity changes, it impacts ecosystem processes. This impact may affect the health of an ecosystem.

Biodiversity also has both economic and ecological **value**. Healthy ecosystems, such as that in **Figure 1**, provide resources and materials that we use. We consume food, fuel, medicines, and fibers from healthy ecosystems.

Academic Vocabulary

What does it mean when someone says that a person was raised with good values? Provide two examples.

....

....

....

....

....

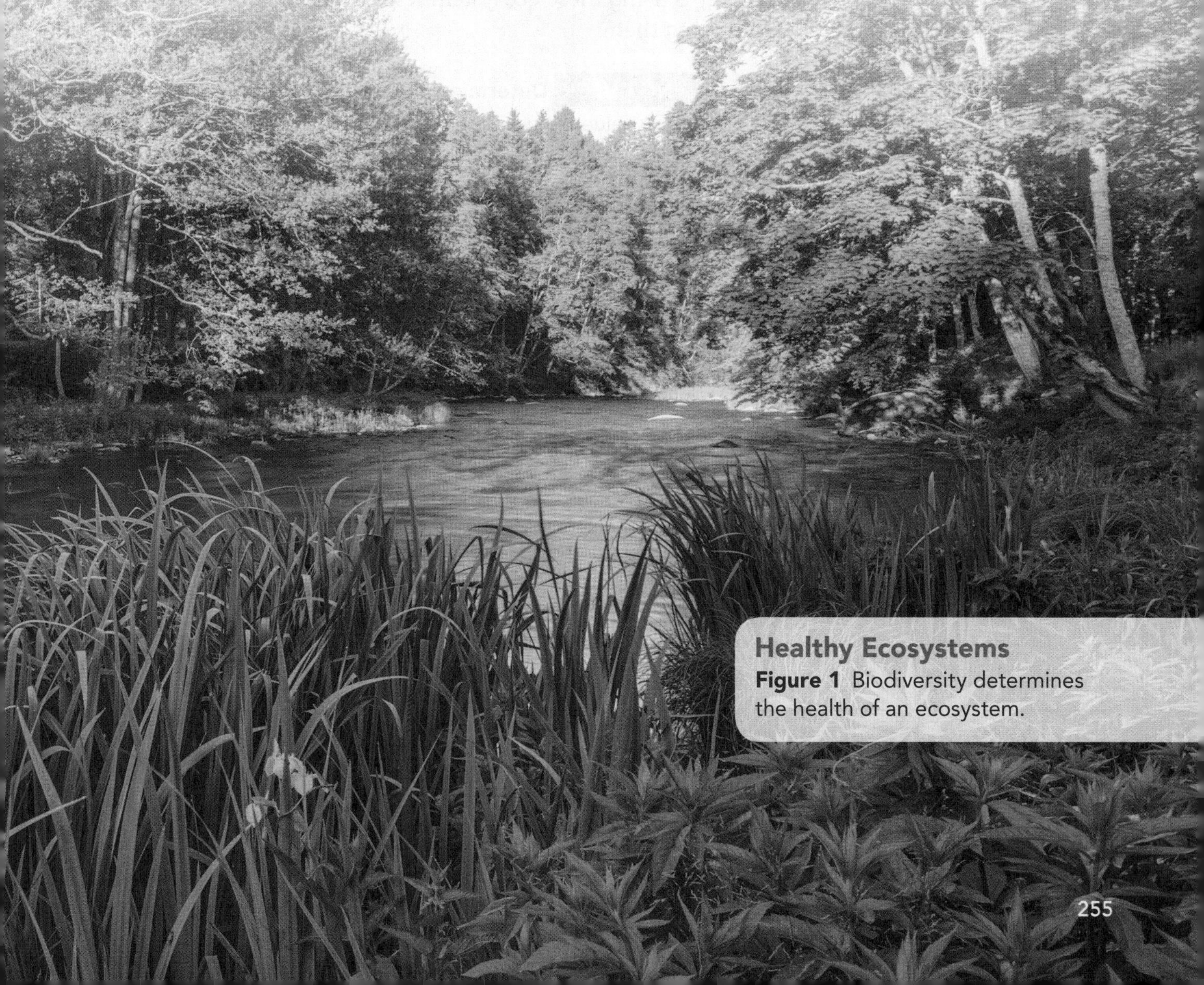

Healthy Ecosystems

Figure 1 Biodiversity determines the health of an ecosystem.

Academic Vocabulary

How would you explain the term *economic* to someone who did not understand the meaning?

....

....

....

....

Literacy Connection

Cite Textual Evidence. As you read, underline the activities discussed in the text that support the idea that biodiversity has value.

Economic Value

Economic Value Humans use ecosystems for our own profit. There is value in using ecosystems to fulfill our basic needs and wants. The products we take from ecosystems have **economic** value, such as providing a household income. People can profit from healthy ecosystems both directly or indirectly.

Resources that are consumed from an ecosystem provide a direct value. For example, the crops you see in **Figure 2** are direct value. The farmer used the land and grew the crops so that she can feed her family and make a profit on their sale. In addition to food, medicines and raw materials provide resources and income. Unfortunately, our demand for certain organisms and resources can harm biodiversity and ecosystems. Humans can use too many resources at once. As a result, many ecosystems do not have time to recover and are damaged.

Some resources in an ecosystem are used, but not consumed. These indirect values also affect the economic value. Shade trees reduce utility bills and provide wind protection. Wetlands reduce soil erosion and control flooding. Hiking, touring unique habitats, and recreational activities provide revenue. The key is using these ecosystem resources for profit without destroying them.

☑ READING CHECK **Determine Central Ideas** What makes crops a direct value from an ecosystem?

....

....

From Farm to Market

Figure 2 Disease and poor weather conditions can cause severe financial losses for farmers.

Form an Opinion Would it be wise for a farmer to grow just one type of crop? Explain.

....

....

....

....

....

....

A Valuable Tree

Figure 3 Elephants eat the fruit of the balanite, or desert date, tree. The elephants then spread the seeds in their waste as they travel.

Apply Scientific Reasoning Consider the interdependence between the tree and the elephant. What would happen if one of the species were to decline in number?

....

....

Ecological Value All species function within an ecosystem. Each species performs a certain role. All species are connected and depend on each other for survival. A **keystone species** is a species that influences the survival of many other species in an ecosystem. One example of a keystone species is the African elephant.

African elephant herds appeared to be stripping vegetation from the ecosystem, thereby harming it. Some park officials wanted to control the elephant population by thinning the herds. Instead, they let the herds range freely. When the elephants uprooted trees, that made way for grasslands and smaller animals. Shrubs grew where the trees once stood and fed the animals unable to reach taller trees. Over time, the park ecosystem, **Figure 3**, returned to an ecological balance. Changes to physical and biological factors of an ecosystem, such as the number of elephants and trees, affect all of the populations within an ecosystem.

Biodiversity sustains ecosystems by protecting land and water resources, and aiding in nutrient cycling. Trees and vegetation hold soil in place to prevent erosion and landslides. Roots break up rocks to allow water to enter the soil. Animal waste sustains soil fertility. A diverse ecosystem is stable, productive, and can easily withstand environmental changes.

HANDS-ON LAB

Investigate Explore the role of keystone species in maintaining biodiversity.

☑ READING CHECK **Evaluate** Why is the elephant considered a keystone species?

....

....

INTERACTIVITY

Explore the diversity of species that live in the Amazon.

Factors Affecting Biodiversity

There are numerous ecosystems on Earth. Biodiversity within these ecosystems varies from place to place. Various factors affect biodiversity, including niche diversity, genetic diversity, extinction, climate, and area.

Niche Diversity Every species in an ecosystem occupies a unique niche. The abiotic and biotic resources that a species needs to survive are provided by its niche. These resources include food, water, and habitat. The niches of different populations within an ecosystem interact with one another. Some species, like the panda in **Figure 4**, live in a narrow niche with only a few food sources. Species that have a narrow niche are more vulnerable to environmental changes. A niche can also be shared by two different species. When this happens, they compete for resources. If resources are low, one species may survive while the other must leave or die out. A healthy ecosystem reflects a balance among different populations and their unique niches.

A Narrow Niche

Figure 4 The panda's diet has no diversity. Its diet consists almost entirely of leaves, stems, and shoots from different bamboo species. Pandas can eat over 30 kg of bamboo a day. Circle the bamboo in the image.

Apply Concepts What would happen to the panda population if there were a decrease in the amount of bamboo available? Explain.

....

....

....

....

....

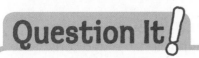

Question It!

Endangered Species

Figure 5 Cheetahs are endangered. Scientists speculate that their near-extinction status could be from their low genetic diversity, loss of natural food resources, or loss of habitat.

Ask Questions A group of scientists visit your school to discuss the importance of saving the cheetah population. They need your help to design a solution to stop their declining numbers. However, you must first understand a little more about the declining cheetah populations. Each person is required to ask at least three questions of the experts to help design a solution. In the space below, write your questions. Consider constraints when developing your questions.

....

....

....

Genetic Diversity You may have heard the expression "gene pool." It is the number of genes available within a population. Genetic diversity, on the other hand, is the total number of inherited traits in the genetic makeup of an entire species. The greater its genetic diversity, the more likely it is that a species can adapt and survive. Species with low genetic diversity lack the ability to adapt to changing environmental conditions. The cheetahs you see in **Figure 5** have low genetic diversity, which may have contributed to their near-extinction status.

Species Extinction According to fossil evidence, over ninety percent of all organisms that have ever lived on Earth are now extinct. The disappearance of all members of a species from Earth is **extinction**. Species in danger of becoming extinct are endangered species. And species that could become endangered in the near future are threatened species. There are two ways in which species can become extinct. Background extinction occurs over a long period of time. It usually involves only one species. Environmental changes or the arrival of a competitor cause background extinctions. Mass extinction can kill many different species in a very short time. Mass extinctions are caused by rapid climate changes (such as from a meteoroid impact), continuous volcanic eruptions, or changes in the air or water.

☑ READING CHECK **Summarize Text** Why are populations with low genetic diversity, like cheetahs, less likely to survive?

....

....

Other Factors The climate and size of an ecosystem also affect biodiversity. Scientists hypothesize that a consistent climate supports biodiversity. One of the most diverse places on Earth is the tropical rainforest. Temperatures do not fluctuate greatly and it receives a large amount of rainfall. Also, plants grow year-round, providing food for animals. An ecosystem's area, or the amount of space that an ecosystem covers, also determines its biodiversity. For example, more species are found in an ecosystem that covers 50 square kilometers, than in one that covers 10 square kilometers. An ecosystem with a larger area will generally have more biodiversity.

Math Toolbox

Room to Roam

A savanna is a grassland ecosystem with few trees. About 65 percent of Africa is covered by savannas. Lions roam where there are fewer than 25 people per square mile. As the human population in Africa increases, the amount of land where lions roam is decreasing. Use the chart and graphs to answer the questions.

1. **Predict** Describe how the green area of the pie chart would change to show the area where lions freely roam today.

....

2. **Draw Conclusions** How has the balance in the African lion population shifted over time? What caused this shift?

....

....

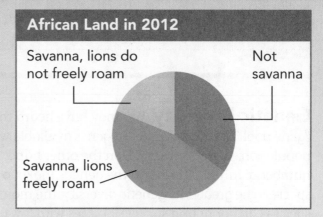

3. **Use Ratio Reasoning** Write a ratio comparing the lion population in 1950 to 2000. Explain the relationship between human population and the lion population.

....

....

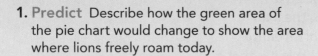

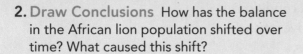

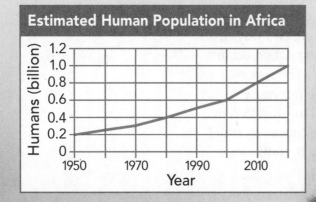

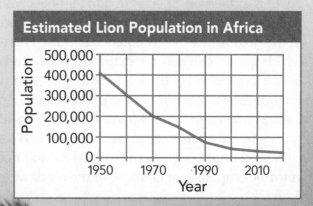

Human Impact

When an ecosystem is harmed in any way, its biodiversity is reduced. Human activities directly impact ecosystems and the organisms that live there. As you see in **Figure 6**, human activities can impact the environment.

Our Impact on Ecosystems

Figure 6 🖉 For each image, determine if the human activities are increasing or decreasing impacts on the environment. Place an "I" in the circle for an increased impact, and a "D" in the circle for a decreased impact. Then, in the space provided, provide evidence to support your determination.

....
....
....

....
....
....

....
....
....

....
....
....

....
....

....
....

Threats to Coral

Figure 7 🖋 These images show two different coral reef ecosystems. One image shows how an increase in water temperature can harm a coral reef through coral bleaching. When water gets too warm, coral can become stressed, causing the algae living in their tissue to leave. Because the coral relies on algae for food, it begins to starve. Circle the image that shows coral bleaching.

✅ **READING CHECK**

Determine Conclusions

What evidence is presented to show that a warming climate can impact biodiversity?

....

....

....

....

....

....

Damaging Biodiversity Human activities cause most of the harm to habitats and ecosystems. The result is a loss of biodiversity. For example, removing natural resources from an ecosystem can reduce its biodiversity.

Scientists agree that increased levels of carbon dioxide gas contribute to climate change. One way humans contribute to climate change is by the removal of resources from ecosystems. For example, people remove trees for farming, houses, and timber. The use of machinery to remove and process the trees increases the amount of carbon dioxide gas in our atmosphere. In addition, the deforested plants are not taking in carbon dioxide. Changes to the climate impact all of Earth's ecosystems. It is easy to observe changes in temperature on land, but ocean water temperature also changes. **Figure 7** shows how a changing climate threatens biodiversity.

Human activities can also introduce non-native species, called **invasive species**, into a habitat. Often, invasive species out-compete native species within an ecosystem. Humans also remove species when poachers illegally kill wildlife for clothing, medicine, or body parts such as horns for ivory.

Protecting Biodiversity We can all take action to protect wildlife on Earth. For example, **Figure 8** shows students collecting data for conservation projects. Captive breeding programs help endangered species reproduce and sustain diversity. States and countries can set aside land to safeguard natural habitats. Finally, international laws and treaties protect the environment and biodiversity.

Habitat Preservation The goal of habitat preservation is to maintain the natural state of an ecosystem. Sometimes, that requires restoring its biodiversity. National parks, marine fisheries, and wildlife refuges are areas that preserve habitats. These areas are wildlife sanctuaries. Laws prevent or severely restrict any removal of resources from wildlife sanctuaries.

🖐 **INTERACTIVITY**

Examine how humans can safeguard and preserve biodiversity.

Citizen Scientists

Figure 8 Scientists often seek help from people like you for preservation and conservation efforts. Citizens are trained to collect data on factors such as water quality, population numbers, and behavior of species. Scientists use data to track populations and to monitor preservation efforts.

Form an Opinion Do you think citizen volunteers should participate in citizen science projects? Explain.

....

....

....

....

Reflect What do you value about being out in nature? Consider the number and variety of species you see when you are outside. What would happen if some of them disappeared?

Global Cooperation

Habitat preservation is critical to maintain our existing species and protect biodiversity globally. There are two treaties that are dedicated to preserving global biodiversity. The Convention on Biological Diversity focuses on conservation. The Convention on International Trade in Endangered Species of Wild Fauna and Flora ensures that the trade of plants and animals does not endanger them. These two treaties protect over 30,000 plant and animal species. We all benefit from global efforts that protect Earth's biodiversity (**Figure 9**). Protection and conservation ensure resources for future generations.

Protecting Our Oceans

Figure 9 ✎ The Sea of Cortez is a protected marine ecosystem. Global support for protecting Earth's marine ecosystems is increasing. However, gathering support is a slow process. The ocean is large and many people do not understand the importance of marine protection. Circle two organisms that could be harmed without marine protection.

☑ **READING CHECK** **Construct Explanations** Why is it important to protect marine ecosystems?

....

....

....

☑ LESSON 3 Check

MS-LS2-4, MS-LS2-5, MS-LS4-1

1. **Describe** What is meant by the value of biodiversity?

....

....

....

....

2. **Distinguish Relationships** How is an ecosystem's biodiversity a measure of its health?

....

....

....

....

3. **Cause and Effect** What consequences might occur if a particular species becomes extinct?

....

....

....

....

4. **Apply Concepts** When scientists analyze the rock record, they look for fossil evidence. How are scientists able to determine that the majority of all organisms are now extinct?

....

....

....

....

....

....

5. **Construct Arguments** Support the argument that biodiversity needs to be protected. Explain.

....

....

....

....

....

....

Quest CHECK-IN

In this lesson, you learned about the value of healthy ecosystems and the importance of biodiversity. You also learned about the factors affecting biodiversity.

Synthesize Information How can road construction affect the biodiversity of an ecosystem?

....

....

....

....

HANDS-ON LAB

Design and Model a Crossing

Go online for a downloadable worksheet of this lab. Build a model of your wildlife crossing. As a class, share your ideas. Evaluate how each model functions to protect biodiversity.

MS-LS2-2, MS-LS2-4

The Dependable Elephant

The African elephant is the largest land mammal on Earth. It can grow to weigh more than 4,500 kilograms (10,000 pounds) and spend most of its days eating. This huge creature often lives in herds of 12 to 15 individuals that are led by a dominant female. An African elephant gives birth every 3 to 4 years, producing one calf after a two-year pregnancy. A calf can weigh about 110 kilograms (250 pounds) at birth.

Elephants serve an ecological role as big as their size. As a keystone species, they directly impact the structure, composition, and biodiversity of their ecosystem—where the vast grassy plains of the African savannas and woodlands meet. Elephants affect the variety and amount of trees that make up a forest. By pulling down trees and tearing up thorny bushes, they create grassland habitats for other species. Elephant dung enriches the soil with nutrients and carries the seeds of many plant species. In fact, some of the seeds need to pass through the elephant's digestive system to germinate! Other seeds are removed from the dung and eaten by other animals. Scientists estimate that at least one-third of Africa's woodlands depend on elephants for their survival in one way or another.

African elephants once numbered in the millions, but the numbers have been dropping. This dramatic decline is a result of poaching. Hunters kill the elephants for their ivory tusks. The valuable ivory is sold or used to make decorative items.

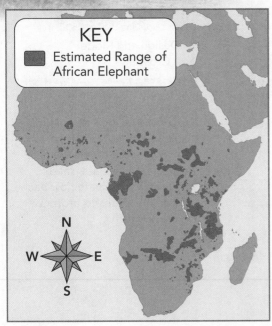

KEY

Estimated Range of African Elephant

N
W · E
S

Saving the Elephants

Various elephant conservation groups suggest that there are scattered pockets of African elephants throughout the southern portions of the continent. While there are efforts being made to protect the elephants, there are just too few people and too much land to cover to be very effective.

The graph to the right shows the estimated African elephant population from 1995 through 2014. Use the graph to answer the questions.

1. **Patterns** Describe any patterns you see in the graph.

   ....
   ....
   ....
   ....
   ....

African Elephant Population Trends, 1995–2014

Source: US National Library of Medicine and National Institutes of Health

2. **Predict** Do you think the trend shown in the graph will continue? Explain.

   ....
   ....
   ....
   ....

3. **Construct Explanations** Based on the data, how might the rest of the elephant's ecosystem be affected long term?

   ....
   ....
   ....
   ....

4. **Solve Problems** What are some ways elephants could be protected in order to preserve the biodiversity of an ecosystem?

   ....
   ....
   ....
   ....

Guiding Questions

- Why is it important to maintain healthy ecosystems?
- Which supporting services are necessary to all other ecosystem services?
- How does biodiversity impact ecosystem services?

Connections

Literacy Write Arguments

Math Graph Proportional Relationships

MS-LS2-3, MS-LS2-5

Vocabulary

ecosystem services
ecology
natural resource
conservation
sustainability
ecological restoration

Academic Vocabulary

regulation

 VOCABULARY APP

Practice vocabulary on a mobile device.

 **CONNECTION**

Consider how road construction impacts ecosystem services.

Connect It!

✏️ **Circle three different organisms interacting with their environment.**

Distinguish Relationships Describe how each organism interacts with the environment. How would they be affected if the environment was disrupted?

....

....

....

....

Ecosystem Services

Ecosystems meet our needs by supplying us with water, fuel, and wellness. **Ecosystem services** are the benefits humans receive from ecosystems. They are often produced without help from humans, and they are free! Ecosystem services occur because systems in an ecosystem interact with one another. Plants interact with the air, sun, soil, water, and minerals. Animals interact with plants, other animals, the air, and water. Because services are exchanged when interactions occur, biodiversity is an important factor.

In an ecosystem, all organisms, including humans, interact with one another and benefit from those interactions. **Ecology** is the study of how organisms interact with their environment. Ecology helps us understand how services emerge from those interactions. For example, the bee in **Figure 1** is pollinating the flower, but it is also getting nectar from the flower. Both interactions can result in services that humans use. Further, their exchange is an example of cycling matter and energy within an ecosystem.

Humans rely on cycling of matter and energy that occurs in diverse ecosystems. Scientists have separated ecosystem services into four categories, based on how they benefit us. The categories are: cultural, provisional, regulatory, and supporting services. Identifying and protecting each service is vital for human life.

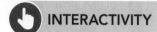

INTERACTIVITY

Explore the services provided by a healthy ecosystem.

Ecosystem Services

Figure 1 Organisms interact with and rely on one another. This bee pollinates the flower, which will turn into a blueberry. Consider some benefits you might get from this ecosystem. Some of these benefits might be obvious, while others may not be.

269

Cultural and Provisional Services

Figure 2 ✏ Cultural services make us feel well, while provisional services provide us with something to use. Circle any photo that shows a provisional service.

Apply Concepts

Which services, cultural or provisional, do humans pay the most money for? Explain.

....

....

....

....

....

Cultural Services Nature has a way of putting a smile on your face. When nature makes you happy, it is providing you with a cultural service. Cultural services include recreational services, such as paddling a canoe at a local lake or going on a hike, and educational services, such as exploring Earth's history in the rock layers. We use cultural services to rest and relax, or learn more about the world around us. We can even learn about history, such as the role of the Mississippi and Missouri Rivers in building our nation. **Figure 2** shows a few examples of the cultural services that give meaning to life and help our wellness.

Provisional Services *Provisional* means useful. Provisional services, also shown in **Figure 2**, are the products obtained from the natural resources in an ecosystem. Anything naturally occurring in the environment that humans use is a **natural resource**, such as drinking water, food, fuel, and raw materials. Filtered ground water and surface water are two sources we tap into for drinking water. Farming provides many of the meats, vegetables, and fruits we eat. Marine and freshwater ecosystems provide us with meat and vegetables. Fuel resources include oil, coal, and natural gas. Plants provide us with timber for buildings and plant-based medicines.

Restoring Water

The water flowing into New York Harbor is polluted due to waste and fertilizer runoff. Scientists have designed a solution that relies on natural filtration and purification. One oyster filters about 150 liters of water a day, while one mussel filters 65 liters a day.

1. Write an Expression Write a formula to show the amount of water filtered by 7 oysters in one day.

....

....

2. Graph Proportional Relationships Use your formula to calculate the amount of water 5, 10, 15, and 20 oysters can filter. Then, calculate that amount of water the same number of mussels can filter. Graph your data. Use a solid line to represent the oysters and a dashed line to represent the mussels.

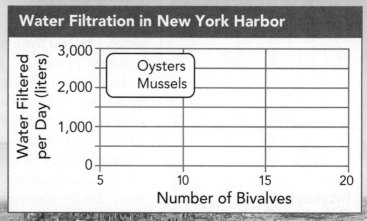

Water Filtration in New York Harbor

Graph: Water Filtered per Day (liters), y-axis from 0 to 3,000 (marks at 0, 1,000, 2,000, 3,000); x-axis Number of Bivalves from 5 to 20. Legend: Oysters, Mussels.

Regulatory Services

Regulatory Services Benefits humans receive from natural processes are regulatory services. An ecosystem needs to function and operate properly to support life. Many of these processes, such as decomposition, go unseen. Regulatory services allow nature to resist or fix problems that may harm the ecosystem. These processes also protect humans from some of the same problems.

Plants and animals play a major role in the regulation of an ecosystem. Plants increase air quality by removing harmful chemicals and releasing useful chemicals. They regulate our climate by absorbing a greenhouse gas—carbon dioxide. The roots of plants prevent soil erosion. Bivalves, such as mussels and oysters, filter polluted and contaminated water. We have fruits to eat because animals pollinate flowers and help disperse seeds. Some animals naturally help with pest and disease control. This natural regulation of pests is biological control.

VIRTUAL LAB

Test and evaluate competing solutions for preventing soil erosion to protect cropland.

✓ READING CHECK **Cite Textual Evidence** How are regulatory services important for ecosystems?

....

....

INTERACTIVITY

Explore the four key ecosystem services.

Supporting Services

The most important ecosystem services are the ones that support all the processes in nature. While supporting services do not directly impact humans, ecosystems would cease to function without them.

Supporting services cycle resources such as water, nutrients, gases, and soil throughout the ecosystem. In the water cycle, water evaporates, travels into the air and forms a part of a cloud, returns to Earth as precipitation, and the cycle continues. When an organism dies, it decomposes and forms nutrient-rich matter that becomes part of the soil. Plants take in the nutrients and store them in their cells. Atmospheric gases also cycle through ecosystems. During photosynthesis, plants take in carbon dioxide and release oxygen. Animals then take in oxygen and release carbon dioxide. Soil is also cycled. It is formed from weathered rock and organic matter. Rock sediment can reform into another rock with added heat and/or pressure. **Figure 3** shows how these different cycles interact with one another. The cycles ensure that matter and energy are endlessly transferred within a healthy ecosystem.

Interactions Between Cycles of an Ecosystem

Figure 3 🖉 Draw two arrows to show the flow of water in this ecosystem.

Explain Phenomena What would happen if any of these services were disrupted?

....

....

....

☑ **READING CHECK** **Determine Central Ideas** Why are supporting services important to the ecosystem?

....

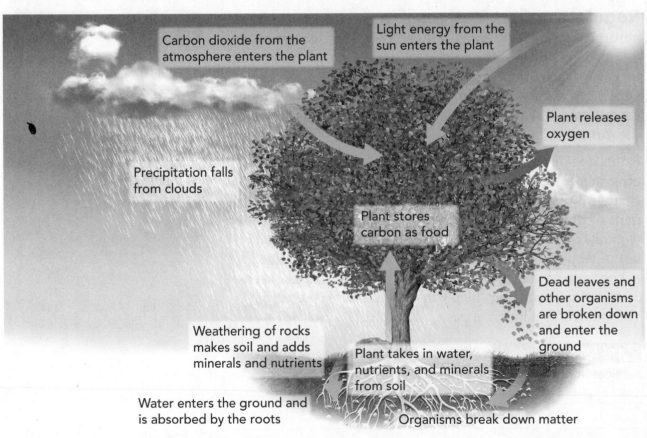

Carbon dioxide from the atmosphere enters the plant

Light energy from the sun enters the plant

Plant releases oxygen

Precipitation falls from clouds

Plant stores carbon as food

Dead leaves and other organisms are broken down and enter the ground

Weathering of rocks makes soil and adds minerals and nutrients

Plant takes in water, nutrients, and minerals from soil

Water enters the ground and is absorbed by the roots

Organisms break down matter

Biodiversity in Ecosystems

Figure 4 The survival of marine ecosystems, like this coral reef, is dependent on the diversity of organisms. Coral reefs provide every type of ecosystem service. But sometimes those services can be in conflict. People who snorkel and scuba dive can damage the corals. Boats can increase water pollution. People can also overfish the area.

Specify Design Constraints Think about ways to preserve this ecosystem. What sort of management plan could maintain the ecosystem services a coral reef provides, while protecting it from the negative impact of human activities?

....

....

....

....

....

....

Factors Impacting Ecosystem Services

Earth needs diverse and healthy ecosystems. All organisms depend on their environment to get food, water, and shelter. Diverse ecosystems provide these basic needs for life.

Biodiversity Ecosystem production increases with biodiversity. When production increases, ecosystem services increase. Coral reefs, such as the one you see in **Figure 4**, cover less than one percent of the ocean. However, over 25 percent of the marine life lives among coral reefs. Each species plays a role within the ecosystem and they benefit from one another. Small fish eat algae, so the coral do not compete for resources with algae. Predators, such as sharks, keep the number of small fish from getting too large. Some fish eat parasites growing on other fish. Organisms like crabs feed on dead organisms.

As you can see, there are many more examples of biodiversity found at coral reefs. This biodiversity helps coral reefs survive changing conditions. However, coral reefs are increasingly threatened by our demand for their resources.

Avocado Farms

Figure 5 Avocado farmers in Mexico did not know that the roots of the native trees filter water. Avocado tree roots are not able to filter the ground water.

Identify Patterns How has this impacted people who rely on naturally filtered drinking water?

....

....

....

....

HANDS-ON LAB

Investigate Model how wetlands help with water purification.

Literacy Connection

Write Arguments Use the Internet to conduct research on the clearing of forests to create farmland. Research two opposing sides of the issue. Select one side of the issue to support. Using evidence, explain why you chose that side.

Human Activities When humans alter or destroy habitats, the natural cycling of the ecosystem is disrupted. The severe impact of human activities is mostly due to our ignorance and greed. Removing species from ecosystems disrupts natural cycling, which decreases ecosystem services. However, many people are working to restore and protect the natural cycling of ecosystems.

We once thought that our oceans could handle anything we dumped in them, from sewage to nuclear waste. We also assumed there would be an endless supply of goods. But by polluting our oceans, we have lost marine organisms. We have also overfished the Atlantic cod, bluefin tuna, and Chilean sea bass. Our demand has caused their populations to decline drastically.

Changing the ecosystem impacts humans because it reduces the ecosystem services we rely on. The development of cities and demand for food further harms ecosystems. When buildings replace wetlands and floodplains, flooding and loss of biodiversity often result. To grow crops, farmers strip the land of native plant species, decreasing biodiversity. In Mexico, this became a problem when avocado farmers cleared native oak and pine trees to grow avocado trees, as shown in **Figure 5**.

READING CHECK **Summarize Text** What impact do farms have on an ecosystem?

....

....

Conservation

Over the past 50 years, human activities have drastically changed Earth's ecosystems. Scientists and engineers are working to design solutions to help save Earth's ecosystems. One way is through **conservation**, or the practice of using less of a resource so that it can last longer. As concerned citizens, we can all participate in conservation to protect and restore Earth's ecosystems.

Protection Healthy ecosystems need protection from the loss of resources. **Sustainability** is the ability of an ecosystem to maintain biodiversity and production indefinitely. Designating protected areas and regulating the amount of resources humans can take from an ecosystem are two main efforts to promote sustainability. The **regulation** of protected areas can be difficult to enforce without monitors.

Restoration **Ecological restoration** is the practice of helping a degraded or destroyed ecosystem recover from damage. Some recovery efforts are easy, like planting native plants. Others are more difficult. For example, toxic chemical spills require bioremediation, a technique that uses microorganisms to breakdown pollutants. Restoring land to a more natural state, or land reclamation, also helps ecosystems (**Figure 6**).

✓ READING CHECK **Determine Central Ideas** Why do scientists prefer to use bioremediation to clean up chemical spills?

....

....

👆 **INTERACTIVITY**

Investigate how biodiversity impacts ecosystem services.

Academic Vocabulary

Why is it important for the school to have regulations?

....

....

....

Design It!

Ecological Restoration

Figure 6 Restoring an ecosystem often takes several years and several regulations.

Design Your Solution Construction of a shopping mall has caused the deterioration of a wetland area. A study conducted showed that runoff from paved areas is disrupting the existing wetland. Create a plan to present to local officials outlining criteria for restoring the remaining wetland.

....

....

....

MS-LS2-3, MS-LS2-5

1. Identify What are the four categories of ecosystem services?

....

....

2. Describe How do cultural services help humans?

....

....

3. Distinguish Relationships How are biodiversity and the cycling of matter related to maintaining ecosystem services?

....

....

....

....

4. Apply Concepts What are several ways that you could conserve water?

....

....

....

....

....

5. Explain Phenomena What are supporting services and why are they important to cultural, provisional, and regulatory services?

....

....

....

....

....

....

....

6. Evaluate Proportion Using your data from the math toolbox, which bivalve is more efficient at filtering water? Provide support.

....

....

....

....

7. Apply Scientific Reasoning What are some other organisms, aside from bivalves, that could be used to purify water? Explain the benefits of using this organism.

....

....

....

....

....

8. Implement a Solution A giant factory farm uses large open lagoons to treat waste from the buildings where hogs are stored. The problem is that the lagoons smell awful and, during rainstorms, they are at risk of spilling into surrounding river systems. Design a solution that resolves the smell and water contamination risk, and allows the farm to continue to raise hogs.

....

....

....

....

....

....

....

....

....

FROM BULLDOZERS To Biomes

INTERACTIVITY

Evaluate design solutions based on how well they meet a task's criteria and constraints.

Do you know how to transform an old clay pit into lush biomes? You engineer it! The Eden Project in Cornwall, England shows us how.

The Challenge: To renew and transform land after humans have damaged it.

Phenomenon A clay pit in Cornwall had been mined for over a hundred years to make fine china and was shutting down. Mining provides access to resources, but can damage ecosystems by removing vegetation and topsoil. Mining can threaten biodiversity by destroying or fragmenting habitats, and increasing erosion and pollution.

Eden Project planners chose the clay pit to build a giant greenhouse to showcase biodiversity and the relationship between plants, people and resources.

The greenhouse represents two biomes: the rain forest biome and the Mediterranean biome. These biomes contain over a million plants and more than 5,000 different species. Visitors can learn how plants are adapted to different climates, how plants play a role in their daily lives, and how to use resources sustainably.

The top photo shows the clay pit that was transformed into the biome structures and lush vegetation of the Eden Project below.

DESIGN CHALLENGE

Can you build a model of a biome structure? Go to the Engineering Design Notebook to find out!

You have limited materials to work with: 30 toothpicks and 15 balls of clay

☑ TOPIC 5 Review and Assess

① Interactions in Ecosystems

MS-LS2-1, MS-LS2-2

1. To reduce competition, the role of an organism in its habitat is called its
   - A. adaption.
   - B. host.
   - C. niche.
   - D. parasite.

2. In which type of interaction do both species benefit?
   - A. predation
   - B. mutualism
   - C. commensalism
   - D. parasitism

3. Four different mammals all live among oak and maple trees in a forest. They don't seem to compete for the same foods or nesting places. Which of the following is a likely explanation for this lack of competition?
   - A. The four species occupy different niches.
   - B. Their small size is a limiting factor that reduces competition among them.
   - C. There is no shortage of food.
   - D. There is no shortage of space.

4. **Cause and Effect** Why is it in the best interest of a parasite not to kill its host? Explain.

   ....

   ....

   ....

5. **Construct Explanations** Describe what a predatory relationship would look like in a forest ecosystem and a wetland ecosystem. Identify any similarities and differences.

   ....

   ....

   ....

   ....

   ....

   ....

② Dynamic and Resilient Ecosystems

MS-LS2-1, MS-LS2-2, MS-LS2-4

6. The series of predictable changes that occur in a community over time is called
   - A. natural selection.
   - B. ecology.
   - C. commensalism.
   - D. succession.

7. A disruption to an established ecosystem can lead to
   - A. new organisms being prevented from moving into the area.
   - B. changes in the populations of the community.
   - C. more resources for all the organisms that make up the community.
   - D. hurricanes or volcanic eruptions.

8. A former farmland that is now home to shrubs and small trees is undergoing
   - A. pioneer succession.
   - B. primary succession.
   - C. secondary succession.
   - D. adaptive succession.

9. After a long time, a mature community is established in an ecosystem. This community will not change unless a component of the ecosystem is ....

10. **Apply Scientific Reasoning** When a disrupted part of a wetland ecosystem is left alone so that nature can help restore it to what it once was, what are people counting on occurring? Explain.

    ....

    ....

    ....

    ....

    ....

    ....

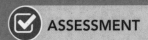

3 Biodiversity

MS-LS2-4, MS-LS2-5

11. A(n) .... is a species that influences the survival of many other species in an ecosystem.

12. A(n) .... is a non-native species that is introduced into an ecosystem and severely disrupts it by competing with native species.

13. **Cause and Effect** Why are species with low genetic diversity at more risk of becoming extinct than species with high genetic diversity?

....
....
....
....
....
....
....
....

14. **Apply Concepts** Describe an example in which humans overuse an ecosystem's resources for their economic value.

....
....
....
....
....
....
....
....

4 Ecosystem Services

MS-LS2-3, MS-LS2-5

15. Going for a hike in a forest where you can breathe fresh air, observe wildlife, and relax is an example of a .... service that an ecosystem can provide.

16. The water cycle, photosynthesis, nutrient cycling, and soil formation are examples of
    A. cultural services.
    B. provisioning services.
    C. regulating services.
    D. supporting services.

17. **Analyze Properties** What are some examples of provisioning services humans get from plants?

....
....
....

18. **Synthesize Information** Describe an example of when land reclamation may be needed on a beach.

....
....
....
....
....
....
....
....

19. **Explain Phenomena** How can bioremediation play a role in cleaning up an oil spill?

....
....
....

279

MS-LS2-1, MS-LS2-4

Evidence-Based Assessment

Like organisms in an ecosystem, the microscopic organisms, or microbiota, living in the human mouth are affected by environmental conditions. One way the human oral environment can change is by a changing diet.

Scientists use fossil evidence to compare the oral microbiota of our ancestors with people living today. Their goal is to gain a better understanding of how the human diet has changed over time. First, they studied the diversity of oral microbiota species. They found that two cavity-causing bacteria appeared more often through time (*S. mutans* and *P. gingivalis*). Then they studied the frequency, or rate, of the two cavity-causing bacteria.

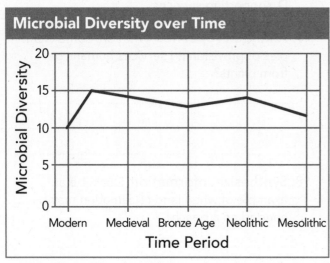

Source: Nature Genetics (2013)

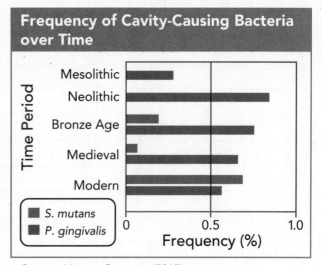

Source: Nature Genetics (2013)

The scientists also considered the changes in human diet and culture that have taken place since ancient times.

- During the Mesolithic period (7,550–5,450 BP), humans were hunter-gatherers.

- During the Neolithic period (7,400–4,000 BP), humans developed farming and adopted a carbohydrate-rich diet.

- During the Bronze Age (4,200–3,000 BP), humans manufactured bronze tools, but did not change their diet.

- During the Medieval period (1,100–400 BP), human diet was based on agricultural products.

- In modern times, humans incorporated mass-produced, commercially processed food into their diet, largely based on flour and sugar.

1. **Analyze Data** According to the study, in which period were mouth microbiota the least diverse?
   A. Mesolithic period
   B. Neolithic period
   C. Bronze Age
   D. Medieval era
   E. Modern times

2. **Identify Patterns** How did the frequency of each cavity-causing bacteria change over time?

   ....
   ....
   ....
   ....
   ....
   ....
   ....
   ....
   ....

3. **Explain Phenomena** According to the information presented in the graphs and text, what is the relationship between diet and the diversity of oral microbiota populations throughout time? Cite evidence from the graph and text.

   ....
   ....
   ....
   ....
   ....
   ....
   ....
   ....

4. **Construct Arguments** Based on the data and information presented, how did the availability of resources cause changes in the population size of cavity-causing bacteria? Explain.

   ....
   ....
   ....
   ....
   ....
   ....
   ....
   ....
   ....
   ....
   ....

Quest FINDINGS

Complete the Quest!

Phenomenon Determine the best way to clearly present your claim with data and evidence, such as graphics or a multimedia presentation.

Cause and Effect If new homes or businesses are constructed when new highways are built, how would an animal crossing affect the changes to the physical and biological components of the ecosystem?

....
....
....
....

INTERACTIVITY

Reflect on Your Animal Crossing

Changes in an Ecosystem

> How can you use a **model** to determine the effects of a **forest fire** on a **rabbit population?**

Background

Phenomenon Forest fires have a bad reputation! Many of these fires damage or destroy habitats and impact the populations of organisms that live there. But forest fires can also play an important role in maintaining the overall health of ecosystems. In this lab, you will develop and use a model to investigate how a forest fire might affect a population of rabbits 50 years after the fire.

Materials

(per pair)
- tree-shadow circles handout
- scissors
- transparent tape

Young Longleaf Pine

Tree Shadow As Seen From Above

Mature Longleaf Pine

Tree Shadow As Seen From Above

Safety

Be sure to follow all safety guidelines provided by your teacher. The Safety Appendix of your textbook provides more details about the safety icons.

Oak Tree

Tree Shadow As Seen From Above

Procedure

1. Predict what will happen to the rabbit population 50 years after the fire. Will the population be smaller, the same size, or larger? Record your prediction.

2. The graph paper represents the forest floor where each square is equal to 10 square meters (m^2). Calculate the total area of the forest floor. Create a data table in the space provided and enter this area in the table.

3. ✂ Cut out the tree shadow circles from the tree-shadow circles handout. Design a longleaf pine forest by arranging the mature pine and oak tree shadow circles on the forest floor. (Do not use the young pine tree shadows yet.) Tape the mature pine tree shadows in place, but not the oak tree shadows.

4. Determine the area of forest floor in sunlight. Add this data to your table.

5. Using a similar method, determine the square meters of shadow. Calculate the percentage of forest floor in shadow and in sunlight. Add this data to your table.

6. Suppose a lightning strike ignites a forest fire. Here's what would happen to some of the populations in the forest:

   - **Oak trees** are not adapted to survive fire so they burn and are destroyed; new trees will grow only if seeds are carried into the forest after the fire

   - **Longleaf pine trees** survive and continue to grow; seeds are released from pine cones and can germinate

   - **Bluestem grasses** are burned, but roots survive

7. Fast forward 50 years. The oak trees did not survive the forest fire, but the longleaf pines did. Use the young pine tree shadows to model the areas where young pine trees have likely grown. Repeat Steps 4 & 5 to gather evidence from your model about what the forest looks like 50 years after the fire.

HANDS-ON LAB

и**Demonstrate** Go online for a downloadable worksheet of this lab.

Prediction

....

....

....

....

....

....

....

Observations

....

....

....

....

....

....

....

....

....

....

Data Table

Analyze and Interpret Data

1. **Explain** What resources are the trees and grass competing for?

   ....

   ....

   ....

2. **Analyze Data** Was your prediction correct? How did resource availability 50 years after the fire impact the rabbit population? (Hint: The rabbits are herbivores that primarily feed on grasses.)

   ....

   ....

   ....

   ....

   ....

3. **Cite Evidence** Use the data you have collected as evidence to support the claim you made in Question 2.

   ....

   ....

   ....

   ....

   ....

4. **Construct Arguments** Longleaf pine forests are important habitats, home to several endangered species. Oak trees are invasive (non-native) species in longleaf pine forests. When there are too many oak trees, they block the sunlight that pine trees need. Construct an argument that it is sometimes necessary to set forest fires in these habitats in order to preserve these endangered species.

   ....

   ....

   ....

   ....

   ....

   ....

   ....

Distribution of Natural Resources

NGSS PERFORMANCE EXPECTATIONS

MS-ESS3-1 Construct a scientific explanation
based on evidence for how the uneven distributions
of Earth's mineral, energy, and groundwater
resources are the result of past and current
geoscience processes.

MS-ESS3-3 Apply scientific principles to design
a method for monitoring and minimizing a human
impact on the environment.

MS-ESS3-4 Construct an argument supported by
evidence for how increases in human population
and per-capita consumption of natural resources
impact Earth's systems.

What is responsible
for these colorful
rock formations?

▶ VIDEO

☝ INTERACTIVITY

🎛 VIRTUAL LAB

☑ ASSESSMENT

📖 eTEXT

📱 APP

HANDS-ON LAB

и**Connect** Observe coal to draw conclusions about its formation.

The Essential Question

How is the distribution of natural resources the result of geological processes?

The Artists Palette is a geological formation in Death Valley National Park in California. The striking colors are caused by mineral deposits in the rock. How do you think the minerals got there?

....

....

....

....

Quest KICKOFF

How could natural resources have saved a ghost town?

Phenomenon In the past, the discovery of valuable or rare natural resources often led to the quick development of towns as people rushed to strike it rich. But many of these boomtowns, as they came to be known, died as quickly as they began. In this problem-based Quest activity, you will investigate how resource availability affected the longevity and success of boomtowns. By applying what you learn in each lesson, you will gather key Quest information and evidence. In the Findings activity, you will choose a boomtown to explore in more detail and explain the role that resource availability played in the fate of the town.

NBC LEARN ▶ VIDEO

After watching the Quest Kickoff video, which explores how resource availability affected the success or failure of boomtowns, think about what made your town or city a desirable location for people to settle in the past.

....

....

....

....

....

....

....

....

....

....

 INTERACTIVITY

Predicting Boom or Bust

MS-ESS3-1 Construct a scientific explanation based on evidence for how the uneven distributions of Earth's mineral, energy, and groundwater resources are the result of past and current geoscience processes.

Quest CHECK-IN

IN LESSON 1
How does the availability of fossil fuels affect the success of a boomtown? Predict which boomtowns could have survived by using coal, oil, and/or natural gas.

 INTERACTIVITY

Surviving on Fossil Fuels

Quest CHECK-IN

IN LESSON 2
What conditions make renewable resources a viable alternative to fossil fuels? Explore how renewable energy resources might have affected the success or failure of the boomtowns.

 INTERACTIVITY

Renewable Energy

Quest CHECK-IN

IN LESSON 3
What effect does the distribution of minerals have on the success of a boomtown? Analyze the distribution of gold, copper, and salt to help you determine the fates of the boomtowns.

 INTERACTIVITY

Surviving on Minerals

Many towns like the one shown here did not have the resources required to sustain growth and development.

BLACKSMITH

Quest CHECK-IN

IN LESSON 4

How does access to water affect the fate of a boomtown? Predict which boomtowns might have survived based on the availability of water resources.

👆 **INTERACTIVITY**

Surviving on Water

Quest FINDINGS

Complete the Quest!

Find out what happened to each boomtown and then create a travel brochure for one of the boomtowns to explain how resource availability affected the fate of that town.

👆 **INTERACTIVITY**

Reflect on Boomtowns

Nonrenewable Energy Resources

Guiding Questions

- What are nonrenewable resources?
- What factors affect the distribution of nonrenewable energy resources?
- How has human activity impacted the distribution of fossil fuels?

Connections

Literacy Cite Textual Evidence

Math Analyze Relationships

MS-ESS3-1, MS-ESS3-4

Vocabulary

natural resource
nonrenewable
 resource
fossil fuels
nuclear fission

Academic Vocabulary

renew

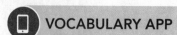

VOCABULARY APP

Practice vocabulary on a mobile device.

Quest CONNECTION

Consider how the availability of energy resources, such as oil and coal, might impact the success or failure of a town.

Connect It!

✎ **Identify and label some the materials that are being used in this construction project.**

Classify Pick one of the materials you identified in the photo and explain whether you think the resource is limited or unlimited.

....

....

Natural Resources

We all rely on natural resources to survive. A **natural resource** is anything occuring naturally in the environment that humans use. We need air to breathe, water to drink, soil in which to grow plants to eat, sunlight to make those plants grow, and other natural resources. Some of these resources are essentially unlimited and renewable regardless of what we do. For example, sunlight and wind are available daily at most places on Earth. Other renewable resources can be reused or replenished, but it may require some care or planning. For example, wood from trees is a renewable resource as long as some trees are spared to reproduce and make the next generation of trees.

Other resources are **nonrenewable resources,** which cannot be replaced. This may be because there is a finite amount of the resource on Earth and we don't have a way to make more of it. The element silver, for example, cannot be made from other substances. The amount of silver on Earth is set. Other resources are considered nonrenewable because it takes very long periods of time for them to form.

✔️ READING CHECK **Cite Evidence** Why is wood considered to be a renewable resource?

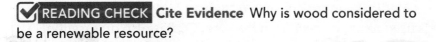

....

....

....

HANDS-ON LAB

Classify resources that you use in a typical day.

📖 **Reflect** In your science notebook, describe how a natural resource could shift from being renewable to nonrenewable.

Resource Use
Figure 1 This construction project relies on a number of natural resources.

Lignite

Bituminous Coal

Anthracite

Types of Coal

Figure 2 Brittle, lustrous anthracite has more energy than crumbly, dull lignite.

Determine Differences Why might one type of coal contain more energy than another type of coal?

....

....

....

....

Fossil Fuels

The sources of energy commonly called fossil fuels include coal, petroleum, and natural gas. **Fossil fuels** are the energy-rich substances made from the preserved remains of organisms. The chemical energy in fossil fuels can be converted to other forms by burning them.

The energy stored in these compounds originally arrived on Earth as sunlight. Photosynthetic organisms such as algae, moss, grasses, and trees converted sunlight into carbon-based compounds. When animals ate the plants, they absorbed some of those compounds. Under certain conditions involving high temperatures and pressures, the remains of these organisms were transformed into new materials, including solid coal, liquid petroleum, and methane gas.

Coal Coal is formed from the remains of plants that died long ago in and around swampy areas. There are different grades, or types, of coal (**Figure 2**). Each grade forms under different conditions, as shown in **Figure 3**. In addition to being a source of energy, coal is used in a wide array of applications. Coal is used in water and air purification systems, as well as medical equipment such as kidney dialysis devices. Coal is used to make steel from iron ore. Coal is also an essential ingredient in carbon fiber, an extremely durable and lightweight material used to construct everything from bicycles to buildings.

Burning coal in coal-fired power plants accounts for about 30 percent of the electricity produced in the United States. Coal has long been used as a fuel because it has twice as much energy per unit of mass as wood. So, when coal can be mined at a large scale, it can be an efficient source of energy.

Unfortunately, burning coal produces pollutants and causes millions of deaths each year from health problems. Coal mining also requires large mines to be dug into the ground, or the removal of mountaintops or other surface layers to access coal beds. Removing coal causes great damage to the surrounding environment.

☑ READING CHECK **Determine Central Ideas** What is the original source of the energy contained in coal? Explain.

....

....

....

Coal Formation and Distribution

Figure 3 Coal only forms under the right conditions. The map shows major deposits of coal around the world.

1. **Use Models** ✏ Circle the three continents that have the most coal resources.

2. **Construct Explanations** Why is coal not found evenly distributed around the world?

....

....

....

....

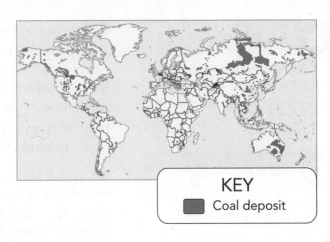

KEY

▨ Coal deposit

Swamp Environment

PEAT
(Partially altered plant material; very smoky when burned, low energy)

Burial

Compaction

LIGNITE
(Soft, brown coal; moderate energy)

Greater burial

Compaction

BITUMINOUS COAL
(Soft, black coal; major coal used in power generation and industry; high energy)

Metamorphasism

ANTHRACITE
(Hard, black coal; used in industry; highest energy)

Stress

INTERACTIVITY

Explore the distribution of different fossil fuels.

VIDEO

Learn more about how fossil fuels form underground.

Oil What we commonly refer to as oil is scientifically known as **petroleum**, from the Latin terms *petra* (rock) and *oleum* (oil). Petroleum is made of the remains of small animals, algae, and other organisms that lived in marine environments hundreds of millions of years ago. Oil deposits form when these remains become trapped underground and are subject to high pressure and temperature.

Because it is a liquid and can be processed into different fuels, petroleum is especially useful for powering engines in automobiles, ships, trains, and airplanes. Petroleum also has many important industrial uses, such as making plastics, lubricants, and fertilizers. Petroleum is also the basis for synthetic fibers, such as rayon and nylon. Many cosmetic and pharmaceutical products such as petroleum jelly and tar shampoos that treat dandruff, contain forms of petroleum.

As with coal, burning oil and natural gas emits carbon dioxide. Oil can also be spilled, which can be disastrous for wildlife and water quality (**Figure 4**). Natural gas leaks contribute to global warming, and can result in explosions if the concentration of gas is high and a spark ignites it.

Oil Impacts

Figure 4 Oil is often drilled from the ocean floor and transported by ship. Major oil spills can harm or kill wildlife, as well as damaging habitats and water quality.

1. **Interpret Tables** What are the two major causes of accidental oil spills?

   ....

2. **Calculate** About how much more oil was spilled as a result of the *Deepwater Horizon* explosion than the *Valdez* running aground?

   ....

Location and Date	Amount Spilled (gallons)	Cause
Trinidad and Tobago, 1979	90 million	Collision of two oil tanker ships
Gulf of Mexico, 1979	140 million	Blown-out *Ixtoc 1* oil well on ocean floor, fire, collapse of drilling platform
Persian Gulf, 1983	80 million	Collision of ship with oil-drilling platform during Iraq-Iran war
Prince William Sound, Alaska, 1989	11 million	*Exxon Valdez* oil tanker ship runs aground, puncturing hull
Angola, 1991	80 million	Oil tanker ship explodes and sinks
Gulf of Mexico, 2010	181 million	Blown-out *Deepwater Horizon* oil well, explosion of platform

Petroleum Formation and Distribution

Figure 5 Petroleum has been drilled for all over the world. Wells or rigs are constructed to tap "fields" of oil hundreds or thousands of meters below Earth's surface, both on land and water.

Apply Concepts ✎ A large sea once existed in the United States. Shade the area of the country where you think the sea likely existed. Then explain your choice.

....

....

....

KEY
- ☐ Onshore basins
- ☐ Offshore basins

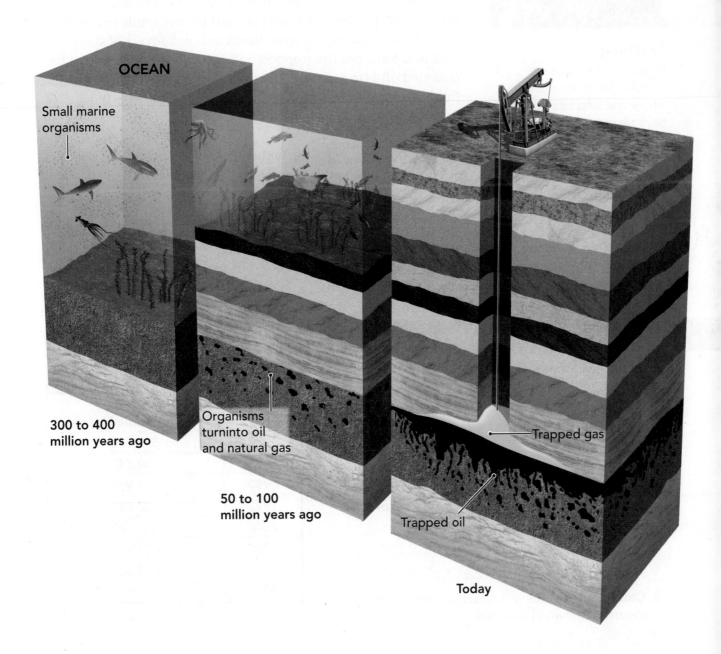

OCEAN

Small marine organisms

300 to 400 million years ago

Organisms turninto oil and natural gas

50 to 100 million years ago

Trapped gas

Trapped oil

Today

Natural Gas

Natural Gas Formed from the same processes that produce oil and found in the same locations, natural gas is trapped in pockets within layers of rock deep below Earth's surface. A drill can tap the trapped gas, and then pipelines carry the gas for processing and transport. Burning petroleum and coal releases more carbon dioxide than burning natural gas. This is one reason many countries have encouraged more use of natural gas and are surveying underground basins of gas for further exploitation. On the other hand, the gas itself is a powerful greenhouse gas that contributes to global warming. This means any leaks of natural gas from wells, pipelines, and other structures pose a pollution problem.

To meet the demand for natural gas, a process called fracking has become popular. Fracking is short for hydraulic fracturing. This involves using pressured fluids to break layers of shale rock and force out the trapped natural gas, which can then be collected and transported. There are concerns that the fracking fluids are contaminating vital stores of groundwater that humans rely on (**Figure 6**).

☑ READING CHECK **Cite Textual Evidence** Natural gas burns cleaner than coal, yet it is considered a pollutant. Why?

....

....

Fracking

Figure 6 Groundwater samples taken from sites where fracking has occurred have tested positive for methane and other hydrocarbons.

Math Toolbox

Natural Gas Consumption in the U.S.

In recent years, consumption patterns of natural gas have changed.

1. **Calculate** What was the percent increase in gas usage from 1980 to 2015? Show your work.

....

....

2. **Analyze Relationships** What trend is shown in the data?

....

....

3. **Cause and Effect** What factors contributed to the trend shown in the data?

....

....

U.S. Annual Natural Gas Consumption	
Year	**Volume (Million Cubic Meters)**
1980	562,862
1985	489,342
1990	542,935
1995	628,829
2000	660,720
2005	623,379
2010	682,062
2015	773,228

Source: U.S. Energy Information Administration

Nuclear Energy

Nuclear power is another nonrenewable energy resource used to generate much of the world's electricity. Nuclear energy provides 20 percent of the electricity in the United States. Inside a nuclear power plant, controlled nuclear fission reactions occur. **Nuclear fission** is the splitting of an atom's nucleus into two nuclei. Fission releases a great deal of energy. This energy is used to heat water, turning it into steam. The steam is then used to turn the blades of a turbine to produce electricity.

Uranium is the fuel used for nuclear fission inside nuclear reactors. It is a heavy metal that occurs in most rocks and is usually extracted through mining. The uranium found on Earth was part of the original cloud of dust and gas from which our solar system formed. Uranium is found throughout Earth's crust. But large ores of the material are formed from geological processes that only occur in certain locations on Earth (**Figure 7**).

Literacy Connection

Cite Textual Evidence As you read, underline text that supports the idea that uranium is a limited resource with finite amounts on Earth.

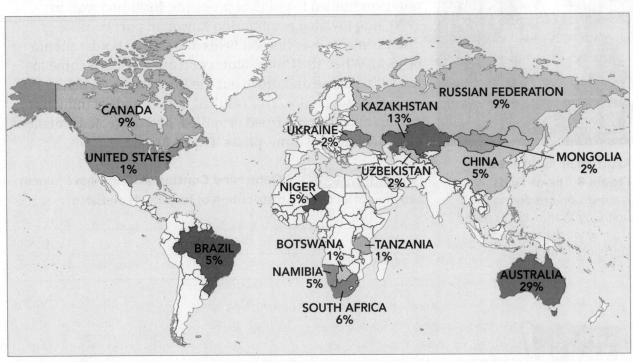

Source: World Nuclear Association

Distribution of Uranium

Figure 7 According to the World Nuclear Association, almost 70 percent of accessible uranium is found in only 5 countries.

1. Use Models ✏ Circle the two countries with the greatest percentage of uranium resources.

2. Patterns What patterns do you observe in the distribution of uranium?

....

....

....

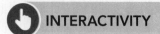

INTERACTIVITY

Learn more about the progression of living matter to petroleum.

Using Energy Resources

Fossil fuels are among the most important nonrenewable resources for humans. As the human population has grown, these resources have become less abundant. Geologists estimate that we have already used about half the petroleum that fossilization, pressure, heat, and time have produced over hundreds of millions of years—and all in just a few centuries.

Pollution Humans are burning fossil fuels at a faster rate than the resulting carbon emissions can be absorbed by natural processes, such as photosynthesis. This is why the concentration of carbon dioxide in the atmosphere is now 45 percent higher than it was just over 200 years ago. Scientists have concluded that this is fueling global warming and climate change.

World Politics The uneven distribution of fossil fuel resources has led to political problems, including war. In 1990, Iraq invaded neighboring Kuwait in part because of disagreements over how oil fields at a shared border should be used. When the United States and other nations came to Kuwait's defense and drove out the Iraqi forces, oil fields and wells were set on fire. This resulted in hundreds of millions of gallons of oil being burned or spilled, and untreated emissions billowing into the atmosphere (**Figure 8**).

Gulf War Oil Fires
Figure 8 The oil fields that were set on fire during the first Gulf War in 1991 caused significant damage to the land and living things.

☑ READING CHECK **Determine Conclusions** How have human activities affected the distribution of fossil fuels on Earth?

....

....

....

Plan It!

Household Energy Use

Use the space to describe how you could determine how much fossil fuel is used in your home and then make recommendations about how to reduce your usage.

....

....

....

....

....

MS-ESS3-1, MS-ESS4-3

1. **Identify** Which fossil fuel is produced from the remains of peat?

....

2. **Cause and Effect** A friend argues that the location of a petroleum deposit is a sign that marine organisms once lived there. Is your friend correct? Explain.

....

....

....

....

3. **Apply Concepts** How does the abundance of a resource, and whether it is renewable or nonrenewable, affect how much it is used?

....

....

....

....

....

....

....

4. **Identify** What advantage does coal have over wood as an energy source? What is the major disadvantage of using coal for energy?

....

....

....

....

....

....

5. **Construct Explanations** Why are oil, coal, and natural gas not found evenly distributed on Earth?

....

....

....

....

....

....

....

....

....

....

....

Quest CHECK-IN

In this lesson, you learned about different types of nonrenewable energy resources called fossil fuels and the impacts of human activities related to extracting and using these resources.

Evaluate Why is access to energy resources such as fossil fuels important to the economic and social development of a town?

....

....

....

....

☞ INTERACTIVITY

Surviving on Fossil Fuels

Go online to examine four different towns in the United States and determine the distribution pattern of the resources and the processes that may have resulted in the resource formation.

② Renewable Energy Resources

Guiding Questions
- What are renewable energy resources?
- How do renewable energy resources reduce human reliance on other natural resources?

Connections
Literacy Draw Evidence

Math Represent Quantitative Relationships

MS-ESS3-1, MS-ESS3-3

Vocabulary
renewable
  resource

Academic Vocabulary
cost

 VOCABULARY APP

Practice vocabulary on a mobile device.

Quest CONNECTION

Think about how using renewable energy resources, such as solar or wind, could affect the future of a boomtown.

Connect It !

✏️ **Draw arrows to indicate how the mirrors in this thermal energy plant direct the sun's rays to a small point on the tower.**

Infer How do you think this thermal energy plant helps reduce reliance on fossil fuels?

....

....

Reducing Fossil Fuel Usage

The abundance of energy-rich fossil fuels has made it easy for humankind to justify using petroleum, coal, and natural gas. However, there are both benefits and costs in terms of the short-term and long-term effects. Even though they are nonrenewable and impact Earth's systems, it was easier and less expensive in the past to mine and drill for coal, oil, and gas than to harness other sources of energy. Due to increased awareness of the consequences of mining and burning fossil fuels, as well as advances in technology, things are beginning to change in favor of alternative sources of energy.

Alternative energy resources, such as the solar power tower in **Figure 1**, are considered **renewable resources** because we cannot run out of them. They are replaced by nature, or with a little help from us.

READING CHECK **Determine Meaning** Why are some energy resources referred to as "renewable"?

....

....

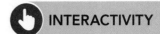

INTERACTIVITY

Identify renewable resources that are most suitable for use in your community.

Thermal Power
Figure 1 This thermal energy plant uses energy from the sun to heat water and produce electricity using steam.

▶ **VIDEO**

Learn more about the sun's role in providing energy that cycles through different processes on Earth.

Alternative Sources of Energy

Using renewable energy resources can reduce our dependence on nonrenewables and avoid some of the problems associated with them.

Solar Energy One of the most basic types of solar energy is passive solar power. It involves letting sunlight pass through glass to heat a room or building to maximize its exposure to sunlight and retain that heat. A greenhouse is a good example of passive solar power.

In an active solar power system, sunlight is captured by solar cells, which can power things as small as wristwatches or as large as entire cities. As shown in **Figure 2**, a solar (or photovoltaic) cell converts the energy from sunlight directly into electrical energy. Solar cells are not a new technology, but they are now much more efficient and less expensive than they were years ago.

Though the sunlight is free, the **costs** of the initial investment can be high. Another drawback is the inconsistency of sunlight. More solar energy is available near the equator and in drier climates that do not experience many cloudy days. Additional technology must be used to store the electrical energy for use at night. Finally, not all places on Earth receive the same amount of sunlight throughout the year.

Academic Vocabulary

What are two different meanings of the term *cost*?

....

....

....

....

....

☑ READING CHECK **Summarize** What is the difference between passive solar power and active solar power?

....

....

Model It !

Solar Cells

Figure 2 When sunlight hits it, each solar cell in a panel generates a small amount of electricity.

Develop Models ✏
Trace the path of a negative particle from the top layer to the bottom layer to indicate how electrical energy is generated.

1. Sunlight hits the solar cell, which is made up of two layers separated by a barrier.

2. Energy from the sun excites the material in each layer. One layer ends up with negative particles and the other layer with positive particles.

2. The negative particles are attracted to the positive particles, but the barrier keeps the particles apart. Instead, the negative particles are guided along a path of wiring to the other layer. This creates electrical energy that can be used to power equipment.

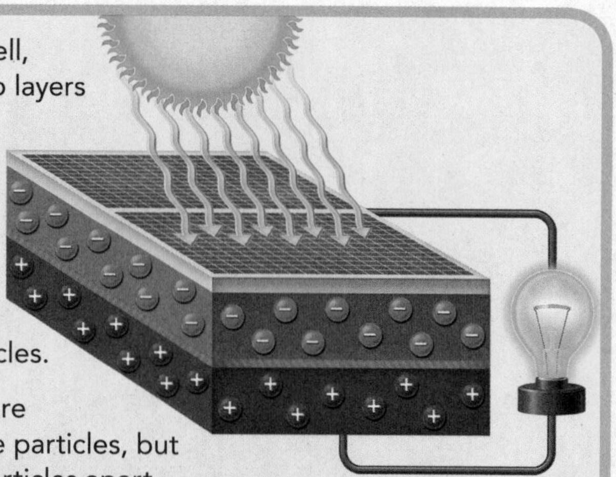

Hydroelectric Resources The sun's energy drives the water cycle, which moves large volumes of water to higher elevations from lower elevations in the form of rain and snow. Gravity pulls water downhill, giving rivers, streams, waterfalls, and tides their movement. Turbines can convert the energy of moving water into electricity.

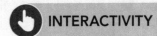

INTERACTIVITY

Learn about renewable resources, their global distributions, and the processes necessary for them to be viable.

Hydroelectric dams restrict the natural flow of a river by controlling how much water passes through turbines, as shown in **Figure 3**. Hydroelectric dams can generate a great deal of power, but they disrupt natural processes such as migrations of fish. Dams also alter habitats by creating reservoirs above the dam and reducing the width and flow of the river below. Most importantly, a dam must be close to a source of moving water.

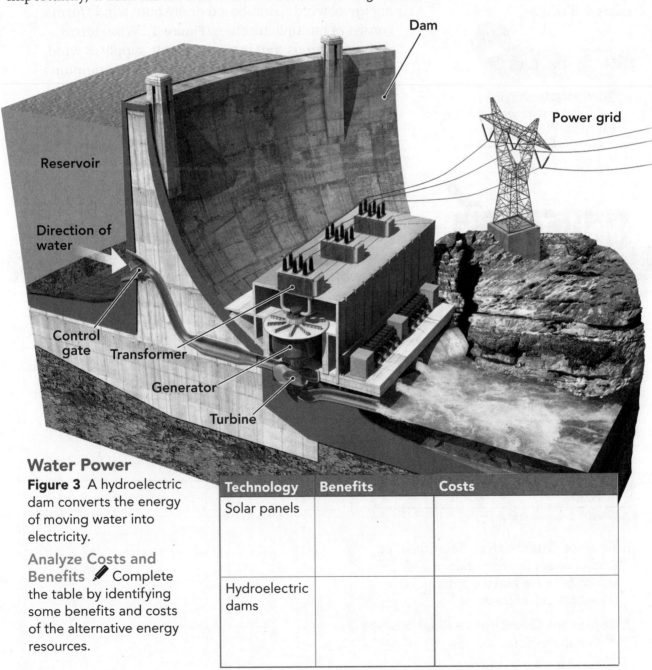

Water Power

Figure 3 A hydroelectric dam converts the energy of moving water into electricity.

Analyze Costs and Benefits ✏ Complete the table by identifying some benefits and costs of the alternative energy resources.

Technology	Benefits	Costs
Solar panels		
Hydroelectric dams		

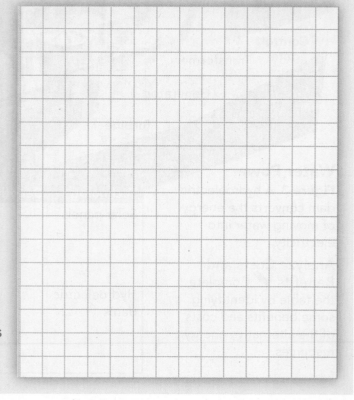

Offshore Wind Farm

Figure 3 Wind is plentiful on the water, but turbines introduce obstacles to both boats and wildlife.

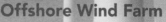

HANDS-ON LAB

Investigate Design, build, and test a model of wind power technology.

Math Toolbox

Wind Power

Wind Energy Like the water cycle, wind is powered by energy from sunlight. An area of Earth's surface warms as sunlight is converted to thermal energy. Warm air rises and expands, allowing cooler, denser air to flow in to fill the void. We know this movement of air masses as wind. Just as turbines can be used to harness the energy in moving water, they can be used to harness the energy of wind. Land-based or offshore wind "farms" consist of multiple turbines (**Figure 3**). Wind farms do best in areas that receive a steady supply of wind. Some farms are found in valleys between mountains that channel and concentrate the wind. Others are found in the ocean, where land and sea breezes provide strong winds. The costs of constructing wind farms are considerable, and some people are concerned that large turbines threaten birds and spoil natural scenery. But wind power is already less expensive than coal power in many parts of the country, and it is the fastest-growing energy source in the world.

The table shows the projected production of industrial wind farms in the U.S. over the coming decades.

Year	Production (gigawatts)
2000	2.5
2010	40.2
2020	113.4
2030	224.1
2040	
2050	404.3

Source: U.S Department of Energy

1. **Analyze Quantitative Relationships** Predict what the production in 2040 should be, based on the pattern. Fill in the empty cell of the table.

2. **Represent Quantitative Relationships** Graph the data.

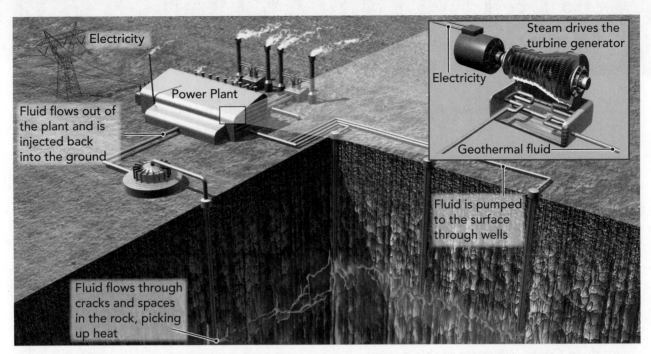

Electricity

Power Plant

Fluid flows out of the plant and is injected back into the ground

Steam drives the turbine generator

Electricity

Geothermal fluid

Fluid is pumped to the surface through wells

Fluid flows through cracks and spaces in the rock, picking up heat

Geothermal Energy

One renewable energy source not originating with the sun is geothermal energy. Deep below Earth's surface, the rock of Earth's crust is hot. In some places on Earth's surface, this heat can be used on a small scale to warm homes. On a larger scale, geothermal energy plants (**Figure 4**) use this heat to generate electricity. One of the biggest drawbacks is that geothermal reservoirs are not easy to find. The site must be located over a geothermal hot spot, where the rock is hot enough to continuously reheat pumped water. The best sites are near volcanic areas. While initial costs to construct the plant and drill the pipes are expensive, the power it can provide in the long run makes up for it.

Bioenergy Resources

Biomass such as wood, grasses, coconut husks, and other plant-based materials have been burned to produce light and heat for thousands of years. These resources are only limited by where they can grow. Scientists have developed ways to turn these resources into biofuels such as ethanol, which is usually made from corn or sugar cane, and biodiesel, which can be made from used cooking oil. Unfortunately, the energy that goes into producing these biofuels is often equal to or greater than the energy they yield. Also, burning biofuels is not much better for the atmosphere than burning fossil fuels.

READING CHECK Summarize In the long run, why might it be less expensive to construct 100 geothermal power plants than to farm the same area for corn to make ethanol?

....

....

....

Geothermal Power Plant

Figure 4 ✎ Draw arrows to indicate the flow of water through the geothermal power plant. Use the information in the text to help you.

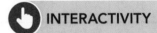 **INTERACTIVITY**

Set up a dairy farm and investigate how much electricity you can generate from biogas.

Literacy Connection

Draw Evidence Underline the text that supports the idea that geothermal energy is a cost-effective solution in the long run.

305

MSS-ESS3-1

1. **Identify** Name five renewable energy resources.

....

....

2. **Cause and Effect** Is wind power a practical source of renewable energy everywhere on Earth? Explain.

....

....

....

3. **Analyze Costs** Which renewable energy source poses problems most similar to those of fossil fuels? Explain.

....

....

....

....

....

4. **Obtain Information** Suppose your state wants to encourage the use of renewable energy resources by investing in a power plant fueled by a renewable energy source. Describe how you would investigate which renewable source would be most suitable for your area.

....

....

....

....

....

....

....

....

....

Quest CHECK-IN

In this lesson, you learned about different renewable energy resources, or renewables, and the costs and benefits of using them.

Construct Arguments What impact might the availability of renewable energy resources, such as water or wind, have on the success of a town?

....

....

....

👆 **INTERACTIVITY**

Renewable Energy

Go online to apply what you have learned about renewable energy to supplying energy to a boomtown.

Micro-Hydro POWER

▶ VIDEO

Examine how hydroelectric power plants and wind farms generate clean energy.

How can people without access to electricity use moving water to generate power? You engineer it!

The Challenge: To generate power from moving water.

Earth's water system is an excellent source of power. Centuries ago, people realized that moving water, properly channeled, can turn wheels that make machinery move. More recently, engineers designed large-scale dams to harness the energy of moving water. Water power's great advantage is that the water is always moving, so electricity can be generated 24 hours a day.

Now engineers have developed hydropower on a small scale, known as micro-hydro power. If there is a small river or stream running through your property, then you need only a few basic things: a turbine, pipes to channel the water to the turbine, and a generator that will transform the energy into electricity.

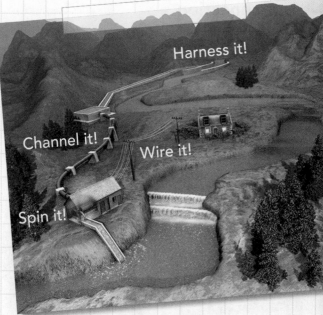

Harness it!

Channel it!

Wire it!

Spin it!

In this micro-hydro system, water from the river is channeled to the generator, which transforms the energy of the moving water into electrical energy.

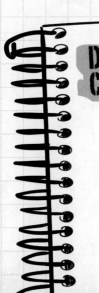

DESIGN CHALLENGE

Can you design a micro-hydro system? Go to the Engineering Design Notebook to find out!

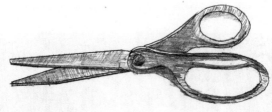

Mineral Resources

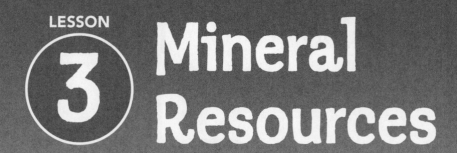

Guiding Questions

- What are mineral resources?
- What factors affect the distribution of minerals on Earth?

Connection

Literacy Determine Meaning

MS-ESS3-1, MS-ESS3-4

Vocabulary

ore
crystallize

Academic Vocabulary

distribution

 VOCABULARY APP

Practice vocabulary on a mobile device.

Quest CONNECTION

Consider how the availability of mineral resources could help a town thrive or cause it to fail.

Connect It !

✎ **Circle some of the objects in the photo that you think contain minerals.**

Construct Explanations How do you think these minerals formed?

....

....

....

Minerals and Ores

You may think that minerals are only found in rocks. It's true that rocks are made from minerals, but if you look around, you will probably see several other things that are made from minerals. Metals are made from one or more minerals. The graphite in a pencil is a type of mineral. Computers, smartphones, and other electronic devices are made with metals and other minerals, too. Even you contain minerals, such as the calcium-bearing minerals that make up your bones and teeth.

But what is a mineral? A mineral is a solid substance that is non-living and made from a particular combination of elements. There are over 5,000 named minerals on Earth. Gold, quartz, and talc are just a few examples. When a mineral deposit is large enough and valuable enough for it to be extracted from the ground, it is known as **ore**. People remove ore from the ground so they can use it or sell it to make money.

HANDS-ON LAB

Investigate Explore the geological processes that form minerals.

Reflect Throughout the day, list some of the things you see and use that are made from minerals. Then, at the end of the day, write a paragraph explaining why minerals are important and describing some of their most important uses.

Stalactite Formation

Figure 1 These stalactites in Carlsbad Caverns National Park in New Mexico formed as minerals deposited by a dripping mineral-rich solution built up over long periods of time.

Determine Meaning

As you read, circle or underline an unknown word in the text and use context clues to help you determine the meaning. Revisit the unknown word at the end of the lesson and use a resource if you still cannot determine the meaning.

How Minerals Form
Minerals form in different ways. They can form from organic materials, from mineral-rich solutions, and from cooling magma and lava.

Organic Material Corals like the ones in **Figure 2** create a hard outer skeleton that provides the coral with shape and protection. This skeleton is made from thin layers of calcium carbonate (also called calcite), a chemical compound similar to the shells of other sea animals. Once the coral is dead, the calcium carbonate skeleton is left behind. It may get buried and broken down into smaller fragments.

Minerals from Living Things
Figure 2 These corals produce a hard outer skeleton made from the mineral calcite. The skeleton will be around for a long time after the coral dies.

Apply Concepts Why wouldn't other body parts of living things, such as skin, become minerals after an organism's death?

....

....

Solutions When water contains dissolved substances it is called a solution. In some cases, the elements in these solutions will **crystallize** to form a new mineral. This can happen within bodies of water and underground. One way this happens on Earth's surface involves the process of evaporation. When the water evaporates, the elements and compounds that are left behind crystallize into new minerals such as salts. This is how the mineral formations in **Figure 3** formed.

Another way that minerals form from solutions is through a process in which a warm solution flows through a crack in existing rock. Elements and compounds leave the solution as it cools and crystallize as minerals in the crack. These form veins of ores that are different from the surrounding rock.

Magma and Lava The molten and semi-molten rock mixture found beneath Earth's surface is known as magma. In its molten, or melted state, magma is very hot. But when it cools, it hardens into solid rock. This rock is made from crystallized minerals. It may form beneath Earth's surface or above Earth's surface when magma (which is known as lava when it breaks the surface) erupts from the ground and then cools and hardens as is shown in **Figure 4.**

The types of minerals that form from magma and lava vary based on the materials and gases in the magma, as well as the rate at which it cools.

☑ READING CHECK **Analyze Text Structure** Examine the way the text on these two pages has been organized. Describe how the author has organized the text so that it supports the reader's comprehension.

....

....

....

....

....

....

Minerals from Solutions
Figure 3 These mineral deposits in Mammoth Hot Springs in Yellowstone National Park formed from a solution.

Make Observations ✏ Draw an X on the solution the minerals formed from. Circle some of the mineral deposits.

Minerals from Magma
Figure 4 As this lava cools, it will harden and crystallize into minerals.

Cause and Effect Where would you expect to find minerals that have formed in this way?

....

....

....

311

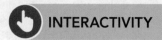

INTERACTIVITY

Find out more about mineral resources and their distributions.

VIDEO

Learn why some minerals are only found in certain places.

Academic Vocabulary

Explain what *distributed* means and give one or two examples of something that is distributed.

....

....

....

....

....

Distribution of Minerals

The distribution of mineral resources on Earth depends on how and when the minerals form. Common minerals, such as the ones that make up most of the rocks in Earth's crust, are found roughly evenly distributed around the planet. Other minerals are rare because they only form as a result of tremendous heat and pressure near volcanic systems. Therefore, these minerals will only be found near subduction zones or other regions associated with volcanic activity. Other minerals may form from evaporation in the ocean or on land, such as in basins called playas. The map in **Figure 5** shows how some minerals are **distributed** around the world.

Gold, for example, is a heavy metal that formed, along with all other atoms other than hydrogen and helium, from stars that went supernova preceding the formation of our solar system. Gold is rare at the surface because most of it sank into the core when the early Earth was molten. Gold gets concentrated when hot fluids pass through the crust and pick up the gold, which doesn't fit well in the crystals of most rocks.

☑ READING CHECK **Determine Meaning** Locate the term concentrated in the second paragraph. Using context clues, what do you think this word means? Explain your thinking.

....

....

....

....

Question It!

Minerals for Dinner?

Minerals are used in many ways in our everyday lives. We even need minerals in our diets to stay healthy. Humans need minerals that contain calcium, potassium, and magnesium to grow, fight illness, and carry out everyday functions.

Apply Scientific Reasoning
Write two or three questions you would like to have answered about the importance of minerals in your diet.

....

....

....

....

....

....

....

....

....

....

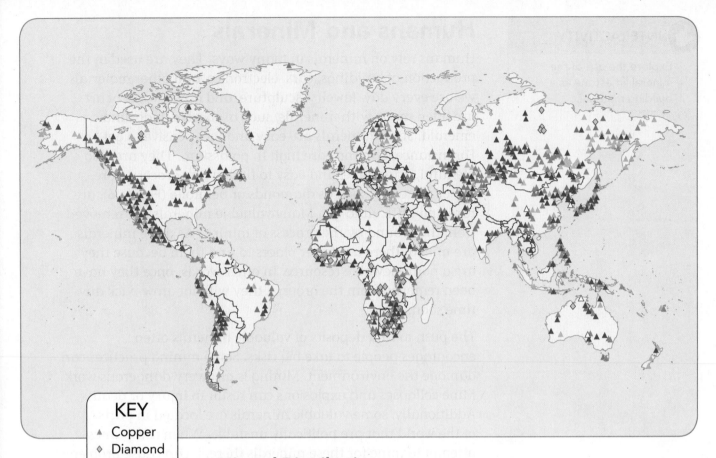

KEY
- ▲ Copper
- ◇ Diamond
- ▲ Gold
- ▲ Iron
- ▲ Lead-Zinc
- ▲ Silver
- △ Uranium

Mineral Distribution

Figure 5 Minerals are distributed unevenly on Earth.

1. **Use Models** ✏ Circle a region on the map that is likely to be rich in silver.

2. **Patterns** Suppose you were to draw the boundaries of tectonic plates and locations of volcanic activity on the map. What patterns would you notice among plate boundaries, volcanic activity, and the distribution of different mineral resources? Explain.

....

....

....

....

....

....

....

....

....

....

....

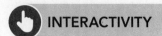

INTERACTIVITY

Explore the use of the mineral limestone as a building material.

Humans and Minerals

Humans rely on minerals in many ways. They are used in the production of buildings, cars, electronics, and other materials we use every day. Jewelry, sculpture, and other works of art are often made with minerals, such as marble, jade, and emerald. Some minerals are easy and inexpensive to get. For instance, bananas are high in potassium. They are also plentiful, affordable, and easy to find in any grocery store. Other minerals, such as diamonds or benitoite (**Figure 6**), are rare and difficult to get. Many valuable minerals are removed from the ground by the process of mining. As more minerals are mined, there are fewer places to find them because they are a nonrenewable resource. In other words, once they have been removed from the ground, they will not grow back any time soon.

The push to find deposits of valuable minerals often encourages people to take big risks. Some mining practices can damage the environment. Mining is also very dangerous work. Mine collapses and explosions can result in injury or death. Additionally, some valuable minerals are located in parts of the world that are politically unstable. When companies attempt to mine for these minerals there, it can cause problems and danger for everyone involved.

✓ **READING CHECK** **Summarize Text** How do humans rely on minerals?

....

....

....

Rare Mineral

Figure 6 Benitoite is a very rare blue mineral that forms as a result of hydrothermal processes in Earth's crust. It has been discovered in a few locations on Earth. But gemstone-quality benitoite can be found in only one place in California.

Connect to Society

Do you think a benitoite ring would be costly or inexpensive? Explain your reasoning.

....

....

....

....

....

....

☑LESSON 3 Check

MS-ESS3-1

1. **Define** What are minerals? List examples.

....

....

....

....

2. **Distinguish Relationships** Explain the relationship between minerals and ores.

....

....

....

....

....

3. **Cause and Effect** What causes minerals to be unevenly distributed on Earth?

....

....

....

....

....

4. **Identify Patterns** 🖊 Use drawings to show one of the ways that minerals can form.

Quest CHECK-IN

In this lesson, you learned why minerals are important resources and about how they form. You also learned that the different ways that minerals form leads to uneven distribution of different types of minerals around the world.

Evaluate Data Why should you consider mineral resources when trying to determine whether a town will boom or become a ghost town?

....

....

....

....

....

👆 **INTERACTIVITY**

Surviving on Minerals

Go online to find out more about how some mineral resources in the United States are distributed. Then, apply this information to your analysis of the town you are researching.

Phosphorus Fiasco

Without phosphorus, living things would not exist on Earth. All animals and plants need phosphorus to produce the energy that keeps them alive. Unfortunately, like all minerals, phosphorus is not a renewable resource. Only a certain amount exists in nature, where it moves in a natural cycle. In recent years, however, that cycle has been broken, and we run the risk of using up Earth's supply of phosphorus.

In the phosphorus cycle, animals and people eat phosphorus-rich plants. The excess phosphorus leaves the bodies of organisms as waste. The waste returns to the soil to enrich the plants, starting the cycle again.

Phosphorus mining has altered the natural phosphorus cycle.

For many centuries, farmers used manure, which is rich in phosphorus, to fertilize their crops. About 175 years ago, as the population grew, farmers looked for new sources of fertilizer to keep up with the demand for food. Engineers and geologists realized that phosphorus might be mined from underground and used to manufacture fertilizers. Most of the world's phosphorus reserves are in the United States, China, Russia, and northern Africa.

The "phosphorus fiasco" is a result of improved technology that has interrupted the natural phosphorus cycle. Because most human waste now ends up in sewer and water treatment systems, phosphorus ends up in the ocean. More manufactured fertilizer is used to fertilize plants and crops. We still get our required phosphorus, but we are using up the natural supply in the process.

World Phosphate Mine Production and Reserves			
Country	Mine Production (tons)		Reserves
	2015	2016	
China	120,000	138,000	3,100,000
Jordan	8,340	8,300	1,200,000
Morocco/Western Sahara	29,000	30,000	50,000,000
Russia	11,600	11,600	1,300,000
United States	27,400	27,800	1,100,000

Source: U.S. Geological Survey, 2017

Use the text and the data table to answer the following questions.

1. Calculate Which country saw the greatest increase in phosphorus production between 2015 and 2016? Describe the amount of the increase as a fraction or percentage.

2. Analyze Costs How have technological developments affected the natural phosphorus cycle? What do you think can be done to address this problem?

3. Evaluate Change Based on its current rate of production, in how many years will the United States use up its known reserves of phosphate?

4. Construct Explanations Morocco/Western Sahara has by far the greatest reserves of phosphorus, but it is not the largest producer. Why do you think this is the case? Do you think the situation might change? Explain.

(4) Water Resources

Guiding Questions

- How do geological processes affect the distribution of groundwater on Earth?
- How is water used as a resource?

Connections

| Literacy | Support Author's Claim |

| Math | Draw Comparative Inferences |

MS-ESS3-1, MS-ESS3-4

Vocabulary

desalination

Academic Vocabulary

component
obtain

 VOCABULARY APP

Practice vocabulary on a mobile device.

Quest CONNECTION

Think about how the availability of water resources would affect whether a town will boom or bust.

Connect It!

✏️ **The drop of water on Earth represents all the water on the planet. Draw a circle inside the drop of water to represent the amount of freshwater you think exists on Earth.**

Apply Scientific Reasoning How does water's role in Earth systems make it an important natural resource?

....

....

....

Water on Earth

Although Earth is known as the water planet, the water that living things rely on represents only a fraction of the planet's total water supply **(Figure 1)**. Most water on Earth is salt water. Freshwater is only found on the surface of our planet as surface ice or water, or within Earth's crust as groundwater.

Water is a limited resource, which means there is a finite amount of it on Earth. In addition, it is not evenly distributed around the planet as a result of meteorological and geological forces. The water cycle circulates water through Earth's ocean and other bodies of water, on and below its surface, and in the atmosphere. A tiny amount of the freshwater on Earth is in the atmosphere, and a fair amount of water is contained underground as groundwater. But most freshwater is locked up as ice at the poles and in glaciers. A very small amount of the water on the surface of the planet is immediately available for human use in lakes and rivers.

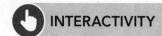

INTERACTIVITY

Predict how much water on Earth is drinkable.

Reflect How is water used in your local environment? In your science notebook, describe some ways your local environment would be affected if there were suddenly less water available.

A Drop to Drink

Figure 1 If all of the water on Earth were collected, it would form a sphere about 1,380 kilometers (860 miles) across.

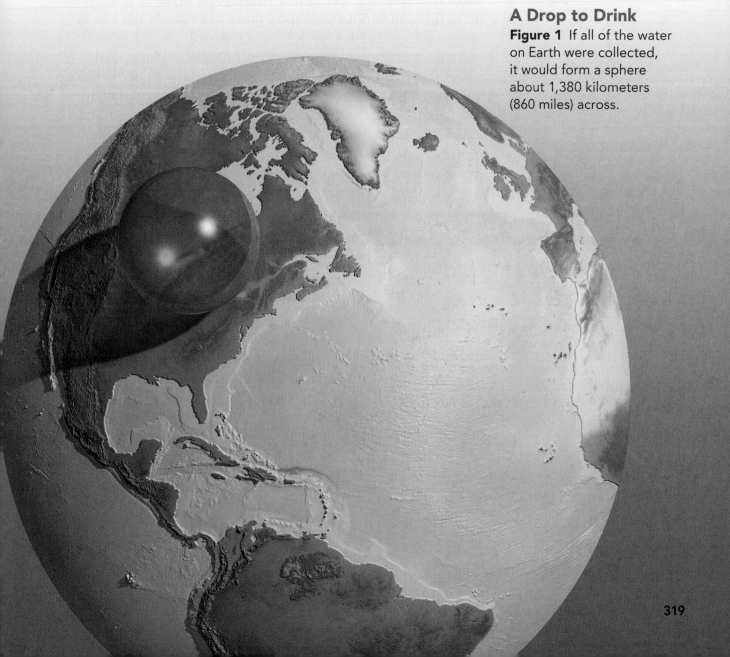

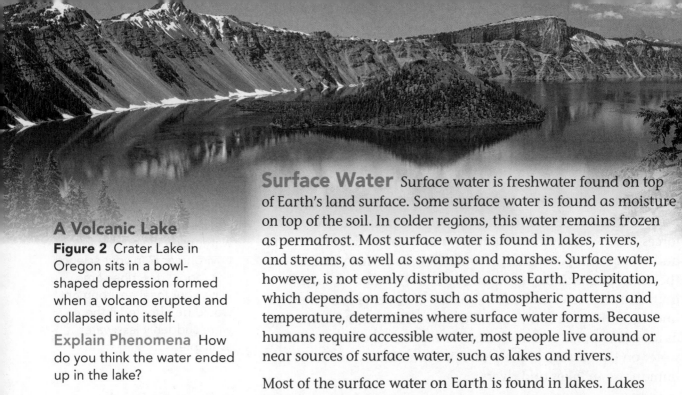

A Volcanic Lake

Figure 2 Crater Lake in Oregon sits in a bowl-shaped depression formed when a volcano erupted and collapsed into itself.

Explain Phenomena How do you think the water ended up in the lake?

....

....

....

....

Surface Water

Surface water is freshwater found on top of Earth's land surface. Some surface water is found as moisture on top of the soil. In colder regions, this water remains frozen as permafrost. Most surface water is found in lakes, rivers, and streams, as well as swamps and marshes. Surface water, however, is not evenly distributed across Earth. Precipitation, which depends on factors such as atmospheric patterns and temperature, determines where surface water forms. Because humans require accessible water, most people live around or near sources of surface water, such as lakes and rivers.

Most of the surface water on Earth is found in lakes. Lakes form through various geological processes when water fills in depressions in Earth's surface, as in **Figure 2.** These can occur as a result of erosion, the movement of tectonic plates, and retreating glaciers. Some lakes form when a river's path erodes away an area or a dam blocks a river's flow. All rivers begin as a small flow of water caused by gravity. Runoff from rain or melting ice collects and flows downhill following the least resistant path. These small flows of water form streams, which combine and grow to form larger rivers and river systems.

Math Toolbox

Distribution of Water Resources

While most of the planet is covered in water, only a small amount of it is available to humans for cooking, drinking, and bathing.

1. **Calculate** Use the data in the graphs to complete the missing values.

2. **Draw Comparative Inferences** About how much more accessible surface freshwater is found in lakes than in the atmosphere as water vapor?

....

....

....

....

....

Distribution of the World's Water

All Water

Oceans 97%   Freshwater %

Freshwater

Ice caps and glaciers 79%   Groundwater %

Accessible surface water 1%

Accessible Surface Water

Lakes %   Soil moisture 38%   Water vapor 8%

Water within living organisms 1%

Rivers 1%

Groundwater As with surface water, groundwater is not evenly distributed across Earth **(Figure 3)**. The presence of groundwater depends on the type of rock layers in Earth's crust. Groundwater forms when gravity causes water from precipitation and runoff to seep into the ground and fill the empty spaces between these rocks. Some rocks are more porous, or have more empty spaces in which water can collect. Once water reaches a dense layer of bedrock that is not porous, it will spread out horizontally. The volume of porous rock that can contain groundwater is called an aquifer. Wells are drilled into aquifers to access the water.

Deep groundwater reservoirs can take hundreds or thousands of years to accumulate, especially in arid regions where there is little rainfall or surface water to supply the aquifer. New studies of Earth's mantle reveal there may be many oceans' worth of water locked hundreds of kilometers below the surface in mineral formations. This groundwater may take millions of years to exchange with surface water through the movement of tectonic plates and mantle convection.

☑ READING CHECK **Summarize** How does the type of rock in Earth's crust affect the distribution of groundwater?

....

....

....

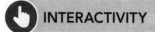

INTERACTIVITY

Explore how groundwater is distributed around Earth.

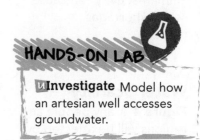

HANDS-ON LAB

🔲 **Investigate** Model how an artesian well accesses groundwater.

Distribution of Groundwater

Figure 3 Groundwater is especially important in areas that do not have immediate access to rivers or lakes for sources of freshwater.

Use Models ✏ Indicate the areas on the map with the greatest groundwater resources with a circle. Indicate the areas with the least groundwater resources with an X.

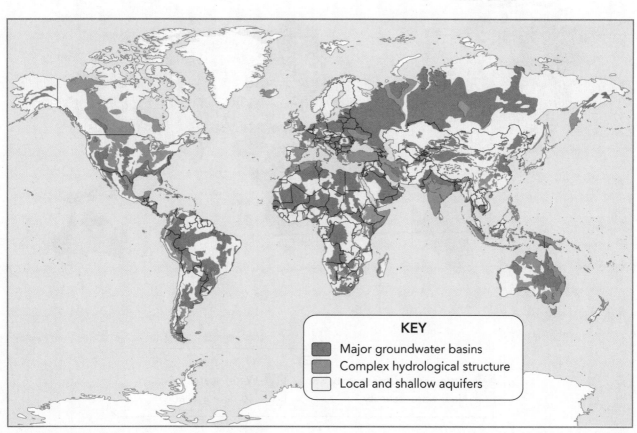

KEY
- ■ Major groundwater basins
- ▨ Complex hydrological structure
- □ Local and shallow aquifers

Water Scarcity

Figure 4 Many people and regions will be affected by water scarcity in the future.

Cause and Effect How might water scarcity affect economic development in an area?

....

....

....

Human Impacts

Humans rely on water not only to live and grow, but also for agriculture and industry. Water is needed to produce our food, manufacture products, and carry out many chemical reactions. The distribution of water resources is a result of past and current geologic processes such as the water cycle, plate tectonics, and the formation of rock. These processes take time, and in some areas humans are depleting water resources faster than they can be replenished. The human impact on water distribution is already a cause of social and economic conflict in some areas.

Using Water Humans use surface water, which often involves changing its natural path, such as with dams. This affects the amount of water that continues to flow and the ecology of the area. Humans access groundwater resources by digging wells in aquifers. But if more water is removed from an aquifer or other groundwater source than is replenished through the water cycle, water shortages can occur. As with surface water, pollution can enter groundwater supplies and impact the quality of the water. Study the effects of water scarcity in **Figure 4.**

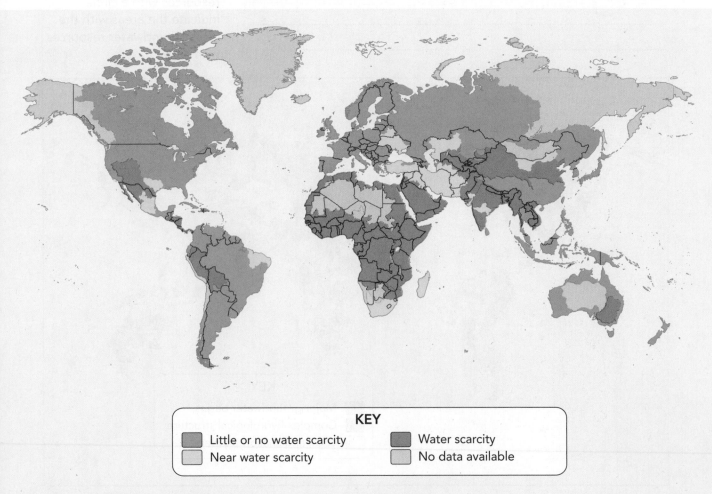

KEY

☐ Little or no water scarcity	☐ Water scarcity
☐ Near water scarcity	☐ No data available

Using Ocean Resources
Figure 5 If too many of these fish are caught, then fewer will survive to produce new generations.

Desalination In the future, humans may look to technology and the ocean to meet their water needs. The process of **desalination** removes salt and minerals from saltwater to make freshwater. Today, desalination plants around the world are costly and require a lot of energy to distill saltwater. We may eventually use solar energy to convert ocean water into freshwater.

Other Water Resources Humans rely on the ocean to provide a number of other important resources besides water, such as sea organisms for food and other products **(Figure 5)**. The ocean also provides salt, minerals, and fuels.

Living resources like fish are replenished through a natural cycle. However, overfishing can result in severe reductions or complete collapses of ocean ecosystems and the resources they provide. In addition, pollution and global climate change can have serious impacts on the living resources we rely on from the ocean.

INTERACTIVITY

Examine the factors that affect water availability on Earth.

READING CHECK

Identify What are some other ocean resources humans use besides water?

....

....

....

....

....

....

Design It

Sustainable Fishing

Fish populations are replenished only if sufficient numbers are allowed to live and reproduce in their ecosystems.

Design Your Solution ✏
Develop a design for a sustainable fishing net. Your net should function to allow only some fish to be caught, leaving others to replenish populations each year. Sketch your design in the space provided and label your sketch to explain how the net allows for sustainable fishing.

MS-ESS3-1, MS-ESS3-4

1. Identify What are the different sources of freshwater on Earth?

....

....

....

2. Construct Explanations What factors account for the uneven distribution of ground-water on Earth?

....

....

....

....

3. Infer Are humans more likely to use surface water or groundwater as a freshwater source? Explain your answer.

....

....

....

....

....

4. Cause and Effect Explain why some regions are more extremely affected by water scarcity than others.

....

....

....

....

....

....

....

5. Connect to Society In what way does water scarcity harm the economic development of an area?

....

....

....

....

....

Quest CHECK-IN

In this lesson, you learned how water is distributed on Earth and what effects geologic processes have on water resources. You also discovered how human activities are affected by water availability and limit its distribution.

Evaluate Why is it important to consider how water is distributed when considering the availability of resources in a new town?

....

....

....

....

☞ INTERACTIVITY

Surviving on Water

Go online to use what you have learned about water resources and relate it to the available resources for a ghost town.

The Pseudoscience of Water Dowsing

It's the early 1800s and you're moving westward across America. When you arrive at your land, you see that there's no nearby river or lake. As you look out, you wonder how to decide where to dig the well that will provide your freshwater. This is where someone known as a water dowser comes in.

Water dowsers claim to be able to use a simple tool to locate underground water. The two arms of a Y-shaped stick are held in the hands, with the end of the stick pointing upward. As the dowser walks around the property, he keeps an eye on the stick. When the stick pulls toward the ground, he claims that water is somewhere below.

Dowsers still work today, usually in areas where there are no easily accessible sources of groundwater. Some people believe the dowsing stick responds to the presence of water. Scientifically, though, the explanation is much simpler. In many places, groundwater is abundant enough that, in a temperate climate, you have an excellent chance of striking water no matter where you dig a well.

Geologists searching for underground water use much sounder methods. In a desert, for example, growing plants indicate there might be water present. Technology like sonar can also reveal if water lies below the ground.

CONNECT TO YOU

Do you think it's important for people to understand the difference between science and pseudoscience? Why? Discuss your ideas with a partner.

☑TOPIC 6 Review and Assess

1 Nonrenewable Energy Resources

1. Which of the following is considered a nonrenewable resource?
   - A. sunlight
   - B. wood
   - C. water
   - D. natural gas *(circled)*

2. Which of the following is *not* an effect of our growing population's use of fossil fuels?
   - A. The distribution of these resources is changing.
   - B. The amount of carbon dioxide in the atmosphere is increasing.
   - C. The resources are now being replaced faster than they are being used. *(circled)*
   - D. Political conflicts occur over control of these resources.

3. Which of the following is directly involved in transforming the remains of organisms into fossil fuels?
   - A. pressure *(circled)*
   - B. wind
   - C. sunlight
   - D. precipitation

4. Fossil fuels are .... resources that are .... distributed on Earth.

5. **Construct Arguments** Why are coal and petroleum resources not commonly found across the planet?

   ....

   ....

   ....

   ....

   ....

   ....

   ....

   ....

2 Renewable Energy Resources

MS-ESS3-1, MS-ESS3-4

6. Which of the following renewable energy resources comes from underground?
   - A. geothermal energy *(circled)*
   - B. hydropower
   - C. wind power
   - D. solar power

7. Which of the following is a drawback of biofuels such as ethanol?
   - A. The energy ethanol can provide is about the same as the energy required to make it. *(circled)*
   - B. It is much more expensive than gasoline.
   - C. There are few places where plants used to make ethanol can be grown.
   - D. When it is burned, ethanol produces even more emissions than coal.

8. **Apply Concepts** What areas on Earth are worst suited for using solar energy to generate electricity?

   ....

   ....

   ....

9. **Develop Models** ✏ Draw a diagram that shows how the sun is responsible for the production of wind energy.

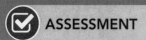
3 Mineral Resources

MS-ESS3-1, MS-ESS3-4

10. Which of the following is an essential
characteristic of a mineral?
A. crystal structure
B. artificially manufactured
C. liquid
D. formed from organic processes

11. Which of the following statements about
minerals and ores is true?
A. Minerals are deposits of valuable ores.
B. Minerals are products that are made
from ores.
C. Minerals form from solutions, but ores
form from volcanoes.
D. All ores are minerals, but not all minerals
are ores.

12. Many minerals are formed from ....
as water ....

13. Construct Explanations Gold is a
valuable mineral that is found underground.
It is brought closer to the surface, where it
can be mined, by volcanic activity. Why do
you think gold is not evenly distributed on
Earth?

....

....

....

....

....

....

....

....

....

4 Water Resources

MS-ESS3-1, MS-ESS3-4

14. The most abundant water resource on
Earth is
A. salt water   B. fresh water
C. groundwater   D. surface water

15. Most fresh water on Earth is
A. in the atmosphere as water vapor.
B. found on the surface in lakes and rivers.
C. locked up in ice.
D. located underground.

16. Factors such as precipitation, ...
and surface features determine where
surface water can form on Earth.

17. Construct Arguments How could
groundwater sources become depleted if
water is constantly being cycled?

....

....

....

....

....

18. Draw Conclusions Why is the distribution
of water resources a concern for the
economic and social welfare of people
around the world?

....

....

....

....

....

....

....

MS-ESS3-1

Evidence-Based Assessment

Van is researching information about the mineral copper and its distribution on Earth. Copper is used in electrical systems and even found in very small amounts in living things. Here is some of the other information Van finds, along with two maps that he finds during his research:

- copper ore can form from different geological processes

- one type of copper, called porphyry copper, is found in large deposits in certain types of rock

- most porphyry copper deposits are 340 million years old or younger

- porphyry copper forms at relatively shallow depths of about 4,500 to 9,000 meters (15,000 to 30,000 feet) in Earth's crust

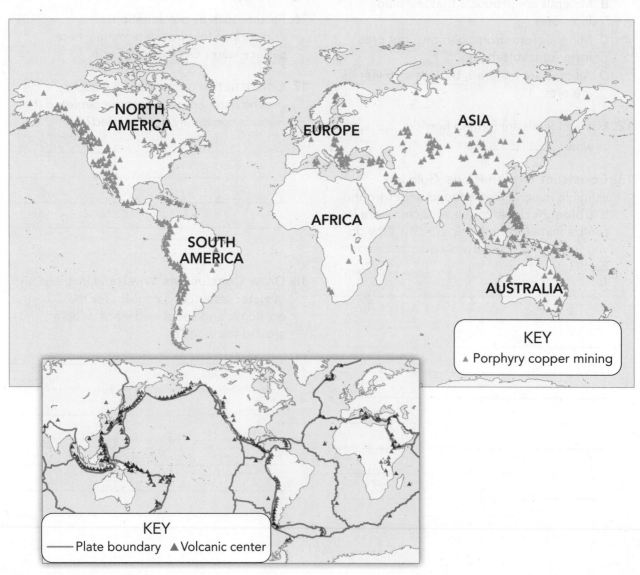

KEY
▲ Porphyry copper mining

KEY
—— Plate boundary ▲ Volcanic center

1. **Analyze Data** Which of these regions seems to have the greatest concentration of porphyry copper mining?
   A. Africa **B.** Australia
   C. Europe **D.** South America

2. **Cause and Effect** Why are there so many volcanoes around the Pacific Ocean? Support your answer with evidence from the volcanic activity map.

   ....

   ....

   ....

   ....

   ....

   ....

   ....

   ....

   ....

   ....

   ....

   ....

   ....

   ....

3. **Patterns** Based on the map of porphyry copper mining, which of the following statements about the distribution of copper is correct? Select all that apply.
   - [ ] Porphyry copper is distributed relatively evenly across most of the continents.
   - [ ] Very little porphyry copper is found in Africa.
   - [ ] A concentration of porphyry copper runs from Europe eastward through Asia and then south into Australia.
   - [ ] Porphyry copper is widely distributed across South America.
   - [ ] A majority of porphyry copper is found on continents that border the Pacific Ocean.
   - [ ] There are fewer sources of porphyry copper in North America than in Asia.

4. **Construct Explanations** Use evidence from the maps to explain why porphyry copper is generally found near areas where volcanic activity, often associated with plate collisions, has occurred in the past.

   ....

   ....

   ....

   ....

   ....

   ....

   ....

   ....

   ....

   ....

Quest FINDINGS

Complete the Quest!

Phenomenon Choose one of the boomtowns you studied and develop a travel brochure to describe what the town was like when it was settled and what it is like now.

Cause and Effect In what ways can proximity to a valuable natural resource affect the success of a town or city?

....

....

....

....

....

....

👆 **INTERACTIVITY**

Reflect on Boomtowns

To Drill or Not to Drill

How can you **use a model** to confirm the location of a **petroleum** deposit?

Background

Phenomenon An energy company wants to drill for oil on the outskirts of a small town. The owners of the energy company have provided evidence that the town is located near an area that was a large sea millions of years ago. Based on that evidence, they believe there is a large deposit of petroleum under the town. Town officials have hired you as an expert to look for evidence of oil under the town.

In this investigation, you will develop a model that you can use to predict whether or not the company will locate any oil below the town.

Materials

(per group)

- aquarium gravel
- glass baking dish
- wax crayons or candles
- plastic knife
- small weight or heavy book
- hot plate

Safety

Be sure to follow all safety guidelines provided by your teacher. The Safety Appendix of your textbook provides more details about the safety icons.

Develop Your Model

☐ 1. Using the available materials, your group must develop a model that meets the following criteria:

- It must show how oil forms from ancient marine plants.
- It must demonstrate the geological forces involved in the formation of oil.
- It must indicate whether or not oil can form below the town.

☐ 2. Work with your group to develop ideas for a model that meets the criteria. Consider the following questions as you develop and design your model:

- What materials can you use to represent the buried organic material that eventually forms oil?
- How can your model demonstrate the geological forces that form oil?
- What observations will you make?

☐ 3. After agreeing on a plan, write out the steps that your group will follow to develop and use the model. Include a sketch of the model that labels the materials you will be using and what they represent.

☐ 4. After getting your teacher's approval, construct your model and use it to demonstrate how oil forms. Record your observations and data in the space provided.

Plan and Sketch

Observations

_____
_____
_____
_____
_____
_____
_____
_____
_____
_____
_____
_____
_____
_____
_____
_____

Analyze and Interpret Data

1. **Use Models** Use your model to explain why oil is a nonrenewable resource.

....

....

....

....

2. **Cause and Effect** What geological forces are involved in the formation of oil? How did you incorporate these forces into your model?

....

....

....

....

....

3. **Construct Explanations** Explain whether or not oil will be found under the town. Use evidence from your model to support your explanation.

....

....

....

....

....

....

4. **Identify Limitations** In what ways is your model not reflective of the actual conditions that lead to the formation of oil? How could your group improve the model?

....

....

....

....

....

....

NGSS PERFORMANCE EXPECTATIONS

MS-ESS3-4 Construct an argument supported by evidence for how increases in human population and per-capita consumption of natural resources impact Earth's systems.

HANDS-ON LAB

uConnect Explore ways that you can reduce the pollution you create.

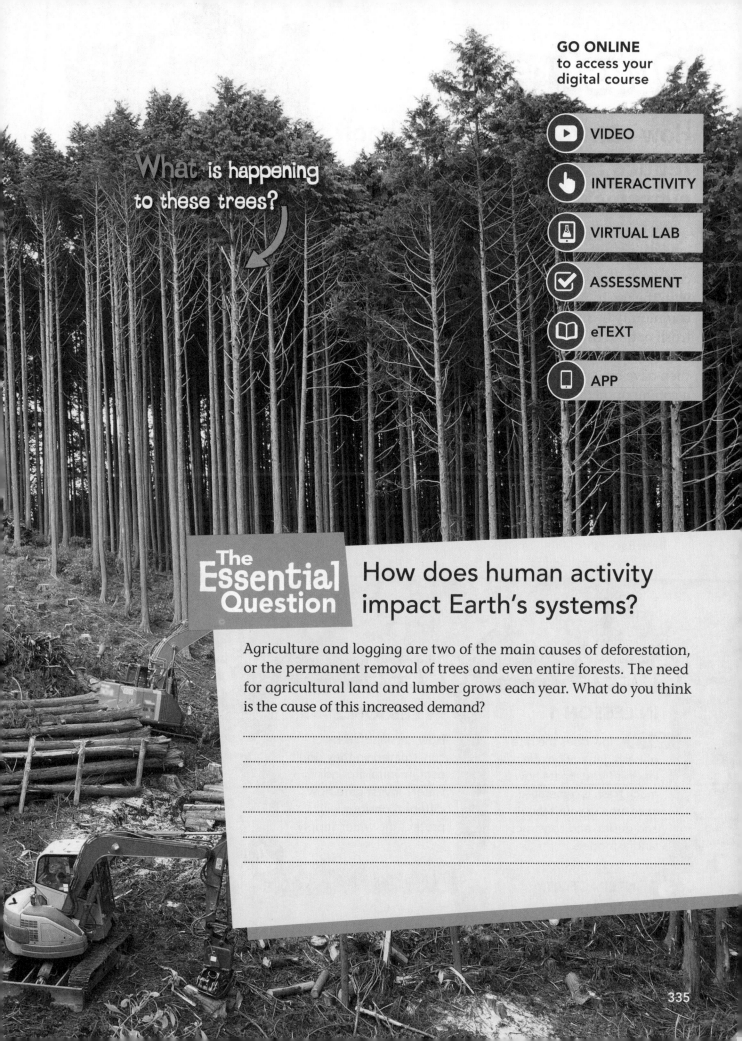

What is happening to these trees?

GO ONLINE
to access your
digital course

▶ VIDEO

👆 INTERACTIVITY

⚗ VIRTUAL LAB

☑ ASSESSMENT

📖 eTEXT

📱 APP

The Essential Question

How does human activity impact Earth's systems?

Agriculture and logging are two of the main causes of deforestation, or the permanent removal of trees and even entire forests. The need for agricultural land and lumber grows each year. What do you think is the cause of this increased demand?

....

....

....

....

....

....

How can you help your school reduce its impact on Earth's systems?

After watching the Quest Kickoff video, which explores the plastic items that end up in the ocean, think about the trash you generate. How can you reduce, recycle, or reuse your trash?

STEM **Phenomenon** The landfill used by your community is running out of space. The community must expand it or find other ways to deal with the trash. Your principal has decided to help the community by finding ways to reduce the school's trash output. In this problem-based Quest activity, you will evaluate the trash output at your school. You will then develop a plan to decrease that output through a combination of reducing, reusing, and recycling. As you work, you should anticipate objections to your plan. Finally, you will present your plan and work to implement it at your school.

Reduce:

....

....

Recycle:

....

....

Reuse:

....

....

 INTERACTIVITY

Trash Backlash

MS-ESS3-4 Construct an argument supported by evidence for how increases in human population and per-capita consumption of natural resources impact Earth's systems.

Quest CHECK-IN

IN LESSON 1

STEM How does the rate of trash generation affect landfills? Investigate how much trash is generated in an area of your school, and design and construct landfill models.

 INTERACTIVITY

More Trash, Less Space

Quest CHECK-IN

IN LESSON 2

How can landfills be constructed so they don't contaminate ground-water? Investigate how different designs will protect the water supply.

HANDS-ON LAB

Trash vs. Water

Quest CHECK-IN

IN LESSON 3

How is a landfill site chosen, and what laws regulate landfill use? Explore the stages of a landfill's life, and conduct research about laws that affect landfills.

INTERACTIVITY

Life of a Landfill

According to the U.S. Environmental Protection Agency, Americans recycled only about 35 percent of their waste in 2014. Much of the rest of the waste ended up in landfills such as this one.

Quest CHECK-IN

IN LESSON 4

How can everyone contribute to reducing waste at your school? Develop a plan to reduce trash output in at least one area of your school.

HANDS-ON LAB

Reducing Waste

Quest FINDINGS

Complete the Quest!

Refine and present your plan to reduce trash output at your school.

INTERACTIVITY

Reflect on Trash Backlash

Population Growth and Resource Consumption

Guiding Questions

- How has the human population changed over time?
- How is the consumption of natural resources by humans affected by changes in population size?

Connections

Literacy Determine Conclusions

Math Draw Comparative Inferences

MS-ESS3-4

Vocabulary

birth rate
death rate
exponential
 growth
pollution
overpopulation
conservation
sustainable use

Academic Vocabulary

estimate
constraints

 VOCABULARY APP

Practice vocabulary on a mobile device.

Quest CONNECTION

Think about how many people are in your school and how many resources, such as food, water, and other materials, each person uses every day.

Connect It!

✏️ **Draw a line to indicate where you think the city limits of Los Angeles were about 100 years ago.**

Apply Scientific Reasoning How do you think the amount of resources used by the human population of Los Angeles has changed in the past 100 years?

....

....

....

The Human Population

There are more humans living on Earth today than any time in our history. Human populations have fluctuated in the past, mostly due to environmental or climate conditions. Around 60,000 years ago, the human population was generally stable at around 600,000 individuals. A warming climate and improvements in hunting and fishing techniques resulted in a rapid increase to about 6 million humans over a few thousand years.

This population remained fairly constant until about 10,000 years ago, when agriculture and livestock breeding gave rise to steady, long-term population growth. This growth dropped occasionally during war, epidemics, or invasions, but maintained a steady climb until the 1700s. Since then, unprecedented population growth has occurred, with the human population reaching 1 billion by the early 1800s. In the last 300 years, the world population has increased tenfold. As of 2017, there were 7.5 billion people on Earth.

HANDS-ON LAB

Explore how food becomes a limiting factor when population size increases.

Reflect How has the population of your community changed in your lifetime? In your science notebook, describe some ways your community would be affected if the population were to suddenly increase or decrease.

Growth of a City

Figure 1 A little over 4 million people call the city of Los Angeles home. The population has grown a great deal since the first Native American tribes settled there thousands of years ago.

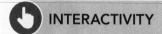
Academic Vocabulary

What other kinds of information might scientists need to estimate?

....

....

....

....

....

Population Changes

Population growth, whether in a town, a country, or the world, is determined by calculating the number of individuals who are born, die, or move into or out of an area. The number of births per 1,000 individuals for a certain time period is called the **birth rate**. On the other hand, the number of deaths per 1,000 individuals for a certain time period is called the **death rate**. When the rates of births and people moving into an area are greater than the rates of deaths and people moving out of an area, the population increases. Otherwise, the population decreases. In 2016, scientists **estimate** there were 280 births and 109 deaths every minute.

In early human history, birth rates and death rates were fairly balanced, which resulted in little change in the size of the human population. For most of human history, birth rates were only slightly higher than death rates, resulting in a slow, steady increase in population.

The graph in **Figure 2** shows human population growth beginning in 1750, around the start of the Industrial Revolution. Human population grew rapidly after the Industrial Revolution because the death rate began to decline. Advances in technology resulted in new farming and transportation methods that increased the availability of resources, such as food and clean water. Improvements in public health and general living standards also played a role in decreasing the death rate.

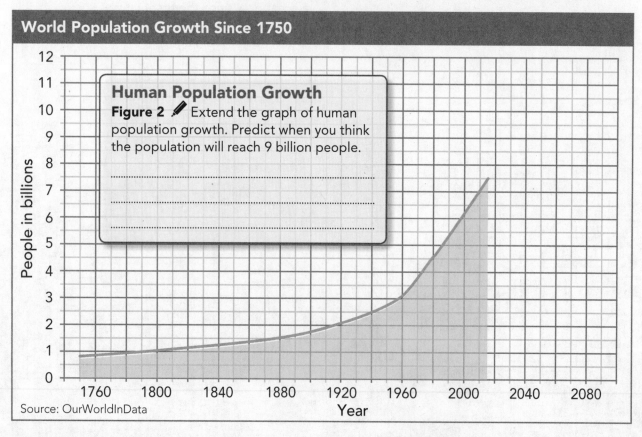

World Population Growth Since 1750

Human Population Growth

Figure 2 ✎ Extend the graph of human population growth. Predict when you think the population will reach 9 billion people.

....

....

....

Source: OurWorldInData

Population Growth Rate

Human population changes do not represent a straight line of increase on a graph. Instead the population increases more and more rapidly over time. This rate of change is called **exponential growth**—a growth pattern in which individuals in a population reproduce at a constant rate, so that the larger population gets, the faster it grows.

However, no living population can experience such extreme exponential growth for very long. Populations are limited by space and resources. Exponential growth will cease when a population reaches the upper limit of organisms its environment can support. At that point, the population will stabilize or possibly decline. Throughout history, human populations have experienced periods of growth and decline, depending on the conditions and resources available.

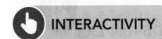
INTERACTIVITY

Learn about how human population growth affects Earth's systems.

☑ READING CHECK **Determine Conclusions** What would happen if the population growth rate reached zero?

....

....

Math Toolbox

Projected Growth Rates

The rate of human population growth is not the same all around the world. Experts use existing data to predict growth rates in different countries. Some areas may experience rapid growth, while others may have no growth or a decline.

1. **Evaluate Data** Which country represented has the highest population growth rate? Lowest?

....

....

2. **Draw Comparative Inferences** What conclusions can you draw from the growth rates of Angola and Germany?

....

....

....

....

Country	Population Growth Rate (%)
Angola	1.9
Australia	1.0
Canada	0.7
Germany	−0.2
Haiti	1.3
Japan	−0.2
South Korea	0.5
United States	0.8
Venezuela	1.2

Source: CIA World Factbook, 2017 estimates

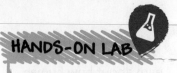
Academic Vocabulary

What are some other words that have the same meaning as *constraint*?

....

....

....

Using Natural Resources

Earth provides many resources that humans rely on to live, such as energy sources, minerals, water, trees, and plants. These resources are needed by all organisms on Earth. Some resources, such as water, are part of systems that affect our planet's climate and other natural cycles.

Human Activity Industries and families alike rely on energy sources such as fossil fuels to provide electricity to power our lives. We use fuel to keep us warm in the winter and cool in the summer, to travel from place to place, and to grow and transport the food we eat. We use wood from trees and minerals that are mined from the ground to build everything from the tiniest computer chips to the tallest skyscrapers. Every human being relies on fresh, clean water to survive.

As the world's population grows, so does our demand for resources. Like the human population, many resources are not evenly distributed around Earth. For example, the availability of fresh, usable water varies in different locations on Earth. It is one of the factors that may act as a **constraint** on human activities in the near future. Currently, more than 700 million people do not have access to safe, clean water. This lack of clean water forces many individuals to consume unsafe water. Experts estimate that by 2025, nearly 1.8 billion people could be suffering from water scarcity.

Question It!

Mining Salt

Salt is not only a necessary part of the human diet, it is used in numerous industrial and agricultural applications. Most of the salt used today is mined from underground deposits.

Ask Questions Develop a list of questions you would ask to help determine the relationship between human population growth and salt mining.

....

....

....

....

....

....

....

....

....

....

....

Impact of Agriculture
Figure 3 In order to grow food for people to eat, farmers use fertilizers and other chemicals. These chemicals often run off the land and pollute lakes, rivers, and the ocean.

Infer What effect does farming food for a growing population have on the environment?

....

....

....

....

....

....

....

Impact on the Earth System

Using resources reduces their amounts, which is a problem for nonrenewable resources like fossil fuels. The way in which we obtain many of these resources involves drilling, mining, or clearing Earth's surface, which damages the land. As some resources such as minerals or fossil fuels become scarce, humans dig deeper and disturb more areas to keep up with our growing population. When we remove resources, it increases the potential to release harmful substances into the environment. For example, using resources creates waste. If left untreated, waste can harm the environment. Motorized vehicles, such as the one shown in **Figure 3,** burn petroleum and release gases and chemicals that can cause **pollution**, which is the contamination of Earth's land, water, or air.

Human activities also affect other life on Earth. When we mine for a mineral or divert water for our use we often destroy valuable habitats. Pollution in land and water habitats endangers the organisms that live there. Also, many organisms are over-exploited as food for growing human numbers. When the number of humans grows beyond what the available resources can support, we reach the point of **overpopulation**. Human overpopulation is a driving force of many environmental and social issues, including climate change, habitat loss, and human conflict. There may come a point at which Earth cannot adequately meet human needs at our current rate of resource use. In some parts of the world, this is already the case.

READING CHECK Determine Conclusions How does a growing population impact land, air, and water resources?

....

....

Literacy Connection

Determine Conclusions As you read, underline evidence in the text that supports your conclusions about how growing populations impact the environment.

INTERACTIVITY

Examine the different types of resources available on Earth.

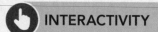

Balancing Needs

Science can identify problems and offer possible solutions, but it is up to individuals, governments, and international organizations to decide how to manage the impacts of a growing population. There are economic, social, and environmental costs and benefits which all must be weighed against one another (**Figure 4**). For example, humans use a variety of resources to produce electricity, from burning fossil fuels to building dams. No single method works in every situation, and there are benefits and costs to each.

The practice of using less of a resource so that it can last longer is called **conservation**. To ensure that future generations have access to the same resources we enjoy now, we need to use resources in ways that maintain them at a certain quality for a certain period of time. This practice is known as **sustainable use** of living resources. It gives resources time to recover and replenish themselves.

Addressing human impacts on the environment also requires engineering new solutions to our problems. These might include using desalination to counter water shortages, or advances in solar power, wind power, and other forms of renewable energy. As human populations continue to rise, the need for new ideas and solutions will increase.

READING CHECK **Develop an Argument** Why is it important to conserve natural resources?

Harvesting Timber

Figure 4 We use timber, but there is an impact of our use on the environment. In the table, list the benefits and costs of logging.

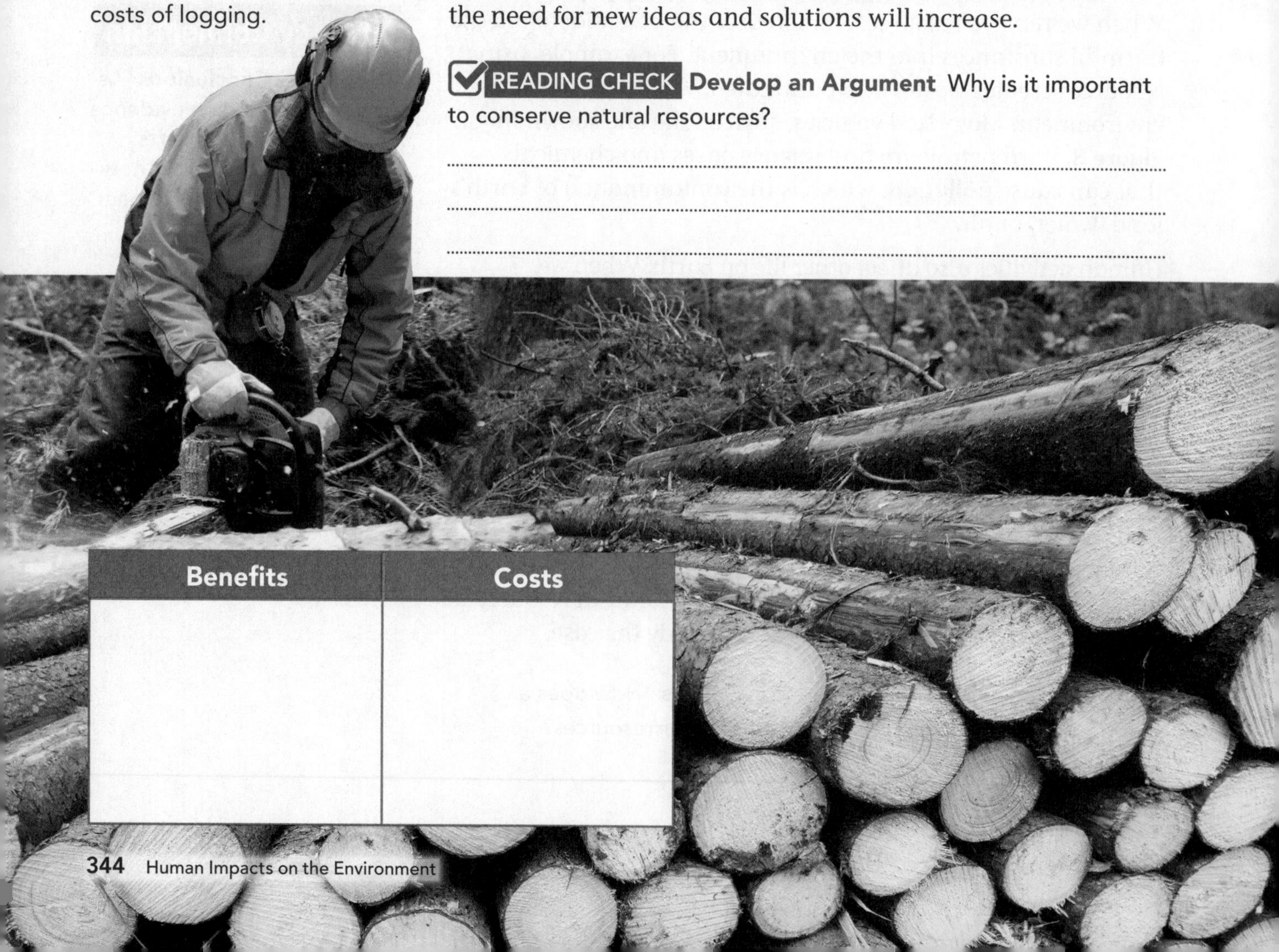

Benefits	Costs

1. Summarize What factors limited human population growth in the past?

....

....

....

....

2. Quantify Change How did the Industrial Revolution affect human population growth?

....

....

....

....

3. Construct Arguments What actions should humans take to conserve natural resources?

....

....

....

....

....

Use the graph to answer question 4.

Human Population 1750–2020

Y-axis: Billions (0–7)
X-axis: 1750, 1800, 1850, 1900, 1950, 2000

4. Cite Evidence Explain how the human population graph shows exponential growth.

....

....

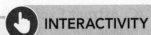

Quest CHECK-IN

In this lesson, you learned how human population has changed over time and how human population growth impacts Earth's systems.

Connect to the Environment Why is it important to consider human population growth when developing strategies for dealing with pollution?

....

....

....

....

INTERACTIVITY

More Trash, Less Space

Go online to learn about the total volume of trash generated in the United States and to determine how much trash is generated at your school.

Guiding Questions

- What are the causes of air pollution?
- What are the long-term negative impacts of air pollution?
- What efforts are being made to decrease the levels of air pollution around the world?

Connections

Literacy Cite Textual Evidence

Math Analyze Quantitative Relationships

MS-ESS3-4

Vocabulary

point source
nonpoint source
emissions
ozone
acid rain

Academic Vocabulary

primary

 VOCABULARY APP

Practice vocabulary on a mobile device.

Quest CONNECTION

Think about how the resources you use and the trash you make at school contribute to air pollution.

Connect It!

✏️ **Circle each mode of transportation that causes air pollution.**

Construct Explanations How do these different forms of transportation pollute the air?

....

....

Make Predictions What is the benefit of walking or riding a bike?

....

....

Causes of Pollution

You are surrounded by air. Air is a mixture of nitrogen, oxygen, carbon dioxide, water vapor, and other gases. Almost all living things depend on these gases to survive. These gases cycle between the biosphere and the atmosphere. The cycles guarantee that the air supply will not run out, but they don't ensure that the air will be clean.

Pollution The contamination of Earth's land, water, or air is called pollution. Pollution is caused by liquids, chemicals, heat, light, and noise. Pollution can have dramatic negative effects on the environment and on living organisms.

Humans affect the levels of pollution by using natural resources and manufactured products. For example, **Figure 1** shows how the burning of gasoline pollutes the air. In addition, when coal and oil-based fuels are burned to generate electricity, carbon dioxide and sulfur dioxide are released into the air.

Types of Pollution A specific, identifiable pollution source is called a **point source**. A sewer that drains untreated wastewater into a river is an example of a point source.

A **nonpoint source** of pollution is widely spread and cannot be tied to a specific origin. For example, the polluted air around big cities is caused by vehicles, factories, and other sources. Because it is difficult to identify the exact source of the pollution, that pollution has a nonpoint source.

☑ READING CHECK **Determine Central Ideas** What is the difference between point and nonpoint sources of pollution?

....

....

....

HANDS-ON LAB

Explore how particles move through the air.

📓 **Write About It** What are the large-scale impacts of breathing polluted air?

Different Sources of Pollution

Figure 1 Pollution can occur naturally or through human activities. Sometimes the level of pollution is so great that it harms people.

Forest fires

Industrial emissions

Motor vehicle emissions

Livestock

Sources of Air Pollution

Figure 2 ✏ Circle the natural sources of pollution. Mark an X on the human-made causes of pollution.

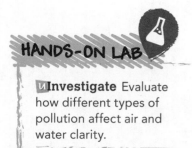

HANDS-ON LAB

ⓤ**Investigate** Evaluate how different types of pollution affect air and water clarity.

Outdoor Air Pollution

The air you are breathing is a combination of different gases. If you are in the mountains, the air might feel fresh and crisp. If you are at the shore, you might smell the salt water. In large cities, however, the air might not be as refreshing. Air pollution can be a big problem in areas where there are a lot of factories or a lot of people.

Emissions Many years ago, the main source of air pollution was the smoke being pumped out of factories. You have probably seen images of these **emissions**, or pollutants that are released into the air, as the dark smoke coming out of a factory's tall chimneys. This smoke is loaded with chemicals that mix with the gases in the air. However, today, most air pollution is released from coal-fired power plants and from motor vehicles, as shown in **Figure 2**. Emissions often contain carbon dioxide, which is also a pollutant. The increasing level of carbon dioxide is the primary contributor to the rise in average global temperatures over the past century.

Not all air pollution is caused by people. There are also some natural causes of air pollution, such as forest fires and volcanic eruptions. For example, the Hawaiian volcano Kilauea releases nearly 1,500–2,000 tons of harmful sulfur dioxide into the atmosphere each day during eruptions. However, human activities emit more than ten times as much sulfur dioxide and more than one hundred times as much carbon dioxide as all volcanoes combined.

Smog If you live in a large city, chances are you have heard the term "smog alert." This is a warning to alert you that the amount of air pollution may make it difficult to breathe outdoors. Smog forms when certain gases and chemicals react with sunlight. This results in a thick, brownish haze that hovers over a city. Smog can cause breathing problems and diseases of the eyes and throat.

The **primary** source of smog is the emissions of cars and trucks. Among these emissions are chemicals called hydrocarbons and nitrogen oxides. These gases react in the sunlight to produce a form of oxygen called **ozone**. Ozone is toxic to humans, and it causes lung infections and harms the body's immune system.

Under normal conditions, air near the ground is heated by Earth's surface and rises up and away from the surface. Pollutants in the air are carried up into the atmosphere by the rising air. However, under certain weather conditions called temperature inversions, the normal circulation of air is blocked. As **Figure 3** shows, cool air becomes trapped below a layer of warm air during an inversion. This keeps the pollutants trapped near Earth's surface and causes them to become more concentrated and dangerous.

✔️ READING CHECK **Cite Textual Evidence** What are the main sources of air pollution and how do they cause smog?

....

....

....

Academic Vocabulary
Write a sentence using the word *primary*.

....

....

....

Temperature Inversion
Figure 3 ✏️ Complete the image on the right by shading in the air pollutants to show how they are trapped during a temperature inversion.

Normal conditions
Cold Air
Cool Air
Warm Air

Temperature inversion
Cold Air
Warm Air
Cool Air

349

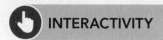
Acid Rain

Acid Rain Precipitation that is more acidic than normal because of air pollution is called **acid rain**. When coal and oil are burned, they produce nitrogen oxide and sulfur dioxide gases. These gases are then released as emissions and react with the water vapor in the air to produce nitric and sulfuric acids. These acids become part of rain, snow, sleet, or fog.

When acidic precipitation falls to Earth's surface, it has damaging effects, as shown in **Figure 4**. As water and soil become more acidic, organisms will die off. Acid rain can also remove nutrients and minerals from the soil, affecting plant growth. Sometimes the effects of acid rain can be reversed by adding chemicals that neutralize the acid, but this is very expensive.

Acid rain also causes damage to nonliving things. The acid reacts with metal and stone of buildings, cars, and statues. It can cause metal to rust at a faster rate and causes the chemical weathering of stone. The effects of acid rain on these materials are irreversible.

Literacy Connection

Cite Textual Evidence
As you read, underline the statements that support the idea that acid rain causes damage to living and nonliving things.

✓ **READING CHECK** **Write Arguments** Suppose your state government does not think that outdoor air pollution is a problem. What evidence could you use to convince your government that air pollution is harmful to people and the environment?

....

....

....

....

....

Effects of Acid Rain

Figure 4 Acid rain can damage nonliving things as well as living things. Explain how acid rain might affect the trees in a forest.

....

....

....

....

....

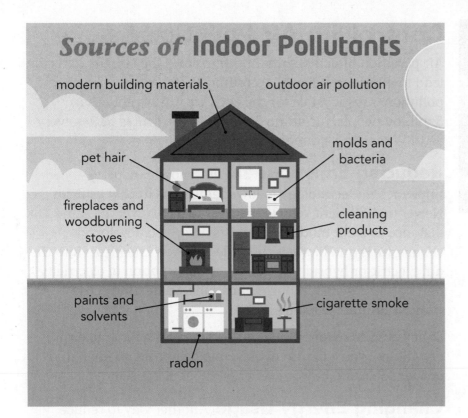

Sources of Indoor Pollutants

modern building materials

outdoor air pollution

pet hair

molds and bacteria

fireplaces and woodburning stoves

cleaning products

paints and solvents

cigarette smoke

radon

Indoor Air Pollution
Figure 5 ✏ Underline the indoor pollutants that are human-made. Circle the pollutants that occur naturally.

Indoor Air Pollution

Sometimes the quality of the air inside a building can be just as bad as the air outside. There are several things that can contribute to indoor air pollution, as shown in **Figure 5**. Some of these can be human-made, while others occur naturally.

Allergens Obvious sources of indoor air pollution include dust, mold, and pet hair. These factors, while quite common, usually affect only people who are sensitive to them. Other sources of indoor air pollution include fumes from glues, paints, and cleaning supplies and tobacco smoke from cigarettes or cigars. These can affect everyone in the home.

Indoor Gases Radon and carbon monoxide are two harmful pollutants often found in homes or other buildings. Radon is a colorless, odorless gas that is radioactive. It forms underground from the decay of certain rocks. Radon enters a home through cracks in the foundation. Breathing this gas over long periods of time can cause lung cancer and other health issues.

Carbon monoxide forms when fuels such as oil, gas, or wood are burned. Breathing carbon monoxide causes respiratory issues, nausea, headaches, and even death.

The best way to protect against carbon monoxide is to install detectors near sleeping areas. These devices alert homeowners if concentrations get too high.

 VIDEO

Explore the misconception that indoor spaces do not suffer from air pollution.

☑ READING CHECK
Integrate With Visuals
What are some ways to reduce the amount of indoor pollution in your home?

....

....

....

....

....

....

....

....

....

351

Controlling Air Pollution

Air pollution affects weather patterns and the climate and can lead to illness and death. According to one recent study, air pollution is responsible for the early deaths of more than 5 million people, including 200,000 in the United States every year. What can be done?

Reducing Emissions The automobile industry implemented technology to lower emissions in new vehicles. Newer fuel-efficient vehicles use less fuel to travel the same distance as older models. Scientists have also developed cleaner fuels and biofuels that release fewer chemicals into the air. Electric or hybrid vehicles use a combination of electricity and gasoline, which reduces emissions. Some all-electric vehicles produce zero emissions.

Other ways to reduce emissions include carpooling, biking, or walking. You can also avoid using gas-powered lawn and garden tools and buy only energy-efficient appliances.

Changing Energy Usage Another way to reduce emissions is to transition away from fossil fuels, such as coal, oil, and natural gas. Solar, wind, hydroelectric, and geothermal energy produce only a small fraction of the harmful emissions that the burning of fossil fuels generates.

Bike Sharing

Figure 6 Bike-sharing programs provide a clean-energy alternative to driving a car or taking a bus. What actions can you take to reduce air pollution in your community?

....

....

....

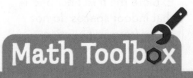

Math Toolbox

Energy Usage

The graphs show how energy consumption has changed in the United States over the past century.

1. **Analyze Quantitative Relationships** By how many times did energy consumption increase from 1908 to 2015?

....

2. **Patterns** Describe any patterns you observe in the graph showing the share of consumption for each energy source. What do you think might explain these patterns?

....

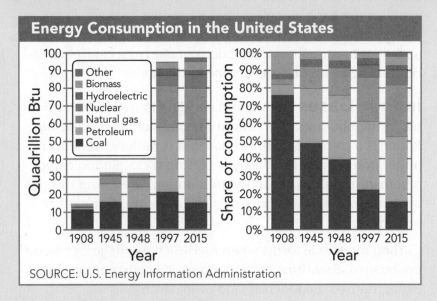

Energy Consumption in the United States

Legend: Other, Biomass, Hydroelectric, Nuclear, Natural gas, Petroleum, Coal

SOURCE: U.S. Energy Information Administration

....

....

Protecting the Ozone Layer If you have ever been sunburned, then you have experienced the effects of the sun's ultraviolet, or UV, radiation. The ozone layer, situated about 15 to 30 km above Earth's surface, works like a shield to protect living things from too much UV radiation.

The Ozone Cycle In the ozone layer, ozone is constantly being made and destroyed in a cycle. An ozone molecule has three oxygen atoms. When sunlight hits a molecule, the ozone absorbs UV radiation. The energy causes the ozone to break apart into an oxygen gas molecule (which has two oxygen atoms) and a single oxygen atom. The oxygen atom hits an oxygen molecule and attaches itself to form a new ozone molecule.

The Ozone Hole In the late 1970s, scientists discovered an area of severe ozone depletion, or a "hole," in the ozone layer over the southern polar region, shown in **Figure 7**. The main cause of the hole was a group of gases called chlorofluorocarbons (CFCs)—human-made gases that destroy ozone molecules. As a result, more UV radiation reached Earth's surface. Nations around the world worked together to ban CFCs to help restore the amount of ozone in the atmosphere.

✓ READING CHECK **Determine Conclusions** Why did countries work together to ban CFCs to help restore the ozone layer?

....

....

....

....

⬆ INTERACTIVITY

Explore how to reduce your carbon footprint.

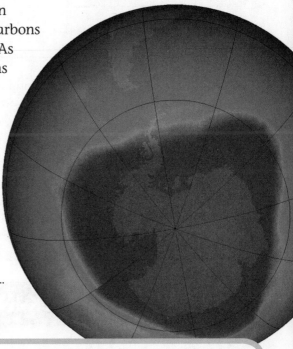

Ozone Hole
Figure 7 A hole in the ozone layer (in blue) allows more harmful UV radiation to reach Earth's surface in the Southern Hemisphere.

Model It!

Ozone Model
Re-read the paragraph about the ozone cycle.

Develop Models ✏ Use the information in the text to create and label a model of an ozone molecule and how it changes during its life cycle. Explain each stage of the cycle.

....

....

....

....

....

☑ LESSON 2 Check

MS-ESS3-4

1. Identify What is the difference between "helpful" and "harmful" ozone?

....

....

....

....

2. Evaluate Reasoning Why is the use of fertilizers on lawns in residential areas an example of a nonpoint source of pollution?

....

....

....

3. Provide Evidence How does burning fossil fuels affect indoor air pollution?

....

....

....

....

....

....

....

4. Cause and Effect What effect does burning fossil fuels during manufacturing and energy production have on outdoor air pollution?

....

....

....

....

....

5. Construct an Argument What evidence supports the claim that walking and biking to work would have a positive effect on air pollution?

....

....

....

....

....

....

....

....

Quest CHECK-IN

In this lesson, you learned how humans affect Earth's systems by producing different forms of air pollution. You also learned how we are working to reduce the impact of air pollution.

Evaluate Why is it important to work toward reducing activities that contribute to air pollution?

....

....

....

....

....

....

HANDS-ON LAB

Trash vs. Water

Download the lab to design and construct a model of a landfill.

MS-ESS3-4

Working Together to Reduce Air Pollution

Air pollution knows no borders. For instance, winds can carry pollution from factories in China nearly 10,000 kilometers to California. Many countries are reducing their own pollution, but they still suffer from the effects of air pollution from other countries. The only way to fight this global problem is by working together across borders.

In 2015, 196 countries came together to make a plan to reduce air pollution around the world. The Paris Agreement, as it is known, sets targets to reduce levels of carbon emissions. Carbon dioxide traps heat in the atmosphere, causing global warming. So, reducing pollution will help mitigate global warming.

It took many years to reach the Paris Agreement. Every country has different needs, industries, and laws. Some groups worry that the agreement doesn't go far enough. Others fear that environmental regulations will damage their national economies. Still, most nations believe that the Paris Agreement is necessary to reduce air pollution and protect Earth.

MY COMMUNITY

What are communities in Florida doing to reduce air pollution? Explore the Florida Climate Center website to find out.

Carbon dioxide, a by-product of burning fossil fuels, is a type of air pollution. It traps heat in Earth's atmosphere, causing global temperatures to rise. Even slight temperature increases can upset the delicate balance of life on Earth.

③ Impacts on Land

Guiding Questions

- What natural resources are obtained from Earth's geosphere?
- Why are natural resources on land so important to Earth's systems?
- How do human activities positively and negatively affect land resources?

Connections

Literacy Cite Textual Evidence

Math Analyze Proportional Relationships

MS-ESS3-4

Vocabulary

natural resource
renewable resource
nonrenewable resource
deforestation
erosion
desertification
sustainable

Academic Vocabulary

resource

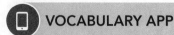 **VOCABULARY APP**

Practice vocabulary on a mobile device.

Quest CONNECTION

Think about the process for choosing a location for a landfill and the steps it takes to create one.

Connect It!

✏️ **Identify and label one unlimited resource and one limited resource shown in the image.**

Cause and Effect What impact do you think the overuse of certain resources might have on Earth's ecosystems?

....

....

Land as a Resource

Did you drink water, turn on a light, or ride in a bus today? All of these activities, and many more, depend on Earth's **resources**. Anything we use that occurs naturally in the environment is called a **natural resource**. As **Figure 1** shows, natural resources include organisms, water, sunlight, minerals, and soil.

A **renewable resource** is either always available or is naturally replaced in a relatively short time. Some renewable resources, such as wind and sunlight, are almost always available. Other renewable resources, such as water and trees, are renewable only if they are replaced as fast as they are used.

Nonrenewable resources are resources that are not replaced within a relatively short time frame. Metals and most minerals are nonrenewable. Oil and coal are also nonrenewable resources. They were formed over millions of years from the remains of long-dead organisms. Humans use these resources faster than they can be replaced. Over time, they will be used up.

While it does not cover as much of the planet's surface as water, land is also a vital resource. Humans use its many resources to survive. As **Figure 2** will show, it is used to grow food, obtain raw materials, and provide shelter.

Academic Vocabulary

A resource is not limited to a material, such as water or trees. What other kinds of resources do you rely on in your life?

....

....

....

....

Reflect What are some renewable and nonrenewable resources that you use? In your science notebook, describe these resources.

Natural Resources

Figure 1 Humans use many different types of resources. Some of these are in limited supply, while others are essentially limitless.

Agriculture Land provides most of the food people eat. The use of land to produce food is called agriculture. Many areas of the world are not suitable for farming. New farmland is often made by draining wetlands, irrigating deserts, or deforestation. **Deforestation** is the removal of forests to use the land for other reasons. This process destroys the habitats of organisms living in these places.

Mining The metals and plastics used to make items such as televisions, cellular phones, building materials, and cars are mined from below Earth's surface. Metals and other resources are obtained through one type of mining called strip mining. Strip mining removes the top layer of dirt, exposing the minerals or ore underneath. When heavy winds and rains come, they can wash soil and land away. With it go all the nutrients it contains. It can take thousands of years for soil to be replaced.

Development Where do you live? It is a good bet that you live in a structure somewhere on the land. Whether it is a house, a camper, or an apartment building, the space your home takes up was once used as a habitat for other organisms. As the human population grows, more and more land is developed and built up with human structures, leaving no room for the living organisms of the original habitat.

☑ READING CHECK

Cite Textual Evidence Which statements from the text support the idea that land is an important resource? Underline them.

clear-cutting

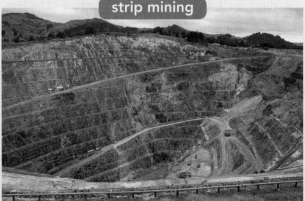
strip mining

development

Land Use

Figure 2 Humans use land is many different ways. How do these activities impact Earth's systems?

....

....

....

....

....

Importance of Soil Management

Healthy, fertile soil is essential for the success of agriculture because it contains the minerals and nutrients that plants require. Soil absorbs, stores, and filters water, which is also necessary for plant growth. Organisms living in soil, such as bacteria, fungi, and earthworms, break down the wastes and remains of living things and return them to the soil as nutrients.

Structure of Soil

If you take a shovel and dig a hole in the ground, you will encounter several layers of soil, such as those shown in **Figure 3**. The first layer is called the litter. This top layer is where dead leaves and grass are found.

The next layer is called the topsoil. Topsoil is a mixture of nutrients, water, air, rock fragments, and dead and decaying organisms. Moving further down, the shovel will hit the subsoil. This layer contains the same water and air as the topsoil, but there are more rock fragments and fewer plant and animal remains here.

Underneath the subsoil is the layer of bedrock. This is the layer that makes up Earth's crust and is the basis for new soil. As time passes, water dissolves the rock, and its freezing and thawing action cracks and breaks apart the bedrock. Plant roots also help to break the bedrock by growing into cracks and then expanding. Animals such as earthworms and moles also help in the process. And as dead organisms break down, their remains contribute to the mixture of new soil.

Soil Layers

Figure 3 Fertile soil is made up of several layers. Label each layer of soil in the photo: *bedrock, litter, subsoil, topsoil.*

Plan It!

Community Considerations

Cause and Effect Suppose you are part of a group that is converting an abandoned lot into a community garden. You need to plan the garden to avoid damaging the local environment further. What harmful effects should you consider and how can you minimize them?

....

....

....

....

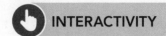
Erosion

Erosion Without soil, life on land could not exist. Soil takes hundreds of years to form. Therefore, every effort must be made to protect Earth's soil. Sometimes, natural forces cause soil loss. Forces such as wind, water, and ice move particles of rocks or soil through a process called **erosion**.

Usually, plant roots growing deep into the soil help to hold it in place. Human activities such as mining, logging, construction, and farming increase erosion by taking away these plants and exposing the soil to wind and precipitation. With nothing to anchor them in place, soil particles easily move. Human activities cause erosion to happen at a much faster rate than naturally-ocurring processes do. **Figure 4** shows some examples of natural and human-caused erosion.

Erosion

Figure 4 ✏ Check the image that shows naturally-ocurring erosion. How did different events cause these areas to form?

....

....

....

....

....

....

....

Nutrient Depletion

Nutrient Depletion Plants make their own food through photosynthesis, but they need to take in nutrients such as nitrogen and phosphorus. Decomposers in the soil break down dead organisms, which add these and other nutrients to the soil. If a farmer plants the same crops in a field every year, the crops may use more nutrients than decomposers can supply. This leads to nutrient depletion; the soil is not adequately fertile. Nutrient depletion can directly affect humans. Crops grown in nutrient-poor soil often have less nutritional value.

Farmers add fertilizers to the soil to provide the needed nutrients. This can produce abundant, nutritious crops, but can also cause damage when rain carries the fertilizers into nearby bodies of water. Farmers often manage the soil by allowing it to sit for a season or two in between plantings. This allows the remnant crops to decompose, which replenishes the soil with nutrients.

Desertification When the soil in a once-fertile area loses its moisture and nutrients, the area can become a desert. The advance of desert-like conditions into areas that were previously fertile is called **desertification**.

One cause of moisture loss is drought. During these prolonged periods of low precipitation, plants, including crops, will dry up or not grow at all. Allowing livestock to overgraze grasslands and cutting down trees without replanting the area can also result in desertification. Without plant roots to hold the soil together, erosion of fertile topsoil will occur. Plant roots also carry water deeper into the soil, so it doesn't dry out as quickly.

From 2010 to 2016, the state of California experienced a severe drought. The people of California took preventive actions to avoid desertification. The state introduced mandatory water restrictions and regulations on the use of groundwater. Farmers also reduced the growing of certain crops to lessen the need for extensive irrigation.

Desertification

Figure 5 Crops cannot grow in arid soil. As a result, many people are unable to grow their own food and must move to a town or city where food is available.

☑️ READING CHECK **Translate Information** What most likely occurred to cause the conditions in **Figure 5**?

....

....

....

Math Toolbox

Causes of Land Degradation

Scientists estimate that there are at least 79.5 million hectares of degraded land in North America. The graph shows the causes of land degradation by percentage.

Analyze Proportional Relationships How many more hectares were degraded by agricultural activities than by deforestation? Show your work.

....

....

....

....

....

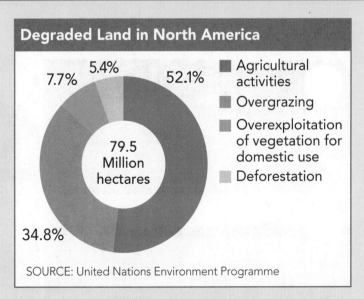

Degraded Land in North America

7.7%   5.4%   52.1%

79.5 Million hectares

34.8%

■ Agricultural activities
■ Overgrazing
■ Overexploitation of vegetation for domestic use
■ Deforestation

SOURCE: United Nations Environment Programme

VIDEO

Learn more about what happens when you throw something "away."

Landfills When you are asked to take out the garbage, where does it go once it leaves your curb? Today much of the solid waste, construction debris, and agricultural and industrial waste we produce is buried in holes called landfills. These areas are designed to protect the surrounding areas from soil and water pollution. If landfills are not managed correctly, they can harm the environment. Materials from waste can leak into the groundwater, making it toxic to drink.

Once a landfill is full, it is covered with soil heavy in clay to keep rainwater from entering the waste. These "capped" landfills can be reclaimed as locations for parks and sports arenas, but they cannot be used for housing or agriculture.

Land Reclamation It is sometimes possible to restore soil that has been lost to erosion, mining, or waste disposal. This process of restoring land to a more productive state is called land reclamation. Land reclamation could involve trucking in soil from another area. Sometimes mine operations reclaim land by storing the soil that they remove from a site, then putting it back after mining operations cease. Land reclamation can restore farming areas as well as wildlife habitats (see **Figure 6**).

Land reclamation is very expensive and difficult. It is much harder to bring back damaged land than it is to protect and conserve those resources before they become damaged.

✅ **READING CHECK** **Draw Evidence** How do human actions impact land? Give one positive and one negative impact.

....

....

....

....

Land Reclamation

Figure 6 🖊 These pictures show an area that was reclaimed to include a stream. Add numbers to put these pictures in chronological order.

Describe Explain what happened to the land in these pictures.

....

....

....

....

Wetlands

A wetland is an area in which water covers the soil for all or most of the year. They are found in all climates and on all continents except Antarctica. Other terms you may have heard for wetland include bog, marsh, and swamp.

Figure 7 shows how wetlands support both land and aquatic ecosystems. They serve as breeding and nursery grounds for many organisms, provide habitats to many species of plants, and are feeding sites for many birds, mammals, and fish.

Human activities have greatly impacted wetlands. The development of homes, businesses, and roads requires controlling the flow of water through these areas. But altering the flow of water in a wetland changes the ecosystem and destroys unique habitats. It can also lead to increases in erosion, flooding, and the pollution of water and soil. Wetland soil acts as a natural "sponge" to collect water. Without wetlands, the large amounts of rain produced by severe storms, such as hurricanes, would flow directly into rivers or populated areas. Wetlands help to protect the quality of water by trapping excess sediments and pollutants before they reach the groundwater or waterways.

☑ READING CHECK **Integrate With Visuals** How would filling in a wetland to create a field affect the surrounding environment?

....

....

....

Literacy Connection

Cite Textual Evidence
When you write an argument, it should be based on factual evidence, not opinions. As you read, underline the evidence that supports the idea that human activities negatively affect the land.

How Wetlands Work
Figure 7 ✏ Wetland plants, soil, and bacteria protect surrounding aspects. Circle the aspects of the wetland that provide benefits to humans.

plants filter out pollutants and sediments

dissipates stream energy

provides critical wildlife habitat

groundwater flow

bacteria break down pollutants

specialized roots stabilize soil

saturated soil stores water

363

Sustainability

Figure 8 Examine the forest closely. Do you think these trees are being managed in a way that maintains the overall health of the forest? Explain.

....

....

....

....

....

....

....

Sustainable Forest Management

Trees and other plants, like the ones in **Figure 8**, are important land resources. They provide food and shelter for many organisms. Through photosynthesis, they release oxygen into the air. They also absorb carbon dioxide and other pollutants from the air. Their roots absorb rainwater and hold the soil together, which helps to prevent erosion and flooding.

Many products are made from the fruit, seeds, and other parts of forest plants. The wood from some trees is used for making paper, and other trees are used to build homes and furniture. Fruits and seeds from trees provide food for people and animals.

All trees, whether cultivated by farmers or growing in the wild, need to be protected and managed sustainably. Because we can plant trees to replace trees that are cut down, forests can be renewable resources. How long a resource lasts depends on how people use it. **Sustainable** use of a resource means using it in ways that maintain the resource for all future generations. Replacing and reserving trees are important ways to sustain a forest. These practices ensure that the ecosystem remains healthy and that people can still depend on forests for the resources they need.

Logging Methods

Logging Methods There are two main methods of logging, or cutting down trees: clear-cutting and selective cutting, illustrated in **Figure 9**. Clear-cutting is the process of cutting down all the trees in an area at once. Selective cutting is the process of cutting down only some trees in a forest and leaving a mix of tree sizes and species behind.

Clear-cutting is usually faster and less expensive than selective cutting. However, selective cutting is less damaging to the forest ecosystem than clear-cutting. When a forest is cleared, all the animals' habitats are suddenly gone. Without the protection of the trees, the soil is more easily eroded by wind and rain. The soil can then be blown or washed away and into nearby streams, harming aquatic ecosystems.

Selective cutting takes much longer, as the loggers need to actively choose which trees will come down and which will remain. It is more dangerous for loggers to selectively cut trees because they have to move heavy equipment and logs around the remaining trees.

Logging Methods

Figure 9 🖉 Clear-cutting and selective cutting are two methods of tree harvesting. Label each method shown as clear-cutting or selective cutting.

Original Forest

INTERACTIVITY

Create a solution for a controversial use of land.

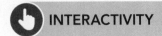

Write About It Collect information about how trees in your state are managed. In your science notebook, write an argument from the position of a conservation organization that says the yield is too high and needs to be reduced.

Sustainable Forestry Forests can be managed to provide a sustainable yield. A sustainable yield is the amount of a renewable resource that can be harvested regularly without reducing the future supply. Planting one tree to replace each one that is cut down ensures that the overall yield remains constant.

In sustainable forestry, after trees are harvested, young trees are planted, as shown in **Figure 10**. Trees must be planted frequently enough to maintain a constant supply. Forests containing fast-growing tree species, such as pines, can be harvested and replanted every 20 to 30 years. Forests containing slower-growing species, such as hickory, oak, and cherry, may be harvested only every 40 to 100 years. One sustainable approach is to log small patches within a forest, so different sections can be harvested every year.

READING CHECK **Draw Evidence** Why is it important to manage forests so that their yield is sustainable?

....

....

....

....

....

....

Replanting

Figure 10 Planting another generation of trees is one technique of sustainable forestry.

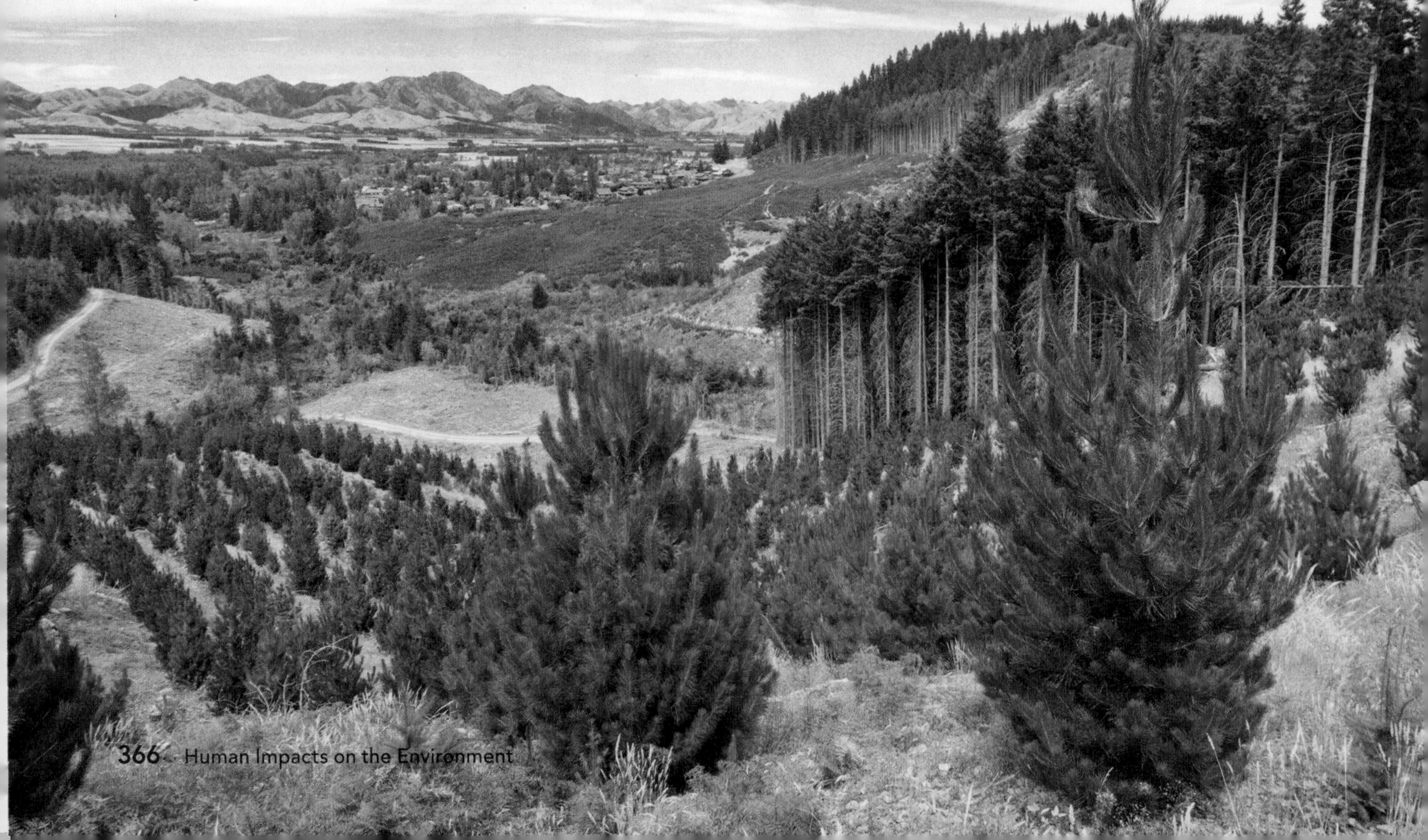

☑ LESSON 3 Check

MS-ESS3-4

1. **Identify** What are three different ways land is used as a resource?

....

....

2. **Cite Evidence** Why are trees considered a renewable resource?

....

....

....

3. **Construct Arguments** How do poor farming methods impact Earth?

....

....

....

....

....

....

....

4. **Defend Your Claim** Give evidence to defend the claim that it is environmentally unsound to change the flow of water in a wetland.

....

....

....

....

....

....

....

....

5. **Cause and Effect** How does the presence of trees maintain the stability of land resources?

....

....

....

....

Quest CHECK-IN

In this lesson, you learned about natural resources found on land and their importance to Earth's systems. You also learned how humans positively and negatively affect these resources.

Evaluate Why is it important to conserve resources and not simply use them in the most convenient way?

....

....

....

....

....

👆 INTERACTIVITY

Life of a Landfill

Go online to learn about where to site a landfill and how a landfill is constructed.

Nothing Goes TO WASTE

One city in Texas is making sure nothing in its sewers goes to waste. The Hornsby Bend Biosolids Management Plant in Austin, Texas, recycles sewage into biosolids. Biosolids are rich in nutrients, so they make great soil and fertilizer.

Every day, Hornsby Bend receives about a million gallons of sewage solids from Austin's water treatment plants, where the sewage is separated from the wastewater. The sewage is screened, and then flows into tanks where bacteria get to work feeding on it. The bacteria break the sewage down, killing most disease organisms as they go. This process is actually not that different from how the human digestive system works. After about 60 days, the sewage is converted into biosolids.

Hornsby Bend also collects Austin's yard trimmings and mixes these with the biosolids to make nutrient-rich soil. The plant sends some soil to nearby farmers who enhance their existing soil with the mix. The rest is used to supplement the soil of Austin's public lawns, gardens, parks, and golf courses. Instead of going to an expensive landfill, the biosolids are put to good use.

Hornsby Bend is also a bird sanctuary with more than 350 types of birds.

All of the water used at the treatment plant is recycled, too. Some of it goes to irrigate the nearby farmland, and the rest goes to ponds at the treatment plant. The nutrient-rich pond water has still another benefit: the treatment plant is also a bird sanctuary. Hornsby Bend is one of the best birding sites in the state. Thanks to the Hornsby Bend Biosolids Management Plant, Austin's waste doesn't go to waste.

Use the table to answer the following questions.

1. **Use Tables** One sample of biosolids contains 18.2 mg/kg mercury, 22.5 mg/kg arsenic, and 29.7 mg/kg cadmium. Are these biosolids safe to use? Why or why not?

   ....

   ....

2. **Calculate** A biosolids plant is picking up waste from a new factory. The level of lead in the plant's biosolids had been 121 mg/kg. With the waste from the new factory, the lead has increased 12 percent. Calculate the new lead level to determine if the biosolid is still safe to use on farmland.

   ....

   ....

   ....

Safe Levels of Pollutants in Soil on Farms Fertilized with Biosolids	
Pollutant	**Risk Assessment Acceptable Soil Concentration (mg/kg-soil)**
Arsenic	23.5
Cadmium	19.7
Copper	769.0
Lead	161.0
Mercury	8.6
Nickel	228.0
Selenium	50.21
Zinc	1,454.0

SOURCE: Environmental Protection Agency

3. **Construct Arguments** Why is a chart like this important?

   ....

   ....

   ....

4. **Engage in Argument** Are biosolids safe to use in agriculture? Make an argument to support your answer.

   ....

   ....

   ....

   ....

Guiding Questions

- Why is fresh water such a limited resource within Earth's systems?
- How do certain human activities cause freshwater and ocean pollution?
- What methods have humans developed to reduce freshwater and ocean pollution?

Connections

Literacy Draw Evidence

Math Analyze Proportional Relationships

MS-ESS3-4

Vocabulary

sewage
sediment
thermal pollution

Academic Vocabulary

distributed

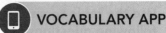 **VOCABULARY APP**

Practice vocabulary on a mobile device.

Quest CONNECTION

Think about how reducing the trash output at your school could reduce water pollution.

 **Connect It!**

✎ **Circle the areas in the photo that contain fresh water.**

Provide Evidence Why is water an important resource?

....

....

Water as a Resource

Water is essential for life on Earth. Most of Earth's surface is covered by some form of water, as shown in **Figure 1**. It serves as a habitat for many species. Approximately 97 percent of the water on Earth is undrinkable because it contains salt. Of the remaining 3 percent, most is frozen solid in the polar ice sheets. That leaves less than 1 percent of all the water on the planet as drinkable.

Earth's water is a renewable resource, but fresh water is a limited resource. Recall that water continually moves between the atmosphere and Earth's surface in the water cycle. However, there is not always enough water in a given place at a given time. When water usage is poorly managed, it can lead to water shortages.

The limited supply of fresh water is not evenly **distributed** around the world. Some areas have an abundant supply, while in others it is quite scarce. Water scarcity occurs when there is not enough water to meet demand. It can be caused by droughts, low levels of groundwater, unequal water distribution, or environmental factors such as water pollution. An area faces water scarcity when the water supply is less than 1,000 cubic meters per person.

✓ READING CHECK **Draw Evidence** Why is water a limited resource even though it is renewable?

....

....

📓 **Write About It** What do you think the world's freshwater supply will look like in another 100 years? In your science notebook, describe how and why our water supply might change.

Academic Vocabulary

What are some items that might get distributed? Can you think of any examples from your school?

....

....

Where is the Fresh Water?

Figure 1 Drinkable fresh water makes up less than one percent of the water on Earth.

Water Pollution

Figure 2 ✏ Most sources of freshwater pollution come from human activities. Mark any examples of nonpoint sources of pollution with a checkmark. Mark any examples of point sources of pollution with an X.

Sources of Freshwater Pollution

With fresh water being so limited, any form of pollution entering the water supply can have drastic results. Most water pollution is directly linked to human activities, as shown in **Figure 2**. Wastes from farming, households, industry, and mining can end up in the water supply. Water pollutants may be point or nonpoint sources, depending on how they enter the water. A point source for water pollution could be a factory output pipe or a leaking landfill. Nonpoint pollution sources could be farm pesticides, farm animal wastes, or runoff of salt and chemicals from roads.

Farming Wastes Animal wastes, fertilizers, and pesticides are sources of pollution. When it rains, animal wastes, fertilizers, and pesticides can wash away into nearby water sources and eventually the ocean. These pollutants can cause overgrowths of algae. The algae block light and deplete the water of oxygen, killing everything else in the water.

Household Pollutants The water and human wastes that are washed down sinks, showers, and toilets are called **sewage**. Sometimes, the sewage can leak into groundwater before it is treated. Because sewage contains many disease-causing bacteria, people will become ill if they drink or swim in water containing them.

Industrial Wastes The waste products of factories and mines may also pollute the water. Many manufacturing processes use or produce toxic chemicals that need to be disposed of properly. During this disposal, chemicals sometimes leak into the groundwater. Some chemicals, such as heavy metals, build up in the bodies of aquatic organisms, making them and the animals that eat them ill.

Sediment

Erosion carries small particles of rocks and sand from the land into the water. These particles are called **sediment**. Sediment can cover up sources of food, nests, and eggs of aquatic organisms. Sediment also blocks sunlight, which prevents photosynthesis in plants.

Heat

When heat negatively affects bodies of water, it is known as **thermal pollution**. Factories and power plants use water to cool their machinery. This heated water is often discharged back into the environment. Because it is so hot, the water can kill organisms.

Oil and Gasoline

Oil and gasoline are often transported in long pipelines, either underground or above ground. Sometimes these pipelines leak into rivers, streams, or groundwater. When oil and gasoline pollute the water, it can take many years for the ecosystem to recover. Oil is difficult to collect and penetrates much of the soil in the area. It also affects the plants that grow along the water's edge. Spilled oil also has both direct and indirect effects on wildlife. It coats their fur or feathers and causes skin irritation, at the least. It kills their food sources as well.

Oil and gasoline leaks from underground storage tanks are also sources of water pollution. These leaks can seep into the groundwater, making it unfit to drink.

☑ READING CHECK **Draw Evidence** Does most water pollution happen as a result of human activities? Explain.

....

....

....

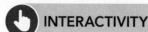 **INTERACTIVITY**

Examine how pollution affects the water cycle.

Literacy Connection

Draw Evidence Sometimes you need to draw evidence to support your analysis of a certain topic. Reread the previous page and the current page. As you read, underline any pieces of evidence that support the idea that most water pollution is directly linked to human activities.

INTERACTIVITY

Investigate whether or not human activity is responsible for odd mutations found in frogs.

Sources of Ocean Pollution

It was once thought that "the solution to pollution is dilution." This meant that whatever was dumped into the ocean would just spread out and eventually go away. Today, we know that isn't true. Dumping large amounts of wastes into the ocean threatens marine organisms and the overall functioning of Earth's systems.

Natural Occurrences There are some pollutants that occur naturally. These include freshwater runoff from land after heavy rains. When this freshwater enters the ocean, the salinity drops. Some organisms cannot tolerate this, so they either move to saltier waters or die.

Human Activities Most ocean pollution is related to human activities. The chemicals, sewage, and other wastes that are dumped into the ocean come from human sources. Fertilizers and pesticides from farms run off and eventually make it to the ocean. When enough of these build up, they can create an ocean dead zone—an area where nothing can live because there is not enough oxygen in the water.

Trash Trash and plastic, as shown in **Figure 3**, are hazardous to marine animals. For example, sea turtles often mistake plastic bags floating in the water for jellyfish. Once consumed, the bags clog up the intestines of the turtles. Fishing line and nets can catch swimming animals and entangle them. One area in the Pacific Ocean contains about 2 million bits of plastic per square mile. When sea creatures consume these tiny pieces, they can become ill and die. The plastic bits can also cause health problems for animals higher up in the food chain that eat small animals with plastic inside of them.

Effects of Pollution

Figure 3 This plastic and trash was recovered from the ocean, where it can harm organisms. What are some ways humans can reduce the amount of plastic that ends up in the ocean?

....

....

....

Sources of Oil Pollution

There are different ways for oil to pollute the ocean.

1. **Construct Graphs** ✏ Create a bar graph of the data.

2. **Analyze Proportional Relationships** How many times greater is the amount of pollution caused by runoff than that caused by oil spills?

....

....

....

Source of Oil Pollution	Oil Pollution (millions of liters)
Offshore drilling	80
Land runoff	1,375
Natural seeps	240
Ship repair	510
Oil spills	125

Oil Spills Oil that is accidentally spilled into the ocean is also a large source of pollution. Oil rigs that drill for oil sometimes leak into the ocean. This oil coats the feathers of birds, reducing their ability to stay warm. Oil also harms animals if they swallow it. Pollutants can build up in organisms' bodies and poison people or other marine life that feed on them.

 VIDEO

Explore the misconception that the ocean cannot be harmed because it is so vast.

Aquaculture The practice of raising fish and other water-dwelling organisms for food is called aquaculture. Fish are often raised in artificial ponds and bays that replace and destroy natural habitats, such as salt marshes. The farms can cause pollution and spread diseases into wild fish populations.

✓ READING CHECK **Determine Conclusions** How can you help to reduce the amount of pollution that ends up in the ocean?

....

....

....

....

HANDS-ON LAB

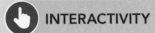Investigate Practice
different techniques for
cleaning up oil spills.

INTERACTIVITY

Take a closer look at water
pollution and solutions.

**Deepwater
Horizon Disaster
Figure 4** In 2010, an oil
rig in the Gulf of Mexico
exploded, leaving an oil
well wide open on the
ocean floor. In the following
days, 210 million gallons
of crude oil spilled into the
Gulf.

Reducing Water Pollution

Everyone needs clean water. But how can the pollution that
currently enters the water be reduced, and what efforts can be
made to prevent future pollution?

The United States and other countries have laws that regulate
water-polluting substances. These laws mandate the types and
amounts of substances that can be dumped into the water.
While these laws help, the keys to keeping water clean are the
prevention of oil and gasoline spills, effective cleanup of spills,
proper sewage treatment, and reduction of pollutants.

Protecting the Ocean

The ocean is a continuous
body of water. Because no one country owns the ocean, it is
every nation's responsibility to do whatever it can to ensure
the water stays clean. To help protect the ocean, the United
Nations set up regulations that say the first 22 kilometers from
the coast are controlled by the nation that owns that coast.
That nation also controls any resources, such as oil, natural
gas, and fish, that are found out to 370 km.

Many nations are helping to protect the ocean by limiting
how much can be taken from it and by establishing marine
protected areas (MPAs). They also are working to reduce the
amount of pollution in their coastal waters.

Cleaning Oil Spills

Oil spills, such as the one in
Figure 4, are one of the worst environmental hazards that can
occur. While nature can clean small amounts of oil from the
water, large spills such as the Deepwater Horizon oil spill are
too much to handle. The bacteria that are able to digest oil
cannot keep up with the volume of oil that is released in such a
spill. Boats deploy skimming devices to collect floating oil, and
barriers are set up to absorb or block oil before it reaches the
shore. Chemical dispersants are also sprayed into the water to
break up the oil. Cleanup of a major oil spill in the ocean can
take many years.

Improved Farming Methods Modern farming practices reduce water pollution. Formerly, farmers would leave fields bare in winter, allowing soil and fertilizers to wash into streams. It was also common to use large amounts of pesticides, herbicides, and fungicides. These chemicals would run off into streams, polluting the water and killing organisms. Today, farmers can reduce erosion and pollution by leaving stalks in the field or planting winter grasses that hold the soil and nutrients in place. Farmers also treat their land with a smaller amount of chemicals, and find natural predators to combat pests.

Reducing Pollutants Another way to protect Earth's waters is to reduce the amount of pollution that is created. Instead of dumping waste products directly into the environment, manufacturers can recycle them. By turning waste products into new things, the companies may even save money. Another method to reduce waste is to change the way materials are produced. Factories can eliminate the use of non-recyclable materials. By figuring out more environmentally-friendly manufacturing methods, they may make less total waste or less hazardous waste.

You can help to prevent water pollution in your home. Common household water pollutants include paints, paint thinner, motor oil, and garden chemicals. Instead of dumping these into the environment, save these materials for your community's hazardous waste collection day (**Figure 5**), or take them to a specialized facility for such wastes.

INTERACTIVITY

Investigate the techniques that work best to restore a coastal wetland.

Hazardous Waste
Figure 5 Many towns and cities have special recycling centers that provide safe and proper disposal of household chemicals, such as paint and cleaning supplies.

✓ READING CHECK **Write Explanatory Texts** What can your community do to reduce water pollution?

....

....

....

Plan It !

Reducing Waste in Factories
Many factories are "going green" and changing the way they manufacture products to create less waste. Suppose there is a manufacturing company in your community that is not reducing its waste.

Construct Arguments Come up with a solution to your community's problem. Plan a presentation to convince the factory owners to "go green." How might changing their policy benefit both the community and the factory? How will making these changes impact the environment?

☑ LESSON 4 Check

MS-ESS3-4

1. Construct an Explanation Why is it so important for sources of fresh water to be protected?

....

....

....

....

2. Cause and Effect How do farming methods cause water pollution?

....

....

....

3. Provide Evidence What evidence suggests that factories sometimes cause water pollution?

....

....

....

....

....

....

4. Analyze Systems How does water pollution in one area affect water and organisms elsewhere?

....

....

....

....

....

5. Construct Arguments Write an argument to defend the idea that oil spills are the worst environmental hazard.

....

....

....

....

....

....

....

....

Quest CHECK-IN

In this lesson, you learned why fresh water is a limited resource within Earth's systems. You also discovered how human activities lead to water pollution and how humans can reduce freshwater and ocean pollution.

Evaluate Why is it important to consider the effects of waste disposal on water sources?

....

....

....

....

👆 INTERACTIVITY

Reducing Waste

Go online to determine how everyone at your school can work together to reduce wastes and help the environment. Then make a plan to reduce the trash output at your school.

FROM WASTEWATER TO
Tap Water

 VIDEO

Walk through the water treatment process.

Fresh water is a precious resource on Earth, so we reuse every drop we can. Wastewater from homes and businesses ends up being recycled for irrigation, manufacturing, and replenishing aquatic ecosystems. But how do you recycle wastewater into drinking water? You engineer it!

The Challenge: To treat wastewater so it can return to the water supply.

Phenomenon In San Diego, California, the Point Loma Wastewater Treatment plant treats wastewater and makes it safe to drink, but it takes several steps. First, water from the sewer system passes through screens that filter out large particles. Next, the water flows into tanks where gravity separates solid waste from the water. Heavy solids sink to the bottom.

The water then flows to a second set of tanks where bacteria digest waste that's still in the water. Then the water is left to settle one more time and the last sediments are removed.

Following that, the water goes through a series of filters to get rid of any small solids or harmful microorganisms. The last step is disinfection using chlorine and UV light. Finally, this water will spend about six months in storage before it arrives at a tap.

DESIGN CHALLENGE

Can you design a model for recycling wastewater or rainwater from your home or school? Go to the Engineering Design Notebook to find out!

A typical wastewater plant has many, many tanks.

Primary Treatment			Secondary Treatment		Disinfection		
Pumping station	Primary screening	Primary sedimentation	Bacteria treatment	Secondary sedimentation	Filtration for micro-organisms	Cleaning with chlorine and UV	Clean water

Wastewater →

☑ TOPIC 7 Review and Assess

1 Population Growth and Resource Consumption

MS-ESS3-4

1. Rather than increasing at a constant rate, human population growth in recent decades has increased more and more rapidly over time. This rate of change is called
A. excessive growth.
B. exponential growth.
C. reverse growth.
D. zero growth.

2. For the global population growth rate to reach zero, the number of births would have to be

....

....

3. Connect to Society Beginning around 1750, the global human population began to grow at a much faster rate than it had in the years before this time. What caused this change in the population growth rate?

....

....

....

....

4. Cause and Effect How does a growing human population affect Earth's resources?

....

....

....

....

....

....

2 Air Pollution

MS-ESS3-4

5. Evaluate Reasoning A classmate tells you that the good thing about renewable resources like trees is that you can use them and use them and they will never run out. What is your classmate misunderstanding about renewable resources?

....

....

....

....

....

....

6. Which is a natural source of air pollution?
A. volcanoes
B. carbon monoxide
C. smog
D. ozone layer

7. Automobiles contribute to air pollution by
A. increasing methane.
B. decreasing oxygen.
C. decreasing carbon dioxide.
D. increasing carbon dioxide.

8. As human populations continue to increase, the demand for natural resources

....

9. Construct Explanations Why did it take international efforts to reduce the impact of air pollution on the ozone layer?

....

....

....

....

....

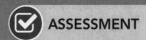
3 Impacts on Land

MS-ESS3-4

10. What is the difference between point and nonpoint sources of water pollution?

A. Point sources can be directly identified, and nonpoint cannot.

B. Point sources involve solid wastes, and nonpoint sources are liquids.

C. Point sources contain animal wastes, while nonpoint sources are human-made chemicals.

D. Point sources break down easily, while non-point sources break down over a long time.

11. Which of these changes can lead to desertification?

A. reduced air quality

B. increased plant life

C. reduced moisture

D. increased nutrient levels

12. What impact does logging have on the land?

A. increased nutrients

B. increased erosion

C. accelerated recycling of organic matter

D. accelerated soil deposition

13. Changing the flow of water, such as filling in a wetland for development, impacts the environment by

A. increasing desertification.

B. increasing flooding and pollution.

C. decreasing erosion.

D. decreasing nutrient depletion.

14. As human populations increase, there is a higher demand for ...., the use of land to produce food.

15. When natural forces such as wind, water, and ice move particles of rocks or soil, the process is called ....

4 Water Pollution

MS-ESS3-4

16. Construct Arguments What evidence could be used in an argument against planting the same crop in the same field year after year?

....

....

....

....

....

....

....

....

17. Which of these is a source of human-made ocean pollution?

A. fresh water

B. ozone

C. plastics

D. sediment

18. Construct an Argument What evidence supports the idea that construction companies should implement protocols that reduce the amount of sediment that runs off from land into the water?

....

....

....

....

....

....

☑ TOPIC 7 Review and Assess

MS-ESS3-4

Lange's metalmark butterfly

Evidence-Based Assessment

In 1976, ecologists made a disturbing discovery in the Antioch Dunes along the banks of the San Joaquin River in San Francisco. A butterfly, formally observed first in 1939 and only found in the dunes, was going extinct. Known as Lange's metalmark butterfly, it became one of the first insects protected as an endangered species by federal law.

Here are some important facts about the butterfly and its habitat.

- Lange's metalmark butterfly produces one crop of offspring each year, and females only lay their eggs on one species of plant, the naked-stem buckwheat plant.

- The dunes where the butterfly lives formed thousands of years ago, when sand deposited by ancient glaciers was moved and shaped by water and wind.

- When the first American settlers arrived in the early 1800s, the dunes ran along the river for about 3 kilometers (2 miles) and reached over 30 meters (100 feet) high in some places.

- As the population of San Francisco grew, parts of the dunes were leveled and developed for industry. Sand from the dunes was mined to produce bricks and other building materials. The data table shows changes in the population of San Francisco from 1850 to 2000.

San Francisco County Population, 1850–2000

Year	Population	Year	Population
1850	21,000	1930	634,394
1860	56,802	1940	634,536
1870	149,473	1950	775,357
1880	233,959	1960	740,316
1890	298,997	1970	715,674
1900	342,782	1980	678,974
1910	416,912	1990	723,959
1920	506,676	2000	776,733

1. **Analyze Data** Which statement about the trends in San Francisco's population growth is valid?
   A. It dropped for a few decades after 1890, but has grown almost every year since then.
   B. It grew slowly each year until 1930, when the population quickly increased.
   C. It increased steadily each year since 1850.
   D. It grew rapidly in the mid to late 1800s and then again in the 1940s.

2. **Cause and Effect** How would mining and extracting sand affect plants that live in the dunes, like the naked-stem buckwheat? Based on the population data, when you do think the most sand was removed from the dunes? Explain.

....

....

....

....

....

....

....

....

....

....

....

3. **Apply Scientific Reasoning** The remaining sand dunes became a national wildlife refuge in 1980. A few years later, researchers began an annual count of the butterflies. Between 1999 and 2008, the number of butterflies fell steadily. What might account for this continued drop?

....

....

....

....

....

4. **Engage in Argument** How could an increase in the human population of San Francisco have impacted the Lange's metalmark butterflies that lived there? Use evidence from the text to support your answer.

....

....

....

....

....

....

....

....

....

....

....

....

Quest FINDINGS

Complete the Quest!

Phenomenon Refine your plan to reduce trash at your school and present the plan.

Cause and Effect We produce a lot of trash that is disposed of in landfills. How would decreasing the trash we generate affect Earth's systems?

....

....

....

....

👆 **INTERACTIVITY**

Reflect on Trash Backlash

Washing Away

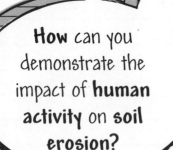

How can you demonstrate the impact of **human activity** on **soil erosion?**

Background

Phenomenon A nearby town is considering a developer's plan to turn riverfront property into shops, restaurants, and apartments. The area is now an undisturbed habitat consisting of trees, bushes, and grasses. Almost all of the natural vegetation will be removed during construction. You will be part of a team tasked with providing an environmental impact report to the town board.

In this lab, you will design and conduct an investigation into the impact of vegetation and ground cover on soil erosion. You will test how quickly water runs off soil in different conditions and how much soil is carried away by the water.

Materials

(per pair)
- two 2-liter beverage bottles, cut lengthwise to form troughs
- about 4 cups of potting soil, divided in half
- grass or radish seedlings
- 2 large plastic cups
- 1 liter of water
- watering can with rain spout
- stopwatch

Plan Your Investigation

HANDS-ON LAB

иDemonstrate Go online for a downloadable worksheet of this lab.

1. Work with your partner to design an experimental setup using the materials provided by your teacher. Your experiment must test how fast water runs off the soil and how much soil is carried away in the runoff. As you design your setup, consider the following questions:

   - How would you describe the condition of the riverbank before the proposed construction?

   - How would you describe the condition of the riverbank during the construction?

   - How can you use the materials to model the condition of the riverbank before and during construction?

   - How can you design your setup so that you will be able to measure how fast the water runs off the soil and how much soil is contained in the runoff?

   - What are your dependent variable and independent variable, and the factors you hold constant?

   - How many tests will you run?

   - What observations will you make and what data will you collect?

2. Write a detailed procedure describing how you will investigate the effects of removing vegetation and ground cover on soil erosion. Include any sketches of your setup.

3. After getting teacher approval for your procedure, conduct your investigation.

4. Record your observations and data in the table provided.

Procedure and Sketches

Data Table

Bottle	Water Poured (mL)	Water Captured (mL)	Time (sec)	Observations of Water Collected
Grass and soil				
Soil only				

Analyze and Interpret Data

1. **Compare Data** Review the data you collected and the observations you recorded. How do the results of your tests compare?

....

....

....

....

2. **Apply Scientific Reasoning** Based on the results of your investigation, describe how soil erosion might affect the ecology of rivers, lakes, and other bodies of water.

....

....

....

....

3. **Refine Your Plan** Examine and evaluate the procedures of other teams. Based on what you learned, how might you modify your own procedure to improve the results of your investigation?

....

....

....

....

....

4. **Engage in Argument** What would you recommend to the town board? Use the data from your investigation as evidence to justify your claim.

....

....

....

....

....

TOPIC

8

Waves and Electromagnetic Radiation

NGSS PERFORMANCE EXPECTATIONS

MS-PS4-1 Use mathematical representations to describe a simple model for waves that includes how the amplitude of a wave is related to the energy in a wave.

MS-PS4-2 Develop and use a model to describe that waves are reflected, absorbed, or transmitted through various materials.

HANDS-ON LAB

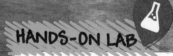

uConnect See how particles on a wave move in this rope experiment.

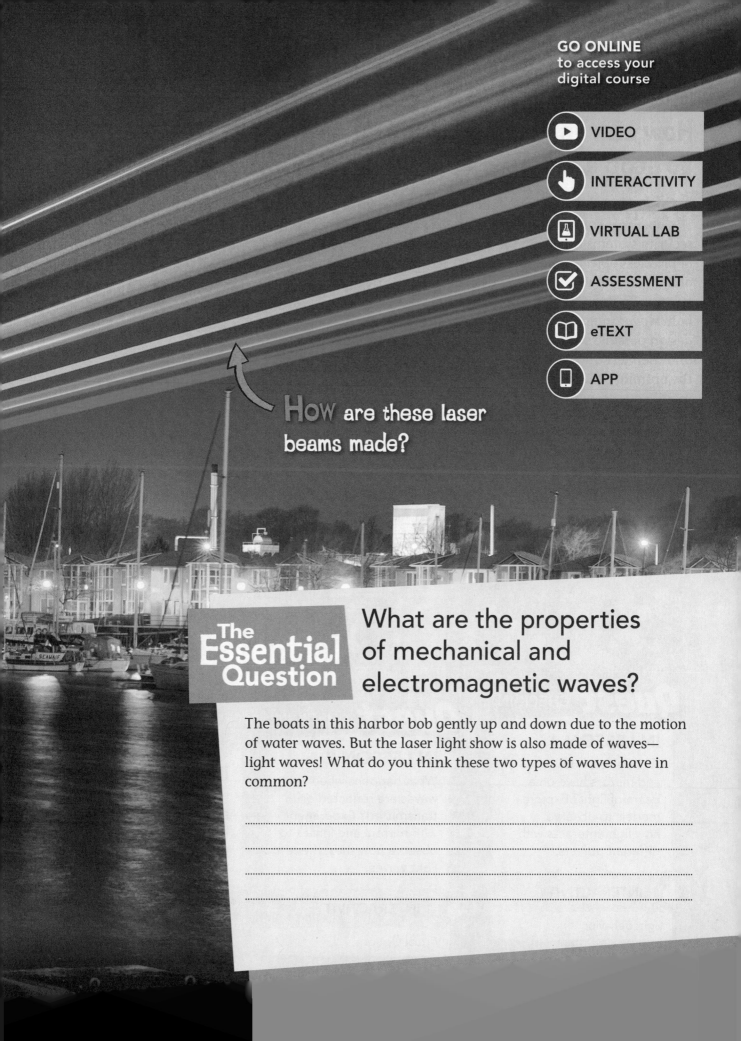

GO ONLINE
to access your
digital course

▶ VIDEO

👆 INTERACTIVITY

⚗ VIRTUAL LAB

☑ ASSESSMENT

📖 eTEXT

📱 APP

HOW are these laser beams made?

The Essential Question

What are the properties of mechanical and electromagnetic waves?

The boats in this harbor bob gently up and down due to the motion of water waves. But the laser light show is also made of waves—light waves! What do you think these two types of waves have in common?

....

....

....

....

Quest KICKOFF

How can you design a system to stop a thief?

NBC LEARN ▶ VIDEO

STEM **Phenomenon** It may seem like something out of the movies, but some security systems use lasers to help prevent the theft of priceless objects. Engineers apply their knowledge of light and how it behaves to design these security systems. In this Quest activity, you will explore how light waves interact with lenses and mirrors. You will design possible solutions for a security demonstration and then test and evaluate your solutions to determine the optimal design. After making any additional modifications, you will demonstrate your expertise by directing a beam of light around an obstacle to reach

After watching the Quest Kickoff video, think about a problem in your community that might be solved with the use of lasers. Record your solutions. Then share your ideas with a partner and discuss how lasers are important to our daily lives.

....
....
....
....
....
....
....
....

MS-PS4-1 Use mathematical representations to describe a simple model for waves that includes how the amplitude of a wave is related to the energy in a wave.
MS-PS4-2 Develop and use a model to describe that waves are reflected, absorbed, or transmitted through various materials.

 INTERACTIVITY

Design to Stop a Thief

Quest CHECK-IN

IN LESSON 1
What effects do lenses and mirrors have on a beam of light? Explore models to observe how light interacts with different objects.

 INTERACTIVITY

Light Behavior

Quest CHECK-IN

IN LESSON 2
What happens when light waves are reflected or transmitted? Experiment with mirrors and lenses to observe how they affect light waves.

 INTERACTIVITY

Virtual Optics

IN LESSON 3
How do the properties of sound waves differ from light waves? Consider the properties of waves in your solution.

Quest CHECK-IN

IN LESSON 4

How can you make a beam of light bend around an object? Develop and evaluate possible solutions to the challenge.

▶ **INTERACTIVITY**

Optical Demonstration

Quest CHECK-IN

IN LESSON 5

STEM How can you apply your knowledge of lenses and mirrors to your solution? Build and test a solution, using lenses and mirrors. Then communicate your solution in a presentation or visual display.

HANDS-ON LAB

An Optimal Optical Solution

Quest FINDINGS

Complete the Quest!

Evaluate your security system designs and reflect on the design and engineering process.

▶ **INTERACTIVITY**

Reflect on Your Demonstration

391

① Wave Properties

Guiding Questions

- How can you use a simple model to describe a wave and its features?
- How can you observe the properties of waves?
- What kinds of patterns can you predict based on wave properties?

Connections

Literacy Integrate Information

Math Use Proportional Relationships

MS-PS4-1

Vocabulary

wave
mechanical wave
medium
electromagnetic
  radiation
transverse wave
amplitude
longitudinal wave
wavelength
frequency

Academic Vocabulary

vacuum

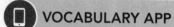

VOCABULARY APP

Practice vocabulary on a mobile device.

Quest CONNECTION

Think about what kind of wave light is, and understand its properties, to prepare you for your quest.

Connect It !

✏ **Read the caption, and then label the photos with different types of waves that are indicated in some way by the photos.**

Engage in Argument How is Earth dependent on the sun for energy?

....

....

....

Connect to Society How is a tsunami warning system a benefit to society?

....

....

....

Types of Waves

When you think of a wave, you probably picture a surface wave on the ocean. Actually, a **wave** is any disturbance that transfers energy from place to place. An ocean wave is one type of wave called a **mechanical wave**, meaning it moves through some type of matter. The matter a wave travels through is called a **medium**. A mechanical wave cannot travel through a **vacuum**, such as space.

Sound waves are another type of mechanical wave. Sound can travel through the ocean, but it can also travel through a solid object, such as a piece of metal, or a gas, such as the air. It cannot travel through a vacuum such as space.

Another type of wave is an electromagnetic wave. This type of wave transfers **electromagnetic radiation**, a type of energy. Examples of electromagnetic radiation include visible light, radio waves, X-rays, and microwaves. Like a mechanical wave, electromagnetic waves transfer energy. However, electromagnetic waves are unique in that they can travel without a medium.

Both types of waves involve a transfer of energy without a transfer of matter. While mechanical waves travel *through* matter, the waves themselves do not move the matter to a new place. The waves are disturbances in matter that transfer energy.

Figure 1 shows several different types of waves at work. Ocean waves cause the buoy to bob in the water. If a seafloor sensor detects a wave called a tsunami (soo NAH mee), it sends a signal to the buoy, which then sends a radio signal to a satellite orbiting Earth. The signal gets relayed to scientists, who can then warn coastal communities. The sunlight that lights this scene is also made of waves.

Academic Vocabulary
A vacuum is completely empty. Why is the space around you not considered a vacuum?

....

....

Reflect Write down some examples of waves that you are familiar with from everyday life. Can you classify them as mechanical or electromagnetic?

World of Waves

Figure 1 A tsunameter is a buoy anchored to the ocean floor. It detects extremely large waves called tsunamis and sends a radio signal to warn people.

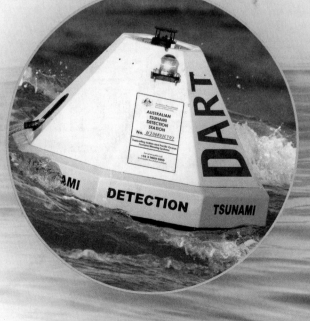

Transverse Waves Waves can be classified by how energy is transmitted. Energy is transmitted through a medium by mechanical waves. Electromagnetic waves are capable of transmitting energy through empty space.

Waves can also be classified by how the particles in a disturbance vibrate. A mechanical wave begins when a source of energy causes a medium to vibrate. The direction of the vibration determines what type of mechanical wave is produced. A **transverse wave** travels perpendicular (at right angles) to the direction of the source's motion. The person in **Figure 2** is using his arms to make up-and-down vibrations in two ropes. Each particle of the rope moves up and down. The direction of the waves he's producing, though, is perpendicular to that up-and-down motion. The energy travels toward the far ends of the ropes.

The curved shape of the rope indicates the main features of a transverse wave. The high point of a wave is its crest, and the low point is the trough. Halfway between the crest and trough is the wave's resting position. The distance between the highest crest and the resting position marks the wave's **amplitude**. In general, the amplitude of a wave is the maximum distance the medium vibrates from the rest position.

Electromagnetic waves, such as sunlight, are also transverse waves. In their case, however, there is no motion of particles, even when light travels through a liquid, such as water, or a solid, such as glass.

Transverse Waves

Figure 2 ✏ Use arrows to indicate the direction the rope is vibrating and the direction energy is flowing. Label a crest and a trough, and indicate the amplitude.

Longitudinal Waves

A wave that travels in the same direction as the vibrations that produce it is called a **longitudinal wave**. Sound is a longitudinal wave. Sound travels from speakers when flat surfaces inside the speakers vibrate in and out, compressing and expanding the air next to them.

Figure 3 shows a longitudinal wave in a spring toy. When the left hand pulls on the toy, the result is a series of stretches and compressions. Gaps between compressions are called rarefactions. Energy moves to the right along the toy.

While the wave travels, the spring particles do not move all the way to the right like the wave does. Each spring particle moves back and forth, like the hand. The small piece of ribbon on the spring moves the same way the particles in the spring move.

Literacy Connection

Integrate Information As you learn about waves, take notes that summarize and categorize the different motions that waves produce.

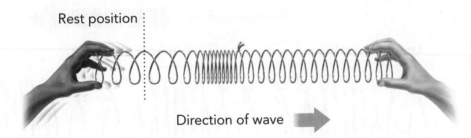

Rest position

Direction of wave

Longitudinal Wave
Figure 3 ✏ Label a compression and a rarefaction.

Surface Waves

Combinations of transverse and longitudinal waves are called surface waves. For example, an ocean wave travels at the surface of water. When a wave passes through water, the water (and anything on it) vibrates up and down. The water also moves back and forth slightly in the direction that the wave is traveling. The up-and-down and back-and-forth movements combine to make each particle of water move in a circle, as shown in **Figure 4**.

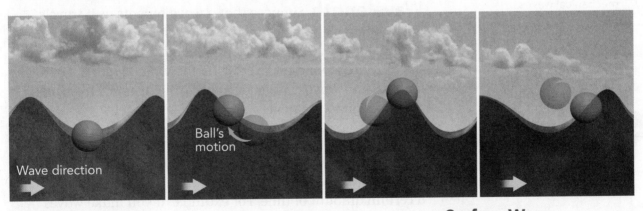

Ball's motion

Wave direction

Surface Wave
Figure 4 As waves move from left to right, they cause the ball to move in a circle.

✅ **READING CHECK** **Compare and Contrast** What is the main difference between a surface wave and a longitudinal wave?

....

....

Properties of Waves

Figure 5 All waves have amplitude, wavelength, frequency, and speed. After you read about these properties, answer the questions on the image.

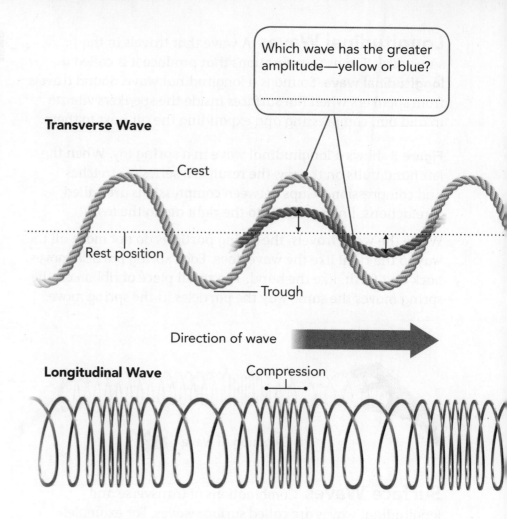

Transverse Wave

Crest

Rest position

Trough

Which wave has the greater amplitude—yellow or blue?

....

Direction of wave

Longitudinal Wave

Compression

HANDS-ON LAB

**Investigate** Model the three different types of mechanical waves.

INTERACTIVITY

See how a wave travels through a coil.

Properties of Waves

In addition to amplitude, all waves have three other properties: wavelength, frequency, and speed. These properties are all related to one another.

Wavelength Suppose that a wave repeats as it travels. Its **wavelength** is determined by the distance it travels before it starts to repeat. The wavelength of a transverse wave is the distance from crest to crest, as shown in **Figure 5**. For a longitudinal wave, the wavelength is the distance from one compression to the next.

Frequency The number of times a wave repeats in a given amount of time is called its **frequency**. You can also think of frequency as the number of waves that pass a given point in a certain amount of time. For example, if you make waves on a rope so that one wave passes by a point every second, the frequency is 1 wave per second. Frequency is measured in units called hertz (Hz). A wave that occurs every second has a frequency of 1 Hz. If two waves pass by in a second, the frequency is 2 Hz.

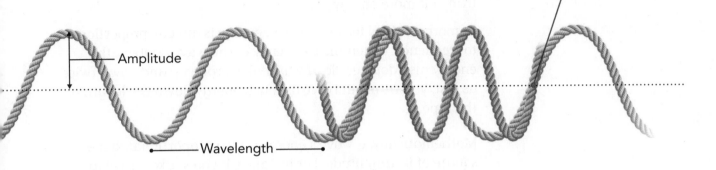

One yellow wave passes by this point each second, so the frequency of the yellow wave is ....

Two green waves pass by this point each second, so the frequency of the green wave is ....

Amplitude

Wavelength

Wavelength

Rarefaction

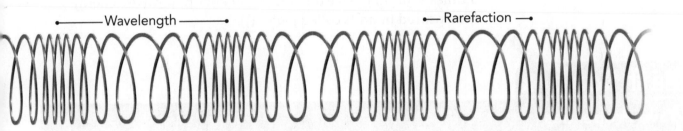

Speed The speed of a wave is determined by the distance it travels in a certain amount of time. Different waves have different speeds. For instance, a light wave travels almost a million times faster than a sound wave travels through air! Waves also travel at different speeds through different materials. For example, light travels faster through water than through glass. Sound travels more than three times faster through water than through air.

To calculate a wave's speed, divide the distance it travels by the time it takes to travel that distance. You can also find a wave's speed if you know its wavelength and frequency—just multiply wavelength times frequency.

Wave speed = **Wavelength** × **Frequency**

✅ READING CHECK **Predict** If you and a friend are standing at opposite ends of a gymnasium and one of you claps, will the other person hear the clap at the same time she sees it happen? Why or why not?

....

....

INTERACTIVITY

Generate virtual waves in a wave pool.

VIDEO

See what happens when balls of different masses are dropped in water.

Wave Energy

Waves transmit energy from place to place. The amount of energy they transmit depends on how much energy was input by the original source of the vibration. Faster vibrations transmit more energy. Larger amplitude vibrations also transmit more energy.

In mathematical terms, a wave's energy is directly proportional to frequency. When the frequency of the wave doubles, the energy also doubles. So, if you shake a rope up and down twice as fast, you transmit twice as much energy down the length of the rope.

Mathematically, a wave's energy is also proportional to the square of its amplitude. For instance, if you shake a rope to make waves and then move your hand three times as high with each shake, the wave energy increases by a factor of 3 times 3, or nine! Like other forms of energy, a wave's energy is measured in units called joules (J).

Math Toolbox

Wave Properties

🖉 The table shows the properties of waves near the beach on one summer day. Use the relationship between speed, wavelength, and frequency to complete the table. Then answer the questions.

Waves at a Beach				
Time	Amplitude	Wavelength	Frequency	Speed
10 AM	0.4 m	10 m	2 Hz	
2 PM	0.2 m		4 Hz	2 m/s
6 PM	0.3 m	12 m		4 m/s

1. **Use Tables** What would happen to the energy of the 10 AM wave if the frequency increased to 6 Hz?

....

2. **Apply Mathematics** If the amplitude of the 6 PM wave increases to 0.6 m, how many times greater would the energy become?

....

....

3. **Use Proportional Relationships** Recall that speed = wavelength × frequency. Assuming that the wavelength of a wave stays the same, would the energy of the wave increase or decrease if the speed of the wave increases? Why?

....

....

....

....

1. **Explain** How can you measure the wavelength of a longitudinal wave?

....

....

....

2. **Calculate** A sound wave's frequency is 4 Hz and its wavelength is 8 meters. What is the wave's speed?

....

3. **Use Models** ✏ Draw a model of a transverse wave. Use lines and labels to show the amplitude and wavelength of the wave.

4. **Use Proportional Relationships** During high tide, ocean waves often become larger. If the amplitude of a wave increases by a factor of 4, by how much does the energy increase?

....

....

....

5. **Cause and Effect** If a musician increases the wavelength of the sound waves she produces without changing their speed, what must be happening to the frequency? Explain your answer.

....

....

....

....

....

....

....

....

Quest CHECK-IN

In this lesson, you learned about the difference between electromagnetic and mechanical waves, including the three different types of mechanical waves that move through and affect the matter around us. You also learned how the properties of waves such as amplitude, frequency, energy, and speed are related.

Evaluate If you were designing a security system that uses light to detect an intruder, why would it be important to know about the different media and materials that would be parts of the system?

....

....

....

👆 INTERACTIVITY

Light Behavior

Go online to learn more about the behavior of light, including how a mirror affects a laser beam.

SOUND AND LIGHT AT THE
Ballpark

It's baseball season! The lights illuminate the field. As the batter swings, there is a whoosh of the bat through the air, and a satisfying CRACK! as he hits a long ball to the outfield.

Fans are yelling and cheering. "PEANUTS! Get your PEANUTS!" shout the vendors as they move through the packed stands. "Take Me Out to the Ball Game" blares over the speakers, and everyone stands up and sings.

A baseball game is a sporting event. But everything that happens there obeys the laws of physics. How do light and sound waves behave at the ball park? Take a look—and listen!

There are runners on all the bases, and the batter hits the ball. It's a ground ball to the shortstop. He throws it to the third baseman, who has his foot on third base. The umpire at third base watches the runner's foot touch the base while listening for the sound of the ball striking the third baseman's glove.

The next batter comes up to the plate and misses the first pitch. You see the catcher catch the ball before you hear the thwack of the ball hitting his glove.

You see the umpire signal a strike before you hear him call "STRIKE ONE!"

On the next pitch, you hear the crack of the bat hitting the ball after you see the batter hit the ball. It's a home run!

You see the bright lights for the night game as soon as the worker throws the switch.

Think about the last time you watched a thunderstorm. The lightning and thunder happen at the same moment—but you may see the lightning several seconds before you hear the thunder. Why does this happen? Because sound waves and light waves are different kinds of energy.

- Sound waves need a medium to travel through, such as water or air. A sound wave is a mechanical disturbance. Sound travels about 332 meters per second in air.

- Light waves can travel through the vacuum of space. A light wave is an electromagnetic disturbance. Light travels about 300,000,000 meters per second in air.

Use what you know about sound and light waves to answer the following questions.

1. **Construct Explanations** How does the time at which you see things happen at a baseball game compare to the time when you hear things happen? Explain your answer.

2. **Infer** The batter hits the ball while runners are on all the bases. Is the umpire making an accurate call if he compares the sound of the ball hitting the third baseman's glove to the time he sees the runner touch the base? Why or why not?

2 Wave Interactions

Guiding Questions

- How do waves interact with different materials?
- How do waves interact with each other?

Connection

Literacy Integrate Information

MS-PS4-2

Vocabulary

reflection
refraction
diffraction
absorption
interference
standing wave
resonance

Academic Vocabulary

transmitted

 VOCABULARY APP

Practice vocabulary on a mobile device.

Quest CONNECTION

Pay attention to how lenses and mirrors affect the motion of light.

Connect It !

🖊 **Look at the goldfish shown swimming in a glass tank. Place an X on any fish that you think is a reflection.**

Use Evidence How many real fish do you think there are?

....

....

Construct Explanations Why is it difficult to count the number of fish in the tank?

....

....

....

....

Reflection, Refraction, and Absorption

If you've ever been to the beach, you've seen how different kinds of waves move. Some ocean waves crash into rocks or piers, while others reach the shore smoothly. Rays of sunlight hit the surface of the water, and some bounce off while others pass through. In general, when waves encounter different media, they are either reflected, transmitted, or absorbed.

Reflection Some waves are completely blocked by an obstruction, but their energy is not absorbed or converted to another form of energy. These types of waves bounce off, or reflect from, those obstructions. In a **reflection**, the wave bounces off and heads in a different direction. The law of reflection states that the angle of incidence equals the angle of reflection. This means that the angle at which the wave strikes the material will match the angle at which the reflected wave bounces off that material, as shown in **Figure 2**. Light reflecting from a mirror is the most familiar example of reflection. The echo of a voice from the walls of a canyon is another example.

Fish Reflection and Refraction
Figure 1 Light waves reflecting off the walls of a tank can create multiple images of the same fish.

Reflection
Figure 2 A flashlight beam reflects off of a mirror at the same angle it strikes.

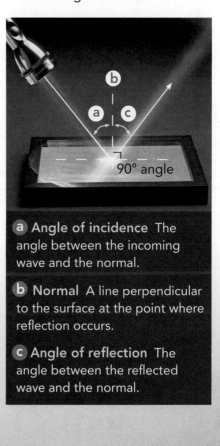

90° angle

a Angle of incidence The angle between the incoming wave and the normal.

b Normal A line perpendicular to the surface at the point where reflection occurs.

c Angle of reflection The angle between the reflected wave and the normal.

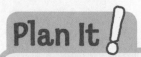

Plan It

Develop Models ✏ Have you ever seen a movie scene in which a character appears to be looking at a mirror, yet the camera is not visible in the mirror? Think about how the director sets up this scene. Draw a set up that shows the position of the actor, the camera, and the mirror, and demonstrate why the camera's image is not visible to the camera.

Refraction

Figure 3 Light rays bend as they enter water because one side of the wave fronts slows down in water while the other side continues at the same speed in air.

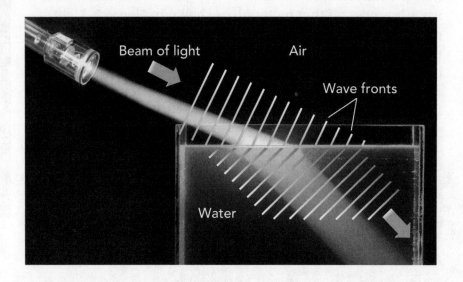

Academic Vocabulary

What is another way for saying that a wave is "transmitted" through a medium?

....

....

....

Refraction
Imagine riding a bike down a smooth asphalt road. When you turn off the road onto a dirt path, the transition can be jarring. You might have to grip the handlebars hard to keep the bike going straight as each wheel is on a different surface.

When light waves are **transmitted** from one medium into another, they also bend in different directions. This bending is due to **refraction**, or the bending of waves due to a change in speed.

When a wave enters a new medium at an angle other than perpendicular, it changes direction. For instance, when light is directed at water at an angle, as in **Figure 3**, the light slows down and bends downward. The wave bends toward the normal, the imaginary line that runs perpendicular from the boundary between the two media.

Diffraction Did you ever wonder how you can hear someone speaking even if they are around the corner of a building or doorway? This is an example of **diffraction**. Waves don't only travel in straight lines. They are also bend around objects.

You can observe diffraction with water waves as well as sound waves. Water waves can diffract around a rock or an island in the ocean. Because tsunami waves can diffract all the way around an island, people on the shores of the entire island are at risk.

Absorption When you think of something being absorbed, you might think of how a paper towel soaks up water. Waves can be absorbed by certain materials, too. In **absorption**, the energy of a wave is transferred to the material it encounters. When ocean waves reach a shoreline, most of their energy is absorbed by the shore.

When light waves encounter the surface of a different medium or material, the light waves may be reflected, refracted, or absorbed. What happens to the waves depends on the type of material they hit. Light is mostly absorbed by dark materials, such as the surface of a parking lot, and mostly reflected by light materials, such as snow.

Literacy Connection

Integrate Information
As you read, classify the phenomena you learn about as either interactions between waves and media or interactions among waves.

Reflect What are some ways in which you use reflection in your everyday life? Are there things you have to keep in mind when you use reflective devices, such as mirrors?

 VIDEO

Discover how reflection and absorption create echoes.

Question It!

Classify ✏ Identify each picture as being an example of reflection, refraction, or absorption.

Wave Interference

Have you ever seen two ocean waves collide from opposite directions so they momentarily form a bigger, hill-like shape before continuing in their original directions? This is an example of wave **interference**. There are two types.

Constructive Interference

The example of two waves of similar sizes colliding and forming a wave with an amplitude greater than either of the original waves is called constructive interference. You can think of it as waves "helping each other," or adding their energies together. As shown in **Figure 4**, when the crests of two waves overlap, they make a higher crest. If two troughs overlap, they make a deeper trough. In both cases, the amplitude of the combined crests or troughs increases.

Types of Interference

Figure 4 ✏ Write captions to describe three parts of destructive interference. Complete the key to explain what the different arrows mean in the images.

Constructive Interference

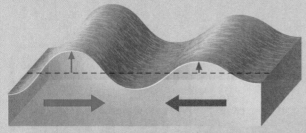

1 Two waves approach each other. The wave on the left has a greater amplitude.

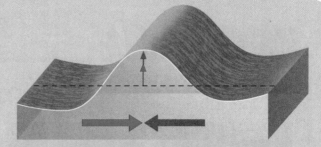

2 The new crest's amplitude is the sum of the amplitudes of the original crests.

Destructive Interference

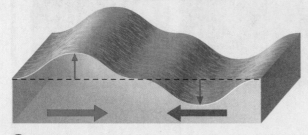

1 ....

....

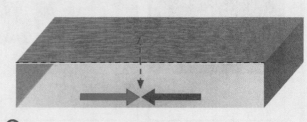

2 ....

....

Destructive Interference

When two waves combine to form a wave with a smaller amplitude than either original wave had, this is called destructive interference. Destructive interference occurs when the crest of one wave overlaps the trough of another wave. If the crest has a larger amplitude than the trough of the other wave, the crest "wins," and part of it remains. If the original trough has a larger amplitude than the crest of the other wave, the result is a trough. If a crest and trough have equal amplitudes, they cancel each other out, as shown in **Figure 4**. Destructive interference is used in noise-canceling headphones to block out distracting noises in a listener's surroundings.

☑ READING CHECK **Infer** Which type of wave interference could cause sound to become louder? Explain your answer.

....

....

....

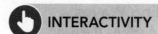

INTERACTIVITY

Observe wave interference in a rope and in surface waves.

Interfering Waves

Figure 5 Ripples created by rain water on a pond interfere with one another in a pattern that exhibits both constructive and destructive interference.

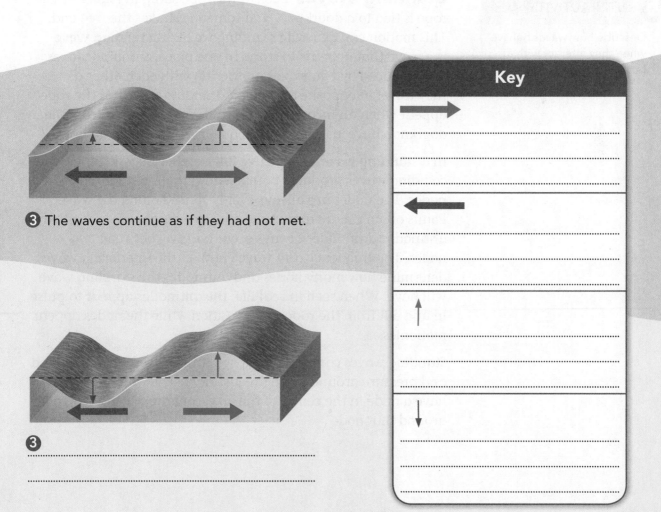

❸ The waves continue as if they had not met.

❸ ....

....

Key
→
←
↑
↓

Standing Waves

Figure 6 ✏ As the hand shown at left increases the frequency, the number of wavelengths present in the standing wave will increase. In a standing wave, it looks like there's a mirror image of both the crest and trough. Label the rest of the nodes and antinodes.

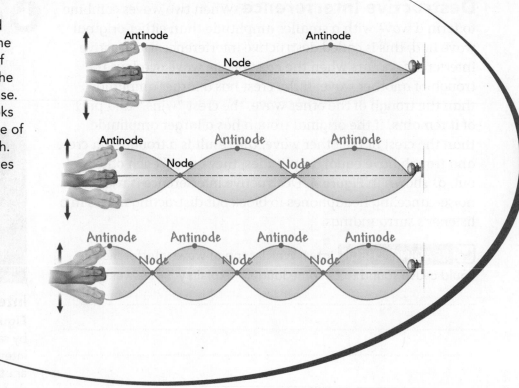

INTERACTIVITY

Describe how waves behave when they interact with a barrier or boundary.

Standing Waves

Look at the rope setup in **Figure 6**. The rope is tied to a doorknob, and someone shakes the free end. This motion can generate standing waves. A **standing wave** is a wave that appears to stand in one place. Standing waves are produced by two waves interfering with each other as they travel in opposite directions. Standing waves on the rope appear when an incoming wave and wave reflected from the doorknob have just the right frequency to interfere as shown.

In a standing wave, destructive interference between the two colliding waves produces points with zero amplitude, called nodes. The nodes are always evenly spaced along the wave. Points of maximum amplitude on a standing wave are called antinodes. Antinodes always occur halfway between two nodes. The frequency and wavelength of the interfering waves determine how many nodes and antinodes the standing wave will have. When seen in real life, the antinodes appear to pulse in and out from the rope's rest position while the nodes appear motionless.

Standing waves can sometimes appear on lakes when the wind and pressure around them are just right. The water appears to have a node in the center of the lake, and the water wave rolls around that node.

Resonance Think about the last time you swung on a swing at a playground. You may have noticed that it is difficult to get yourself going. Once you are in motion, you can pull on the chains of the swing and pump your legs at the right time to keep yourself swinging. The swing has a natural frequency, and your actions match that frequency to create greater amplitudes in your motion.

Most objects have at least one natural frequency of vibration. Standing waves occur in an object when it vibrates at one of these natural frequencies. If a nearby object vibrates at the same frequency, it can cause resonance. **Resonance** is an increase in the amplitude of a vibration that occurs when external vibrations match an object's natural frequency.

When engineers build a bridge, they have to make sure that bridge supports are not placed at potential nodes for a standing wave. Otherwise, wind could cause the bridge to swing wildly like the rope in **Figure 6** and collapse.

Understanding the resonance of different materials is also useful for people who build guitars, violins, or other wood-based stringed instruments. If the wood in a guitar, such as the one in **Figure 7**, resonates too much with a certain note, it may sound too loud when that particular note is struck. Likewise, if the wood does not resonate with any particular note, the instrument may lack volume or "presence" and sound dull.

☑ **READING CHECK** **Summarize** In general, why is it risky to build something whose natural frequency can be matched by external vibrations?

....

....

....

📖 **Make Meaning** Make a two-column chart in your notebook. Use it to record descriptions of constructive interference, destructive interference, standing waves, and resonance.

Musical Resonance
Figure 7 The types of wood and construction techniques used to make a guitar affect aspects of its sound, including its resonance.

409

☑LESSON 2 Check

MS-PS4-2

1. Relate Cause and Effect Explain what happens to light when it is refracted at the surface of water.

....

....

....

....

2. Interpret Diagrams The diagrams below show two waves interfering to form a dark blue result. Which of the diagrams depicts constructive interference? Explain your choice using the term *amplitude*.

A.   B.

....

....

....

....

....

3. Explain What does it mean for waves to be absorbed by a certain medium? Make sure to include energy in your explanation.

....

....

....

....

4. Construct Explanations Why does the transition of light waves from water to air make it seem as if fish and other things in a pond are shallower than they actually are?

....

....

....

....

....

....

....

....

....

....

....

Quest CHECK-IN

In this lesson, you learned how waves interact with their surroundings and with each other. Waves can reflect, refract, and be absorbed depending on the media they travel through and the materials they strike. They can also interfere with each other in ways that are destructive or constructive, resulting in phenomena such as standings waves and resonance.

Apply Concepts Think about the ways that light can change direction. What are two ways that you could change the path of light? What materials would you need to do it?

....

....

....

INTERACTIVITY

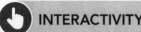

Virtual Optics

Go online to experiment with light and its transmission or reflection.

Say "CHEESE!"

INTERACTIVITY

Find out how cameras work.

For hundreds of years, people who traveled took sketch pads and pencils to record their memories. This all changed in the nineteenth century with the invention of photography.

The Challenge To continue to improve the ways in which people can record images.

Phenomenon Early cameras were large and clumsy objects that printed images on glass. In the twentieth century, engineers experimented with smaller and lighter cameras that used film. Today we have digital cameras. But they all use the same process to create images.

Cameras have changed a lot over the years!

Today, cameras all have three main parts for capturing light:

- The **lens** is the camera's eye. It detects the light reflected off of what you want to photograph.

- The **aperture** lets light in through the lens. The wider the aperture, the more light is let in.

- The **shutter** is like a curtain that opens when you take the photo.

In a film camera, the light changes the film both physically and chemically to create an image. In a *digital* camera, the light reaches photosensors, which convert the image to a string of numbers.

DESIGN CHALLENGE

Can you build your own simple camera using just a box? Go to the Engineering Design Notebook to find out!

LESSON

3 Sound Waves

Guiding Questions

- How are sound waves reflected, transmitted, or absorbed by materials?
- What factors affect the speed of sound waves?

Connections

Literacy Integrate With Visuals

Math Reason Quantitatively

MS-PS4-2

Vocabulary

loudness
intensity
decibel
pitch
Doppler effect

Academic Vocabulary

differentiate

 VOCABULARY APP

Practice vocabulary on a mobile device.

Quest CONNECTION

Think about how the properties of sound waves differ from light waves in your quest.

Connect It!

🖊 **When someone strikes a cymbal, the cymbal vibrates to produce sound. Draw compressions and rarefactions of the air particles as the sound waves travel away from the cymbal.**

Ask Questions Is sound a mechanical wave or an electromagnetic wave? Explain your answer.

....

Predict What do you think happens to a sound wave when the volume of sound increases?

....

The Behavior of Sound

All sound waves begin with a vibration. Look at the woman in **Figure 1.** When she hits a drum or a cymbal with her drumstick, the drum or cymbal vibrates rapidly, disturbing the air particles around the drum set. When the drum or cymbal moves away from its rest position, it creates a compression by pushing air particles together. When it moves back toward its rest position, it creates a rarefaction by causing air particles to spread out.

Recall that sound waves are mechanical waves that require a medium through which to travel. In the case of the drummer and the drum set, the compressions and rarefactions that are created travel through the air. Sound waves, however, travel more easily through liquids and solids. When you set a glass down on a table, for example, the sound waves that are generated travel first through the glass and the table and then are released into the air.

Sound waves are also longitudinal—they travel in the same direction as the vibrations that produce them. Like other types of mechanical waves, sound waves can be reflected, transmitted, absorbed, and diffracted.

HANDS-ON LAB

Discover how the amplitude of a guitar string affects its loudness.

Making Waves
Figure 1 The vibrations caused by hitting drums and cymbals generate sound waves.

413

Reflection and Transmission

Reflection and Transmission Like other mechanical waves, sound waves that pass through a surface are called transmitted waves, and sound waves that bounce off a surface are called reflected waves. When a sound wave travels through the air and comes into contact with a solid surface, such as a wall, a portion of the wave passes through the surface. Most of the wave, however, is reflected away from the surface.

Absorption Have you ever been to a concert in a large indoor theater? If so, you may have noticed panels on the walls. Most large theaters have acoustic panels to help with sound absorption. Sound absorption describes the process of sound waves striking a surface and quickly losing energy. The energy is converted to thermal energy in the surface. Acoustic panels in theaters are porous, meaning they are full of small holes, and they absorb a portion of the sound waves. In the case of a theater, absorption of sound waves improves the listening experience for people at the concert. More sound energy is absorbed than reflected, so the audience does not experience as much interference from reflected sound waves. See **Figure 2** for another example of absorption. Any material with a porous surface can act as a sound absorber.

A Quiet, Snowy Night
Figure 2 Have you noticed that it's quieter outside when there is snow on the ground? Why do you think this is?

....

....

....

If you've ever yelled loudly into an open space, such as a canyon or a courtyard, then you may have heard an echo. An echo occurs when sound waves are reflected off a hard surface, such as the wall of a rocky mountain. The sound you hear is delayed because it takes time for the sound waves to reflect off the surface and reach your ears.

Develop Models 🖊 Draw a picture of sound waves when an echo is created. In addition to reflected waves, your model should also indicate waves that are transmitted or absorbed.

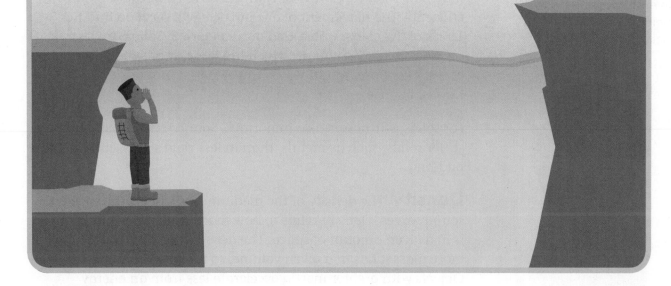

Diffraction It is usually easy to hear someone talking if they are in the same room as you, but you can also hear people in other rooms nearby. Why is this? You can hear them because sound waves can bend around the edges of an opening, such as a doorway. This is called sound diffraction. Sound waves, like water waves, spread out after passing through an opening.

How much sound waves are transmitted, reflected, absorbed, or diffracted depends greatly upon the medium through which they travel. If sound waves travel through air and hit a solid surface, such as a concrete wall, much of the energy in the waves is reflected back toward the source. If the surfaces they hit are softer or more porous, then more sound waves will be absorbed. Sound waves will be diffracted around corners and through passageways between hard surfaces.

HANDS-ON LAB

Investigate Use models to examine how sound waves travel through different media.

✓ **READING CHECK Summarize** What are four things that can happen to sound waves when they reach a barrier?

....

....

VIDEO

Explore what thunder is and how to determine your distance from an approaching storm.

Speed of Sound

Figure 3 Rate the speed of sound through the medium in each container, with "1" being the fastest and "3" being the slowest.

Factors Affecting the Speed of Sound

As you have read, sound waves are mechanical waves that require a medium through which to travel. The characteristics of the medium have an effect on the speed of the sound waves traveling through them. The main factors that affect the speed of sound are compressibility, stiffness, density, and temperature.

Stiffness In general, sound waves travel faster in materials that are harder to compress. This is because of how efficiently the movement of one particle will push on another. Think of the coins, water, and air in **Figure 3**. Solids are less compressible than liquids, which are less compressible than gases. Therefore, sound waves travel fastest in solids and slowest in gases.

For solids, stiffness is also important. Sound travels faster in stiffer solids, such as metals, than in less rigid solids, such as pudding.

Density The density of the medium also affects the speed of sound waves. Density refers to how much matter or mass there is in a given amount of space. The denser the material, the more mass it has in a given volume, so the greater its inertia. Objects with greater inertia accelerate less from an energy disturbance than objects with less inertia, or less massive objects. Therefore, in materials of the same stiffness, sound travels more slowly in the denser material.

Temperature The temperature of a medium also affects the speed at which sound waves travel through it, though in more complicated ways. For solids, an increase in temperature reduces the stiffness, so the sound speed decreases. For fluids, such as air, the increase in temperature reduces the density, so the sound speed generally increases.

✓ READING CHECK **Hypothesize** Would sound waves travel slower through air at the North Pole or at the equator? Explain.

....

....

....

....

....

Loudness and Pitch

How might you describe a sound? You might call it loud or soft, high or low. When you turn up the volume of your speakers, you increase the loudness of a sound. When you sing higher and higher notes, you increase the pitch of your voice. Loudness and pitch depend on different properties of sound waves.

Factors Affecting Loudness You use the term **loudness** to describe your awareness of the energy of a sound. How loud a sound is depends on the energy and intensity of the sound waves. If someone knocks lightly on your front door, then you might hear a quiet sound. If they pound on your door, then you hear a much louder sound. Why? The pounding transfers much more energy through the door than a light knock does. That's because a hard knock on a door produces a much greater amplitude in the sound waves than a softer knock does. Increased energy results in greater intensity of the waves. **Intensity** is the amount of energy a sound wave carries per second through a unit area. The closer the sound wave is to its source, the more energy it has in a given area. As the sound wave moves away from the source, the wave spreads out and the intensity decreases.

Intensity of Sound

Figure 4 ✎ Sound waves spread out as they travel away from the source producing the sound. For each of the locations in the image, rank the intensity of the sound waves coming from the band on a scale of 1 to 3, with 1 being the greatest intensity.

Academic Vocabulary

What is the root word in *differentiate*? How does this help you figure out the word's meaning?

....

....

....

....

....

....

Measuring Loudness

Measuring Loudness So, how do our ears **differentiate** between a light knock and a hard knock on a door? Loudness can be measured by a unit called a **decibel** (dB). The greater the decibels of the sound, the louder that sound seems to a listener. The loudness of a sound you can barely hear, such as a pin dropping to the floor, is about 0 dB. When someone lightly taps on your door, the loudness is about 30 dB. But if someone pounds on your door, that loudness might increase to 80 dB! Sounds louder than 100 dB, such as the sound of a chainsaw, can cause damage to people's ears, especially if they are exposed to the sounds for long periods of time. Music technicians use equalizers to change the loudness levels of different frequencies of sound, as in **Figure 5**.

Using an Equalizer

Figure 5 You can use an equalizer to adjust the loudness of sound waves at different frequencies. Raising the decibel level of low frequencies increases the bass tones of music.
How might you increase the high-pitched tones of music?

....

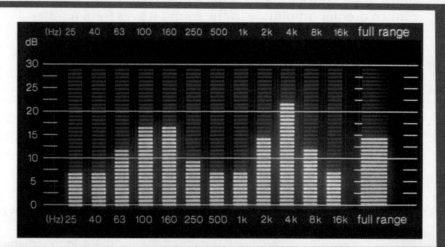

Math Toolbox

Decibel Levels

Every 10-decibel increase represents a tenfold increase in intensity and power. For example, when loudness increases from 20 to 30 decibels, a sound's power is multiplied by 10. If loudness increases by 10 again, power increases by another factor of 10. Therefore, when loudness increases from 20 to 40 decibels, power increases by a factor of 100!

1. **Reason Quantitatively** If a sound's power level increases from 20 decibels to 50 decibels, by what factor does its power increase?

....

....

2. **Cause and Effect** If you want to lower the loudness of the bass tones in your music by 20 decibels, by how much does the intensity need to decrease?

....

....

Thickness Affects Pitch

Figure 6 On a standard 6-string guitar, the strings range in thickness.

✎ On the photo, draw an X on the guitar string that has the lowest pitch.

Factors Affecting Pitch Have you ever heard someone describe a note on a piano as "high-pitched" or "low-pitched"? The **pitch** of a sound refers to how high or low the sound seems. Pitch depends upon the frequency of the sound waves. Sound waves with a high frequency have a high pitch, and waves with a low frequency have a low pitch.

The frequency of a sound wave depends upon how fast the source of the sound is vibrating. For example, when people speak or sing, the air from their lungs moves past their vocal cords and makes the cords vibrate, producing sound waves. When vocal cords vibrate more quickly, they produce higher-frequency sound waves with higher pitches. When vocal cords vibrate more slowly, they produce lower-frequency sound waves with lower pitches.

This phenomenon happens with all things that vibrate and produce sound waves. Guitars produce sound when someone strums or plucks their strings. If you've ever studied a guitar, then you may have noticed that its strings vary in thickness. The thicker strings of a guitar vibrate more slowly than the thinner strings do, and so the thicker strings have a lower frequency, and therefore a lower pitch, than the thinner strings (**Figure 6**).

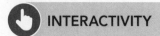
Literacy Connection

Integrate With Visuals
Do you think the motorcyclist would hear a change in pitch of the motorcycle's sound as he passes by you? Why or why not?

....

....

....

....

....

The Doppler Effect

Have you ever had a loud motorcycle drive by you and heard the pitch of the engine noise change? Change in pitch occurs because the movement of the source of the sound causes a sound wave to either compress or stretch. As the motorcycle approaches, the peaks of the emitted sound waves are scrunched together. When the peaks are closer together, the sound waves have a higher frequency. As the motorcycle moves away, the peaks of the emitted sound waves are spread out. The sound waves then have a lower frequency.

A change in frequency is perceived by a listener as a change in pitch. This change in frequency (and therefore, in pitch) of the sound wave in relation to an observer is called the **Doppler effect. Figure 7** shows the Doppler effect when a firetruck rushes by a person on the sidewalk.

☑ **READING CHECK** **Summarize** What property of a sound wave determines the pitch of a sound?

....

The Doppler Effect

Figure 7 As a firetruck speeds by, an observer detects changes in the pitch of the truck's siren. The firetruck approaches the observer in the first image. It then passes her and continues on.
✏ Draw the sound waves as the truck moves away.

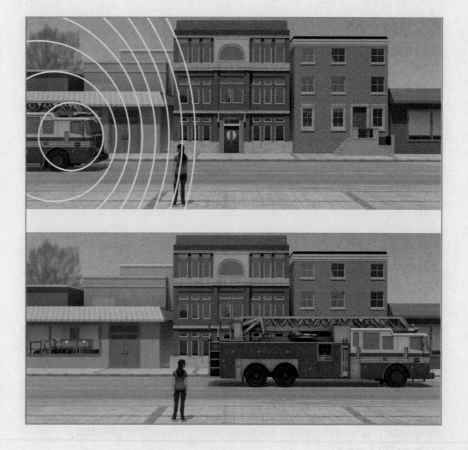

1. **Identify** What is the cause of any sound wave?

....

2. **Construct Explanations** Explain why sound waves are mechanical waves rather than electromagnetic waves.

....

....

3. **Apply Scientific Reasoning** Why does sound travel more quickly through a solid than through a liquid or a gas?

....

....

....

....

....

....

4. **Form a Hypothesis** Dogs can hear higher-pitched whistles that humans do. How do you think the sound frequencies that dogs can hear compare to the frequencies that humans can hear?

....

....

....

....

....

5. **Cause and Effect** What effect might spending years working on a construction site have on a person's hearing? Why?

....

....

....

....

....

6. **Apply Concepts** Ultrasound, also known as sonography, is a technology that uses high-frequency sound waves to produce images. It is used in medical applications to help doctors see inside patients' bodies. How do you think the sound waves can be used to image bones, muscles, and other internal structures?

....

....

....

....

....

....

....

7. **Develop Models** ✎ Imagine a person is sitting on a beach, and a speedboat passes by on the water. Draw a model of this situation, and indicate how the Doppler effect would influence how the sound waves coming from the boat would be perceived by the person on shore.

....

....

....

....

....

....

....

Electromagnetic Waves

Guiding Questions

- What makes up an electromagnetic wave?
- How can you model electromagnetic wave behavior?
- What kinds of waves make up the electromagnetic spectrum?

Connections

Literacy Translate Information

Math Draw Comparative Inferences

MS-PS4-2

Vocabulary

electromagnetic wave
electromagnetic spectrum
radio waves
microwaves
visible light
ultraviolet rays
infrared rays
X-rays
gamma rays

Academic Vocabulary

transverse

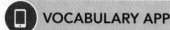 **VOCABULARY APP**

Practice vocabulary on a mobile device.

Quest CONNECTION

Keep thinking about how your security system might work based on the characteristics of electromagnetic waves.

Connect It!

✏️ **Look at the image of this ship. Imagine that an airplane some 25 kilometers in front of the ship is sending out radar waves to detect vessels. Recall the law of reflection from Lesson 2. Draw arrows to represent the radar waves and to show how they would reflect off this unusually angular ship.**

Infer Do you think the reflected waves would ever return to the airplane that transmitted them? Explain.

....

....

....

Characteristics of Electromagnetic Waves

As you read this book, you are surrounded by waves. There are radio waves, microwaves, infrared rays, visible light, ultraviolet rays, and tiny amounts of X-rays and gamma rays. These waves are all electromagnetic waves. An **electromagnetic wave** is made up of vibrating electric and magnetic fields that can move through space at the speed of light. The energy that electromagnetic waves transfer through matter or space is called electromagnetic radiation.

Electromagnetic waves do not require a medium such as air, so they can transfer energy through a vacuum. This property makes them different from mechanical waves, which do require a medium. Mechanical waves are caused by a disturbance or vibration in the medium, while electromagnetic waves are caused by a source of electric and magnetic fields. Those fields are produced by the movement of charged particles.

Radar is a technology that uses microwaves, a type of electromagnetic wave, to detect objects in the atmosphere. The vessel in **Figure 1** is the U.S. Navy's attempt at using stealth technology to deflect radar. Its angular surface causes the microwaves to deflect away from the radar source.

Reflect Think about the devices you use every day. What are some examples of technology that use electromagnetic waves?

Stealth Ship
Figure 1 The U.S.S. Zumwalt is the first in a class of "stealth" destroyers. Much of its hull and other structures have surfaces that are angled upward. This means radar waves will be deflected away from the source of the radar.

Academic Vocabulary

The term *transverse* means "situated across." It is always applied to something that has a specific orientation or direction. Is there a part of the term *transverse* that signals this meaning?

....

....

....

....

Models of Electromagnetic Wave Behavior

Light is mysterious in that it can behave as either a wave or a particle depending on the situation. A wave model can explain most of the behaviors, but a particle model best explains others. Light is an electromagnetic wave, which is a transverse wave. Light has many properties of **transverse** waves, but it can sometimes act as though it is a stream of particles.

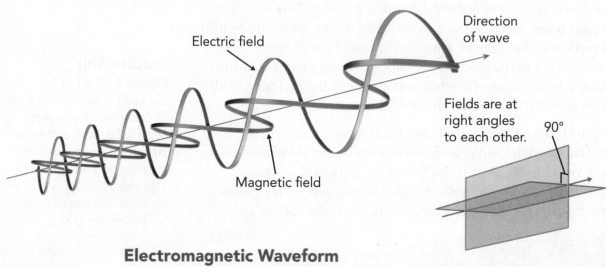

Electromagnetic Waveform
Figure 2 An electromagnetic wave consists of vibrating electric and magnetic fields.

INTERACTIVITY

Find out more about the differences between light waves and sound waves.

Wave Model of Light

One way to visualize light is using a wave model. The wave originates due to a disturbance of a charged particle. The disturbance results in vibrating electric and magnetic fields, which are oriented perpendicular to each other as shown in **Figure 2.** The two vibrating fields reinforce each other, causing energy to travel as light through space or through a medium. A ray of light consists of many of these traveling disturbances, vibrating in all directions.

A polarizing filter acts as though it has tiny slits aligned in only one direction. The slits can be horizontal or vertical. When light enters the filter, only waves whose vibrating electric fields are oriented in the same direction as the slits can pass through it. The light that passes through is called polarized light. Polarized sunglasses block out some waves of light so that your eyes are not exposed to as much radiation.

Model It

Polarizing Glasses

✎ These sunglasses allow light through only if the light waves are oriented vertically. Draw the light wave that passes through each lens.

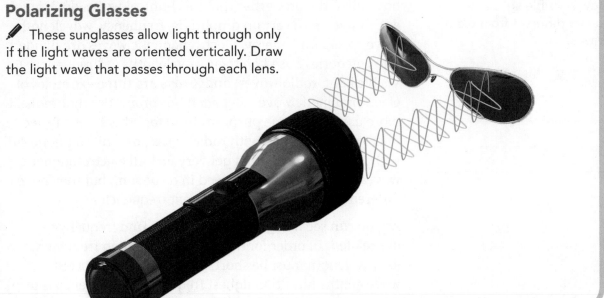

Particle Model of Light

The wave model of light does not explain all of its properties. For example, when a beam of high-frequency light shines on some metals, it knocks some tiny particles called electrons out of the metal. This is called the photoelectric effect. However, lower-frequency light such as red light doesn't have enough energy to knock the electrons out.

The photoelectric effect can be explained by thinking of light as a stream of tiny packets, of energy instead of as a wave. Each packet of light energy is called a photon. For the effect to occur, each photon must contain enough energy to knock an electron free from the metal.

One property of light that the wave model explains but the particle model does not is diffraction. When light passes through a narrow enough slit, instead of forming one image of the slit on a screen, it spreads out and produces a striped pattern of light and dark areas. This is similar to a water wave passing through a narrow channel and then spreading out on the other side.

☑ READING CHECK **Summarize** Light is described as what two things in the two models you just read about?

....

....

 VIDEO

Watch this video to compare the wave and particle models of light.

 **INTERACTIVITY**

Explore the particle model of light yourself.

Translate Information
How is visible light similar to and different from radio waves?

....

....

....

....

....

Wavelength and Frequency

If you use a wave model for electromagnetic waves, the waves have all of the properties that mechanical waves do. Namely, each wave has a certain amplitude, frequency, wavelength, wave speed, and energy. Electromagnetic waves are divided into categories based on their wavelengths (or frequencies). Visible light, radio waves, and X-rays are three examples of electromagnetic waves. But each has properties that make it more useful for some purposes than for others. If you tried to microwave your food with radio waves, or make a phone call with X-rays, you wouldn't get very far! All electromagnetic waves travel at the same speed in a vacuum, but they have different wavelengths and different frequencies.

As you can see in **Figure 3**, wavelength and frequency are related. In order for a wave to have a high frequency, its wavelength must be short. Waves with the shortest wavelengths have the highest frequencies. Frequency is also related to energy. Higher frequency waves have more energy, while lower frequency waves have less energy.

Visible light is the only range of wavelengths your eyes can see. A radio detects radio waves, which have much longer wavelengths than visible light. X-rays, on the other hand, have much shorter wavelengths than visible light.

✓ READING CHECK **Draw Conclusions** Of X-rays, radio waves, and visible light, which wave type has the most energy? Explain.

....

....

Wavelengths and Frequencies

Figure 3 ✏ Use the information from the text to label the three wavelength ranges shown in the diagram as either X-rays, radio waves, or visible light.

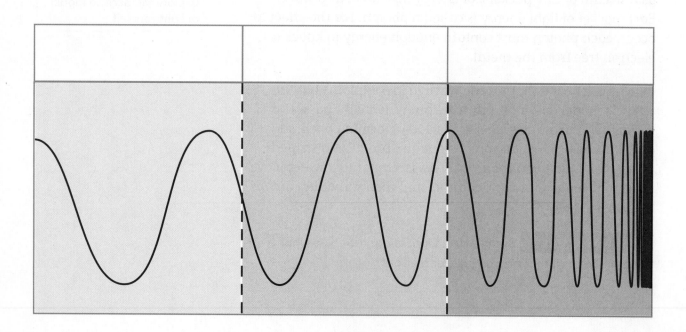

The Electromagnetic Spectrum

There are many different types of electromagnetic waves. The complete range of electromagnetic waves placed in order of increasing frequency is called the **electromagnetic spectrum**. The electromagnetic spectrum is made up of radio waves, microwaves, infrared rays, visible light, ultraviolet rays, X-rays, and gamma rays. The full spectrum is shown in the Math Toolbox.

Radio Waves Electromagnetic waves with the longest wavelengths and the lowest frequencies are **radio waves**. Radio waves are used in mobile phones. Towers, such as the one in **Figure 4**, receive and transmit radio waves along a network that connects mobile phones to each other, to the Internet, and to other networks.

Mobile Phones
Figure 4 Mobile phones depend on a network of towers to transmit, receive, and relay radio signals.

Math Toolbox

Frequencies and Wavelengths of Light

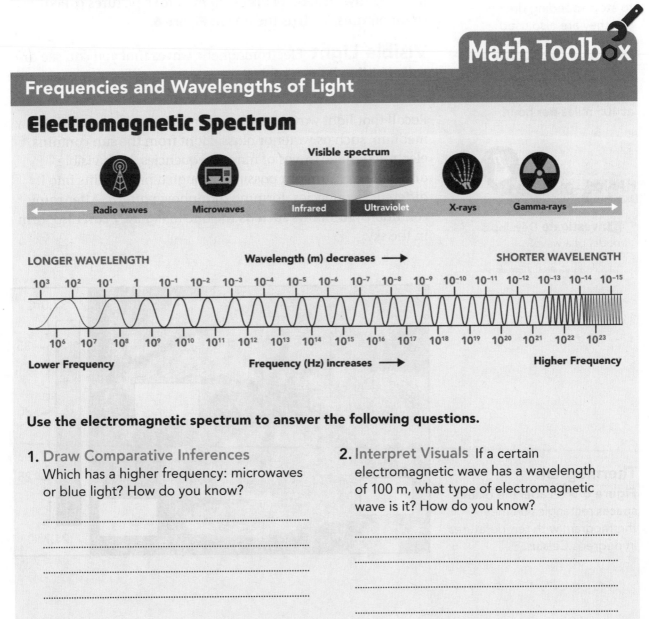

Use the electromagnetic spectrum to answer the following questions.

1. Draw Comparative Inferences
   Which has a higher frequency: microwaves or blue light? How do you know?

   ....
   ....
   ....
   ....

2. Interpret Visuals If a certain electromagnetic wave has a wavelength of 100 m, what type of electromagnetic wave is it? How do you know?

   ....
   ....
   ....
   ....

427

Lighting Up the Radar Gun

Figure 5 Radar guns are used in law enforcement to stop speeding drivers, but they are also used to measure the speeds of pitches in a game of baseball. Some pitchers' fastballs have been clocked at 105 miles per hour!

HANDS-ON LAB

иInvestigate Develop a model of a wave.

Microwaves

Microwaves have shorter wavelengths and higher frequencies than radio waves. When you think about microwaves, you probably think of microwave ovens. But microwaves have many other uses, including radar. Radar is a system that uses reflected microwaves to detect objects and measure their distance and speed. Radar guns, such as the one in **Figure 5**, are used to measure the speed of a baseball pitch. Police also use them to detect cars that are traveling over the speed limit.

Infrared Rays

If you turn on an electric stove's burner, you can feel it warm up before the heating element starts to glow. The invisible heat you feel is infrared radiation, or infrared rays. **Infrared rays** are electromagnetic waves with wavelengths shorter than those of microwaves. An infrared camera uses infrared rays instead of visible light to take pictures called thermograms, such as the one in **Figure 6.**

Visible Light

Electromagnetic waves that you can see are called **visible light**. Visible light waves have shorter wavelengths and higher frequencies than infrared rays.

Recall that light waves bend, or refract, when they enter a new medium, such as water or glass. Light from the sun contains electromagnetic waves of many frequencies, both visible and invisible. Sunlight passing through a prism splits into its different frequencies, forming a rainbow pattern. After rainy conditions, rainbows such as the one in **Figure 7** can also form in the sky.

Thermogram

Figure 6 ✎ Label the blank spaces rectangles on the thermogram with temperatures in degrees Celsius.

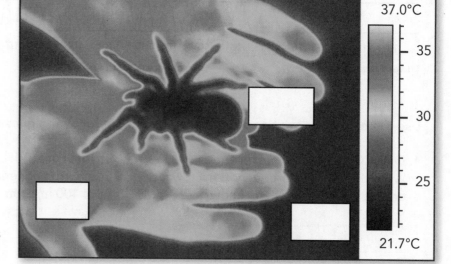

Ultraviolet Rays Electromagnetic waves with wavelengths just shorter than those of visible light are called **ultraviolet rays**, or UV rays for short. UV rays have higher frequencies than visible light, and carry more energy. Sunscreen helps protect your skin from some of the sun's harmful UV rays.

X-rays Electromagnetic waves with wavelengths shorter than those of ultraviolet rays are **X-rays**. Because of their high frequencies, X-rays carry more energy than ultraviolet rays and can penetrate most matter. However, dense matter, such as bone, absorbs X-rays. Therefore, X-rays are used to make images of bones and teeth in humans and animals.

Gamma Rays Electromagnetic waves with the shortest wavelengths and highest frequencies are **gamma rays**. They have the greatest amount of energy of all the electromagnetic waves. Gamma rays are dangerous, but they do have beneficial uses. Radiosurgery shown in **Figure 8,** is a tool that uses several hundred precisely focused gamma rays to target tumors, especially in the brain. The blast of radiation at the point where the beams cross destroys the targeted tumor cells.

Rainbow

Figure 7 Label the rainbow to show which colors have the highest frequency and which have the lowest frequency.

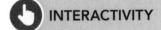 **INTERACTIVITY**

Observe how electromagnetic and mechanical waves differ.

Radiosurgery

Figure 8 The combination of 200 beams of gamma rays can leave tumor cells unable to reproduce, which can stop tumors from growing.

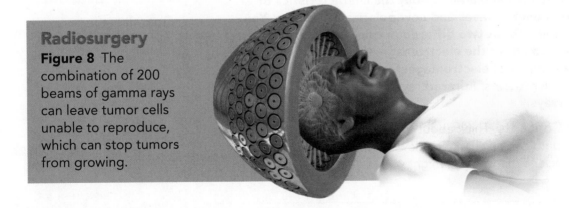

✔ READING CHECK **Draw Conclusions** Can radio waves be used to form images of your bones like x-rays are? Why or why not?

....

....

MS-PS4-2

1. Organize Information In order from lowest to highest frequency, list the different waves along the electromagnetic spectrum.

....

....

....

....

....

....

2. Summarize Describe the electromagnetic spectrum in a few sentences.

....

....

....

....

....

....

....

3. Explain Compare the particle model of light to the wave model of light.

....

....

....

....

....

....

4. Connect to Society How would you describe the connection between the amount of energy a type of electromagnetic wave has and how that wave is used in technology and society?

....

....

....

....

....

....

....

Quest CHECK-IN

In this lesson, you learned about the characteristics of electromagnetic waves and how polarization works. You also learned about two different models of light. Finally, you learned about the electromagnetic spectrum and the different types of electromagnetic waves, including radio waves, microwaves, infrared rays, ultraviolet rays, x-rays, and gamma rays.

Apply Concepts Think about the properties of visible light and how its path can be changed. How might you move light around an obstacle? What devices might you use in your design?

....

....

....

INTERACTIVITY

Optical Demonstration

Go online to plan your demonstration.

Lights! Camera!
ACTION!

A lighting designer plans how to light a stage or performance space. The designer uses three factors—color, intensity, and motion—to light a show in the most striking and effective way possible.

There are three primary, or basic colors. For pigments, the primary colors are red, yellow, and blue. In lighting, the primary colors are red, green, and blue. When the three primary colors are mixed in equal amounts, a painter ends up with black paint, but a lighting designer creates white light!

Lighting designers use gels to change the colors of stage lights. A gel is a thin sheet of plastic polymer that slides into grooves at the front of the light. Gels come in every color of the rainbow.

Lighting designers can use lots of instruments and a variety of gels to light the stage. By mixing gels, the designer creates new colors. Red and purple gels, used together, make magenta light.

Lighting designers need a good understanding of physics and engineering, as well as dramatic performance, to create effective displays. Lighting designers are called on to illuminate many kinds of spectacles and events. Ice shows, movie sets, political appearances, and concerts are only a few examples of situations in which lighting designers create the right mood and appearance.

> ▶ **VIDEO**
>
> Explore how lighting designers use and manipulate light to communicate with an audience.

MY CAREER

What kinds of decisions do you think lighting designers have to make? Write down your thoughts and think about whether lighting design might be a good career for you.

A lighting designer shines lights at different angles all around the stage to set a bright and lively mood for this concert.

LESSON 5 Light

Guiding Questions

- How are the transmission, reflection, and absorption of light related to the transparency and color of objects?
- What happens to light when it is strikes different types of mirrors?
- What happens to light when it passes through different types of lenses?

Connection

Literacy Evaluate Media

MS-PS4-2

Vocabulary

transparent
translucent
opaque
diffuse reflection
convex
focal point
concave

Academic Vocabulary

compare

 VOCABULARY APP

Practice vocabulary on a mobile device.

Quest CONNECTION

Think about how the behavior of light and how its interaction with objects can help you complete your quest.

Connect It!

✏️ **Shadows are made by different objects in the picture. Label two shadows with the names of the objects that made them.**

Apply Scientific Reasoning Why do some objects make shadows, while others do not?

....

....

....

....

Light, Color, and Objects

When people talk about light, they are usually referring to the part of the electromagnetic spectrum that is visible to humans. This light interacts with the world around us to determine what we see and how it appears.

Materials can be classified based on how much light transmits through them. A material that transmits most of the light that strikes it is **transparent**. You can see through a transparent object, such as a window pane or the plastic wrap on a package.

A **translucent** material scatters the light that passes through it. You might be able to see through a translucent material, but the image will look blurred. Waxed paper and gelatin dessert are examples of translucent materials.

A material that reflects or absorbs all of the light that strikes it is called **opaque**. A book, a marshmallow, and a hippopotamus are all opaque—you can't see through them because light does not transmit through them. **Figure 1** shows an example of what happens when light strikes transparent and opaque objects.

Reflect Explain why you have a shadow, but a window pane does not.

Shadows

Figure 1 You can see shadows of both the person and the window frame. There is no shadow of the panes of glass in the window because light passes through them.

433

INTERACTIVITY

Observe and describe the behavior of light in various situations.

The Color of Objects

Recall that white light is a mixture of all of the colors in the rainbow. When white light shines on an object, some of the colors of light are reflected and some are absorbed.

The color of an opaque object is the color of light that the object reflects. It absorbs all other colors. Under white light, the soccer ball in **Figure 2** appears blue and red. It reflects blue and red wavelengths of light and absorbs all other colors. Other objects, such as a brown tree trunk, do not appear as basic colors of light. These objects reflect more than one color of light. Brown is a combination of red and green, so a brown object reflects both red and green light, and it absorbs all other colors. If an object appears black, then it absorbs all colors of light. A white object reflects all light.

The color of a transparent or a translucent object is the color of light that passes through it. For example, the color of a clear, green drinking glass is green because green light is the only color of light that passes through it.

☑ READING CHECK **Determine Central Ideas** Why does snow appear white?

....

Light and Color

Figure 2 When light shines on an object, some wavelengths of light are reflected and some are absorbed. ✎ Circle the answers that correctly complete the sentences. The color of an opaque object is the color of light it (absorbs / reflects). If the object (absorbs / reflects) all of the light, the object appears black.

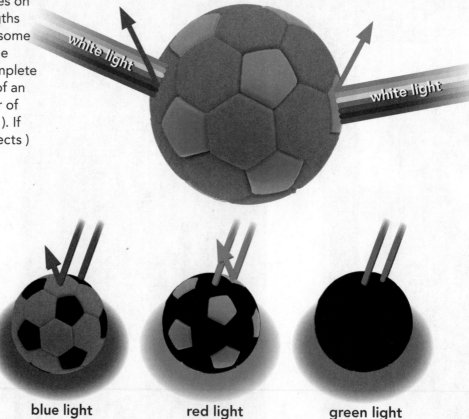

blue light   red light   green light

Color Filters Perhaps you have looked at an object that has a colored light shining on it. You might have noticed that the color of the object looks different than it does when white light shines on it. The color of the light might come from white light shining through a colored filter—a tinted piece of glass or plastic. A red filter, for example, transmits only red light. When light shines through a red filter onto an object, any part of the object that is red, looks red. Any other color looks black. **Figure 3** shows several different color filters and what happens when white light shines on them.

Color filters are often used in photography and movies. They are part of the special effects that create different moods for scenes. Use what you know about filters to complete the activity in **Figure 3**.

INTERACTIVITY

Explore how color filters affect the appearance of different objects.

Literacy Connection

Evaluate Media Describe an image you've seen with a filter on it, and write about how the filter altered the image.

....

....

....

....

Photography and Color Filters

Figure 3 🖉 Color filters can be used in photography to bring out certain colors or create dramatic moods. For each of the inset images, write the color of the filter that produced the altered images.

Reflecting Light

You have seen that sometimes light is transmitted through materials. Like other electromagnetic radiation, light can also be reflected. The reflection of light occurs when parallel rays of light bounce off a surface. Reflected light is how you see your image in a mirror, but reflected light is also why you see a distorted image or no image at all in the surface of rippling water on a lake. The difference lies in whether the light undergoes regular reflection or diffuse reflection.

Regular reflection occurs when parallel rays of light hit a smooth surface. As shown in **Figure 4**, the trees are reflected because light hits the smooth surface of the water, and the rays all reflect at the same angle. As a result, the reflection is a clear image.

In **diffuse reflection**, parallel rays of light hit an uneven surface. The angle at which each ray hits the surface equals the angle at which it reflects. The rays, however, don't bounce off in the same direction because the light rays hit different parts of the surface at different angles. **Figure 4** shows why light undergoes diffuse reflection when it hits choppy water on a lake.

Regular and Diffuse Reflection

Figure 4 Light reflects off the surface of water.
✏️ For each type of reflection, circle the terms that correctly complete the sentence.

You (can / cannot) see an image in the still water because the light undergoes (regular / diffuse) reflection.

You (can / cannot) see an image in the choppy water because the light undergoes (regular / diffuse) reflection.

Mirror Images

The most common way to form a clear image using reflected light is with a mirror. There are three different types of mirrors—plane, convex, and concave. The types of mirrors are distinguished by the shape of the surface of the mirror.

The mirror you have hanging on a wall in your home probably is a flat mirror, also known as a plane mirror. The image you see in the mirror is called a virtual image, which is an image that forms where light seems to come from. **Figure 5** shows an example of a virtual image in a plane mirror. This image is upright and the same size as the object that formed the image, but the right and left sides of the image are reversed.

Convex Mirrors

To visualize a convex mirror, think about a metal bowl. A **convex** mirror is like the outside of the bowl because it is a mirror with a surface that curves outward. If you look at an image in the outside of the bowl, it is smaller than the image in a plane mirror. **Figure 6** shows an example of an image in a convex mirror. To understand how these images form, look at the optical axis and the focal point of the mirror. The optical axis is an imaginary line that divides a mirror in half. The **focal point** is the location at which rays parallel to the optical axis reflect and meet. The light reflects off the curved surface such that the image appears to come from a focal point behind the mirror.

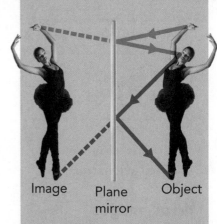

Image   Plane   Object
mirror

Plane Mirror Image

Figure 5 In this virtual image, the reflected light rays appear to come from behind the mirror, where the image forms. The distance from the image to the mirror is the same as the distance from the object to the mirror.

Convex Mirror Image

Figure 6 Most rear-view mirrors are convex. Light rays bend when they hit the surface of the mirror in such a way that the object appears smaller than it is.

Optical axis

Focal point

437

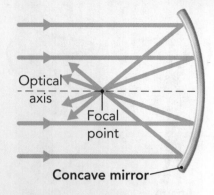

Concave Mirrors Just as a convex mirror is like the outside of a shiny bowl, a concave mirror is like the inside of the bowl. The surface of a **concave** mirror curves inward. **Figure 7** shows that the focal point of a concave mirror is on the reflecting side of the mirror. The image that forms from a concave mirror depends on whether the object is between the focal point and the mirror or farther away from the mirror than the focal point. If the object is farther from the mirror than the focal point is, then reflected light rays cross past one another, and the image is inverted. This image is called a real image. If the object is between the focal point and the mirror, then the image is not inverted and is larger than the actual object. This image is a virtual image.

☑ READING CHECK **Classify** If a mirrored image is inverted, what type of image is it?

....

Mirror Images

Figure 7 The images formed by mirrors depend upon the shape of the mirror. Examine the diagram, and then identify the type of image in each example.

The object is located farther from the mirror than the focal point is. It forms a .... image.

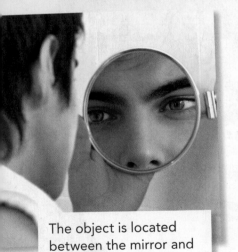

The object is located between the mirror and the focal point. It forms a .... image.

Model It !

Fun with Mirrors

In a fun house, mirrors are often used to change the appearance of objects.

Develop Models ✏ Suppose you want to use a mirror to make a door look smaller and rounder. In the space below, draw the mirror and the door, along with the focal point. Label the mirror with the type of mirror it is.

Lenses

Light not only reflects, as it does with a mirror, but it also bends, or refracts. A lens is a curved piece of transparent material that refracts light. Every time you look through a telescope, a microscope, or a pair of eyeglasses, you are looking through a lens. Just like a mirror, a lens is either convex or concave, based on its shape.

Convex Lenses Look at **Figure 8** to see what convex lenses look like, how they refract light, and what type of image is produced. You can see that convex lenses are thicker in the middle and thinner at the edges. As light passes through the lens, it refracts toward the center of the lens. The more curved the lens is, the more the light refracts.

A convex lens can produce either a virtual image or a real image depending on where the object is located relative to the focal point of the lens. If the object is between the lens and the focal point, then a virtual image forms. This image is larger than the actual object. You may have observed this when using a magnifying glass. If the object is farther away from the lens than the focal point is, then a real image forms. This image can be larger, smaller, or the same size as the object.

Does this description of a convex lens sound familiar? **Compare** a convex lens and a concave mirror. Both a convex lens and a concave mirror focus light, and the type of image formed depends on the location of the object compared to the location of the focal point.

 VIDEO

Explore the effects of different lenses and filters in cameras.

Academic Vocabulary

How does comparing items differ from contrasting them?

....

....

....

....

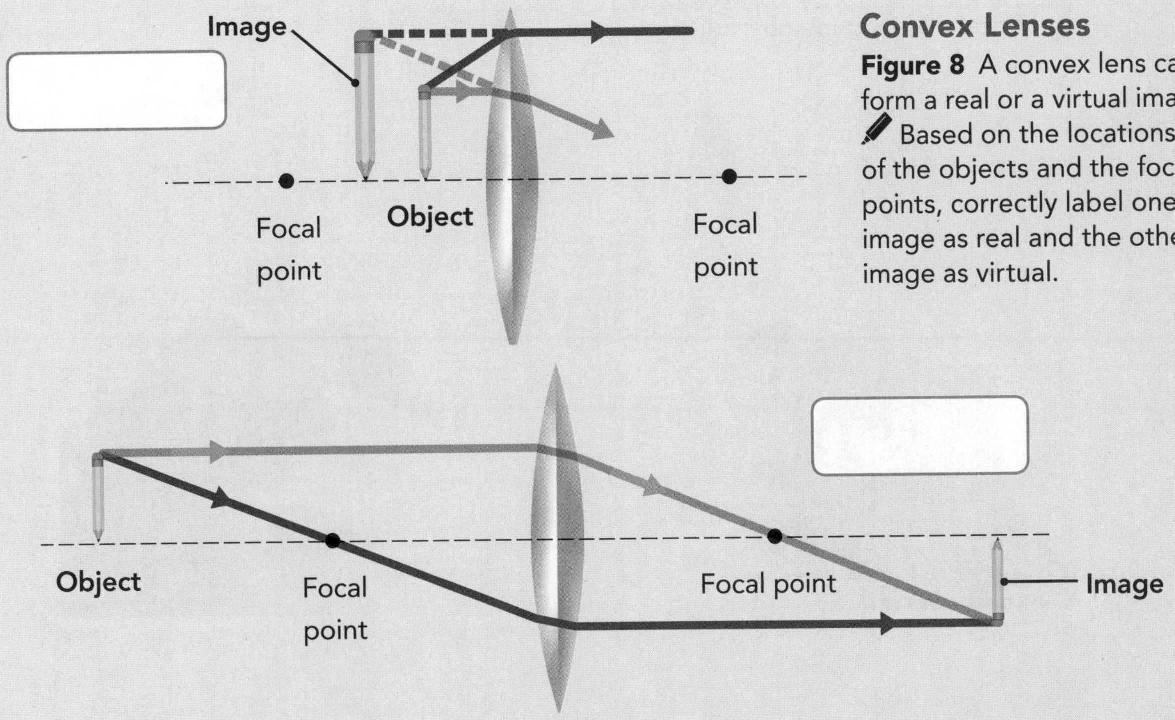

Convex Lenses

Figure 8 A convex lens can form a real or a virtual image.
✏ Based on the locations of the objects and the focal points, correctly label one image as real and the other image as virtual.

Image

Focal point   Object   Focal point

Object   Focal point   Focal point   Image

439

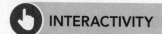

INTERACTIVITY

Predict the behavior of light rays as they encounter different objects and substances.

Concave Lenses Concave lenses are thinner at the center than they are at the edges. When light rays travel through the lens, the rays are bent away from the optical axis, so the rays never meet. Because the rays never meet, concave lenses form only virtual images, and these images are upright and smaller than the objects. **Figure 9** shows how concave lenses form images.

✓ READING CHECK **Compare and Contrast** In what ways is a convex lens like a concave mirror? In what ways are they different?

....

....

....

....

Concave Lenses

Figure 9 When looking through a concave lens, a virtual image forms which is always smaller than the object itself. ✏ After examining the diagrams, circle the photo in which the image is formed by using a concave lens.

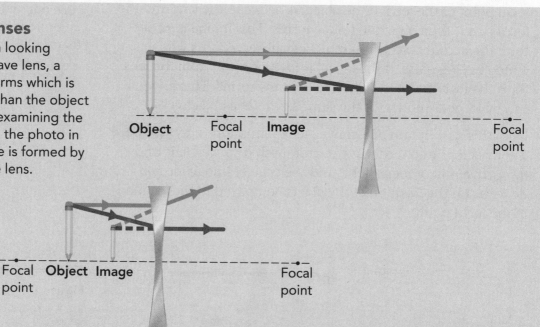

☑ LESSON 5 Check

1. **Classify** What kind of material transmits some light, making objects behind it appear blurry?

....

....

....

2. **Identify** A bird runs into the window of a building because it sees the reflection of the sky in the window. The sky does not appear distorted in this window. What type of mirror or lens is the window acting as? Explain your answer.

....

....

....

....

3. **Apply Scientific Reasoning** When a person is nearsighted, an eyeglass lens is needed to bend light entering the eye away from the optical axis. What type of lens will do this?

....

....

4. **Cause and Effect** Why might some rear-view mirrors in a car state, "Objects are closer than they appear"?

....

....

....

....

....

5. **Construct Explanations** Suppose a movie director is filming on a set that should look like a hot desert. He wants the scene to appear warmer, such that the red and yellow tones are the most apparent. What color filters should he use? What color will the blue sky appear when he uses those filters, and why?

....

....

....

....

....

....

....

Quest CHECK-IN

In this lesson, you observed how light behaves when it encounters transparent, translucent, and opaque objects. You saw how the color of light or filters affects the color of objects. You also discovered the ways that light can reflect from mirrors or refract through lenses.

How might you apply this knowledge to choose the objects and their placement in your quest?

....

....

....

....

HANDS-ON LAB

An Optimal Optical Solution

Go online to download the lab worksheet. Build and test your optical security system.

1 Wave Properties

MS-PS4-1

1. Which of the following is a property of a mechanical wave?

A. amplitude B. weight
C. incidence D. color

2. The sound wave frequency of an F-sharp in music is 370 Hz, and its wavelength is 0.93 m. What is the wave's speed?

A. 34.4 m/s B. 397.9 m/s
C. 344.1 m/s D. 300,000 km/s

3. Which statement about the speed of sound is correct?

A. Sound travels faster through water than air.
B. Sound travels at the same speed through water and air.
C. Sound travels faster through space than air.
D. Sound travels at the same speed through space and air.

4. If the amplitude or frequency of a wave increases, the energy of the wave ....

5. Construct Explanations It's been said that you can estimate how far away a lightning bolt is by counting the number of seconds that elapse between seeing the flash and hearing the thunderclap, and then dividing that number by five to get a distance in miles. In terms of the physics of light and sound waves, does this method make sense?

....
....
....
....
....
....
....

2 Wave Interactions

MS-PS4-2

6. Refraction is the bending of waves that occurs due to a change in

A. speed. B. frequency.
C. height. D. amplitude.

7. Which of the following pairs of terms describes the two different wave interactions depicted below?

A. constructive and destructive interference
B. moving and standing waves
C. mechanical and electromagnetic waves
D. sound waves and light waves

8. When a ray of light strikes a surface, it can be

................................, ...,

or ....

9. Construct Arguments Why is it important for engineers to understand the natural frequency of vibrations in building materials when planning to build a bridge in an area with high winds or frequent earthquakes?

....
....
....
....
....
....

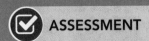
3 Sound Waves

MS-PS4-2

10. When a sound wave is absorbed by an object,
    A. it quickly gains energy.
    B. it quickly loses energy.
    C. it slowly gains energy.
    D. its energy does not change.

11. **Analyze Properties** How do stiffness, density, and temperature affect sound waves?

    ....

    ....

    ....

    ....

    ....

4 Electromagnetic Waves

MS-PS4-2

12. Which electromagnetic wave type has the highest frequency?
    A. visible light
    B. infrared rays
    C. gamma rays
    D. microwaves

13. Of all of the colors in the visible part of the electromagnetic spectrum, red light has the lowest frequency, the .... wavelength, and the .... energy.

14. **Use Models** Describe how you could use a simple rope to teach someone about the different waves along the electromagnetic spectrum.

    ....

    ....

    ....

    ....

    ....

5 Electromagnetic Radiation

MS-PS4-2

15. Which statement is correct?
    A. A red apple reflects green light.
    B. A blue ball absorbs blue light.
    C. A green leaf reflects green light.
    D. A black shirt reflects all colors of light.

16. What happens when light rays encounter a concave lens?
    A. The light rays are reflected back.
    B. The light rays travel through the lens and refract away from the center of the lens.
    C. The light rays travel through the lens and refract toward the center of the lens.
    D. The light rays travel through the lens without bending.

17. When an object is located between a concave mirror and the focal point, a .... image is produced.

18. **Develop Models** ✏ Draw a model to show what happens to light when it meets a convex mirror.

MS-PS4-1, MS-PS4-2

Evidence-Based Assessment

Bianca is helping the theater director at her school with lighting, sound, and set design for a school play. She will be choosing the materials that will be used on stage and on the walls of the theater. After she reads the script and makes observations inside the theater, she makes the following list of the factors to consider in her design.

- The echoes throughout the theater need to be reduced.

- The set should not reflect too much light into the audience's eyes.

- The only lights available are white, purple, and yellow. The filters available are red and blue.

- The blue sky on the set should appear black for Act 2.

Bianca draws a detailed illustration of her plan to show the theater director. She labels it with the materials she plans to use.

1. **Apply Scientific Reasoning** Bianca plans to shine a few spotlights on the sky for Act 2 and use a filter to change the color. Which filter should Bianca use on the white light to make the blue sky appear black?

   A. a red filter

   B. a blue filter

   C. a white filter

   D. no filter at all

2. **Identify Criteria** Which of the following considerations does Bianca need to take into account as she works on the set and lighting design? Select all that apply.

   ☐ Two different sets are needed for Act 2.

   ☐ The set materials should not be too shiny or glossy.

   ☐ Only the colors white, purple, and yellow can be used to paint the sets.

   ☐ The walls have hard surfaces that reflect sound waves.

   ☐ Only the white lights can be used for Act 2.

3. **Use Models** Based on Bianca's illustration, did she choose the appropriate material on the walls for reducing echoes? Why or why not?

   ....

   ....

   ....

   ....

4. **Develop Models** As sound waves travel away from the speaker, their amplitudes and energy decrease. Where will the sound be the most quiet? If you were to move the speaker, where would you place it and why?

   ....

   ....

   ....

   ....

   ....

   ....

5. **Provide Critique** Based on Bianca's criteria and model, which materials would you change on stage? Explain your reasoning.

   ....

   ....

   ....

   ....

   ....

   ....

   ....

   ....

Quest FINDINGS

Complete the Quest!

Phenomenon Reflect on your demonstration and answer questions about modifying and improving your design. List some other kinds of jobs that may require a good knowledge of light and its behavior.

Apply Concepts You've seen how light can bend and move. How might a grocery store manager use the properties of light and set up objects to make sure the entire store can be visible from one location without using cameras?

....

....

....

....

👆 **INTERACTIVITY**

Reflect on Your Demonstration

Making Waves

How can you use a **model** to demonstrate what happens when **waves interact** with barriers or other waves?

Background

Phenomenon A wave breaker is a large wall made of rocks or concrete objects that extends into the ocean. Breakers often are built near beaches to make the water calmer for swimmers. These barriers help to diminish the force of incoming waves by scattering them and interfering with their movements.

In this lab, you will model the behavior of water waves and explain how the waves interact with each other and with objects in their paths. You will then decide on the best method and materials for diminishing waves.

Materials

(per group)

- water
- plastic dropper
- metric ruler
- paper towels
- modeling clay
- plastic knife
- cork or other small floating object
- ripple tank (aluminum foil lasagna pan with mirror on the bottom)

Safety

Be sure to follow all safety guidelines provided by your teacher.

This rock barrier helps to block big waves and make the beach more enjoyable for swimmers.

Design an Investigation

HANDS-ON LAB

Demonstrate Go online for a downloadable worksheet of this lab.

☐ One way to generate waves is to squeeze drops of water from an eyedropper into a pan of water. How can you use the dropper to control how forceful the waves are?

....

....

....

☐ What questions will you explore in your investigation? Some questions to explore include:

- What happens when waves hit a solid surface?

- What happens when waves travel through a gap between two solid objects?

- How does a floating object react to waves?

- What happens when one wave meets another wave?

☐ Record any additional questions you hope to answer in your investigation.

....

....

....

☐ Design an experiment to show how waves behave when they interact with different objects or with each other. Write out a procedure. Then decide what information to record and design a data table to record your observations.

447

Procedure

Data

Analyze and Interpret Data

1. **Identify** Are the waves in water mechanical waves or electromagnetic waves? How do you know?

   ....

   ....

   ....

2. **Make Observations** In what situations did you observe waves interfering with one another? How did it affect the amplitude of the waves?

   ....

   ....

   ....

   ....

   ....

3. **Evaluate Your Tests** Repetition is when you repeat a step of the procedure a few times to see if you get the same results. Did you use repetition in your experiment? Why or why not?

   ....

   ....

   ....

4. **Relate Structure and Function** Which material and set-up was best for diminishing waves? Which was the worst? What evidence led you to these conclusions?

   ....

   ....

   ....

   ....

   ....

5. **Provide Critique** Share your results with members of another group. What did they do differently? In what ways would you suggest that the other group members revise their procedure?

   ....

   ....

   ....

   ....

TOPIC 9

Electricity and Magnetism

NGSS PERFORMANCE EXPECTATIONS

MS-PS2-3 Ask questions about data to determine
the factors that affect the strength of electric and
magnetic forces.

MS-PS2-5 Conduct an investigation and evaluate
the experimental design to provide evidence that
fields exist between objects exerting forces on
each other even though the objects are not in
contact.

MS-PS3-2 Develop a model to describe that
when the arrangement of objects interacting at a
distance changes, different amounts of potential
energy are stored in the system.

HANDS-ON LAB

u**Connect** Make observations to
determine the north and south poles
of a magnet.

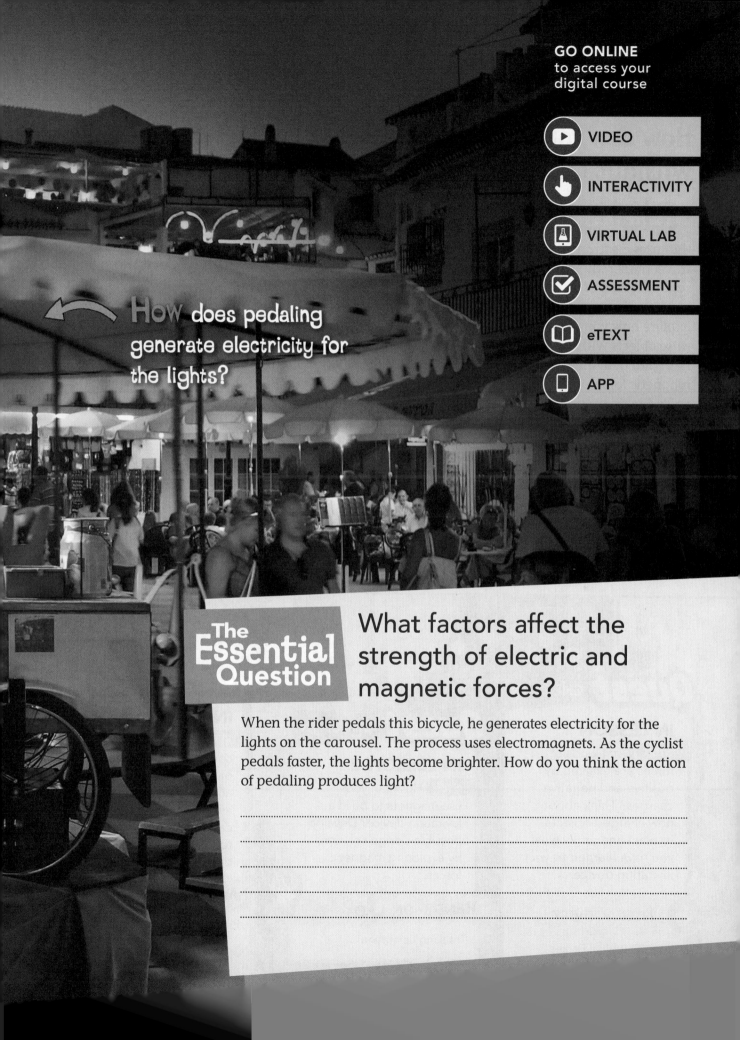

GO ONLINE
to access your
digital course

▶ VIDEO

👆 INTERACTIVITY

📱 VIRTUAL LAB

☑ ASSESSMENT

📖 eTEXT

📱 APP

← How does pedaling generate electricity for the lights?

The Essential Question

What factors affect the strength of electric and magnetic forces?

When the rider pedals this bicycle, he generates electricity for the lights on the carousel. The process uses electromagnets. As the cyclist pedals faster, the lights become brighter. How do you think the action of pedaling produces light?

....

....

....

....

....

Quest KICKOFF

How can you lift an object without making contact?

STEM **Phenomenon** In Japan, South Korea, and China, you can hop on a train that uses electromagnets to levitate above a rail and travel at incredibly high speeds. The technology is the result of years of research and testing by electric and mechanical engineers. In this STEM Quest, you will explore how you can use electromagnetism to lift or raise objects without coming into contact with them. In digital activities, you will investigate electric and magnetic forces. By applying what you have learned, you will design, build, and test a device that can levitate objects.

 INTERACTIVITY

Light as a Feather?

MS-PS2-3 Ask questions about data to determine the factors that affect the strength of electric and magnetic forces. **MS-PS2-5** Conduct an investigation and evaluate the experimental design to provide evidence that fields exist between objects exerting forces on each other even though the objects are not in contact. **MS-PS3-2** Develop a model to describe that when the arrangement of objects interacting at a distance changes, different amounts of potential energy are stored in the system.

NBC LEARN ▶ VIDEO

After watching the video, which examines some industrial applications of magnets and electromagnets, list two examples of objects that you use every day that rely on magnets or electromagnets.

Example 1

....

....

....

Example 2

....

....

....

Quest CHECK-IN

IN LESSON 1

STEM What kinds of forces are exerted by positive and negative charges? Think about how charged objects interact and apply what you have learned to your levitating device.

👆 **INTERACTIVITY**

Apply Electrical Forces

Quest CHECK-IN

IN LESSON 2

STEM How can you use magnets to build a levitation device? Develop possible design solutions by exploring magnetic forces.

HANDS-ON LAB

Tracking Levitation

Quest CHECK-IN

IN LESSON 3

STEM How can you control the strength of your device? Build an electromagnet and explore how you can incorporate the technology into your device.

HANDS-ON LAB

Building an Electromagnet

Magnetism is used to elevate this "maglev" train several centimeters above the tracks and also to propel it forward. The absence of friction between the train and the track allows the maglev train to achieve speeds up to 600 kilometers per hour!

Quest CHECK-IN

IN LESSON 4

STEM How can you refine your levitating device to improve your results? Redesign and retest your device using electromagnets.

HANDS-ON LAB

Electrifying Levitation

Quest FINDINGS

Complete the Quest!

Apply what you've learned by describing other scenarios in your daily life in which electromagnets could be used to make a task easier.

👆 **INTERACTIVITY**

Reflect on Your Levitating Device

① Electric Force

Guiding Questions

- What causes electric fields and electric forces?
- How is potential energy affected by positions of charges?
- How is static electricity different from current?

Connection

Literacy Integrate with Visuals

MS-PS2-5, MS-PS3-2

Vocabulary

electron
electric force
electric field
electric current
conductor
static electricity

Academic Vocabulary

charge
neutral

 VOCABULARY APP

Practice vocabulary on a mobile device.

Quest CONNECTION

As you read, think about how electric forces and fields might be used to develop your levitation device.

Connect It !

✏️ **Identify the parts of this picture that you think show the transfer of electric charges. Draw dots to indicate the paths of the moving electric charges from a cloud to the ground.**

Explain Why do you think lightning is so dangerous if it comes in contact with a person?

....

....

....

Electric Force, Fields, and Energy

Did you know that there are electric **charges**, forces, and fields inside your body? You might not see them or feel them, but they are in every atom, everywhere!

Atoms are made up of protons, neutrons, and electrons, as shown in **Figure 1**. Protons are positively charged particles, and **electrons** are negatively charged particles. Neutrons are **neutral**, meaning that they do not have a charge. Most objects are made of atoms in which the number of protons is equal to the number of electrons. As a result, the positive and negative charges cancel out and the atoms are neutral. However, electrons can move from one atom or object to another. If an object loses electrons, it is left with more protons than electrons. It has an overall positive charge. If an object gains electrons, it will have an overall negative charge.

If you have ever watched a lightning storm, as in **Figure 2**, you have seen a dramatic display of electric charges. The lightning bolts are made up of moving electrons.

✓ **READING CHECK** **Summarize Text** How can a neutral object become negatively charged?

....

....

Academic Vocabulary

Charge is a basic property of matter that creates a force and accounts for electric interactions. Some particles and atoms have no charge, so they are neutral. Is the atom in **Figure 1** neutral or charged?

....

Model of an Atom
Figure 1 Charged particles make up atoms.

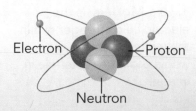

Electron — Proton

Neutron

Lightning Storm
Figure 2 Lightning bolts can travel from clouds to the ground. They can also travel within a cloud and between clouds. These streaks of light are the result of the movement of electric charges.

Electric Field Lines

Figure 3 Images A and B show the field lines around single charges. Image C shows the field lines around a positive charge and a negative charge next to each other. Where field lines are closer together, the electric field is stronger.

1. Use Models Is the electric field stronger within the white rectangle or within the blue rectangle in image C?

2. Draw Conclusions Is the electric field stronger close to the charges or further away from the charges?

☑ **READING CHECK** In which direction would a positive charge move if it were placed in between the positive and negative charges in image C?

Electric Force

The force between charged particles or objects is called **electric force**. If a proton and an electron come close together, the opposition of their positive and negative forces creates an attraction that draws them together. On the other hand, if two electrons come close together, they repel each other because they both are negatively charged. The electric force causes them to move apart. In general, opposite charges attract, and like charges repel.

The strength of the electric force depends on the distance between the charges. For example, when a positively-charged particle or object is close another positively-charged particle, a strong force between them pushes them away from each other. As they move apart, the force between them becomes weaker. The strength of the electric force also depends on the amount of charge present. When more charge is involved, the electric force is stronger. For instance, three protons attract an electron more strongly than one proton alone.

Electric Fields

Two charged particles will experience electric forces between them without even touching. How is this possible? An electric charge has an invisible **electric field** around it—a region around the charged particle or object where the electric force is exerted on other charged particles or objects. Electric fields can be represented by field lines, as in **Figure 3**. They point in the direction that the force would push a positive charge. Field lines around a positively charged object point away from the object. They indicate that the object would repel a positive charge. Field lines around a negatively charged object point toward the object. The negatively charged object would attract a positive charge. When multiple charges are in the same area, the field lines show a slightly more complicated combination of the two fields.

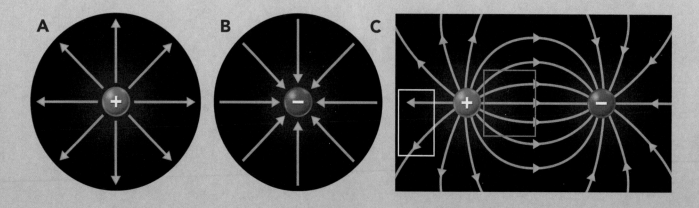

A   B   C

Charges and Potential Energy When forces are in action, you can be sure that energy is also involved. Suppose you have a system that consists of two opposite charges and their interaction. If you pull the opposite charges away from each other, the potential energy of the system increases. You can understand this by comparing it to gravitational potential energy. Gravity is an attractive force. When you lift an object higher above the ground, you apply a force and transfer energy to it. The object's gravitational potential energy increases. When you drop the object, the force of gravity pulls the object to the ground and its gravitational potential energy decreases. The force between opposite charges is also an attractive force. As you apply a force to move opposite charges away from each other, the electric potential energy of the system increases. When the electric force between opposite charges pulls them together naturally, the potential energy of the system decreases, as shown in **Figure 4**.

Potential energy changes in a different way between two like charges. Two like charges naturally repel each other. An outside force is not needed to move them apart. Therefore, as the electric force between two like charges pushes them away from each other, the potential energy of the system decreases.

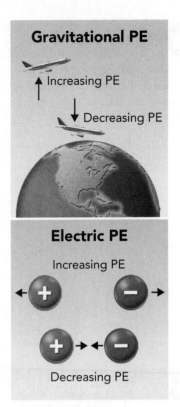

Gravitational PE

↑ Increasing PE

↓ Decreasing PE

Electric PE

Increasing PE

Decreasing PE

Potential Energy
Figure 4 Electric potential energy behaves a lot like gravitational potential energy.

Question It !

Students are conducting an experiment to provide evidence that electric fields exert forces on objects even when the objects are not in contact. They use pith balls hanging from strings. Pith balls are small balls that pick up charge easily. These pith balls have been charged by touching another charged object. The students drew this diagram to show the result of their experiment.

1. **Cause and Effect** When the two pith balls have opposite charges, they are naturally pulled together due to the attractive electric force between them. If you pull the two pith balls away from each other, what happens to the potential energy of the system? Explain.

   ....

   ....

   ....

2. **Cite Evidence** How do the results of this experiment provide evidence that electric fields exert forces on the pith balls, even when they are not in contact?

   ....

   ....

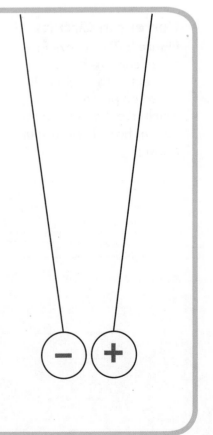

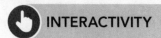

INTERACTIVITY

Discover the properties of electric current, conductors, and insulators.

Electric Current and Circuits

Electric charges play a major role in daily life. Any time you use electricity, you are using energy from electric charges that are in motion. The charges flow through materials like water flows down a stream. The continuous flow of charge is known as **electric current**. Current is measured as a rate in units called amperes. The abbreviation for this unit is A. The number of amperes describes the amount of charge that passes by a given point each second.

Current flows through paths known as circuits. A circuit is a path that runs in a loop. A basic electric circuit contains a source of energy connected with wires to a device that runs on electricity. Current flows from the source of energy, through the wires, through the electric device, and back to the source.

Voltage Why do charges flow through a circuit? They move because of differences in potential energy. Current flows from a point of higher potential energy to a point of lower potential energy in the circuit. For instance, a battery, like the one shown in **Figure 5**, has one end where current has a higher potential energy per charge than it has at the other end of the battery. This difference in electric potential energy per charge is called voltage. The voltage acts like a force that causes current to flow. Voltage is measured in units of volts. The abbreviation for this unit is V.

Literacy Connection

Integrate with Visuals
✎ Draw dots and arrows to represent current flowing through the circuit.

Current in Circuits

Figure 5 The following circuit shows a battery connected to a light bulb. Based on potential energy, which direction should the current flow? Explain your answer.

....
....
....
....
....
....
....
....

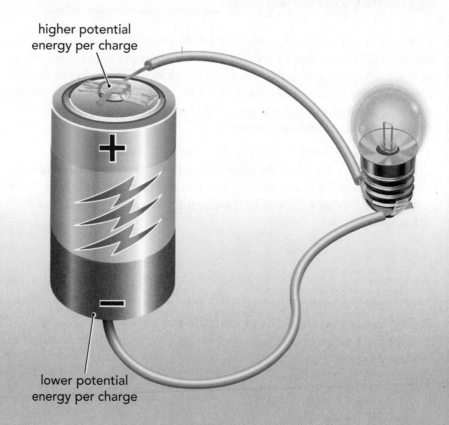

higher potential energy per charge

lower potential energy per charge

Energy in Circuits You can compare a charge in a circuit to an object in the gravitational field of Earth. When an object falls, the force of gravity pulls the object from a position of higher potential energy to a position of lower potential energy. You give that potential energy back when you lift the object up to its initial position. A battery gives energy back to charges as well. Inside the battery, the energy from chemical substances is converted to electric energy. That electric energy becomes the potential energy of the charges. They return to a position of higher potential energy, from which they flow through the circuit.

Current and Resistance

What are the charges that flow through a circuit? They are electrons. Historically, the current is described as flowing in the direction in which positive charges would move. However, electrons are negatively charged. So the direction of current is opposite to the direction of electron flow.

Some materials have electrons that are tightly bound to their atoms. Their electrons are difficult to move. Those materials, called insulators, do not allow charge to flow. Therefore, they have a high resistance to electric current. On the other hand, some materials have electrons that are more loosely bound to their atoms. Those materials are **conductors**—they allow charge to flow more freely (**Figure 6**). Just as there are insulators and conductors of heat, there are insulators and conductors of charge. Insulators of charge are materials such as rubber, wood, and glass, while conductors include materials such as silver, copper, and gold.

☑ READING CHECK **Explain** Describe why current flows through a circuit, and explain why some materials allow charges to flow more easily than others.

....

....

....

....

Conductors and Insulators of Charge

Figure 6 Conductors and insulators of charge are all around you. Label each of these common items as a conductor or an insulator.

Integrate Information Which of the materials used to make these objects would you use in a circuit? Explain why.

....

....

....

....

Charging by Induction

Figure 7 If your finger has a build-up of charge, it may induce a charge in a doorknob. Electrons in the doorknob move away from your finger to the opposite side of the doorknob.

Static Electricity

Recall that most objects are made of atoms in which the number of protons is equal to the number of electrons. As a result, these atoms are neutral. By the law of conservation of charge, charge cannot be created or destroyed, but it can be transferred. The transfer of charge happens by moving electrons from one object to another or from one part of an object to another. When charges build up on an object, they do not flow like current. Instead, they remain static, meaning they stay in place. This buildup of charge on an object is called **static electricity**.

Methods of Charging
Objects can become charged by four methods: conduction, friction, induction, and polarization. Charging by conduction is simply the movement of charge by direct contact between objects. The object that is more negatively charged transfers electrons to the other object. Charging by friction occurs when two objects rub against each other and electrons move from one object to the other. Objects become charged by induction without even touching. The electric field of one charged object repels the electrons of the other object. So the second object ends up with a buildup of charge on its opposite side, as in **Figure 7**. Polarization is similar except the electrons only move to the opposite side of their atoms rather than to the opposite side of the entire object. See if you can identify the methods of charging in **Figure 8**.

Interactions with Static Electricity
Figure 8 Label the method of charging in each image as conduction, friction, induction, or polarization.

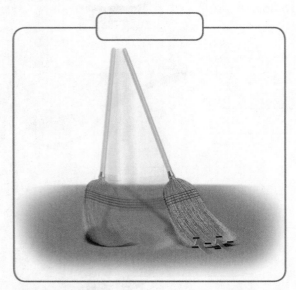

The broom becomes charged as it sweeps across the floor.

Bits of paper are attracted to the broom's negative charge. In the paper, electrons of the atoms move to the opposite side of each atom, away from the broom.

Balloon and Paper
Figure 9 The balloon attracts the paper because of static electricity. Draw the charges on the balloon and on the bits of paper. Then, describe what happens to potential energy as you pull the bits of paper off of the balloon.

....

....

....

....

....

Potential Energy and Static Electricity
If you rub a balloon, you might be surprised that it can pick up bits of paper. The balloon attracts the paper because of static electricity. Rubbing the balloon causes electrons to transfer to it. The charged balloon polarizes the bits of paper. Because the surface of the balloon is negatively charged and the surface of the paper is positively charged, they attract each other as in **Figure 9**. As the bits of paper move toward the balloon, the potential energy between the balloon and paper decreases. When you pull the bits of paper off of the balloon, you apply a force to them. The potential energy between the balloon and the paper increases the further you move them apart.

Static Discharge
Most objects that become charged eventually lose their charge to the air. Charge transfers to or from the air until the charged object is neutral. The process of discharging can sometimes cause a spark or shock when the electrons transfer. If you have ever reached to pet a cat and experienced a shock, it was the result of static discharge.

Lightning is also the result of static discharge. Water droplets in the clouds become charged due to all of the motion within the air during a storm. Electrons then move from areas of negative charge to areas of positive charge. The movement of charge produces the intense spark that we see as a lightning bolt.

✓ READING CHECK **Describe** What happens to charges during static discharge?

....

▶ **VIDEO**

Watch and learn how lightning works.

👆 **INTERACTIVITY**

Develop a model to show the potential energy of a system involving electric forces.

📓 **Reflect** Describe a time when you experienced a shock from static electricity. Explain what happened in terms of electric charges.

MS-PS2-5, MS-PS3-2

1. Describe Why are conductors better than insulators for the flow of electric current?

....

....

....

....

2. Explain A proton is placed next to an negatively charged object. In which direction would the proton move? Explain why.

....

....

....

....

3. Cause and Effect If you move two objects with opposite charges apart, what happens to the potential energy between them? Explain your response.

....

....

....

....

4. Develop Models ✏ After Sandra combs her hair, she notices that her hair moves toward the comb. Draw a model of the comb and Sandra's hair. Show the charges on both the comb and the hair. Describe the types of charges that you think occurred to charge the comb and then to charge the hair.

....

....

....

....

....

....

....

Quest CHECK-IN

In this lesson, you learned about the interactions of electric charges through forces and fields. You also discovered how potential energy plays a role in the flow of current. Additionally, you explored how charges behave in static electricity.

Apply Scientific Reasoning How might electric fields become involved in your levitation device?

....

....

....

👆 INTERACTIVITY

Apply Electrical Forces

Go online to explore how the interaction between charged particles could be used to develop a design for a levitation device.

MS-PS2-5, MS-PS3-2

Bumblebees and Electric Flowers

Most people assume that bumblebees are attracted to certain flowers only because of their colors and scents. As it turns out, there's more to it!

Bumblebees also respond to flowers' electric fields! While the bee has a positive electric charge, the flower and its pollen usually have a negative charge. The opposite charges make the pollen cling to the bee's body.

Scientists believe that bumblebees can use the strength of a flower's electric field to tell how much pollen is there. If they can sense that the field has changed and another bee has already taken all the pollen, then they will move to another flower. Given the number of flowers a bee visits, this information would be really useful!

Bumblebees may use this electric sense for many things, such as recognizing landmarks or identifying which bees have been in a garden before them. Although the bumblebee population is declining, perhaps scientists can find a way to use the bees' electric sense to help save them.

MY DISCOVERY

With a classmate, come up with some questions you have about the relationship between bees and flowers. How might this information be helpful in restoring the bumblebee population? What sources might you investigate to find answers?

② Magnetic Force

Guiding Questions

- How can you change the magnetic force and potential energy between objects?
- How can you detect and describe a magnetic field?

Connection

Literacy Verify

MS-PS2-5, MS-PS3-2

Vocabulary

magnet
magnetism
magnetic force
magnetic pole
magnetic field

Academic Vocabulary

interaction

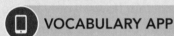 **VOCABULARY APP**

Practice vocabulary on a mobile device.

Quest CONNECTION

As you read, consider how magnets might be used in a levitation device.

Connect It !

✎ **Magnetic field lines are drawings that represent the invisible force around a magnet. Trace one of the magnetic field lines on this page.**

Translate Information How can you describe the shape of Earth's magnetic field?

....

Use Models What does the model show about Earth's magnetic field?

....

....

Identify Limitations What is a limitation of this two-dimensional model?

....

Magnetic Force and Energy

You may use magnets to display notes or pictures on the door of the refrigerator. A **magnet** attracts iron and materials that contain iron. Magnets can be any size, from the ones you use in the kitchen to the entire Earth and beyond. People can use magnetic compasses in navigation because the whole planet acts as a magnet (**Figure 1**).

Magnets attract iron and some other materials—usually metals. They attract or repel other magnets. This attraction or repulsion is called **magnetism**. The **interaction** between a magnet and a substance containing iron is always an attraction. Magnets themselves can either attract or repel one another, depending on how they are placed.

Magnetism can be a permanent or temporary property of a material. Some materials, containing iron or certain other metals, can become permanent magnets after interacting with other magnets. On the other hand, temporary magnetism can occur in different ways. An iron or steel object that is touching a magnet can become a magnet itself as long as the contact exists. For example, you can make a chain of paper clips that hangs from a permanent magnet. Another type of temporary magnet is created when an electric current flows through a conductor. This kind of magnet exists as long as the current is flowing.

Academic Vocabulary

The term *interaction* comes from words meaning *action* and *between two* things. Describe an interaction that you had today.

....

....

....

Magnetic Force

Figure 1 Lines and arrows show the direction of the magnetic field around Earth.

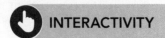
Magnetic Force

Magnetism is caused by a force that can act at a distance. This **magnetic force** is a push or pull that occurs when a magnet interacts with another object. Some large magnets can attract objects from many meters away and are powerful enough to lift a car or truck.

How do you know if the magnetic force between two objects will be a push or a pull? A magnet always exerts a pull on a magnetic object that is not itself a magnet. If you place the ends of the horseshoe magnet in **Figure 2** near a pile of paper clips, the paper clips always move toward the magnet. They never move away. Every magnet has two ends, called **magnetic poles**, where the magnetic force is strongest. One pole is known as the north pole and the other is known as the south pole.

The arrangement of magnets determines which type of force exists between them. If you bring two magnets together so that *like* poles—either both north or both south—are near one another, the magnets repel. If you bring the magnets together so that opposite poles are close to one another, the magnets attract. **Figure 2** shows two ways in which bar magnets can interact.

Push or Pull

Figure 2 ✎ Magnets can either push or pull. Draw arrows on the paperclips and on the bar magnets to show the direction of the magnetic force.

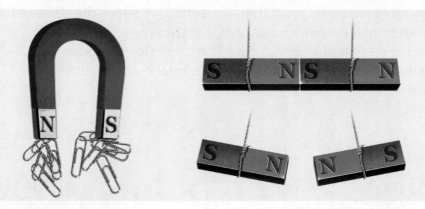

Magnets and Potential Energy

Recall the ways in which the potential energy of a system of electrical charges can change. As you apply a force to move opposite charges away from each other, the electric potential energy of the system increases. The same is true of magnets. Opposite poles naturally attract each other, so you must put energy into the system to pull them apart. As you apply a force to separate the two opposite poles, the potential energy of the system increases. When the magnetic force between opposite poles pulls them together the potential energy of the system decreases. On the other hand, like poles repel each other. To push them together, you have to transfer energy to the system. This increases the potential energy of the system. Use the **Figure 3** activity to summarize these changes in potential energy.

HANDS-ON LAB

☑**Investigate** Discover how you can use a magnet to tell the difference between real and fake coins.

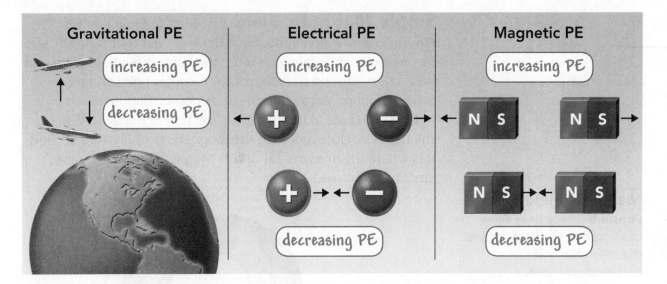

Gravitational PE	Electrical PE	Magnetic PE
increasing PE	increasing PE	increasing PE
decreasing PE	decreasing PE	decreasing PE

Magnetic Fields

The magnetic force is strongest at a magnet's poles. That is why the paper clips tend to stick to the horseshoe magnet at its ends. There is an area of magnetic force that surrounds a magnet. This area of force is the **magnetic field** of the magnet. This field is the source of magnetic energy. It allows magnets to attract objects at a distance. The magnetic field extends from one pole to the other pole of the magnet. You cannot see a magnetic field, but if you place tiny pieces of iron near a magnet, they will arrange themselves along the magnetic field. Their arrangement looks a lot like lines, so illustrations of magnetic fields are drawn with lines, as shown in **Figure 4**.

Objects containing iron, such as steel paper clips, experience a force when they are in a magnetic field. These objects line up with the field around them. Particles inside the objects can also line up with the field. When the particles in an object line up with the field, the object becomes a temporary magnet.

Potential Energy

Figure 3 The gravitational force between the plane and Earth is an attractive force. The forces between opposite charges and opposite magnetic poles are also attractive. Label the locations of increasing and decreasing potential energy in the images.

Visualizing Magnetic Fields

Figure 4 The magnetic field around a bar magnet causes iron filings to form the arrangement shown. This arrangement can also be represented by magnetic field lines. The field is strongest where the lines are closest together.

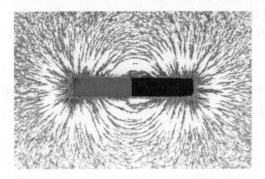

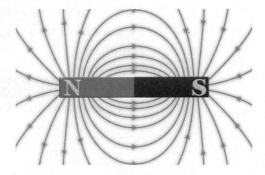

467

Single Magnetic Field

The lines in **Figure 4** and **Figure 5** show a single magnetic field—a field that is produced by one magnet. Single magnetic field lines spread out from one pole, curve around the magnet to the other pole, and make complete loops. Arrows on the lines point from the north pole to the south pole to indicate the direction of the field. When the lines are close together, the magnetic field is stronger than it is where the lines are far apart. Magnetic field lines never cross one another.

Magnetic Field Lines

Figure 5 These lines show the shape of the field around the magnetic poles of a horseshoe magnet.

1. Patterns Add labels to the illustration to show where the magnetic field is strongest and where it is weakest.

2. Use Models Could you pick up a nail using the curved part of the horseshoe magnet farthest from the poles? Explain your answer.

....

....

....

....

....

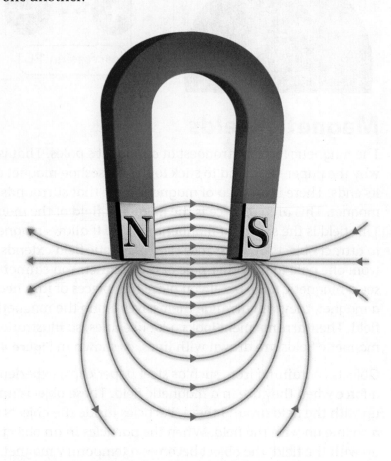

Combined Magnetic Field

The magnetic fields of two magnets placed near each other will interact with one another. When two like poles are close together, the poles and the magnetic fields around them repel one another. When two opposite poles are close together, the fields combine to form a strong magnetic field between the two magnets, as shown in **Figure 6**. As in a single magnetic field, the lines never cross one another.

✔ READING CHECK **Identify** What does the distance between magnetic field lines indicate?

....

....

Combined Magnetic Field Lines

Figure 6 The image on the left shows the combined magnetic field when opposite poles of bar magnets face each other.

Develop Models What would the magnetic field look like if like poles faced each other?

✎ Draw a model of the magnetic field lines in the image on the right.

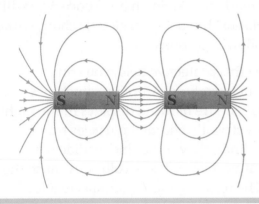

Earth's Magnetic Field

Earth itself acts as a very large magnet. Materials in the core of the planet generate a magnetic field that surrounds the planet. This magnetic field is very similar to the field that surrounds a bar magnet. The magnetic poles of Earth are located near the geographic poles. These are the points where the magnetic field is strongest. The magnetic field lines pass out of the core and through the rocky mantle. They also loop through the space surrounding Earth. The magnetic field is three-dimensional and it is shaped like a donut, as shown in **Figure 7**.

People have used this magnetic field for many centuries for navigation. A compass, shown in **Figure 7**, is a magnetized needle that can turn easily. The needle interacts with Earth's magnetic field. One end is attracted to the north magnetic pole and the other end to the south magnetic pole. People can use a compass to determine the direction in which they are traveling.

 **VIDEO**

See how magnetic fields interact.

Compass

Figure 7 Sailors and hikers use a compass to determine direction. The needle always points toward the geographic north pole. This is the pole that we call the North Pole, but because it is actually a south magnetic pole, the magnetic field lines point toward it.

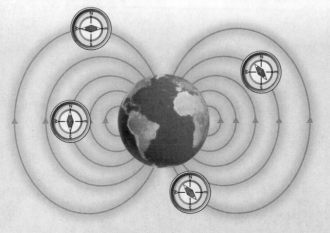

Literacy Connection

Verify Use a reliable Internet source to verify that Earth's magnetic field is caused by substances inside the planet. Which source did you use? How do you know that it's reliable?

....

....

....

....

Aurora Borealis

Figure 8 Auroras form when Earth's magnetic field pushes charged particles toward the poles. The high-energy particles interact with molecules in the atmosphere.

Protecting Life on Earth

Protecting Life on Earth There is a constant stream of particles that flows from the sun toward Earth. This stream is known as the solar wind. These particles have electric charges and they have a lot of energy as they move very rapidly through space. If they were to reach the surface of Earth, the particles in the stream could harm living things. Fortunately, Earth's magnetic field protects us. Electrically charged particles interact with magnetic forces. Earth's magnetic field changes the motion of the charged particles. They flow toward the north and south poles and then past Earth into space. You will learn more about the relationship between electric charges and magnetic fields in the following lessons.

Although you cannot see this protective field, you can sometimes see evidence of it working. Auroras, sometimes called the "Northern Lights," are glowing displays in the night sky. As these energetic electrically charged particles travel along the magnetic field lines, they sometimes collide with gas atoms in the upper atmosphere. These collisions cause the atoms to give off light. The result is often more spectacular than a fireworks show (**Figure 8**).

☑ **READING CHECK** **Use Evidence** Describe how the Aurora Borealis is evidence that the Earth has a magnetic field.

....

....

....

MS-PS2-5, MS-PS3-2

1. **Identify** How can you identify the magnetic north pole of an unlabeled magnet by using a labeled magnet?

....

....

....

....

2. **Patterns** How would increasing the magnetic force of a magnet change the pattern of magnetic field lines between its poles?

....

....

3. **Apply Concepts** Explain how potential energy changes when you pull a magnet off a refrigerator door.

....

....

....

....

4. **Construct an Explanation** Why is the electrical charge on particles in the solar wind an important element of the protection that Earth's magnetic field provides?

....

....

....

5. **Develop Models** 🖊 Draw the magnetic field lines around a nail which has its head as its north pole and its point as its south pole.

Quest CHECK-IN

In this lesson, you discovered magnetic fields and how to draw the lines that represent them. You also learned how potential energy changes when a magnet is present.

Describe how you could orient two magnets so that they repel each other. How might this apply to your levitation device?

....

....

....

....

HANDS-ON LAB

Tracking Levitation

Go online to download the lab worksheet. You will consider how a stable train and section of track can be built using permanent magnets.

Guiding Questions

- How does electricity relate to magnetism?
- How can you describe the magnetic field produced by a current?
- What are the properties of solenoids and electromagnets?

Connections

Literacy Cite Textual Evidence

Math Draw Comparative Inferences

MS-PS2-3

Vocabulary

electromagnetism
solenoid
electromagnet

Academic Vocabulary

produce

📱 VOCABULARY APP

Practice vocabulary on a mobile device.

Quest CONNECTION

Consider how the relationship between electricity and magnetism might come into play when you build your levitation device.

Connect It !

🖉 **Circle the magnet in the photo.**

Explain Phenomena How do you know that the object picking up the metal beams is a magnet?

....

....

Support Your Explanation What material do you think makes up this magnet?

....

Electromagnetic Principles

Have a look at **Figure 1**. How is this crane's magnet strong enough to lift these heavy metal beams? The answer may surprise you. The magnetic field of this crane is actually generated by an electric current! The relationship between electricity and magnetism is called **electromagnetism**.

Electromagnetism was first discovered by a scientist named Hans Christian Ørsted. During a class he was teaching, he brought a compass near a wire that had an electric current running through it. He noticed that the compass needle changed direction when it was near the wire. He placed several different compasses near a wire and found out that the compass needles changed direction when a current passed through the wire. The compass needles did not change direction when no current flowed. Ørsted concluded that an electric current produces a magnetic field, so electricity and magnetism are related.

Literacy Connection

Cite Textual Evidence
What evidence did Ørsted use to conclude that an electric current produces a magnetic field?

....

....

....

....

....

Write About It In your science notebook, describe a time that you drew a new conclusion from your observations.

Magnetic Strength
Figure 1 A regular magnet is not strong enough to pick up these heavy beams. This special type of magnet, called an electromagnet, has the strength to do it.

Magnetism from Electricity

Figure 2 🖋 This figure shows how the direction of a current in a straight wire affects the magnetic field that forms. In the image on the left, the current flows upward. Draw your predicted magnetic field lines in the image on the right, in which the current flows downward.

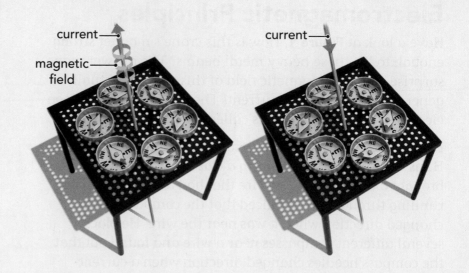

current —
magnetic field

current —

HANDS-ON LAB

☑**Investigate** Explore the relationship between electricity and magnetism.

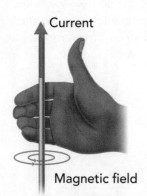

Current

Magnetic field

The Right-Hand Rule

Figure 3 Imagine that you are holding the wire in your right hand with your thumb pointing in the direction the current flows. The direction of the magnetic field is the same as the direction that your fingers curl.

Magnetic Fields and Current

When you examine **Figure 2**, you can see that the magnetic field produced by a current has a certain direction. This field also has a certain strength. How can the field change? It can change in direction and strength, and it can be turned off or on. To turn the magnetic field off or on, simply turn the current off or on.

Magnetic Fields Around Straight Wires In a straight wire, the field's direction depends on the direction of the current. How do you determine the direction of a magnetic field based on the direction of current through a straight wire? You can use what is known as the right-hand rule, as shown in **Figure 3**.

To change the strength of a magnetic field around a current-carrying straight wire, change the amount of current running through the wire. If current is increased, the magnetic field becomes stronger. If the current is decreased, the strength of the magnetic field decreases.

☑ READING CHECK **Determine Central Ideas** How do electric currents relate to magnetic fields?

....

....

Magnetic Fields Around Wire Loops

Suppose you have a loop of wire rather than a straight wire. The magnetic field formed around the loop of wire is in many ways like the field formed when a current flows through a straight wire. The direction of the field depends on the direction of the current and can be determined by using the right-hand rule. The field can be turned off or on by turning the current off or on. The strength of the field depends on the strength of the current.

There is one main difference, however, when a current flows through a loop of wire. Look at **Figure 4**, which shows a current flowing through a loop of wire and the magnetic field it produces. Shaping a wire into a loop can increase the strength of the magnetic field within the loop.

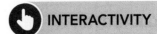
INTERACTIVITY

Predict the direction of magnetic field lines around a current-carrying wire.

✓ **READING CHECK** **Cause and Effect** You have a straight wire with a current running through it. What effect will looping the wire have on the magnetic field?

....

Model It!

Magnetic Field Strength

Figure 4 The overhead view of a magnetic field formed by a current flowing through a single wire is shown. The magnetic field lines are closest together in the center of the loop, where the magnetic field is stronger. The number of loops in a wire can control the strength of a magnetic field.

1. **Develop Models** ✏ Draw the magnetic field lines around the two stacked loops of wire.

2. **Use Models** Is the strength of the magnetic field inside the loop greater or less than the strength when there was just one loop of wire? Justify your answer.

....

....

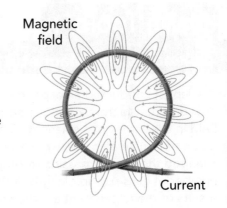

Magnetic field

Current

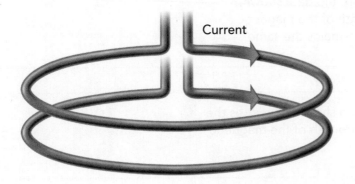

Current

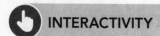
INTERACTIVITY

Design and build a virtual electromagnet that can pick up objects.

Solenoids and Electromagnets

There are many practical uses of coiling a current-carrying wire to make a strong magnetic field. Two devices that strengthen a magnetic field by running a current through coiled wire are solenoids and electromagnets. A **solenoid** is a coil of wire with a current running through it, as shown in **Figure 5**. It is similar to stacked loops of wire. In a solenoid, the magnetic field is strengthened in the center of the coil when a current runs through the coil. One end of a solenoid acts like the north pole of a magnet, and the other end acts like the south pole.

Solenoids

Figure 5 The image shows the magnetic field lines around a solenoid.

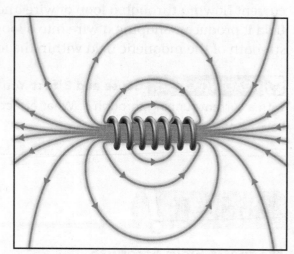

Math Toolbox

Solenoids and Magnetic Fields

A scientist conducted an experiment to investigate how different factors affect the strength of a magnetic field in the center of a solenoid. The solenoid was made of iron wire. In the experiment, the scientist changed the current passing through the wire and the number of coils per unit length of the solenoid. The results of the experiment are shown in the table. Tesla is the SI unit for the strength of a magnetic field.

Number of Coils per meter	Current (amps)	Magnetic Field Strength (Tesla)
100	1	20,000
200	1	40,000
100	2	40,000
200	2	80,000

1. **Draw Comparative Inferences** From the data shown, how does the current affect the strength of the magnetic field, if the number of coils per meter remains the same?

_____

_____

2. **Reason Quantitatively** From the data shown, how does the number of coils per meter affect the strength of the magnetic field, if current is constant?

_____

_____

Field Strength and Solenoids You can increase the strength of the magnetic field inside a solenoid by increasing the number of coils or loops of wire. Winding the coils closer together also produces a stronger magnetic field. As in a straight wire, increasing the current through the solenoid wire will also increase the magnetic field.

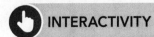

INTERACTIVITY

Apply your knowledge of electromagnets and factors that affect electromagnetic force.

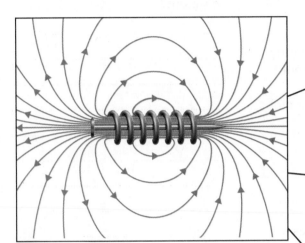

Electromagnets

Figure 6 A solenoid with a nail in the core is a simple electromagnet. More advanced electromagnets have many practical uses.

Some doors are locked with electromagnets and can only be unlocked electronically.

Electromagnets are used both to lift this train off the track and to propel it forward.

Electromagnets

What else can you do to a solenoid to make the magnetic field even stronger? You add a ferromagnetic material to it. A ferromagnetic material is a substance that becomes a magnet when exposed to a magnetic field. The elements iron, nickel and cobalt are ferromagnetic. As shown in **Figure 6**, a solenoid with a ferromagnetic core is called an **electromagnet**. When a ferromagnetic material is placed within a solenoid, both the current and the magnetized material **produce** a magnetic field. This combination produces a magnetic field that is stronger than that produced by the solenoid alone. As in a solenoid, the magnetic field of an electromagnet increases when the number of coils , the closeness of the coils, or the current increases.

Think back to the electromagnet you saw in **Figure 1**. How might you get the electromagnet to drop the metal beams? Just as with other magnetic fields caused by currents, you turn off the current. The magnetic field no longer exists, and the beams drop. Some other uses for electromagnets are shown in **Figure 6**.

An electromagnet helps to produce the vibrations in these earphones. These vibrations carry sound to your ears.

Academic Vocabulary

The term *produce* has several meanings. What does it mean in the text on this page?

....

....

☑ READING CHECK Summarize What is the structural difference between a solenoid and an electromagnet?

....

☑ LESSON 3 Check

MS-PS2-3

1. **Explain** What did Ørsted discover about electricity and magnetism?

....

....

2. **Cause and Effect** Suppose that an electric current flows in a straight wire. The current changes so that it flows in the opposite direction. What changes occur in the magnetic field, and what stays the same?

....

....

....

3. **Develop Models** 🖊 A straight wire has a current running through it. Draw the current-carrying wire and the magnetic field that it produces.

4. **Compare and Contrast** Compare and contrast a solenoid and an electromagnet. What do they have in common? How are they different?

....

....

....

....

....

....

....

....

5. **Apply Concepts** An MRI machine uses an electromagnet to obtain scans of the human body. It uses these scans to generate images. What advantage is there in using an electromagnet instead of a solenoid in an MRI machine?

....

....

....

....

Quest CHECK-IN

In this lesson, you learned about electromagnetism and how electric currents generate magnetic fields. You also discovered how solenoids and electromagnets increase the strength of the magnetic fields.

Use Information How might you apply the principles of electromagnetism when building your levitating device?

....

....

....

....

HANDS-ON LAB

Building an Electromagnet

Go online to download the lab worksheet. Build an electromagnetic and determine how to control the strength of the electromagnetic force.

ELECTROMAGNETISM
In Action

▶ VIDEO

Explore examples of electromagnetism.

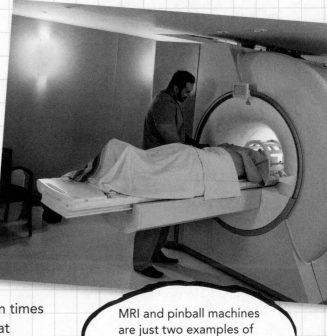

How can you combine electric and magnetic forces to play a game or accomplish a task? You engineer it!

The Challenge: To engineer devices that rely on elecromagnetic force.

Phenomenon People have known for centuries that electricity sparks and that magnets attract. The magnetic compass, for example, has been around since at least the 13th century, and possibly a great deal longer. But it was only in modern times that scientists and engineers began to understand that electricity and magnetism could affect each other.

Electromagnets differ from ordinary magnets because they only attract or repel when an electric current runs through them. An engineer can control an electromagnet, making it useful in industrial applications.

Electromagnetics govern a wide variety of devices and games, from a simple pinball machine to the Large Hadron Collider, an underground experimental facility that physicists are using to study particles. Hospitals use electromagnetics in procedures such as Magnetic Resonance Imaging (MRI). The music industry has found many uses for electromagnets—in speakers, headphones, complex percussion instruments, and recording equipment. Transportation is another field that makes extensive use of electromagnetic technology. The high-speed maglev trains use electromagnetic force to hover above the train tracks and whisk passengers to their destinations at speeds up to 600 kilometers per hour.

MRI and pinball machines are just two examples of the many devices that use electromagnets!

DESIGN CHALLENGE What can you design and build with an electromagnet? Go to the Engineering Design Notebook to find out!

4 Electric and Magnetic Interactions

Guiding Questions

- How do magnetic fields affect moving charges?
- How can current be produced in a conductor?
- How do generators and transformers work?

Connections

Literacy Draw Evidence

Math Understand Ratio Concepts

MS-PS2-3

Vocabulary

galvanometer
electric motor
electromagnetic
  induction
generator
transformer

Academic Vocabulary

source

 VOCABULARY APP

Practice vocabulary on a mobile device.

Quest CONNECTION

As you read, think about how your knowledge of electric and magnetic interactions could help you improve your levitation device.

Connect It!

✎ **Circle the part of the image that shows that electrical energy has been transformed into mechanical energy.**

Construct Explanations Explain how you think the fan works.

....

....

Identify List two other examples in which electrical energy transforms into mechanical energy.

....

....

Magnetic Force on Moving Charges

If a charged particle is at rest in a magnetic field, it is not affected by the field. But if the charged particle moves, it experiences a magnetic force. Why does this happen?

Recall that electric current is charged particles in motion. Suppose you have a wire with a current flowing through it, and you place it at rest in a magnetic field between two magnets. In this situation, there are two magnetic fields at play. The first field is caused by the magnets. The second field is caused by the current flowing through the wire. The magnetic field of the magnets interacts with the magnetic field around the wire. This interaction results in a force on the wire and causes the wire to move in the same direction as the force. The resulting force on the wire is perpendicular to the magnetic field, as given by another right-hand rule. This right-hand rule explains the direction a current-carrying wire moves in a magnetic field, as shown in **Figure 1**.

How does the fan in **Figure 2** work? Inside the fan is an electric motor. The motor uses interactions between magnetic fields around loops of wire and magnetic fields between magnets. To understand how the motor works, take a look at how a current-carrying loop of wire is affected by a magnetic field.

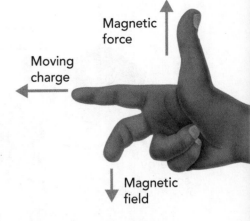

Magnetic force

Moving charge

Magnetic field

Right-Hand Rule #2

Figure 1 Point your index finger in the direction of the current, and bend your middle finger so that it points in the direction of the magnetic field. Your thumb points in the direction of the magnetic force on the moving charges.

Transforming into Mechanical Energy

Figure 2 The blades of this fan start moving when current flows into the fan.

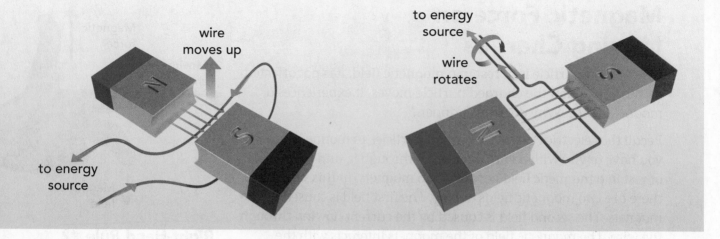
wire
moves up

to energy
source

to energy
source

wire
rotates

Current in a Magnetic Field

Figure 3 A straight wire moves in one direction in a magnetic field. A loop of wire rotates.

INTERACTIVITY

Design and build a virtual motor for a model airplane.

Galvanometer

Figure 4 An electromagnet in the galvanometer turns the pointer to indicate the amount of current present. Why does an electromagnet act like a loop of wire in a magnetic field?

....

....

....

Loop of Current in a Magnetic Field If a
straight wire with a current through it moves in the direction of the force on it, what happens when that wire forms a loop? Compare the two situations in **Figure 3**. When a single wire of current is placed in a magnetic field, it moves in one direction. But when a loop of current is placed in that same field, it rotates. In the loop, the current flows in one direction on one side of the loop. On the other side of the loop, the current flows in the opposite direction. As a result, the magnetic force on one side of the loop points up, and on the other side, the force points down. Because of the directions of these forces, the loop does not rotate in a complete circle. It rotates only half a turn, moving from horizontal to vertical.

Galvanometers This type of rotation is the basis of a
galvanometer, which is a device that measures small currents. Showing how much current is flowing has many uses, such as in fuel gauges or even lie detectors. **Figure 4** shows a galvanometer. In this device, an electromagnet is suspended between two permanent magnets and is attached to the needle of the galvanometer. Recall that one way the strength of an electromagnet is determined is by the amount of current supplied to it. In a galvanometer, the current supplied to the electromagnet is the current that is being measured. If the current is extremely small, the force created is also small, and the needle rotates only a small amount. For a larger current, the force is greater, and the needle moves more.

Electric Motors Recall the fan you saw in **Figure 1**, which contains a motor. An **electric motor** is a device that uses an electric current to turn an axle. In doing that, it transforms electrical energy into mechanical energy.

Examine **Figure 5** to learn the parts that make up an electric motor and how they work together to produce mechanical energy. Recall that a simple loop of wire in a magnetic field can only rotate half a turn because the current flows in only one direction. However, the brushes and the commutator enable the current that flows through the armature to change direction. Each time the commutator moves to a different brush, the current flows in the opposite direction. Thus, the side of the armature that just moved up will now move down, and the armature rotates continuously in one direction. Just picture the armature of a motor attached to an axle to which the blades of a fan are connected. Start the current, and feel the breeze!

READING CHECK **Determine Differences** What is the only part of a motor through which a current does not flow?

....

VIDEO

See what it's like to be an electrical engineer.

HANDS-ON LAB

Investigate Discover the factors that affect the strength of electric and magnetic forces in a motor.

How a Motor Works

Figure 5 🖊 A motor is made of several basic parts, each of which is described below. Study the information about each part. Then, write the number of each description in the appropriate circle on the image.

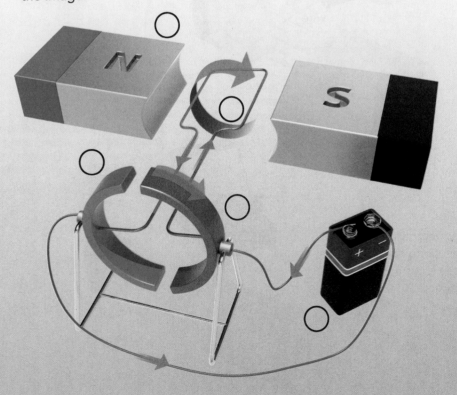

1. **Permanent magnets** produce a magnetic field. This causes the armature to turn.

2. The **commutator** consists of two semicircular pieces of metal. It conducts current from the brushes to the armature.

3. **Brushes,** which do not move, conduct current to the rest of the commutator.

4. The **armature** is a loop of wire that current flows through.

5. The **battery** is the energy source that supplies the current to the brushes.

Literacy Connection

Draw Evidence Underline
the sentence in the
text which identifies
the transformation of
energy that occurs during
electromagnetic induction.

Electromagnetic Induction

You've seen how a current flowing through a wire produces a
magnetic field, and how electrical energy can be transformed
into mechanical energy. In fact, the opposite is also possible. A
magnetic field can be used to produce a current. If a conductor
is moving through a magnetic field, a current is generated in
the conductor. **Electromagnetic induction** is the process of
generating an electric current from the motion of a conductor
through a magnetic field. In this case, mechanical energy is
transformed into electrical energy. The resulting current is
called an induced current.

Induced Current and Moving Conductors By

experimentation, scientists discovered that when a conductor
is moved in a magnetic field, a current flows through the
conductor. Current can be induced if the conductor is a straight
wire, as shown in **Figure 6**. The same principle applies if the
conductor is a coil of wire. Induced current is present any time
that a conductor moves through a magnetic field.

Induction from a Moving Wire

Figure 6 When a conductor (such as a
metal wire) moves through a magnetic
field, current will be induced in the
conductor.

Interpret Diagrams
Examine the image. Then,
use the term *clockwise* or
counterclockwise to complete
each sentence correctly.

When the conductor moves
upward through the magnetic
field, the induced current
flows _____.
When the conductor moves
downward, the induced current
is _____.

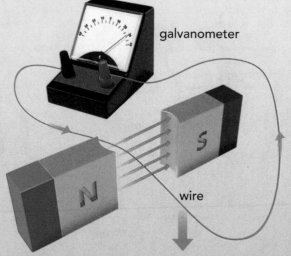

galvanometer

A wire conductor moving up
through a magnetic field induces
a current in one direction.

wire

magnetic
field

galvanometer

A wire conductor moving down
through the same magnetic
field induces a current in the
opposite direction.

wire

Induced Current and Moving Magnets As you have read, an electric current is induced when a conductor moves through a magnetic field. A current also is induced when a magnet moves through a loop of conductive wire. Examine **Figure 7**, which shows what happens when a magnet moves through a loop of wire.

In summary, electric current is induced in a conductor whenever the magnetic field around the conductor is changing. When a conductor is in a magnetic field, a current is induced in the conductor whenever either the conductor or the magnetic field is moving.

✓ READING CHECK **Integrate with Visuals** Based on Figure 6 and Figure 7, what are the two ways that a magnetic field can change, relative to a conductor?

....

....

....

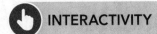
INTERACTIVITY

Predict the direction of a current through a wire near a moving magnet.

Induction from a Moving Magnet

Figure 7 Current will be induced in a conductor in a magnetic field when the magnetic field moves in relation to the conductor.

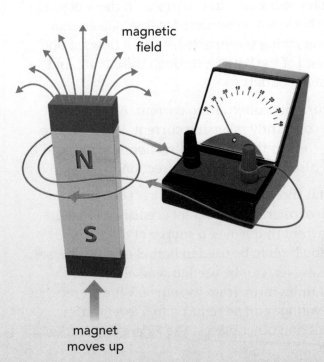

magnetic field

magnet moves up

A magnetic field moving up through a wire conductor induces a current in one direction.

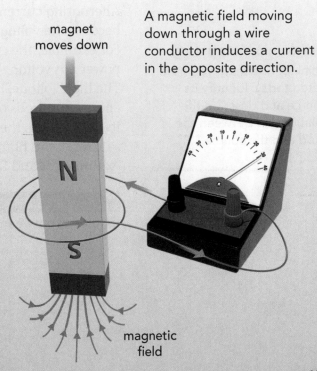

magnet moves down

A magnetic field moving down through a wire conductor induces a current in the opposite direction.

magnetic field

485

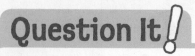

Types of Current

Figure 8 It is not uncommon for one object to require both direct and alternating currents to operate.

Ask Questions An electric car is one item that requires both AC and DC. Write a question about the use of AC and DC in the car.

....

....

....

Academic Vocabulary

Think of one thing you have eaten today. Identify its source and describe the relationship between the food and the source.

....

....

....

Alternating and Direct Current You have probably noticed that not all electrical currents are alike. The type of current that comes from a battery is direct current. Direct current, or DC, has charges that flow in only one direction. Objects that run on batteries use direct current. In these objects, opposite ends of the battery are connected to opposite ends of the circuit. When everything is connected, current flows in one direction from one end of the battery, through the circuit, and into the other end of the battery.

The other type of current is alternating current. Alternating current, or AC, is a constantly reversing current. When a wire in a magnetic field constantly changes direction, the induced current it produces also keeps changing direction.

Alternating current is more common than direct current because the voltage of alternating current is easily changed. For example, the current that leaves a **source** of electrical power has voltage too high to be used in homes and businesses. The high voltage, however, can be used to send electrical energy hundreds of miles away from its source. When it reaches its destination, the voltage can be reduced to a level that is safe for use in homes and other places. Use **Figure 8** to further examine AC and DC.

☑ READING CHECK **Determine Central Ideas** What is the main difference between AC and DC?

....

....

Generators and Transformers

Two common and important devices that use induced current are generators and transformers. Generators and transformers are alike in that an electrical current leaves both of them. They differ in that generators produce electricity, and transformers change the voltage to make the electricity useful.

How Generators Work An electric generator transforms mechanical energy into an electric current. The movement of a conductor within a magnetic field produces a current. The essential parts of a generator are the armature, slip rings, magnets, brushes, and a crank. **Figure 9** shows what these parts are and how they all work together to produce an alternating electric current. The basic operation of a small home generator is the same as that of a large generator that provides current to many homes and businesses.

Although a generator contains some of the same parts as an electric motor, the two devices work in reverse. In an electric motor, an existing current produces a magnetic field, and electrical energy is transformed into mechanical energy. In a generator, the motion of a coil of wire through a magnetic field produces a current and mechanical energy is transformed into electrical energy.

INTERACTIVITY

Construct a virtual generator that can charge a cell phone.

INTERACTIVITY

Explore how electricity and magnetism affect the motion of various materials.

How a Generator Works

Figure 9 A generator works when its component parts operate in the correct order. Number the part names in the correct order to show the operation of a generator from the magnets to the moment when the current is produced. Then, circle the names of the parts of the generator that you would also find in an electric motor.

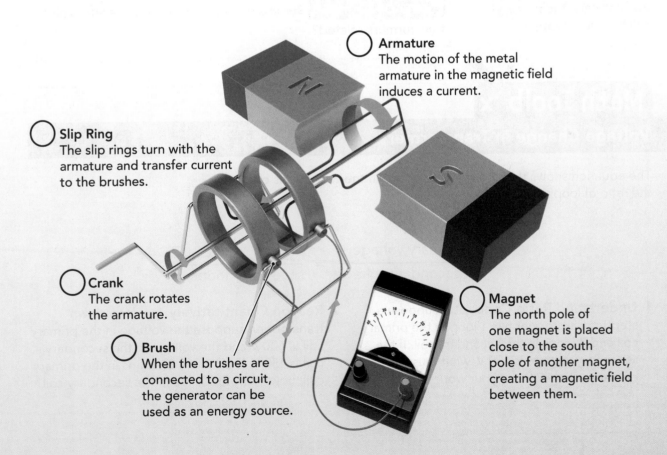

Armature
The motion of the metal armature in the magnetic field induces a current.

Slip Ring
The slip rings turn with the armature and transfer current to the brushes.

Crank
The crank rotates the armature.

Brush
When the brushes are connected to a circuit, the generator can be used as an energy source.

Magnet
The north pole of one magnet is placed close to the south pole of another magnet, creating a magnetic field between them.

Step-Up Transformer

Step-Down Transformer

Types of Transformers

Figure 10 In step-up transformers, the primary coil has fewer loops than the secondary coil. In step-down transformers, the primary coil has more loops.

How Transformers Work You have probably heard the word *transformer* before. What does it mean when a transformer refers to electric current? This type of **transformer** is a device that increases or decreases voltage using two separate coils of insulated wire that are wrapped around an iron core.

The first coil that the current goes through is called the primary coil. This coil is connected to a circuit with a voltage source and alternating current. The other coil is called the secondary coil. It is connected to a circuit, but it does not have a voltage source. The coils share an iron core. Because the primary coil is connected to alternating current, the direction of the current constantly changes. As a result, the magnetic field around it also changes, and it induces a current in the secondary coil.

There are two types of transformers. As shown in **Figure 10**, the type depends on which coil has more loops. Step-up transformers, such as those used to help transmit electricity from generating plants, increase voltage. Step-down transformers, such as those used in phone chargers, decrease voltage. The phone charger plugs into an outlet and reduces the voltage to what is needed to charge a cell phone. The greater the difference between the number of loops in the primary and secondary coils in a transformer, the more the voltage will change.

☑ READING CHECK **Summarize Text** How are generators and transformers related?

....

....

Math Toolbox

Voltage Change in Transformers

The equation shows that the ratio of voltage in the two coils is equal to the ratio of loops.

$$\frac{\text{primary voltage}}{\text{secondary voltage}} = \frac{\text{primary loops}}{\text{secondary loops}}$$

1. **Understand Ratio Concepts** Suppose a step-up transformer has 1 loop in the primary coil and 8 loops in the secondary coil. If the secondary voltage is 120 V, what must be the primary voltage? Show your work.

....

....

2. **Reason Quantitatively** In a step-down transformer, suppose the voltage in the primary coil is 600 V and the voltage in the secondary coil is 150 V. If there are 36 loops in the primary coil, how many loops are in the secondary coil?

....

....

MS-PS2-3

1. Calculate What will be the primary voltage of a transformer if the secondary voltage is 60 V and there are 40 loops on the primary coil and 120 loops on the secondary coil? Show your work.

3. Construct an Explanation In many areas electricity is produced by big generators within dams. What function does large volumes of moving water have in generating electricity?

....

....

....

....

....

4. Apply Scientific Reasoning Suppose you build model airplanes. Use what you know from this lesson to draw a model of a device that would keep a propeller turning as the plane flew.

2. Compare and Contrast How are electric motors and generators similar? How are they different?

....

....

....

....

....

....

....

....

Quest CHECK-IN

In this lesson, you discovered how an electric charge in motion experiences a magnetic force in a magnetic field. You also learned how charges can be set in motion within a conductor by moving the conductor through a magnetic field. A moving magnetic field can also induce a current through a wire. Additionally, you discovered how motors, generators, and transformers work.

Apply Concepts How might a motor, generator, or transformer be used as part of your levitation device?

....

....

....

HANDS-ON LAB

Electrifying Levitation

Go online to download the lab worksheet. Test your levitation device and see how an optimal design can be achieved.

This is an artist's conception of the X-57 Maxwell, showing the electric motors on the extra-thin wings.

THE X-57 Maxwell

Airplanes fly people, mail, and cargo all over the world. Fossil fuels supply the power that planes need in order to fly. With the reserves of fossil fuels dropping, engineers and scientists continue to look for alternative sources of power for planes and other forms of transportation.

NASA's X-57 Maxwell, which is nearing the completion of a long development process, has proved that a battery-powered plane is a possibility. NASA engineers nicknamed the plane "Maxwell" in honor of Scottish physicist James Clerk Maxwell, whose discoveries in physics rank him right behind Einstein and Newton.

The X-57 won't just have electric motors instead of engines; it will have many design features that distinguish it from a traditional plane. The wings will be much smaller, which will reduce the plane's weight and wind resistance. The electric motors will weigh about half as much as traditional combustion engines, and there will be fourteen of them instead of one or two. Twelve of the motors will shut down once the plane is at cruising altitude. There will be special design elements to reduce drag while the plane is aloft.

There are disadvantages to the battery-propelled plane, however. Because the batteries are heavy, the plane won't be able to carry much weight, or many passengers. The plane would also fly more slowly than fuel-power planes, and have a flight distance of about 160 kilometers before its batteries would have to be recharged.

Still, a battery-propelled plane would have many advantages over one that is powered by fossil fuels. Generating the electricity to power the batteries could release less carbon dioxide, which is good news for the climate. Electric motors would also make far less noise than traditional combustion engines.

	X-57 Maxwell	Combustion-Engine Version of Same Plane
Aircraft Weight	1360 kg	819 kg
Cruising Speed	277 km/h	278 km/h
Takeoff Speed	109 km/h	65 km/h
Range	160 km	1240 km

Use the text and the data table to answer the following questions.

1. Summarize Describe the physical features that will make the X-57 Maxwell unique.

2. Calculate What fraction of the plane's full speed would be needed for the plane to get off the ground?

3. Evaluate What factor, aside from the reliance on a battery, do you think makes the range of the X-57 Maxwell shorter than the range of the combustion-engine version of the same plane?

4. Apply Concepts Suppose that the technology pioneered by the X-57 were applied to passenger airliners. What is one advantage that passengers would experience by flying on an X-57 instead of a traditional combustion-engine plane? What would be one disadvantage of passengers flying on an X-57?

☑ TOPIC 9 Review and Assess

1 Electric Force

MS-PS2-5, MS-PS3-2

1. The area around a charge in which the electric force is experienced by other charged objects is the
   A. electric charge. B. electric field.
   C. electric force.   D. electric current.

2. Charges flow through a circuit due to differences in
   A. resistance.   B. potential energy.
   C. conductivity.   D. insulation.

3. Why would two electrons repel each other if they were close together?
   A. They have like charges, so they experience an attractive force.
   B. They have opposite charges, so they experience a repulsive force.
   C. They have like charges, so they experience a repulsive force.
   D. They have opposite charges, so they experience an attractive force.

4. In _____, current flows more easily because electrons are more loosely bound to their atoms than they are in insulators.

5. **Construct Explanations** Suppose a blanket has a sock stuck to it due to static electricity. When you pull the sock off of the blanket, what happens to the potential energy between them? Explain your response.

   ....

   ....

   ....

   ....

   ....

   ....

2 Magnetic Force

MS-PS2-5, MS-PS3-2

6. The push or pull that occurs when a magnet interacts with another object is known as the
   A. magnetic force.   B. magnetic field.
   C. magnetism.   D. magnet.

7. How is a magnet able to pick up bits of metal without actually touching them?
   A. The magnet is surrounded by an electric field that attracts the metal.
   B. The metal exerts a repulsive force on the magnet.
   C. There is an invisible magnetic field around the magnet where it exerts magnetic force.
   D. The electric force from the magnet attracts the bits of metal.

8. **Explain Phenomena** A magnet is placed on a refrigerator to hold up a calendar. As the magnet approaches the refrigerator, the potential energy between the magnet and the refrigerator decreases. Explain why.

   ....

   ....

   ....

   ....

   ....

9. **Develop Models** ✏ Draw the magnetic field lines around a bar magnet, and label the places where the magnetic field is the strongest.

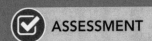
3 Electromagnetic Force

MS-PS2-3

10. What do you call the relationship between electricity and magnetism?
A. static electricity   B. magnetic current
C. electric force   D. electromagnetism

11. A(n) .... is a coil of wire with a current running through it. If you wrap the coil around a ferromagnetic material, it becomes a(n) ....

12. Use Models In the diagram, the direction of a current and the magnetic field around it are shown. Describe what would happen to the magnetic field if you increased the number of turns in the coil and reversed the direction of the current.

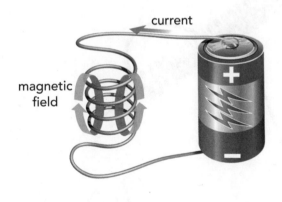
current

magnetic field

....
....
....
....
....
....
....
....
....
....

4 Electric and Magnetic interactions

MS-PS2-3

13. Which of the following descriptions describes electromagnetic induction?
A. Current running through a wire creates a magnetic field.
B. Moving a conductor through a magnetic field generates a current through the conductor.
C. Connecting a conductive wire to both ends of a battery allows current to flow.
D. Moving north poles of two magnets away from each other decreases potential energy.

14. A step-down transformer has a voltage of 400 V through the primary coil and 200 V through the secondary coil. There are 5 loops in the secondary coil. How many loops are in the primary coil?
A. 2 loops   B. 5 loops
C. 10 loops   D. 20 loops

15. Increasing the number of magnets within an electric motor will .... (increase/decrease) the speed of the motor.

16. Determine Differences Electric motors and generators have similar parts but are considered to be opposites. Describe how they are different in terms of electromagnetism and the transformations of energy involved.

....
....
....
....
....
....
....

MS-PS2-3, MS-PS2-5, MS-PS3-2

Evidence-Based Assessment

Manny is investigating factors that affect electric and magnetic forces. He needs to design an experiment to show that objects can exert forces on each other even when they are not in direct contact.

After doing some additional research, Manny decides to make an electromagnet with a battery, some wire, an iron nail, and a switch. He uses a rubber eraser as an insulator to open and close the switch. He uses the electromagnet to see if he can pick up some paperclips.

The diagram shows the setup of Manny's experiment.

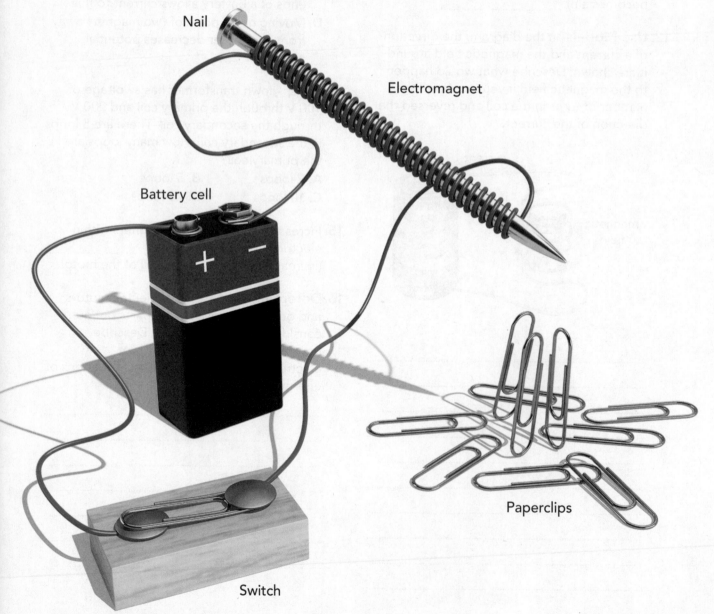

Nail

Electromagnet

Battery cell

Paperclips

Switch

1. **Analyze Data** What is one of the benefits of Manny's electromagnet?

   A. It can only repel objects.

   B. It produces a current through electromagnetic induction.

   C. The magnetic field can be turned on and off.

   D. Its strength cannot be changed.

2. **Cause and Effect** What could Manny do to increase the strength of the electromagnetic force? Select all that apply.

   ☐ Increase the number of coils around the nail.

   ☐ Increase the current by using a battery with a greater voltage.

   ☐ Decrease the number of coils around the nail.

   ☐ Decrease the current by using a battery with a smaller voltage.

3. **Cite Evidence** What evidence is there that the electromagnet exerts a force on the paper clips, even though they are not touching each other?

   ....

   ....

   ....

   ....

   ....

   ....

4. **Analyze Systems** Manny detaches the two wires from the battery and reattaches them to the opposite terminals. Explain how this changes the current and magnetic field.

   ....

   ....

   ....

   ....

   ....

   ....

5. **Explain Phenomena** Suppose you pull the paperclips away from the nail. Explain how the potential energy between the paperclips and the nail changes.

   ....

   ....

   ....

   ....

   ....

   ....

   ....

   ....

Quest FINDINGS

Complete the Quest!

Phenomenon Reflect on the engineering and design work you did building your levitating device.

Connect to Technology Magnets are used in a variety of industrial and medical applications. How do you think magnet technology might be applied to sports?

....

....

....

....

....

👆 **INTERACTIVITY**

Reflect on Your Levitating Device

Planetary Detective

How can you **build** a device to **detect** magnetic fields on distant planets?

Materials

(per pair)

- 3 planet models
- iron filings, 50 mL
- paper cups, 2–3
- pieces of cardboard or small cardboard box
- string, 60 cm
- clear tape
- scissors
- plastic wrap, 2–3 sheets
- copy paper, 3–4 sheets
- small bar magnet

Safety

Be sure to follow all safety guidelines provided by your teacher. The Safety Appendix of your textbook provides more details about the safety icons.

Background

A group of astronomers has approached you for assistance. They are studying three exoplanets, or planets that orbit a star outside our solar system. The three planets orbit in the habitable zone of the star. This means that liquid water can potentially exist on the planets, which is one requirement for life as we know it. The astronomers want to know whether or not the planets have magnetic fields, which will help them determine each planet's capacity for supporting life.

In this investigation, you will build a simple magnetometer, a device that detects magnetic fields, to test models of the three planets. Using evidence from your investigation, you will decide which of the planets have magnetic fields and which one most likely could support life.

Earth's magnetic field helps to deflect charged particles in dangerous solar wind. Without this magnetic field, life would not be possible on our planet.

Design Your Investigation

1. In your investigation, you must build a magnetometer and use it to look for evidence of magnetic fields for models of the three exoplanets, provided by your teacher. Space probes and satellites use this technology to look for evidence of magnetic fields and metals on planets throughout our solar system without coming into contact with the planets.

2. Think about how you can use the available materials to build a magnetometer. Consider the following questions as you work with your group to design your device:

   • How can you use the iron filings to help you detect and observe magnetic forces?

   • How can you use the cups or cardboard along with paper or plastic wrap to design a device that keep the iron filings contained and allows you to safely observe them?

   • How can you make sure that your device's design allows it to detect magnetic fields without coming into contact with the model?

   • How can you use the magnet to test your device?

3. Sketch your design in the space provided and be sure to label the materials you are using to construct the magnetometer. Then build your device.

4. Plan your investigation by determining how you will use the magnetometer to test the models. Record your plan in the space provided. Consider the following questions as you develop your plan:

   • How can you determine whether or not the planet you are studying has a magnetic field?

   • If you detect magnetic fields, how can you compare the strength of the planets' magnetic forces?

5. After getting your teacher's approval, carry out your investigation. Make a table to record your observations and data in the space provided.

uDemonstrate Lab

Sketch and Procedure

Data Table and Observations

Analyze and Interpret Data

1. **Apply Concepts** What characteristics do you think a planet
   needs in order to generate a magnetic field?

   ....

   ....

   ....

   ....

2. **Use Models** Look at your data and observations for the
   planet with the strongest magnetic field. The iron filings in your
   magnetometer were attracted to the magnetic material inside
   the model. Where does the greatest amount of potential energy
   exist—when the magnetometer is 10 cm from the surface of the
   planet or when the magnetometer is 3 cm the surface of the
   planet? Explain.

   ....

   ....

   ....

   ....

   ....

3. **Cause and Effect** How do the results of your investigation
   provide evidence that the magnetic force inside the planet
   interacts with the iron filings in the magnetometer even though
   they do not come into contact with each other?

   ....

   ....

   ....

   ....

   ....

4. **Construct Arguments** Which of the three planets most likely
   could support life? Support your response with evidence from
   your investigation.

   ....

   ....

   ....

   ....

   ....

Information Technologies

NGSS PERFORMANCE EXPECTATIONS

MS-PS4-3 Integrate qualitative scientific and technical information to support the claim that digitized signals are a more reliable way to encode and transmit information than analog signals.

What do these tiny circuits do?

HANDS-ON LAB

uConnect Consider ways to represent the terms *continuous* and *discrete*.

GO ONLINE
to access your
digital course

▶ VIDEO

👆 INTERACTIVITY

📱 VIRTUAL LAB

☑ ASSESSMENT

📖 eTEXT

📱 APP

The Essential Question

Why are digital signals a reliable way to produce, store, and transmit information?

Circuit boards are found in all kinds of electronics devices, from toasters to televisions. How is information transmitted through these boards?

....

....

....

....

....

....

Quest KICKOFF

What is the best way to record sound for my scenario?

STEM ▶ **Phenomenon** Sound engineers work on all kinds of audio recordings, from television shows and movies to music albums. If you wanted to record people's voices and manipulate them to use as sound effects, then how would you do it? In this Quest activity, you will identify the most reliable way to encode and transmit an audio recording. You will explore differences between analog and digital technologies with a hands-on lab and digital activities. By applying what you have learned, you will create a multimedia display that communicates your findings.

🖱 INTERACTIVITY

Testing, Testing . . . 1, 2, 3

MS-PS4-3 Integrate qualitative scientific and technical information to support the claim that digitized signals are a more reliable way to encode and transmit information than analog signals.

🍥 NBC LEARN ▶ VIDEO

After watching the video, which looks at how an audio engineer records sound, describe how attending a live concert is different than listening to an album recorded in a studio.

....

....

....

....

....

....

....

....

Quest CHECK-IN

IN LESSON 1

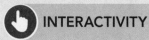 How does a microphone convert sound waves into electrical signals? Design and build a model of a microphone to learn how.

HANDS-ON LAB

Constructing a Microphone

Quest CHECK-IN

IN LESSON 2

How has recording technology changed? Consider the advantages and disadvantages of analog and digital recording technologies.

🖱 INTERACTIVITY

Analog and Digital Recordings

Microphones are just one of the many kinds of technology used to record sound.

Quest CHECK-IN

IN LESSON 3

What type of recording technology would best suit your scenario? Design a multimedia presentation that communicates your choices and reasons.

👆 INTERACTIVITY

Evaluate Recording Technologies

Quest FINDINGS

Complete the Quest!

Reflect on your work and identify fields or careers that require knowledge of analog and digital signals.

👆 INTERACTIVITY

Reflect on Your Recording Method

1 Electric Circuits

Guiding Questions

- What are the components of a circuit?
- How does Ohm's law apply to circuits?
- What is the difference between a series circuit and a parallel circuit?

Connections

Literacy Determine Central Ideas

Math Use Proportional Relationships

MS-PS4-3

Vocabulary

electrical circuit
voltage
resistance
Ohm's law
series circuit
parallel circuit

Academic Vocabulary

diameter

 VOCABULARY APP

Practice vocabulary on a mobile device.

Quest CONNECTION

Think about how electrical circuits might be used in recording technology.

Connect It!

✎ **Circle an object in the image that you think contains a circuit.**

Analyze Systems What provides the energy for the circuit?

....

....

Explain Phenomena Describe any transformations of energy that occur in the circuit.

....

....

Parts of a Circuit

The wall clock in **Figure 1** is part of an electrical circuit. An **electrical circuit** is a complete, unbroken path that electric charges can flow through.

A circuit consists of a few basic parts: a source of electrical energy, conducting wires, and a device that runs on the electrical energy. In a wall clock batteries are the source of electrical energy. Conducting wires connect the batteries to a motor attached to the clock's arms. The motor runs on electrical energy—converting the batteries' energy to the clock's motions. Circuits sometimes also contain switches. When a switch is closed, charges can flow through the circuit. When a switch is open, the circuit is broken and charges cannot flow. A light switch in your home is used to open and close the circuit that sends electrical energy from a power plant to your light bulb.

Even though energy in circuits is used to power devices, the energy is always conserved. The electrical energy does not get used up—instead, it is transformed from one form to another. For example, in a table lamp, the electrical energy is transformed into light and heat.

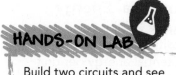

HANDS-ON LAB

Build two circuits and see what happens when some of the lights are unscrewed.

Electric Circuits in a Home

Figure 1 Many devices in a typical home contain circuits and use electricity.

505

Potential Energy

Figure 2 Objects at higher positions have greater potential energy per unit of mass. Similarly, a battery with a higher voltage has greater electrical potential energy per charge.

Develop Models ✏ Draw an X on the water slide where a person would have the greatest gravitational potential energy per unit of mass. Draw an X on the circuit where it has the greatest electric potential energy per charge.

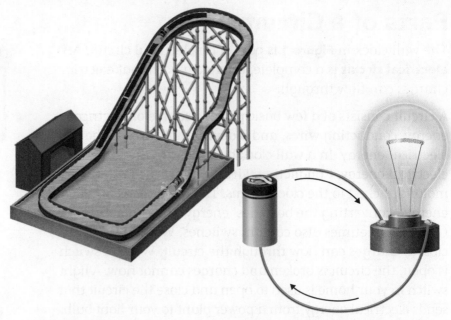

Voltage Electric current flows through a circuit because of differences in electric potential energy in the electric charges. In circuits, it is helpful to think about the electric potential energy per charge, or electric potential, at different points in a circuit. **Voltage** is the difference in electric potential energy per charge between two points in a circuit. So, voltage is the difference in electric potential. Voltage is measured in volts (V).

A typical battery has two ends. One end has a higher electric potential than the other. The end with higher electric potential is called the positive end, and the end with lower electric potential is the negative end. The difference in electric potential is the battery's voltage. For example, the positive end of a 12-volt battery has an electric potential 12 volts higher than the negative end. When the battery is connected within a circuit, this voltage causes current to flow. The current moves from the positive end through the circuit and back to the negative end. The current flows naturally, much like water on a water slide (**Figure 2**).

As the current flows through the circuit, the electric potential energy is converted to other forms of energy. As a result, the electric potential drops as the charges move through the circuit. When the charges reach the battery, they need to regain potential energy if the current is going to continue. The battery supplies the charges with energy by converting chemical energy (from chemicals within the battery) to electrical energy.

The directions of current and voltage were originally defined for positive charges. It was later discovered that negatively-charged electrons flow through a wire circuit. It can be confusing, but remember that what we call electric current goes in the opposite direction of the actual flow of electrons.

Resistance Objects that run on electricity act as resistance to the flow of current. **Resistance** is a measure of how difficult it is for current to flow through an object. It takes more energy for charges to move through objects with higher resistance. Therefore, there is a greater drop in electric potential as the current flows through the circuit. Objects that provide resistance are called resistors. A light bulb, for example, acts as a resistor (**Figure 3**).

The resistance of an object depends on its **diameter**, length, temperature, and material. Objects with a smaller diameter and longer length are more difficult to flow through. In the same way, it is more difficult to sip a drink through a narrow and long straw than a wide and short straw. Current also flows more easily through an object when it is cold than when it is hot. Warmer particles vibrate more and obstruct the flow of current. Current also flows more easily through materials that are good conductors. The conductors have electrons that are more loosely bound, so the charges can move more easily.

READING CHECK Summarize What kind of device in a circuit supplies voltage? What kind of device acts as a resistor?

....

....

....

....

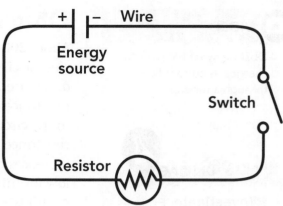

Potential Energy
Figure 3 The diagrams show a circuit with a battery, conducting wires, a switch, and a light bulb.

Academic Vocabulary

The diameter of a circle is the distance across the center. This is the full width of the circle. How would you describe the diameter of a round wire?

....

....

....

Model It

Drawing Circuit Diagrams
As shown in **Figure 3**, symbols are used in a diagram to show the parts of a circuit.

1. Develop Models 🖊 In the space provided, draw what the circuit in **Figure 3** would look like if another battery and another light bulb were added.

2. Predict Will the total resistance in the circuit increase or decrease when more light bulbs are added? Explain.

   ....

   ....

   ....

VIDEO

Observe what happens to charges as current flows through a resistor.

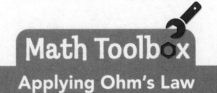

HANDS-ON LAB

Investigate Explore Ohm's law in action with your own circuit.

Ohm's Law

About 200 years ago, scientist Georg Ohm experimented with electric circuits. He measured the resistance of a conductor and varied the voltage to find the relationship between resistance and voltage. He found that changing the voltage in the circuit changes the current but does not change the resistance of the conductor. When voltage increases, current increases but resistance does not change. Ohm came up with a law for this relationship. **Ohm's law** states that resistance in a circuit is equal to voltage divided by current.

$$\text{Resistance} = \frac{\text{Voltage}}{\text{Current}}$$

Resistance is measured in ohms (Ω). This means that one ohm of resistance is equal to one volt (V) divided by one amp (A). If you increase voltage without changing resistance, then current must increase as well.

Solving this equation for voltage, you obtain:

$$\text{Voltage} = \text{Current} \times \text{Resistance}$$

If you increase the resistance of a circuit without changing the voltage, then the current must decrease.

Math Toolbox
Applying Ohm's Law

A stereo converts electrical energy into sound energy. The stereo is plugged into a wall outlet. The voltage is supplied by a power plant, and the current is carried through electrical wires to the stereo.

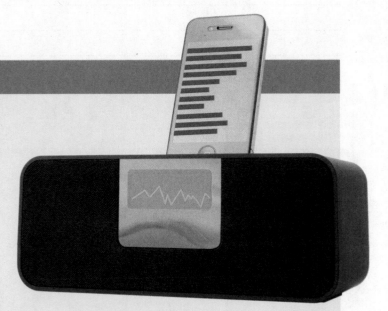

1. **Use Proportional Relationships** When you turn up the volume on a stereo, the voltage increases. Assuming the resistance of the stereo remains the same, what happens to the current?

....

2. **Use Equations** Suppose you turn up the volume on a stereo so that the voltage increases to 110 V while the resistance remains at 55 Ω. Calculate the current after this voltage increase.

....

....

Series and Parallel Circuits

Different situations may call for different types of circuits. Suppose a factory uses multiple machines in an assembly line to recycle glass bottles. If the glass-melting machine breaks down but the bottles keep moving, there could be a major safety hazard as the bottles pile up! To prevent this problem, the machines can be wired so that if one machine breaks, then the circuit is broken and all other machines stop working as well. This is called a series circuit.

Series Circuits

In a **series circuit**, all parts of the circuit are connected one after another along one path (**Figure 4**). There are advantages to setting up a circuit this way, as in the example of the recycling factory. However, it can sometimes be a disadvantage. The more devices you add to the circuit, the more resistance there is. As you learned with Ohm's law, if voltage remains the same and resistance increases, then current decreases. Adding more light bulbs to a string of lights causes them to shine less brightly. The circuit would have more resistance and the current would decrease, causing the bulbs to appear dimmer.

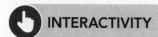

INTERACTIVITY

Explore the similarities and differences between series and parallel circuits.

Write About It Give one example of a situation in your life in which a series circuit is an advantage, and another example in which it could be a disadvantage.

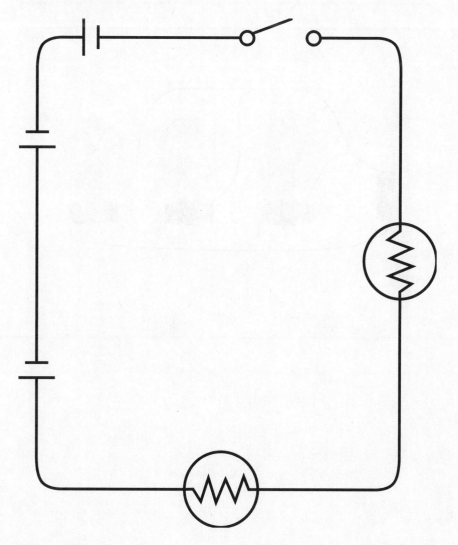

Correcting Circuit Diagrams

Figure 4 ✏ An electrical engineer draws a circuit diagram of a series circuit that includes three resistors, two batteries, and a switch. Find the engineer's mistake, and mark the drawing with your correction.

INTERACTIVITY

Review the parts of a circuit and fix a set of broken lights.

Parallel Circuits In other situations, you may want each device in a circuit to be wired so that if one device breaks, the others still work. For instance, when one overhead light burns out in the kitchen, you don't expect the other lights to go out, leaving you in the dark. In situations like this, you should use a **parallel circuit**, in which different parts of the circuit are on separate branches. As shown in **Figure 5**, there are several paths for the current to take in a parallel circuit.

Surprisingly, adding resistors in parallel to the circuit actually causes resistance to decrease. How is this possible? Adding a branch opens up another path for current to flow. This is similar to adding another pipe for water to flow through. Therefore, resistance in the circuit decreases and current increases. However, the additional current flows down the new path, so it does not affect the other devices. If a string of lights is set up along a parallel circuit, then each new bulb you add will glow as brightly as those originally on the strand.

☑ READING CHECK **Determine Central Ideas** Describe the main difference between a series circuit and a parallel circuit.

....

....

Light Bulbs in Parallel
Figure 5 The circuit diagram shows three light bulbs in parallel.

1. **Cause and Effect** What happens to the other two light bulbs when one light bulb goes out? Explain.

   ....

   ....

   ....

   ....

   ....

   ....

2. **Develop Models** ✏
   Draw the circuit again, adding one switch to each branch so that the bulbs can be controlled separately.

At the Boardwalk

Figure 6 ✏ Many activities at the boardwalk involve circuits. Circle the places where circuits would be.

Construct Explanations Why do you think five of the last lights on the Ferris wheel have gone out?

....

....

....

MS-PS4-3

1. Identify What are the three main parts that must be present to make up a circuit?

....

....

....

2. Define How is voltage related to electric potential energy?

....

....

....

....

3. Develop Models ✏ Draw a series circuit diagram that contains a battery, a switch, and three resistors. Label the parts of the circuit.

4. Use Information A long, narrow resistor is placed in a series circuit along with a short, wide resistor made of the same material. Which will have a greater electric potential drop across it? Explain your reasoning.

....

....

....

....

....

5. Cause and Effect Suppose you construct a parallel circuit consisting of a battery, a switch, and four light bulbs. One of the light bulbs goes out. What happens to the brightness of the remaining bulbs? Explain.

....

....

....

....

....

....

....

Quest CHECK-IN

You have discovered the meaning of voltage and resistance and how they relate to current as described by Ohm's law. You've also read about the different parts of a circuit and how to connect them in series or in parallel.

Communicate How might your understanding of circuits help you decide what type of recording device to use?

....

....

....

HANDS-ON LAB

Constructing a Microphone

Go online to download the lab worksheet. Develop and use a model that shows how a simple microphone converts sound waves into electrical signals.

A LIFE-SAVING
Mistake

👆 **INTERACTIVITY**

Explore what makes up a pacemaker and how it works.

How do you create a tiny device that saves hundreds of thousands of lives? You engineer it! The story of Wilson Greatbatch shows us how.

The Challenge: To develop the first successful cardiac pacemaker.

Phenomenon In 1956, Greatbatch was working at the University of Buffalo, in New York, as an assistant professor in electrical engineering. He was building an electronic device to record the heart rhythms of cardiac patients. While tinkering with the circuitry, he made a mistake and put a resistor into the circuit that was the wrong size.

When Greatbatch added the resistor, he did not get the outcome he expected. The circuit periodically buzzed with electrical pulses that reminded the engineer of a human heartbeat.

Greatbatch's error turned out to be a happy accident. He realized that the device could help cardiac patients whose hearts beat irregularly. He used the idea to develop the first successful pacemaker, a device that delivers small electrical shocks to the heart muscle to keep it beating regularly and pumping blood normally.

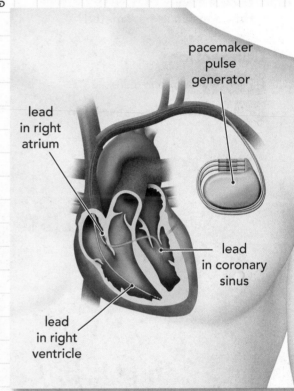

pacemaker pulse generator

lead in right atrium

lead in coronary sinus

lead in right ventricle

A pacemaker uses a pulse generator implanted below a patient's skin to send electric pulses to the heart. The pulses travel through wires called leads.

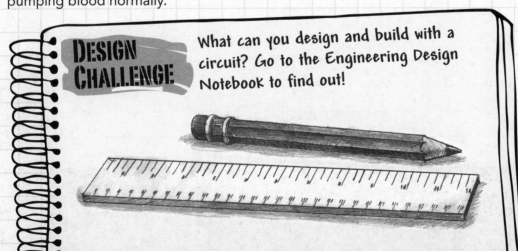

DESIGN CHALLENGE What can you design and build with a circuit? Go to the Engineering Design Notebook to find out!

(2) Signals

Guiding Questions
- How is information sent as signals?
- What are digital and analog signals?
- How are signals transmitted?

Connections
Literacy Summarize Text

Math Draw Comparative Inferences

MS-PS4-3

Vocabulary
wave pulse
electronic signal
electromagnetic
  signal
digital signal
analog signal
pixel

Academic Vocabulary
transmission

 VOCABULARY APP

Practice vocabulary on a mobile device.

Quest CONNECTION

Consider how different signals can be recorded, processed, and transmitted.

Connect It !

✎ **Circle the visual signal that is being used to communicate information.**

Construct Explanations Why do you think hand signals are useful for communicating with a dog?

....

....

....

....

....

Signals and Information

An electric circuit can be used to power a device like a light bulb. However, circuits can also be used to send information. Think about a doorbell, which is usually a circuit. When someone presses a button outside a door, the circuit is complete and the electricity powers a bell that chimes. If you understand the meaning of the chime (a signal that someone is at the door), then you can respond by going to the door. For any signal to be understood, there needs to be agreement between the sender and the receiver about what the signal means. In some cases, the signal can be simple, such as a doorbell or basic hand signals, like the one the pet owner is using in **Figure 1**. Others are more complex. For example, you are reading a specific sequence of letters and spaces on this page to learn about signals.

For much of the 1800s, people communicated with each other over great distances using electrical signals. Samuel Morse patented a version of the electrical telegraph in 1837, and by the Civil War in 1861, there were telegraph lines that carried Morse code from one side of the United States to the other.

HANDS-ON LAB

Compare and contrast analog and digital clocks.

Signaling

Figure 1 A human can teach a dog to respond to visual signals.

Morse Code

Figure 2 In Morse code, combinations of short (dot) and long (dash) wave pulses are sent and each combination is translated into a letter.

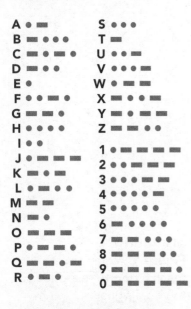

Electronic Signals

An electrical telegraph is used to send Morse code as an **electronic signal**, information that is sent as a pattern in a controlled flow of current through a circuit. The telegraph turns the current on and off as the operator taps a device to close and open the circuit, as shown in **Figure 2**. In Morse code, combinations of short (dot) and long (dash) wave pulses stand for the letters of the alphabet and punctuation marks. A **wave pulse** is a pulse of energy that travels through the circuit when it is closed. In Morse code, the letter *A* is sent and received as "•—", *B* is "—•••", and so on. This code can be used to send messages, but it is very slow.

Electronic signaling became more useful and widespread when inventors developed ways to transmit information without translating them into code. In 1876, Alexander Graham Bell patented the first telephone. In Bell's telephone, two people spoke into devices that were part of the same circuit. A microphone converted soundwaves in the in air—a caller's voice—into electronic signals that would be carried to the receiver somewhere else. At the time, switchboard operators manually connected two telephones into the same circuit. Eventually, switchboards became fully automated.

Model It !

Be a Telegraph Operator

1. **Interpret Visuals** Use the Morse code chart in **Figure 2** to decode the following four lines of code.

   •—— •••• •— — ....

   •• ••• ....

   ••—• ——— •—• ....

   •—•• ••— —• —•—• •••• ....

2. **Use a Model** ✎ Use Morse code to provide an answer to the message you decoded.

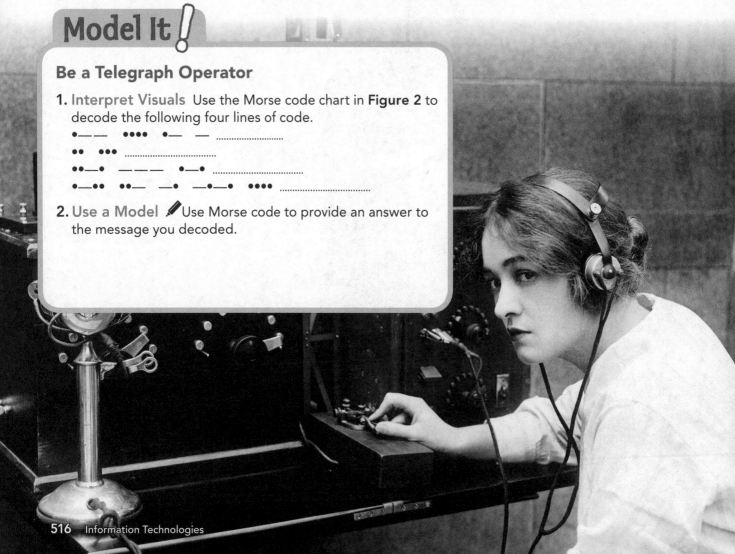

Electronic Signals	Electromagnetic Signals

Electromagnetic Signals

Information sent as patterns of electromagnetic waves such as visible light, infrared waves, microwaves, and radio waves are **electromagnetic signals**. Modern information technologies use a combination of electronic and electromagnetic signals. In 1895, the first radio station transmitted radio wave signals between two points without using an electrical circuit. This launched wireless forms of communication that allowed messages to be transmitted across the globe. Wireless technologies, such as the ones shown in **Figure 3**, now dominate the telecommunications industry. Electromagnetic signals travel at the speed of light, which is much faster than the speed at which current flows through a circuit.

Different types of electromagnetic signals are used for different purposes. Modern mobile phones communicate using microwaves, which are in the ultra-high frequency (UHF) band of the electromagnetic spectrum. Submarines communicate underwater with extremely low frequency (ELF) waves. Optical fibers use visible and infrared light to transmit large amounts of information.

✓ READING CHECK **Determine Central Ideas** What is an electronic signal?

....

....

From Wired to Wireless

Figure 3 The transition from wired to wireless telecommunications has allowed people to communicate and share information with each other with greater convenience, speed, and quality.

Compare and Contrast
✏ Complete the table to compare and contrast electronic and electromagnetic signals.

517

Types of Signals

Figure 4 Analog signals are continuous, whereas digital signals are discrete.

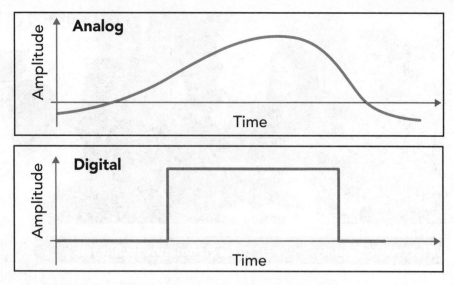

VIDEO

Compare analog sound recording devices to newer digital technologies.

Literacy Connection

Summarize Texts
Underline the sentences that summarize the differences between analog and digital signals.

Analog and Digital Signals

Electronic and electromagnetic signals can carry information from one place to another in two different ways: as analog signals or as digital signals. Both analog and digital signals have strengths and weaknesses, but the power and flexibility of digital signals have made them the foundation of modern information technologies.

Analog Signals An **analog signal** allows for a continuous record of some kind of action (**Figure 4**). For example, when seismic waves from an earthquake cause the ground to move, a seismograph records that continuous motion as an analog signal. The advantage of analog signals is that they provide the highest resolution of an action by recording it continuously. But analog signals can be difficult to record. The signals processed by a seismograph must be recorded with ink on paper as a seismogram. Other examples of analog signals are the recordings of music on vinyl records. You can slow down a record and still hear continuous music. However, vinyl records scratch and warp very easily. Analog media also take up a lot of space, compared to digital media.

Digital Signals A **digital signal** allows for a record of numerical values of an action at a set of continuous time intervals (**Figure 4**). This results in a series of numbers. For example, a digital seismometer can record ground motion by recording the numerical value of the ground height at each second. This produces a list of numbers that shows the ground motion, second by second. The disadvantage of digital signals is that you do not have a record of any signals that occurred in between each sampling. One advantage is that once you have recorded the signal as a set of numbers, you can store it on a computer or other digital device. Digital recordings can also be edited easily by just changing the numbers.

Sampling Rate

The quality of digital media depends on the length of the recording intervals. The term *sampling rate* refers to how often a signal is recorded or converted to digital code. More data are captured and recorded the more times the event is sampled (**Figure 5**). For example, a digital music file with a high sampling rate may sound richer and more detailed than a file with a lower sampling rate. The downside of a higher sampling rate is that the file size is larger.

Scientists and music producers have conducted tests with people to find a sampling rate that will produce digital music files that sound realistic without having more data than humans can perceive. If the sampling rate is too high and the files are too large, then the files will waste space on music players, mobile phones, computers, or storage services.

INTERACTIVITY

Compare analog and digital signals, and learn about signal noise.

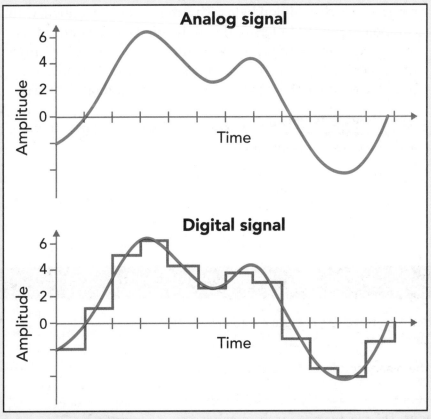

Analog-to-Digital Processing

Figure 5 When an analog signal is converted to a digital signal, what was continuous must be broken into discrete pieces. The higher the sampling rate, the closer the digital signal will come to the analog signal.

Develop Models ✏ Draw two digital versions of the original analog signal in the blank graphs: one based on sampling the analog signal 24 times, and the other based on sampling 32 times.

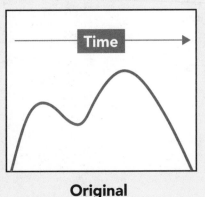

Original

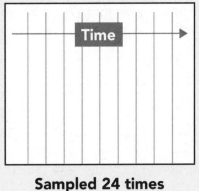

Sampled 24 times

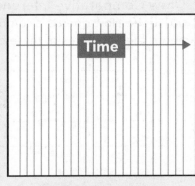

Sampled 32 times

HANDS-ON LAB

иInvestigate Explore how analog signals can be converted to digital information.

Binary Code

Figure 6 The binary codes, or bytes, for the first five letters of the alphabet are shown here. Notice that there are different codes for lowercase and uppercase letters.

a = 01100001   A = 01000001
b = 01100010   B = 01000010
c = 01100011   C = 01000011
d = 01100100   D = 01000100
e = 01100101   E = 01000101

Interpret Data What would the code be for the word *Dad*?

Binary Signals

Recall that Morse code has just two signals—dots and dashes—that are used in different combinations to communicate letters. Computers use a similar system called binary, which consists of ones and zeros. The information that we store on computers is encoded with binary, whether it's a song, a text document, or a movie.

Each number in binary code is a bit of information. Bits are arranged into groups of eight, called bytes. The code for each letter of the alphabet has its own unique byte, as shown in **Figure 6**. The code for a word consists of bytes strung together. For example, as the author wrote this page, a computer program translated the keyboard strokes for the letters in the word *"code"* into bytes.

01100011011011110110010000110101

The basic unit of a computer's storage capacity is the byte. A megabyte is one million bytes. This means one megabyte (MB) can hold a million letters of the alphabet. Digital storage has improved so much in recent years that we now use even larger units such as gigabyte (billion bytes) and terabyte (trillion bytes) to describe the storage capacities of our digital devices.

☑ READING CHECK **Summarize Text** How are signals stored and processed on computers?

Math Toolbox

Cryptography

Cryptography is the study of codes. Use the chart in **Figure 6** to answer the following questions and "break" the codes.

1. Patterns What do you think the binary codes for the letters *f* and *F* are?

....

2. Draw Comparative Inferences The binary code for the number 6 is 00110110. How does this compare to the code for *f*? What can you infer about the structures of these codes?

....

....

....

....

Transmitting Signals

Modern forms of communication involve the **transmission** of electronic or electromagnetic signals. Many transmissions are now in digital formats. In some cases, the transmission consists of an entire file, such as a digital song file saved to your phone. In other cases, the transmission is more like a broadcast, such as a live stream.

Sound Information Analog telephones transmit signals by first converting sound waves to electronic wave pulses. Those travel along wires to another phone, which converts the wave pulses back to sound waves. Modern mobile phones convert sound waves to digital data in the form of binary code. The data are transmitted as microwaves, which are converted back to sound waves by another mobile phone. If someone records and sends a voice message from one mobile phone to another, or to a computer, the process is basically the same. Sound waves are the initial signal and the ultimate product.

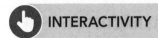
INTERACTIVITY

Analyze a model of how phone calls are made with mobile devices.

Academic Vocabulary

In your science notebook, record other uses of the term *transmission* in science. In those other contexts, what's being transmitted?

Digital Audio

Figure 7 To transmit a sound signal from one place to another, the signal must be processed and converted into different forms.

Develop Models 🖊 Complete the diagram by identifying the type of signals that are being transmitted.

Pixels and File Size

Figure 8 The three images of the flower are copies of the same file. The leftmost image has a low resolution and small file size. The middle image has higher resolution and a larger file size. The rightmost image has the highest resolution and largest file size.

Visual Information Photographs, printed documents, and other visuals can be digitized and transmitted as well. A digital visual consists of **pixels**, or small uniform shapes that are combined to make a larger image (**Figure 8**). The information that determines a pixel's color and brightness is coded in bytes. The more pixels that are used, the more bytes the digital image file will require. For example, a digital image that is meant to take up a few centimeters on a mobile phone screen may be far less than a megabyte, whereas an image that is meant to be shown on a high-resolution display or printed as a poster can be 50 megabytes and more. Just as audio engineers and music producers try to balance file size with detail that will be audible to human ears, visual artists and engineers must strike a balance too. They don't want their images to appear too "pixilated," but they don't want to waste device storage with too much detail either.

☑ READING CHECK **Summarize Text** How are pixels used to capture and convey visual information with digital technology?

....

....

....

☑ LESSON 2 Check

1. **Identify** Sound waves move from a guitar to a microphone. The microphone converts the sound waves to electronic wave pulses that are transmitted through a wire to a computer. The computer converts the wave pulses to a series of 1's and 0's. The 1's and 0's are packaged as a file and posted online for sale to the guitarist's fans. In this process, when were the signals digital?

....

....

....

....

....

2. **Calculate** If one letter of the alphabet is one byte, and the average word consists of five letters, how many words could be encoded in binary and stored on a 1-GB memory card?

....

....

....

....

....

3. **Make Comparative Inferences** How is the sampling rate used in recording digital music similar to the number of pixels in a digital image?

....

....

....

....

....

....

4. **Summarize Text** Compare and contrast Morse code and binary code.

....

....

....

....

....

....

....

....

....

Quest CHECK-IN

In this lesson, you learned about different types of signals and how they are used to record and transmit information.

Evaluate Why is it important to know the different types of signals that can be used to record information?

....

....

....

....

....

INTERACTIVITY

Analog and Digital Recordings

Go online to investigate and identify advantages and disadvantages of digital music.

MS-PS4-3

Super Ultra High Definition!

If your family has purchased a new television recently, you know there are many digital options. In fact, many consumers and digital media providers have sometimes struggled to keep up with the technological changes.

Video resolution is one of the most important factors in digital TV technology. Resolution refers to the number of pixels on the TV screen. The diagram shows the different resolutions currently in use. The numbers shown for each resolution refer to the dimensions of the screen image in pixels. For example, standard-definition resolution (SD) has a 640 × 480 pixel dimension. The image is made up of 480 horizontal lines. Each line contains 640 pixels, for a total of 307,200 pixels.

As resolution increases, image quality increases because there are more pixels to form the image. However, as resolution and image quality increase, file size increases too. Each pixel in the image takes up 1 byte of storage. This means that one frame of an SD image takes up 307,200 bytes, or about 0.3 megabytes (MB) of storage. A moving TV image runs at 30 frames per second, so a one-hour program would take up about 32,400 MB in storage. This is where video codecs come in. A codec is software that digitally encodes and compresses the video signal to reduce its file size without affecting image quality very much.

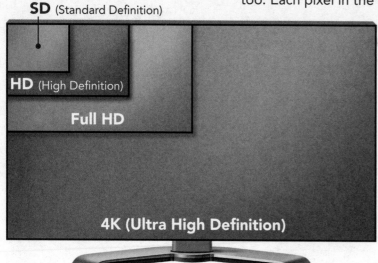

SD (Standard Definition)

HD (High Definition)

Full HD

4K (Ultra High Definition)

A Streaming Society

Today, many people download or stream TV shows and movies to their televisions and smart devices. Because the higher-quality signals are larger in file size, fast Internet speeds are required to move all the data. Internet speed is generally measured in megabits per second (Mbps). The amount of data that can be transferred at three different speeds is shown here.

Mbps speed	MB transferred per second
1	0.125
50	6.25
100	12.5

Use the text and data to answer the following questions.

1. **Use Models** A 4K image contains 8,294,400 pixels. What is the corresponding file size?

2. **Calculate** Suppose you're downloading a movie that is 3.2 GB. Your Internet speed is 50 Mbps. About how long will it take to download the file? Show your work.

3. **Patterns** Some video engineers are already touting 8K resolution, the next advance in video technology. The image quality of an 8K signal is equal to taking four 4K TVs and arranging them in a 2 × 2 array. What are the dimensions of an 8K image? Explain.

4. **Analyze Properties** Television programs used to be transmitted using analog signals. As more people began to buy HD televisions and watch HD programming, TV broadcasters and cable providers switched to digital signals. Why do you think this switch occurred? What advantage does a digital signal have over an analog signal when transmitting HD video?

5. **Construct Explanations** Most televisions sold now are 4K Ultra HD capable. However, most streaming services and digital TV providers offer little 4K programming. Why do think this is the case?

3 Communication and Technology

Guiding Questions

- What technologies are used for communication?
- What are the advantages of using digital signals for communications technology?

Connections

Literacy Cite Textual Evidence

Math Analyze Relationships

MS-PS4-3

Vocabulary

information technology
software
noise
bandwidth

Academic Vocabulary

hardware

 VOCABULARY APP

Practice vocabulary on a mobile device.

Quest CONNECTION

Consider how hardware and software affect the types of signals that are used in information technology.

Connect It!

🖊 **Circle a symbol on the clay tablet that appears more than once.**

Compare and Contrast How is the ancient clay tablet similar to a digital tablet of today? How is it different?

....

....

....

....

The Information Age

The invention of writing was one of the first examples of information technology. Using a sharpened stick or a finger and some kind of medium such as clay (**Figure 1**) or a stone wall, people were able to record ideas, observations, and other information.

Fast forward to today. Information technology is everywhere, and there many forms and modes of writing. For example, one person typed the text on this page into a computer. The file was then sent via the internet to reviewers and editors. Edited text was then combined with the photograph in a different computer application. Finally, a file was sent to a printer, and a series of pages were put together as a book. What would have taken hours to inscribe in clay or rock can now be recorded and shared much faster, thanks to information technology. Modern **Information technology** consists of computer and telecommunications **hardware** and software that store, transmit, receive, and manipulate information. **Software** refers to programs that encode, decode, and interpret information, including browsers, apps, games, and operating systems. The invention of electronic computers around 1940 helped usher in the information age.

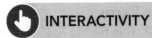

INTERACTIVITY

Discuss the encoding and decoding of information with classmates.

Academic Vocabulary

Hardware is an older term. What do you think "hard" refers to in the information technology usage of *hardware*?

....

....

....

Sumerian Tablet

Figure 1 This clay tablet was used to record information 6,500 years ago in Sumer, part of Mesopotamia.

Server Farm

Figure 2 This facility has thousands of computers that store and share the data of millions of people.

Ask Questions Why do think this facility is called a server farm?

....
....
....
....

Literacy Connection

Cite Textual Evidence
Underline text that supports the idea that we are in a period of exponential data growth.

Information Technologies Every day, hundreds of millions of e-mails, and billions of text messages are sent. Files are also exchanged online through "clouds" that are accessible from thousands of networks. Every year, trillions of gigabytes of information are produced on Earth, ranging from high-definition movies to printable text documents to brief messages about what to buy at the supermarket.

The software and hardware that power modern information technology (IT) depend on each other. IT hardware is the modern version of clay or stone. It serves as the physical medium where information is stored and altered. Processor chips, batteries, disks, wiring, and other components compose the physical place where software operates. In some cases, the hardware you depend on is "local," such as the processor, display, built-in memory, and other components of your mobile device or computer. Other hardware that you probably use is housed elsewhere, such as the cell phone tower that may be in or near your town, and the "farms" of servers that major telecommunications and computer companies use to store some of your information (**Figure 2**). By accessing data held on a server that is somewhere else, you can watch, listen to, read, or otherwise experience media without actually storing the data locally. We are now in a period of exponential growth of digital information production.

✅ READING CHECK **Summarize Text** What are some examples of hardware used in information technology?

....
....
....

Communications Systems

Before the industrial and information ages, long-distance communication methods included smoke signals and handwritten messages carried by pigeons. Today, we depend on three types of transmissions: electronic signals carried by wires, electromagnetic transmissions through the atmosphere, and electromagnetic transmissions through fiber-optic cables.

VIDEO

Learn about the career of a network administrator.

Math Toolbox

Digital Data Explosion

With ever-growing numbers of people accessing the Internet, greater and greater amounts of information and data are being produced. The graph shows data production and expected projections for the future.

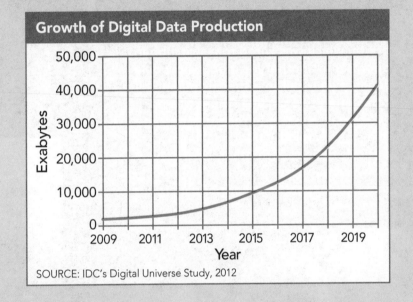

Growth of Digital Data Production

SOURCE: IDC's Digital Universe Study, 2012

1. **Interpret Data** Compare the rate of growth from 2011 to 2013 with the rate of growth from 2015 to 2017.

   ....

   ....

   ....

   ....

   ....

2. **Analyze Relationships** What do you think accounts for the exponential growth of data in recent years?

   ....

   ....

   ....

   ....

   ....

3. **Patterns** If the trend continues, how much data will be produced in 2030?

   ....

   ....

   ....

   ....

   ....

Roger That!

Figure 3 Communications technologies all have one thing in common—they must move vast amounts of data in our digital world.

Connect to Technology For each type of communications technology, identify a benefit and a drawback of using analog signals and digital signals.

For many years, radio and television broadcasts were transmitted using radio waves. Analog televisions and radios depended on tall towers to broadcast signals over the air. In recent years, television has switched over to digital signal transmissions. Televisions can now handle high definition media.

Making a telephone call used to involve a large device mounted on a wall or in a booth, which was wired to a switchboard operator in another location, who would connect your call to a specific person by connecting two circuits. There was no "voicemail" system to record a message. The signal could be poor, making it difficult to hear each other. Nowadays, many people carry phones in their pockets that can connect to other people around the world.

Benefit
....
....

Drawback
....
....

Benefit
....
....

Drawback
....
....

Telecommunications satellites that orbit Earth can relay signals that cannot be transmitted by wires or towers. Some satellites are used to broadcast television stations and other media, and others are used by government agencies and the military.

Benefit
....
....

Drawback
....
....

Fiber optic technology is based on glass or plastic cables that transmit light at speeds around 200,000 kilometers per second. Fiber-optic cables can carry about a thousand times more information per second than standard copper cable.

Benefit
....
....

Drawback
....
....

The Internet is a complex set of interconnected networks that transmits information, largely through the World Wide Web. The Internet is usually accessed through an application called a browser, which allows people to navigate through the millions of pages. Internet connection used to require a cable plugged into a computer, but now many connections are achieved over wireless "WiFi" networks, or even mobile cellular networks.

Benefit
....
....

Drawback
....
....

HANDS-ON LAB

Investigate Observe the structure of a vinyl record and predict how it functions.

Advantages of Digital Signals

Although they are not continuous signals, digital signals are more reliable and efficient overall than analog signals, for several reasons.

Compatibility with Computers Computers process digital signals, and computers are everywhere—on laps and desktops, tucked in pockets, in car dashboards, and even on refrigerator doors. It's easier for computers and digital devices to do what we want them to do without having to convert analog signals first. Using digitals signals is more efficient.

Noise When an analog signal is transmitted, it can incorporate **noise**—random signals from the environment. This noise can then stay with the signal and alter the output. Static is an example of noise. Because digital signals consist of 0's and 1's, it is more difficult for noise to alter the signal, because binary code is essentially a choice between on and off. Unless noise causes a one to become a zero or vice versa, noise shouldn't affect how the digital signal is received or read.

Model It

Noise? No Problem!
The first graph shows an analog signal accompanied by noise during transmission. The second graph shows a digital signal also accompanied by noise during transmission.

Develop Models ✏️
Complete the models by drawing the received analog and digital signals to show how noise affects each one.

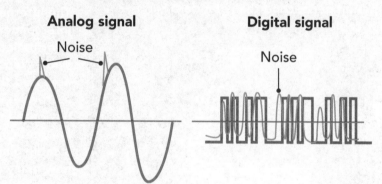

Original signal with noise

Analog signal
Noise

Digital signal
Noise

Received signal

Distortion caused by noise   Restored digital signal

Security Although digital signals are encrypted—hidden by binary coding—both analog and digital signals are vulnerable to security breaches. It's relatively easy for someone to tap into an analog phone line and listen to or record the conversation, because the signal is not encrypted. It's more difficult to access digital phone signals or communications, but hacking—stealing of digital information by breaking the codes—is on the rise. Tech experts are continually working to improve digital security.

Bandwidth As illustrated in **Figure 4**, the amount of information that can be transmitted and measured in bits per second is called **bandwidth**. Digital signals carry less information than comparable analog signals, so digital information technology solutions typically have greater bandwidth than analog solutions. For example, a cable that provides a home with television and Internet service can provide those services faster, and allow more data to be downloaded and uploaded, if it carries digital signals. Compression can help with bandwidth as well. For example, if a 1-gigabyte file can be compressed to a smaller file size for transmission and then uncompressed by a computer, the file should download faster.

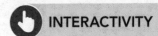
INTERACTIVITY

Research the advantages and disadvantages of analog and digital signals.

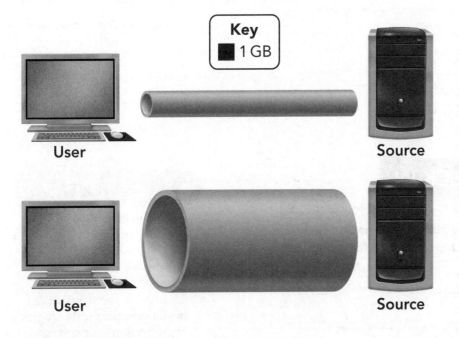

Bandwidth

Figure 4 Narrow bandwidth means slower data transmission, which likely means slower download times.

Develop Models ✏ Using the information in the key, model the transmission of 5 GB of data from each source to each user. Your model should demonstrate why narrower bandwidth results in slower download times.

✓READING CHECK **Cite Textual Evidence** Why are there so many different types of communications technology?

....

....

☑ LESSON 3 Check

MS-PS4-3

1. Identify List five different technologies or types of hardware that are used today in communications.

....

....

....

....

....

2. Cause and Effect Describe how increasing bandwidth and improving compression software can result in a higher quality of hardware and media of higher resolution.

....

....

....

....

....

....

....

....

3. Summarize What role does software play in information technology?

....

....

....

4. Construct Explanations Explain why digital signals are somewhat harder to hack or spy on than analog signals.

....

....

....

....

....

....

....

....

....

....

....

....

Quest CHECK-IN

In this lesson, you learned about information technology and the advantages of using digital signals for communication.

Evaluate How do hardware and infrastructure affect how we use signals?

....

....

....

....

....

INTERACTIVITY

Evaluate Recording Technologies

Go online to research scientific and technical information about analog and digital recording technologies. Then, present your findings in a poster.

Beam Me Up!

It may be hard to believe, but using your phone to make a video call to a friend or family member on the other side of the planet was the stuff of science fiction until about a decade ago. Although the idea for video calls can be traced back to the late 1800s, it required a great deal of scientific advancement and technological progress to become a reality.

In the 1930s, following the development of television, German scientists developed a closed-circuit TV system that allowed people to talk to each other in different cities. Despite plans to expand, the system was shut down in 1940 following the outbreak of World War II.

At the 1964 World's Fair in New York, an American telecommunications company unveiled a picture phone to the world. The system used a regular telephone line with a separate video screen. Since it was very expensive, it did not catch on with the public.

In the 1980s and 1990s, technological advancements, spurred on by the growing popularity of personal computers, led to the development of videoconferencing technology. As electronic devices shrank, it was only a matter of time before the technology made it to the palms of our hands.

MY DISCOVERY

Type "video telephony" into an online search engine to learn more about the history of this technology.

☑TOPIC 10 Review and Assess

1 Electric Circuits

MS-PS4-3

1. Which of the following is *not* a basic part of an electric circuit?
  A. conducting wires
  B. a transformer
  C. a source of electrical energy
  D. a device that runs on electrical energy

2. In a typical battery,
  A. the negative end has more electrical potential energy than the positive end.
  B. the negative end has the same amount of electrical potential energy as the positive end.
  C. the positive end has more electrical potential energy than the negative end.
  D. voltage determines which end of the battery has more electrical potential energy.

3. The measure of how hard it is for current to flow through an object is called ....

4. **Develop Models** 🖍 Draw a diagram of a circuit that consists of two lights. The circuit must allow for one light to remain lit if the other light bulb goes out.

2 Signals

MS-PS4-3

5. Digital signals rely on a coding system known as
  A. megabytes.   B. transmission.
  C. wave pulse.   D. binary.

6. Which of the following comparisons between analog and digital signals is correct?
  A. Analog signals are electronic signals, while digital signals are electromagnetic signals.
  B. Analog signals are continuous signals, while digital signals are discrete signals.
  C. Analog signals can be stored on computers, while digital signals cannot.
  D. Analog signals store information as numbers, while digital signals do not.

7. **Evaluate Claims** A friend says that digital signals are more exact representations than analog signals. Do you agree? Explain.

....
....
....
....
....

8. **Communicate** Using a real-world example, identify one advantage of a digital signal over an analog signal.

....
....
....
....
....
....
....
....

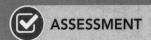
3 Communication and Technology

MS-PS4-3

9. Which of the following is *not* an advantage of sending an email over sending a letter through the postal service?
   A. The email is encrypted, making it harder for someone to intercept and read.
   B. The email is easier to store and retrieve, making it less likely to get lost.
   C. The email is more likely to get destroyed.
   D. The email will arrive much faster than the mailed letter.

10. Which of the following statements about signal noise is true?
   A. It affects analog and digital signals in similar ways.
   B. It affects digital signals more than analog signals.
   C. It affects analog signals more than digital signals.
   D. It has little effect on either analog or digital signals.

11. The amount of information that can be transmitted as digital signals over some amount of time is known as
   A. bandwidth. B. hardware.
   C. resolution. D. noise.

12. Information technology consists of
   .... and ....that store, manipulate, and transmit information.

13. **Analyze Systems** Why is fiber optic technology an improvement over standard copper cable?

   ....
   ....
   ....

14. **Connect to Nature of Science** Choose an example of a digital technology and describe how it has helped to advance science and scientific investigations.

   ....
   ....
   ....
   ....
   ....
   ....
   ....
   ....

15. **Construct Explanations** Explain why digital signals are a more reliable way to conduct a telephone conversation.

   ....
   ....
   ....
   ....
   ....
   ....
   ....
   ....
   ....
   ....

MS-PS4-3

Evidence-Based Assessment

A friend of yours lives in a nearby town. The town needs to purchase new two-way radios for its emergency first responders. Town board members are considering replacing the two-way analog radios with digital radios.

However, the digital radios are more expensive. Board members want to know whether the increased costs will bring any benefits before they will vote to approve the measure. Many residents are opposed to spending additional money on new technology.

You and your friend research the issue and find the graph shown here, which compares the range and quality of analog radio signals with digital radio signals.

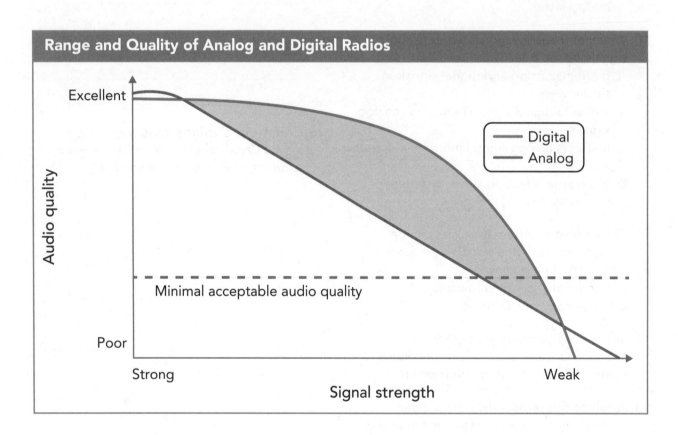

Range and Quality of Analog and Digital Radios

1. **Interpret Data** What does the shaded part of the graph represent?

    A. area in which the audio quality of both radios is not affected by signal strength

    B. area of the digital radio's improved performance over the analog radio

    C. area in which there is no difference in quality between the analog and digital radios

    D. area of the analog radio's improved performance over the digital radio

2. **Characterize Data** Which of the following statements about the data in the graph are correct? Select all that apply.

    ☐ The audio quality of the analog radio is slightly better with a very strong signal.

    ☐ The digital radio has improved audio quality with the very weakest signals.

    ☐ Both the analog and digital radio have almost the same quality with moderate signal strengths.

    ☐ The audio quality of the analog radios drops more sharply as signal strength weakens.

3. **Use Graphs** How are signal strength and audio quality related for both analog and digital signals?

    ....

    ....

    ....

    ....

4. **Cite Evidence** Use evidence from the graph to explain why the digital radio signals are more reliable than the analog radio signals.

    ....

    ....

    ....

    ....

    ....

5. **Construct Arguments** What can your friend tell the town board members and residents to persuade them to purchase the digital radios?

    ....

    ....

    ....

    ....

    ....

    ....

    ....

    ....

    ....

Quest FINDINGS

Complete the Quest!

Phenomenon **Determine the best way to present your claim in a multimedia presentation.**

Connect to Society Are there situations in which recording with an analog signal would be more reliable than a digital signal? Explain.

....

....

....

👆 **INTERACTIVITY**

Reflect on Your Recording Method

Over and Out

How can you demonstrate that **digital** signals are a more efficient way to send **information**?

Background

The Center for Information Technology Education will soon open its doors to the public. The center houses a library for students and researchers, as well as a large multimedia theater and exhibit areas. The center has devoted space for hands-on exhibits where visitors can explore communication technology and its history. The center wants you to develop an interactive exhibit that compares and contrasts analog and digital signals. The exhibit's models will allow visitors to send a coded signal designed for each transmission method.

In this investigation, you will design models that help visitors recognize that digital signals are a more reliable way than analog signals to transmit data and information.

Materials

(per group)

- spring coil
- small light bulb and socket
- battery (9-volt or type C)
- electrical wire, 10 strips
- electrical switch

Safety

Be sure to follow all safety guidelines provided by your teacher. The Safety Appendix of your textbook provides more details about the safety icons.

1885

1920

1985

2015

In just over 125 years, telephone technology has evolved from large boxes with a lot of wires to small, wireless powerhouses.

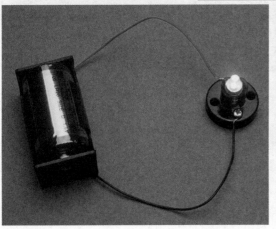
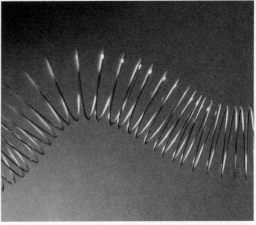

Design Your Exhibit Model

HANDS-ON LAB

Demonstrate Go online for a downloadable worksheet of this lab.

☐ 1. Plan the models you will use in the exhibit. Think about how you can use the available materials to represent two different communication systems: one that models how analog signals send information using continuous wave pulses and one that models how digital signals send information using discrete wave pulses. Consider the following questions as you plan and design your model:

  • Is the spring coil or an electric circuit a better choice to represent the continuous nature of analog signals?

  • Which of these materials is more appropriate to model the discrete nature of digital signals?

☐ 2. Develop a code that can be used for the analog system and another one that can be used for the digital system. The data you will transmit is a word made up of four letters: E, T, A, and S. You will need to create a code for each letter. Think about the following questions as you develop the codes:

  • How can you use continuous wave pulses of different amplitudes to represent each letter for the analog system?

  • How can you use discrete wave pulses to represent each letter for the digital system?

☐ 3. Sketch your models in the space provided and label the materials you will use. Include descriptions of how the models will operate. Then, complete the table with the codes you developed.

☐ 4. After getting your teacher's approval, carry out your investigation. One team member is the transmitter and the other member is the receiver. The transmitter should choose a word, refer to the code, and then transmit the word using the analog system. Repeat the process using a different word for the digital system. You may want to consider using commands to indicate the start and end of transmissions, such as "start transmission" and "end transmission." Run the trial again using the same procedure for each system.

uDemonstrate Lab

Model Sketches

Data Table and Observations

Letter	Analog Code	Digital Code
E		
T		
A		
S		

Analyze and Interpret Data

1. **Use Models** Describe the results of your investigation and your observations about using each system to transmit information. Which system did you find easier to use? Which system was more accurate? Explain.

....

....

....

....

2. **Explain Phenomena** Think about the issue of signal noise. How could you incorporate this concept into your models? What effect do you think signal noise would have on the analog system? What effect might it have on the digital system?

....

....

....

....

3. **Communicate** How do your models for the exhibit demonstrate that digital signals are a more reliable way to encode and transmit information than analog signals? Explain.

....

....

....

....

4. **Identify Limitations** What are some of the challenges you faced as you designed your models and codes? What are some of the drawbacks or limitations of your models?

....

....

....

....

....

....

SEP.1, SEP.8

The Meaning of Science

Science Skills

Reflect Think about a time you misplaced something and could not find it. Write a sentence defining the problem. What science skills could you use to solve the problem? Explain how you would use at least three of the skills in the table.

Science is a way of learning about the natural world. It involves asking questions, making predictions, and collecting information to see if the answer is right or wrong.

The table lists some of the skills that scientists use. You use some of these skills every day. For example, you may observe and evaluate your lunch options before choosing what to eat.

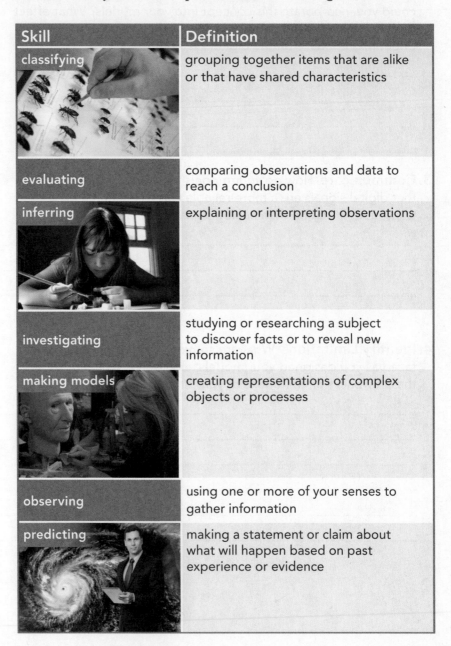

Skill	Definition
classifying	grouping together items that are alike or that have shared characteristics
evaluating	comparing observations and data to reach a conclusion
inferring	explaining or interpreting observations
investigating	studying or researching a subject to discover facts or to reveal new information
making models	creating representations of complex objects or processes
observing	using one or more of your senses to gather information
predicting	making a statement or claim about what will happen based on past experience or evidence

Scientific Attitudes

Curiosity often drives scientists to learn about the world around them. Creativity is useful for coming up with inventive ways to solve problems. Such qualities and attitudes, and the ability to keep an open mind, are essential for scientists.

When sharing results or findings, honesty and ethics are also essential. Ethics refers to rules for knowing right from wrong.

Being skeptical is also important. This means having doubts about things based on past experiences and evidence. Skepticism helps to prevent accepting data and results that may not be true.

Scientists must also avoid bias—likes or dislikes of people, ideas, or things. They must avoid experimental bias, which is a mistake that may make an experiment's preferred outcome more likely.

Scientific Reasoning

Scientific reasoning depends on being logical and objective. When you are objective, you use evidence and apply logic to draw conclusions. Being subjective means basing conclusions on personal feelings, biases, or opinions. Subjective reasoning can interfere with science and skew results. Objective reasoning helps scientists use observations to reach conclusions about the natural world.

Scientists use two types of objective reasoning: deductive and inductive. Deductive reasoning involves starting with a general idea or theory and applying it to a situation. For example, the theory of plate tectonics indicates that earthquakes happen mostly where tectonic plates meet. You could then draw the conclusion, or deduce, that California has many earthquakes because tectonic plates meet there.

In inductive reasoning, you make a generalization from a specific observation. When scientists collect data in an experiment and draw a conclusion based on that data, they use inductive reasoning. For example, if fertilizer causes one set of plants to grow faster than another, you might infer that the fertilizer promotes plant growth.

Make Meaning
Think about a bias the marine biologist in the photo could show that results in paying more or less attention to one kind of organism over others. Make a prediction about how that bias could affect the biologist's survey of the coral reef.

Write About It
Suppose it is raining when you go to sleep one night. When you wake up the next morning, you observe frozen puddles on the ground and icicles on tree branches. Use scientific reasoning to draw a conclusion about the air temperature outside. Support your conclusion using deductive or inductive reasoning.

SEP.1, SEP.2, SEP.3, SEP.4, CCC.4

Science Processes

Scientific Inquiry

Scientists contribute to scientific knowledge by conducting investigations and drawing conclusions. The process often begins with an observation that leads to a question, which is then followed by the development of a hypothesis. This is known as scientific inquiry.

One of the first steps in scientific inquiry is asking questions. However, it's important to make a question specific with a narrow focus so the investigation will not be too broad. A biologist may want to know all there is to know about wolves, for example. But a good, focused question for a specific inquiry might be "How many offspring does the average female wolf produce in her lifetime?"

A hypothesis is a possible answer to a scientific question. A hypothesis must be testable. For something to be testable, researchers must be able to carry out an investigation and gather evidence that will either support or disprove the hypothesis.

Scientific Models

Models are tools that scientists use to study phenomena indirectly. A model is any representation of an object or process. Illustrations, dioramas, globes, diagrams, computer programs, and mathematical equations are all examples of scientific models. For example, a diagram of Earth's crust and mantle can help you to picture layers deep below the surface and understand events such as volcanic eruptions.

Models also allow scientists to represent objects that are either very large, such as our solar system, or very small, such as a molecule of DNA. Models can also represent processes that occur over a long period of time, such as the changes that have occurred throughout Earth's history.

Models are helpful, but they have limitations. Physical models are not made of the same materials as the objects they represent. Most models of complex objects or processes show only major parts, stages, or relationships. Many details are left out. Therefore, you may not be able to learn as much from models as you would through direct observation.

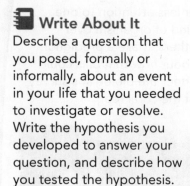

Write About It
Describe a question that you posed, formally or informally, about an event in your life that you needed to investigate or resolve. Write the hypothesis you developed to answer your question, and describe how you tested the hypothesis.

Reflect Identify the benefits and limitations of using a plastic model of DNA, as shown here.

Science Experiments

An experiment or investigation must be well planned to produce valid results. In planning an experiment, you must identify the independent and dependent variables. You must also do as much as possible to remove the effects of other variables. A controlled experiment is one in which you test only one variable at a time.

For example, suppose you plan a controlled experiment to learn how the type of material affects the speed at which sound waves travel through it. The only variable that should change is the type of material. This way, if the speed of sound changes, you know that it is a result of a change in the material, not another variable such as the thickness of the material or the type of sound used.

You should also remove bias from any investigation. You may inadvertently introduce bias by selecting subjects you like and avoiding those you don't like. Scientists often conduct investigations by taking random samples to avoid ending up with biased results.

Once you plan your investigation and begin to collect data, it's important to record and organize the data. You may wish to use a graph to display and help you to interpret the data.

Communicating is the sharing of ideas and results with others through writing and speaking. Communicating data and conclusions is a central part of science.

Scientists share knowledge, including new findings, theories, and techniques for collecting data. Conferences, journals, and websites help scientists to communicate with each other. Popular media, including newspapers, magazines, and social media sites, help scientists to share their knowledge with nonscientists. However, before the results of investigations are shared and published, other scientists should review the experiment for possible sources of error, such as bias and unsupported conclusions.

Write About It

List four ways you could communicate the results of a scientific study about the health of sea turtles in the Pacific Ocean.

SEP.1, SEP.6, SEP.7, SEP.8

Scientific Knowledge

Scientific Explanations

Suppose you learn that adult flamingos are pink because of the food they eat. This statement is a scientific explanation—it describes how something in nature works or explains why it happens. Scientists from different fields use methods such as researching information, designing experiments, and making models to form scientific explanations. Scientific explanations often result from many years of work and multiple investigations conducted by many scientists.

Scientific Theories and Laws

A scientific law is a statement that describes what you can expect to occur every time under a particular set of conditions. A scientific law describes an observed pattern in nature, but it does not attempt to explain it. For example, the law of superposition describes what you can expect to find in terms of the ages of layers of rock. Geologists use this observed pattern to determine the relative ages of sedimentary rock layers. But the law does not explain why the pattern occurs.

By contrast, a scientific theory is a well-tested explanation for a wide range of observations or experimental results. It provides details and describes causes of observed patterns. Something is elevated to a theory only when there is a large body of evidence that supports it. However, a scientific theory can be changed or overturned when new evidence is found.

Write About It

Choose two fields of science that interest you. Describe a method used to develop scientific explanations in each field.

Compare and Contrast Complete the table to compare and contrast a scientific theory and a scientific law.

	Scientific Theory	Scientific Law
Definition		
Does it attempt to explain a pattern observed in nature?		

Analyzing Scientific Explanations

To analyze scientific explanations that you hear on the news or read in a book such as this one, you need scientific literacy. Scientific literacy means understanding scientific terms and principles well enough to ask questions, evaluate information, and make decisions. Scientific reasoning gives you a process to apply. This includes looking for bias and errors in the research, evaluating data, and identifying faulty reasoning. For example, by evaluating how a survey was conducted, you may find a serious flaw in the researchers' methods.

Evidence and Opinions

The basis for scientific explanations is empirical evidence. Empirical evidence includes the data and observations that have been collected through scientific processes. Satellite images, photos, and maps of mountains and volcanoes are all examples of empirical evidence that support a scientific explanation about Earth's tectonic plates. Scientists look for patterns when they analyze this evidence. For example, they might see a pattern that mountains and volcanoes often occur near tectonic plate boundaries.

To evaluate scientific information, you must first distinguish between evidence and opinion. In science, evidence includes objective observations and conclusions that have been repeated. Evidence may or may not support a scientific claim. An opinion is a subjective idea that is formed from evidence, but it cannot be confirmed by evidence.

Write About It
Suppose the conservation committee of a town wants to gauge residents' opinions about a proposal to stock the local ponds with fish every spring. The committee pays for a survey to appear on a web site that is popular with people who like to fish. The results of the survey show 78 people in favor of the proposal and two against it. Do you think the survey's results are valid? Explain.

Make Meaning
Explain what empirical evidence the photograph reveals.

SEP.3, SEP.4

Tools of Science

Measurement

Making measurements using standard units is important in all fields of science. This allows scientists to repeat and reproduce other experiments, as well as to understand the precise meaning of the results of others. Scientists use a measurement system called the International System of Units, or SI.

For each type of measurement, there is a series of units that are greater or less than each other. The unit a scientist uses depends on what is being measured. For example, a geophysicist tracking the movements of tectonic plates may use centimeters, as plates tend to move small amounts each year. Meanwhile, a marine biologist might measure the movement of migrating bluefin tuna on the scale of kilometers.

Units for length, mass, volume, and density are based on powers of ten—a meter is equal to 100 centimeters or 1000 millimeters. Units of time do not follow that pattern. There are 60 seconds in a minute, 60 minutes in an hour, and 24 hours in a day. These units are based on patterns that humans perceived in nature. Units of temperature are based on scales that are set according to observations of nature. For example, 0°C is the temperature at which pure water freezes, and 100°C is the temperature at which it boils.

Measurement	Metric units
Length or distance	meter (m), kilometer (km), centimeter (cm), millimeter (mm) 1 km = 1,000 m 1 cm = 10 mm 1 m = 100 cm
Mass	kilogram (kg), gram (g), milligram (mg) 1 kg = 1,000 g 1 g = 1,000 mg
Volume	cubic meter (m^3), cubic centimeter (cm^3) 1 m^3 = 1,000,000 cm^3
Density	kilogram per cubic meter (kg/m^3), gram per cubic centimeter (g/cm^3) 1,000 kg/m^3 = 1 g/cm^3
Temperature	degrees Celsius (°C), kelvin (K) 1°C = 273 K
Time	hour (h), minute (m), second (s)

📓 Write About It

Suppose you are planning an investigation in which you must measure the dimensions of several small mineral samples that fit in your hand. Which metric unit or units will you most likely use? Explain your answer.

Math Skills

Using numbers to collect and interpret data involves math skills that are essential in science. For example, you use math skills when you estimate the number of birds in an entire forest after counting the actual number of birds in ten trees.

Scientists evaluate measurements and estimates for their precision and accuracy. In science, an accurate measurement is very close to the actual value. Precise measurements are very close, or nearly equal, to each other. Reliable measurements are both accurate and precise. An imprecise value may be a sign of an error in data collection. This kind of anomalous data may be excluded to avoid skewing the data and harming the investigation.

Other math skills include performing specific calculations, such as finding the mean, or average, value in a data set. The mean can be calculated by adding up all of the values in the data set and then dividing that sum by the number of values.

Hour	Number of Ducks Observed at a Pond
1	12
2	10
3	2
4	14
5	13
6	10
7	11

Calculate The data table shows how many ducks were seen at a pond every hour over the course of seven hours. Is there a data point that seems anomalous? If so, cross out that data point. Then, calculate the mean number of ducks on the pond. Round the mean to the nearest whole number.

Graphs

Graphs help scientists to interpret data by helping them to find trends or patterns in the data. A line graph displays data that show how one variable (the dependent or outcome variable) changes in response to another (the independent or test variable). The slope and shape of a graph line can reveal patterns and help scientists to make predictions. For example, line graphs can help you to spot patterns of change over time.

Scientists use bar graphs to compare data across categories or subjects that may not affect each other. The heights of the bars make it easy to compare those quantities. A circle graph, also known as a pie chart, shows the proportions of different parts of a whole.

Write About It
You and a friend record the distance you travel every 15 minutes on a one-hour bike trip. Your friend wants to display the data as a circle graph. Explain whether or not this is the best type of graph to display your data. If not, suggest another graph to use.

SEP.1, SEP.2, SEP.3, SEP.6

The Engineering and Design Process

Engineers are builders and problem solvers. Chemical engineers experiment with new fuels made from algae. Civil engineers design roadways and bridges. Bioengineers develop medical devices and prosthetics. The common trait among engineers is an ability to identify problems and design solutions to solve them. Engineers use a creative process that relies on scientific methods to help guide them from a concept or idea all the way to the final product.

Define the Problem

Reflect Write about a problem that you encountered in your life that had both immediate, obvious causes as well as less-obvious and less-immediate ones.

To identify or define a problem, different questions need to be asked: *What are the effects of the problem? What are the likely causes? What other factors could be involved?* Sometimes the obvious, immediate cause of a problem may be the result of another problem that may not be immediately apparent. For example, climate change results in different weather patterns, which in turn can affect organisms that live in certain habitats. So engineers must be aware of all the possible effects of potential solutions. Engineers must also take into account how well different solutions deal with the different causes of the problem.

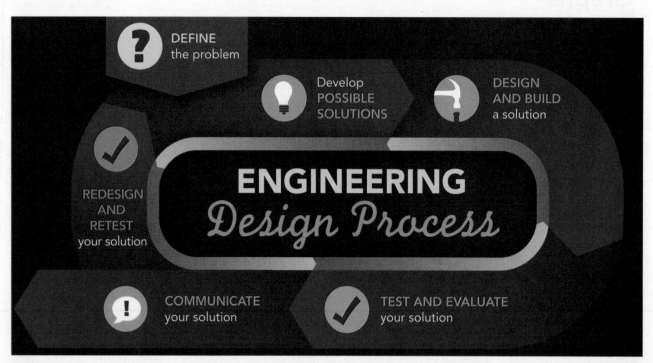

DEFINE the problem

Develop POSSIBLE SOLUTIONS

DESIGN AND BUILD a solution

REDESIGN AND RETEST your solution

ENGINEERING *Design Process*

COMMUNICATE your solution

TEST AND EVALUATE your solution

As engineers consider problems and design solutions, they must identify and categorize the criteria and constraints of the project.

Criteria are the factors that must be met or accomplished by the solution. For example, a gardener who wants to protect outdoor plants from deer and rabbits may say that the criteria for the solution are "plants are no longer eaten" and "plant growth is not inhibited in any way." The gardener then knows the plants cannot simply be sealed off from the environment, because the plants will not receive sunlight and water.

The same gardener will likely have constraints on his solution, such as budget for materials and time that is available for working on the project. By setting constraints, a solution can be designed that will be successful without introducing a new set of problems. No one wants to spend $500 on materials to protect $100 worth of tomatoes and cucumbers.

Develop Possible Solutions

After the problem has been identified, and the criteria and constraints identified, an engineer will consider possible solutions. This often involves working in teams with other engineers and designers to brainstorm ideas and research materials that can be used in the design.

It's important for engineers to think creatively and explore all potential solutions. If you wanted to design a bicycle that was safer and easier to ride than a traditional bicycle, then you would want more than just one or two solutions. Having multiple ideas to choose from increases the likelihood that you will develop a solution that meets the criteria and constraints. In addition, different ideas that result from brainstorming can often lead to new and better solutions to an existing problem.

Make Meaning
Using the example of a garden that is vulnerable to wild animals such as deer, make a list of likely constraints on an engineering solution to the problem you identified before. Determine if there are common traits among the constraints, and identify categories for them.

Design a Solution

Engineers then develop the idea that they feel best solves the problem. Once a solution has been chosen, engineers and designers get to work building a model or prototype of the solution. A model may involve sketching on paper or using computer software to construct a model of the solution. A prototype is a working model of the solution.

Building a model or prototype helps an engineer determine whether a solution meets the criteria and stays within the constraints. During this stage of the process, engineers must often deal with new problems and make any necessary adjustments to the model or prototype.

Test and Evaluate a Solution

Whether testing a model or a prototype, engineers use scientific processes to evaluate their solutions. Multiple experiments, tests, or trials are conducted, data are evaluated, and results and analyses are communicated. New criteria or constraints may emerge as a result of testing. In most cases, a solution will require some refinement or revision, even if it has been through successful testing. Refining a solution is necessary if there are new constraints, such as less money or available materials. Additional testing may be done to ensure that a solution satisfies local, state, or federal laws or standards.

Make Meaning Think about an aluminum beverage can. What would happen if the price or availability of aluminum changed so much that cans needed to be made of a new material? What would the criteria and constraints be on the development of a new can?

A naval architect sets up a model to test how the the hull's design responds to waves.

Communicate the Solution

Engineers need to communicate the final design to the people who will manufacture the product. This may include sketches, detailed drawings, computer simulations, and written text. Engineers often provide evidence that was collected during the testing stage. This evidence may include graphs and data tables that support the decisions made for the final design.

If there is feedback about the solution, then the engineers and designers must further refine the solution. This might involve making minor adjustments to the design, or it might mean bigger modifications to the design based on new criteria or constraints. Any changes in the design will require additional testing to make sure that the changes work as intended.

Redesign and Retest the Solution

At different steps in the engineering and design process, a solution usually must be revised and retested. Many designs fail to work perfectly, even after models and prototypes are built, tested, and evaluated. Engineers must be ready to analyze new results and deal with any new problems that arise. Troubleshooting, or fixing design problems, allows engineers to adjust the design to improve on how well the solution meets the need.

Communicate Suppose you are an engineer at an aerospace company. Your team is designing a rover to be used on a future NASA space mission. A family member doesn't understand why so much your team's time is taken up with testing and retesting the rover design. What are three things you would tell your relative to explain why testing and retesting are so important to the engineering and design process?

....

....

....

....

....

....

....

....

Safety Symbols

These symbols warn of possible dangers in the laboratory and remind you to work carefully.

 Safety Goggles Wear safety goggles to protect your eyes in any activity involving chemicals, flames or heating, or glassware.

 Lab Apron Wear a laboratory apron to protect your skin and clothing from damage.

 Breakage Handle breakable materials, such as glassware, with care. Do not touch broken glassware.

 Heat-Resistant Gloves Use an oven mitt or other hand protection when handling hot materials, such as hot plates or hot glassware.

 Plastic Gloves Wear disposable plastic gloves when working with harmful chemicals and organisms. Keep your hands away from your face, and dispose of the gloves according to your teacher's instructions.

 Heating Use a clamp or tongs to pick up hot glassware. Do not touch hot objects with your bare hands.

 Flames Before you work with flames, tie back loose hair and clothing. Follow your teacher's instructions about lighting and extinguishing flames.

 No Flames When using flammable materials, make sure there are no flames, sparks, or other exposed heat sources present.

 Corrosive Chemical Avoid getting acid or other corrosive chemicals on your skin or clothing or in your eyes. Do not inhale the vapors. Wash your hands after the activity.

 Poison Do not let any poisonous chemical come into contact with your skin, and do not inhale its vapors. Wash your hands when you are finished with the activity.

 Fumes Work in a well-ventilated area when harmful vapors may be involved. Avoid inhaling vapors directly. Test an odor only when directed to do so by your teacher, and use a wafting motion to direct the vapor toward your nose.

 Sharp Object Scissors, scalpels, knives, needles, pins, and tacks can cut your skin. Always direct a sharp edge or point away from yourself and others.

 Animal Safety Treat live or preserved animals or animal parts with care to avoid harming the animals or yourself. Wash your hands when you are finished with the activity.

 Plant Safety Handle plants only as directed by your teacher. If you are allergic to certain plants, tell your teacher; do not do an activity involving those plants. Avoid touching harmful plants such as poison ivy. Wash your hands when you are finished with the activity.

 Electric Shock To avoid electric shock, never use electrical equipment around water, when the equipment is wet, or when your hands are wet. Be sure cords are untangled and cannot trip anyone. Unplug equipment not in use.

 Physical Safety When an experiment involves physical activity, avoid injuring yourself or others. Alert your teacher if there is any reason you should not participate.

 Disposal Dispose of chemicals and other laboratory materials safely. Follow the instructions from your teacher.

 Hand Washing Wash your hands thoroughly when finished with an activity. Use soap and warm water. Rinse well.

 General Safety Awareness When this symbol appears, follow the instructions provided. When you are asked to develop your own procedure in a lab, have your teacher approve your plan.

Using a Laboratory Balance

The laboratory balance is an important tool in scientific investigations. Different kinds of balances are used in the laboratory to determine the masses and weights of objects. You can use a triple-beam balance to determine the masses of materials that you study or experiment with in the laboratory. An electronic balance, unlike a triple-beam balance, is used to measure the weights of materials.

The triple-beam balance that you may use in your science class is probably similar to the balance depicted in this Appendix. To use the balance properly, you should learn the name, location, and function of each part of the balance.

Triple-Beam Balance

The triple-beam balance is a single-pan balance with three beams calibrated in grams. The back, or 100-gram, beam is divided into ten units of 10 grams each. The middle, or 500-gram, beam is divided into five units of 100 grams each. The front, or 10-gram, beam is divided into ten units of 1 gram each. Each gram on the front beam is further divided into units of 0.1 gram.

Apply Concepts What is the greatest mass you could find with the triple-beam balance in the picture?

....

Calculate What is the mass of the apple in the picture?

....

The following procedure can be used to find the mass of an object with a triple-beam balance:

1. Place the object on the pan.

2. Move the rider on the middle beam notch by notch until the horizontal pointer on the right drops below zero. Move the rider back one notch.

3. Move the rider on the back beam notch by notch until the pointer again drops below zero. Move the rider back one notch.

4. Slowly slide the rider along the front beam until the pointer stops at the zero point.

5. The mass of the object is equal to the sum of the readings on the three beams.

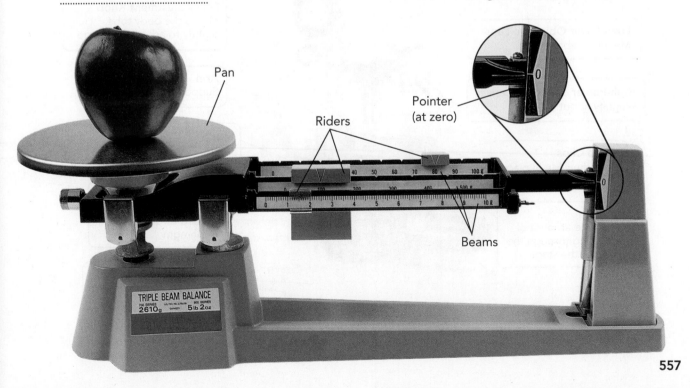

Pan

Riders

Pointer (at zero)

Beams

TRIPLE BEAM BALANCE
750 SERIES   U.S. PAT. NO. 3,709,458   800 SERIES
2610g   CAPACITY   5 lb 2 oz

Using a Microscope

The microscope is an essential tool in the study of life science. It allows you to see things that are too small to be seen with the unaided eye.

You will probably use a compound microscope like the one you see here. The compound microscope has more than one lens that magnifies the object you view.

Typically, a compound microscope has one lens in the eyepiece (the part you look through). The eyepiece lens usually magnifies 10×. Any object you view through this lens will appear 10 times larger than it is.

A compound microscope may contain two or three other lenses called objective lenses. They are called the low-power and high-power objective lenses. The low-power objective lens usually magnifies 10×. The high-power objective lenses usually magnify 40× and 100×.

To calculate the total magnification with which you are viewing an object, multiply the magnification of the eyepiece lens by the magnification of the objective lens you are using. For example, the eyepiece's magnification of 10× multiplied by the low-power objective's magnification of 10× equals a total magnification of 100×.

Use the photo of the compound microscope to become familiar with the parts of the microscope and their functions.

The Parts of a Microscope

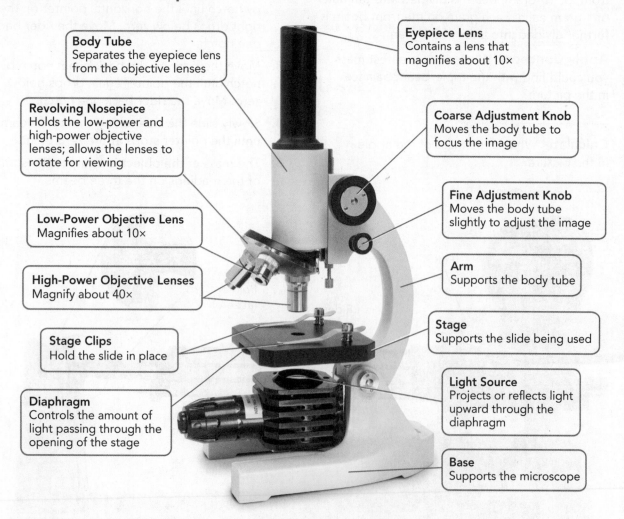

Body Tube
Separates the eyepiece lens from the objective lenses

Revolving Nosepiece
Holds the low-power and high-power objective lenses; allows the lenses to rotate for viewing

Low-Power Objective Lens
Magnifies about 10×

High-Power Objective Lenses
Magnify about 40×

Stage Clips
Hold the slide in place

Diaphragm
Controls the amount of light passing through the opening of the stage

Eyepiece Lens
Contains a lens that magnifies about 10×

Coarse Adjustment Knob
Moves the body tube to focus the image

Fine Adjustment Knob
Moves the body tube slightly to adjust the image

Arm
Supports the body tube

Stage
Supports the slide being used

Light Source
Projects or reflects light upward through the diaphragm

Base
Supports the microscope

Using the Microscope

Use the following procedures when you are working with a microscope.

1. To carry the microscope, grasp the microscope's arm with one hand. Place your other hand under the base.

2. Place the microscope on a table with the arm toward you.

3. Turn the coarse adjustment knob to raise the body tube.

4. Revolve the nosepiece until the low-power objective lens clicks into place.

5. Adjust the diaphragm. While looking through the eyepiece, adjust the mirror until you see a bright white circle of light. **CAUTION:** Never use direct sunlight as a light source.

6. Place a slide on the stage. Center the specimen over the opening on the stage. Use the stage clips to hold the slide in place. **CAUTION:** Glass slides are fragile.

7. Look at the stage from the side. Carefully turn the coarse adjustment knob to lower the body tube until the low-power objective almost touches the slide.

8. Looking through the eyepiece, very slowly turn the coarse adjustment knob until the specimen comes into focus.

9. To switch to the high-power objective lens, look at the microscope from the side. Carefully revolve the nosepiece until the high-power objective lens clicks into place. Make sure the lens does not hit the slide.

10. Looking through the eyepiece, turn the fine adjustment knob until the specimen comes into focus.

Making a Wet-Mount Slide

Use the following procedures to make a wet-mount slide of a specimen.

1. Obtain a clean microscope slide and a coverslip. **CAUTION:** Glass slides and coverslips are fragile.

2. Place the specimen on the center of the slide. The specimen must be thin enough for light to pass through it.

3. Using a plastic dropper, place a drop of water on the specimen.

4. Gently place one edge of the coverslip against the slide so that it touches the edge of the water drop at a 45° angle. Slowly lower the coverslip over the specimen. If you see air bubbles trapped beneath the coverslip, tap the coverslip gently with the eraser end of a pencil.

5. Remove any excess water at the edge of the coverslip with a paper towel.

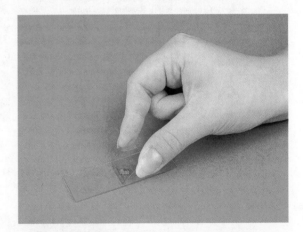

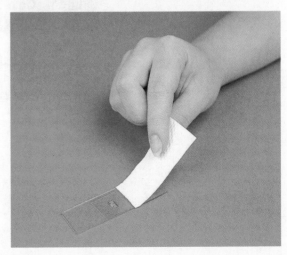

APPENDIX D

Periodic Table of Elements

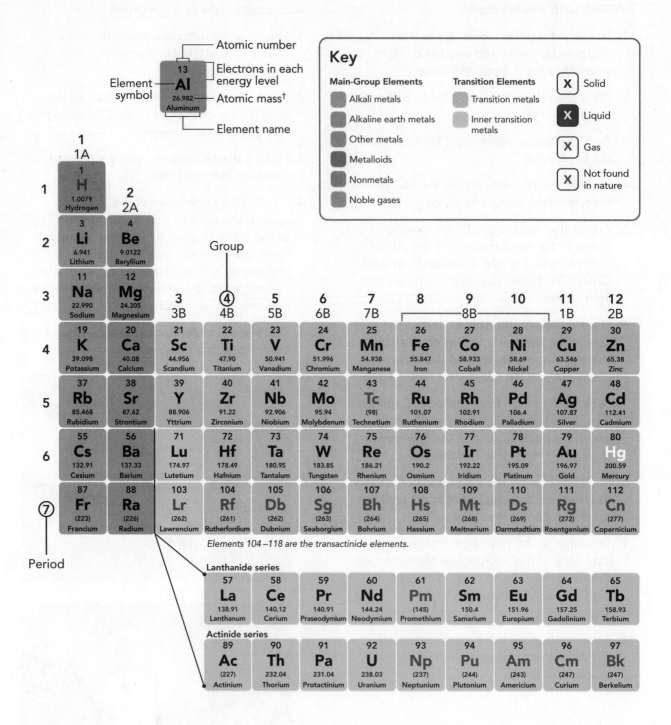

Key

Main-Group Elements
- Alkali metals
- Alkaline earth metals
- Other metals
- Metalloids
- Nonmetals
- Noble gases

Transition Elements
- Transition metals
- Inner transition metals

- X — Solid
- X — Liquid
- X — Gas
- X — Not found in nature

Elements 104–118 are the transactinide elements.

†The atomic masses in parentheses are the mass numbers of the longest-lived isotope of elements for which a standard atomic mass cannot be defined.

18 8A					
					2 **He** 4.0026 Helium

13 3A	14 4A	15 5A	16 6A	17 7A	
5 **B** 10.81 Boron	6 **C** 12.011 Carbon	7 **N** 14.007 Nitrogen	8 **O** 15.999 Oxygen	9 **F** 18.998 Fluorine	10 **Ne** 20.179 Neon
13 **Al** 26.982 Aluminum	14 **Si** 28.086 Silicon	15 **P** 30.974 Phosphorus	16 **S** 32.06 Sulfur	17 **Cl** 35.453 Chlorine	18 **Ar** 39.948 Argon
31 **Ga** 69.72 Gallium	32 **Ge** 72.59 Germanium	33 **As** 74.922 Arsenic	34 **Se** 78.96 Selenium	35 **Br** 79.904 Bromine	36 **Kr** 83.80 Krypton
49 **In** 114.82 Indium	50 **Sn** 118.69 Tin	51 **Sb** 121.75 Antimony	52 **Te** 127.60 Tellurium	53 **I** 126.90 Iodine	54 **Xe** 131.30 Xenon
81 **Tl** 204.37 Thallium	82 **Pb** 207.2 Lead	83 **Bi** 208.98 Bismuth	84 **Po** (209) Polonium	85 **At** (210) Astatine	86 **Rn** (222) Radon
113 **Nh** (284) Nihonium	114 **Fl** (289) Flerovium	115 **Mc** (288) Moscovium	116 **Lv** (292) Livermorium	117 **Ts** (294) Tennessine	118 **Og** (294) Oganesson

66 **Dy** 162.50 Dysprosium	67 **Ho** 164.93 Holmium	68 **Er** 167.26 Erbium	69 **Tm** 168.93 Thulium	70 **Yb** 173.04 Ytterbium
98 **Cf** (251) Californium	99 **Es** (252) Einsteinium	100 **Fm** (257) Fermium	101 **Md** (258) Mendelevium	102 **No** (259) Nobelium

GLOSSARY

A

abiotic factor A nonliving part of an organism's habitat. (196)

absorption The transfer of energy from a wave to a material that it encounters. (405)

acid rain Rain or another form of precipitation that is more acidic than normal, caused by the release of molecules of sulfur dioxide and nitrogen oxide into the air. (350)

aggression A threatening behavior that one animal uses to gain control over another animal. (163)

allele A different form of a gene. (144)

alveoli Tiny sacs of lung tissue specialized for the movement of gases between air and blood. (112)

amplitude The maximum distance the particles of a medium move away from their rest positions as a longitudinal wave passes through the medium. (394)

analog signal A signal that allows for a continuous record of some kind of action. (518)

artery A blood vessel that carries blood away from the heart. (109)

asexual reproduction A reproductive process that involves only one parent and produces offspring that are genetically identical to the parent. (141)

autotroph An organism that is able to capture energy from sunlight or chemicals and use it to produce its own food. (43)

auxin A hormone that controls a plant's growth and response to light. (172)

B

bandwidth The amount of information that can be transmitted in bits per second. (533)

behavior The way an organism reacts to changes in its internal conditions or external environment. (161)

biodiversity The number and variety of different species in an area. (255)

biotic factor A living or once living part of an organism's habitat. (196)

birth rate The number of people born per 1,000 individuals for a certain period of time. (340)

brain The part of the central nervous system that is located in the skull and controls most functions in the body. (121)

bronchi The passages that direct air into the lungs. (112)

C

capillary A tiny blood vessel where substances are exchanged between the blood and the body cells. (109)

carbohydrates An energy-rich organic compound, such as a sugar or a starch, that is made of the elements of carbon, hydrogen, and oxygen. (96)

cell The basic unit of structure and function in living things. (5)

cell cycle The series of events in which a cell grows, prepares for division, and divides to form two daughter cells. (34)

cell membrane A thin, flexible barrier that surrounds a cell and controls which substances pass into and out of a cell. (17)

cell theory A widely accepted explanation of the relationship between cells and living things. (8)

cell wall A rigid supporting layer that surrounds the cells of plants and some other organisms. (16)

cellular respiration The process in which oxygen and glucose undergo a complex series of chemical reactions inside cells, releasing energy. (51)

chlorophyll A green photosynthetic pigment found in the chloroplasts of plants, algae, and some bacteria. (44)

chloroplast An organelle in the cells of plants and some other organisms that captures energy from sunlight and changes it to an energy form that cells can use in making food. (19)

circulatory system An organ system that taransports needed materials to cells and removes wastes. (107)

commensalism A type of symbiosis between two species in which one species benefits and the other species is neither helped nor harmed. (242)

community All the different populations that live together in a certain area. (197)

competition The struggle between organisms to survive as they attempt to use the same limited resources in the same place at the same time. (239)

concave A mirror with a surface that curves inward or a lens that is thinner at the center than at the edges. (438)

condensation The change in state from a gas to a liquid. (217)

conductor A material that allows electric charges to flow. (459)

cones The reproductive structures of gymnosperms. (155)

conservation The practice of using less of a resource so that it can last longer. (275, 344)

consumer An organism that obtains energy by feeding on other organisms. (206)

convex A mirror that curves outward or lens that is thicker in the center than at the edges. (437)

courtship behavior Activty that prepares males and females of the same species for mating. (163)

crystallize To form a crystal structure. (311)

cytokinesis The final stage of the cell cycle, in which the cell's cytoplasm divides, distributing the organelles into each of the two new daughter cells. (38)

cytoplasm The thick fluid region of a cell located inside the cell membrane (in prokaryotes) or between the cell membrane and nucleus (in eukaryotes). (18)

D

death rate The number of deaths per 1,000 individuals in a certain period of time. (340)

decibel (dB) A unit used to compare the loudness of different sounds. (418)

decomposer An organism that gets energy by breaking down biotic wastes and dead organisms and returns raw materials to the soil and water. (207)

deforestation The removal of forests to use the land for other reasons. (358)

desalination A process that removes salt from sea water to make fresh water. (323)

desertification The advance of desert-like conditions into areas that previously were fertile; caused by overfarming, overgrazing, drought, and climate change. (361)

diffraction The bending or spreading of waves as they move around a barrier or pass through an opening. (405)

diffuse reflection Reflection that occurs when parallel light rays hit an uneven surface and all reflect at different angles. (436)

diffusion The process by which molecules move from an area of higher concentration to an area of lower concentration. (27)

digestion The process that breaks complex molecules of food into smaller nutrient molecules. (95)

digital signal A signal that allows for a record of numerical values of an action at a set of continuous time intervals. (518)

Doppler effect The change in frequency of a wave as its source moves in relation to an observer. (420)

dormancy A period of time when an organism's growth or activity stops. (173)

E

ecological restoration The practice of helping a degraded or destroyed ecosystem recover from damage. (275)

ecology The study of how organisms interact with each other and their environment. (269)

ecosystem The community of organisms that live in a particular area, along with their nonliving environment. (197)

ecosystem services The benefits that humans derive from ecosystems. (269)

electric current The continuous flow of electrical charges through a material. (458)

electric field The region around a charged object where the object's electric force is exerted on other charged objects. (456)

electric force The force between charged objects. (456)

electric motor A device that transforms electrical energy to mechanical energy. (483)

electrical circuit A complete, unbroken path through which electric charges can flow. (505)

electromagnet A magnet created by wrapping a coil of wire with a current running through it around a core of material that is easily magnetized. (477)

electromagnetic induction The process of genrating an electric current from the motion of a conductor through a magnetic field. (484)

electromagnetic radiation The energy transferred through space by electromagnetic waves. (393)

electromagnetic signal Information that is sent as a pattern of electromagnetic waves, such as visible light, microwaves, and radio waves. (517)

electromagnetic spectrum The complete range of electromagnetic waves placed in order of increasing frequency. (427)

electromagnetic wave A wave that can transfer electric and magnetic energy through the vacuum of space. (423)

electromagnetism The relationship between electricity and magnetism. (473)

electron A tiny particle that moves around the outside of the nucleus of an atom. (455)

electronic signal Information that is sent as a pattern in a controlled flow of current through a circuit. (516)

emissions Pollutants that are released into the air. (348)

endocytosis The process by which the cell membrane takes particles into the cell by changing shape and engulfing the particles. (30)

energy pyramid A diagram that shows the amount of energy that moves from one feeding level to another in a food web. (210)

enzyme A type of protein that speeds up chemical reactions in the body. (99)

erosion The process by which water, ice, wind, or gravity moves weathered particles of rock and soil. (360)

evaporation The process by which molecules at the surface of a liquid absorb enough energy to change to a gas. (216)

excretion The process by which wastes are removed from the body. (114)

exocytosis The process by which the vacuole surrounding particles fuses with the cell membrane, forcing the contents out of the cell. (30)

exponential growth A rate of change that increases more and more rapidly over time. (341)

external fertilization When eggs are fertilized outside a female's body. (165)

extinction The disappearance of all members of a species from Earth. (259)

GLOSSARY

F

fermentation The process by which cells release energy by breaking down food molecules without using oxygen. (55)

fertilization The process in sexual reproduction in which an egg cell and a sperm cell join to form a new cell. (142)

focal point The point at which light rays parallel to the optical axis meet, after being reflected (or refracted) by a mirror (or lens). (437)

food chain A series of events in an ecosystem in which organisms transfer energy by eating and by being eaten. (208)

food web The pattern of overlapping feeding relationships or food chains among the various organisms in an ecosystem. (208)

fossil fuel Energy-rich substance formed from the remains of organisms. (292)

frequency The number of complete waves that pass a given point in a certain amount of time. (396)

fruit The ripened ovary and other structures of an angiosperm that enclose one or more seeds. (156)

G

galvanometer A device that uses an electromagnet to detect small amounts of current. (482)

gamma rays Electromagnetic waves with the shortest wavelengths and highest frequencies. (429)

gene A sequence of DNA that determines a trait and is passed from parent to offspring. (142)

generator A device that transforms mechanical energy into electrical energy. (487)

germination The sprouting of the embryo out of a seed; occurs when the embryo resumes its growth following dormancy. (157)

gland An organ that produces and releases chemicals either through ducts or into the bloodstream. (86, 124)

H

habitat An environment that provides the things a specific organism needs to live, grow, and reproduce. (195)

heterotroph An organism that cannot make its own food and gets food by consuming other living things. (43)

hormone The chemical produced by an endocrine gland. (86); A chemical that affects growth and development. (172)

I

information technology Computer and telecommunication hardware and software that store, transmit, receive, and manipulate information. (527)

infrared rays Electromagnetic waves with shorter wavelengths and higher frequencies than microwaves. (428)

inheritance The process by which an offspring receives genes from its parents. (144)

instinct A response to a stimulus that is inborn. (161)

intensity The amount of energy per second carried through a unit area by a wave. (417)

interference The interaction between waves that meet. (406)

internal fertilization When eggs are fertilized inside a female's body. (165)

interphase The first stage of the cell cycle that takes place before cell division occurs, during which a cell grows and makes a copy of its DNA. (36)

invasive species Species that are not native to a habitat and can out-compete native species in an ecosystem. (262)

K

keystone species A species that influences the survival of many other species in an ecosystem. (257)

L

law of conservation of energy The rule that energy cannot be created or destroyed. (215)

law of conservation of mass The principle that the total amount of matter is neither created nor destroyed during any chemical or physical change. (215)

limiting factor An environmental factor that causes a population to decrease in size. (200)

longitudinal wave A wave that moves the medium in a direction parallel to the direction in which the wave travels. (395)

loudness The perception of the energy of a sound. (417)

lymph Fluid that travels through the lymphatic system consisting of water, white blood cells, and dissolved materials. (111)

M

magnet Any material that attracts iron and materials that contain iron. (465)

magnetic field The region around a magnet where the magnetic force is exerted. (467)

magnetic force A force produced when magnetic poles interact. (466)

magnetic pole The ends of a magnetic object, where the magnetic force is strongest. (466)

magnetism The force of attraction or repulsion of magnetic materials. (465)

mating system Behavior patterns related to how animals mate. (162)

mechanical wave A wave that requires a medium through which to travel. (393)

medium The material through which a wave travels. (393)

metamorphosis A process in which an animal's body undergoes major changes in shape and form during its life cycle. (177)

microscope An instrument that makes small objects look larger. (6)

microwaves Electromagnetic waves that have shorter wavelengths and higher frequencies than radio waves. (428)

migration The regular, seasonal journey of an animal from one place to another and back again. (167)

mitochondria Rod-shaped organelles that convert energy in food molecules to energy the cell can use to carry out its functions. (19)

mitosis The second stage of the cell cycle during which the cell's nucleus divides into two new nuclei and one set of DNA is distributed into each daughter cell. (37)

mutualism A type of symbiosis in which both species benefit from living together. (242)

N

natural resource Anything naturally occuring in the environment that humans use. (270, 291, 357)

negative feedback A process in which a system is turned off by the condition it produces. (126)

nephron Small filtering structure found in the kidneys that removes wastes from blood and produces urine. (115)

neuron A cell that carries information through the nervous system. (119)

niche How an organism makes its living and interacts with the biotic and abiotic factors in its habitat. (238)

noise Random signals from the environment that can alter the output of a signal. (532)

nonpoint source A widely spread source of pollution that is difficult to link to a specific point of origin. (347)

nonrenewable resource A natural resource that is not replaced in a useful time frame. (291, 357)

nuclear fission The splitting of an atom's nucleus into two nuclei, which releases a great deal of energy. (297)

nucleus In cells, a large oval organelle that contains the cell's genetic material in the form of DNA and controls many of the cell's activities. (18)

nutrients Substances in food that provide the raw materials and energy needed for an organism to carry out its essential processes. (95)

O

Ohm's law The law that staes that resistance in a circuit is equal to voltage divided by current. (508)

opaque A type of material that reflects or absorbs all of the light that strikes it. (433)

ore A mineral deposit large enough and valuable enough for it to be extracted from the ground. (309)

organ A body structure that is composed of different kinds of tissues that work together. (75)

organ system A group of organs that work together to perform a major function. (75)

organelle A tiny cell structure that carries out a specific function within the cell. (15)

organism A living thing. (195)

osmosis The diffusion of water molecules across a selectively permeable membrane. (28)

overpopulation A condition in which the number of humans grows beyond what the available resources can support. (343)

ovule A plant structure in seed plants that produces the female gametophyte; contains an egg cell. (155)

ozone A form of oxygen that has three oxygen atoms in each molecule instead of the usual two; toxic to organisms where it forms near Earth's surface. (349)

GLOSSARY

P

parallel circuit An electric circuit in which different parts of the circuit are on separate branches. (510)

parasitism A type of symbiosis in which one organism lives with, on, or in a host and harms it. (244)

peristalsis Waves of smooth muscle contractions that move food through the esophagus toward the stomach. (98)

petroleum Liquid fossil fuel; oil. (294)

pheromone A chemical released by one animal that affects the behavior of another animal of the same species. (163)

photoperiodism A plant's response to seasonal changes in the length of night and day. (173)

photosynthesis The process by which plants and other autotrophs capture and use light energy to make food from carbon dioxide and water. (42)

pioneer species The first species to populate an area during succession. (247)

pitch A description of how a sound is perceived as high or low. (419)

pixel A small, uniform shape that is combined with other pixels to make a larger image. (522)

point source A specific source of pollution that can be identified. (347)

pollination The transfer of pollen from male reproductive structures to female reproductive structures in plants. (153)

pollution Contamination of Earth's land, water, or air through the release of harmful substances into the environment. (343)

population All the members of one species living in the same area. (197)

precipitation Any form of water that falls from clouds and reaches Earth's surface as rain, snow, sleet, or hail. (217)

predation An interaction in which one organism kills another for food or nutrients. (240)

producer An organism that can make its own food. (205)

R

radio waves Electromagnetic waves with the longest wavelengths and lowest frequencies. (427)

reflection The bouncing back of an object or a wave when it hits a surface through which it cannot pass. (403)

reflex An automatic response that occurs rapidly and without conscious control. (123)

refraction The bending of waves as they enter a new medium at an angle, caused by a change in speed. (404)

renewable resource A resource that is either always available or is naturally replaced in a relatively short time. (301, 357)

replication The process by which a cell makes a copy of the DNA in its nucleus before cell division. (36)

resistance The measurement of how difficult it is for charges to flow through an object. (507)

resonance The increase in the amplitude of a vibration that occurs when external vibrations match an object's natural frequency. (409)

response An action or change in behavior that occurs as a result of a stimulus. (85)

S

saliva A fluid produced in the mouth that aids in mechanical and chemical digestion. (99)

sediment Small, solid pieces of material that come from rocks or the remains of organisms; earth materials deposited by erosion. (373)

selectively permeable A property of cell membranes that allows some substances to pass across it, while others cannot. (26)

series circuit An electic circuit in which all parts are connected one after another along one path. (509)

sewage The water and human wastes that are washed down sinks, toilets, and showers. (372)

sexual reproduction A reproductive process that involves two parents that combine their genetic material to produce a new organism which differs from both parents. (142)

software Programs that encode, decode, and interpret information. (527)

solenoid A coil of wire with a current. (476)

spinal cord A thick column of nervous tissue that links the brain to nerves in the body. (121)

standing wave A wave that appears to stand in one place, even though it is two waves interfering as they pass through each other. (408)

static electricity A buildup of charges on an object. (460)

stimulus Any change or signal in the environment that can make an organism react in some way. (85)

stress The reaction of a person's body to potentially threatening, challenging, or disturbing events. (90)

succession The series of predictable changes that occur in a community over time. (247)

sustainability The ability of an ecosystem to maintain bioviersity and production indefinitely. (275)

sustainable Using a resource in ways that maintain it at a certain quality for a certain period of time. (364)

sustainable use The practice of allowing renewable resources time to recover and replenish. (344)

symbiosis Any relationship in which two species live closely together and that benefits at least one of the species. (242)

synapse The junction where one neuron can transfer an impulse to the next structure. (120)

T

territory An area occupied and defended by an animal or group of animals. (163)

thermal pollution A type of pollution caused by factories and power plants releasing superheated water into bodies of water. (373)

tissue A group of similar cells that perform a specific function. (74)

trait A specific characteristic that an organism can pass to its offspring through its genes. (142)

transformer A device that increases or decreases voltage, which often consists of two separate coils of insulated wires wrapped around an iron core. (488)

transluscent A type of material that scatters light as it passes through. (433)

transparent A type of material that transmits light without scattering it. (433)

transverse wave A wave that moves the medium at right angles to the direction in which the wave travels. (394)

tropism A plant's growth response toward or away from a stimulus. (172)

U

ultraviolet rays Electromagnetic waves with wavelengths shorter than visible light but longer than X-rays. (429)

V

vacuole A sac-like organelle that stores water, food, and other materials. (20)

vein A blood vessel that carries blood back to the heart. (109)

visible light Electromagnetic radiation that can be seen with the unaided eye. (428)

voltage The difference in electrical potential energy per charge between two places in a circuit. (506)

volume The amount of space that matter occupies. (15)

W

wave A disturbance that transfers energy from place to place. (393)

wave pulse A pulse of energy that travels through an electric circuit when it is closed. (516)

wavelength The distance between two corresponding parts of a wave, such as the distance between two crests. (396)

X

X-rays Electromagnetic waves with wavelengths shorter than ultraviolet rays but longer than gamma rays. (429)

Z

zygote A fertilized egg, produced by the joining of a sperm and an egg. (152)

INDEX   Page numbers for key terms are printed in boldface type.

X

Z

ACKNOWLEDGEMENTS

Photographs

Photo locators denoted as follows: Top (T), Center (C), Bottom (B), Left (L), Right (R), Background (Bkgd)

Front Cover: Damselfly, Theo Bosboom/Nature Picture Library/Getty Images

Back Cover: blank notes and papers Marinello/DigitalVision Vectors/Getty Images

Front Matter

iv: Clari Massimiliano/Shutterstock; vi: NIBSC/Science Photo Library/Getty Images; vii: Stefan Schurr/Getty Images; viii: Robert Harding/Alamy Stock Photo; ix: Brian J. Skerry/National Geographic/Getty Images; x: Kong Act/Shutterstock; xi: Panpilas L/Shutterstock; xii: KPG Payless2/Shutterstock; xiii: Paul Melling/Alamy Stock Photo; xiv: Perry Van Munster/Alamy Stock Photo; xv: Raimundas/Shutterstock; xvi: Brian J. Skerry/National Geographic/Getty Images; xvii: Steve Byland/Shutterstock

Topic 1

xviii: NIBSC/Science Photo Library/Getty Images; 003: Richard Cummins/Getty Images; 004: Steve Gschmeissner/Science Photo Library/Getty Images; 006: World History Archive/Alamy Stock Photo; 007 TC: World History Archive/Alamy Stock Photo; 007 TCR: Dr Jeremy Burgess/Science Source; 007 TL: Science and Society/SuperStock; 007 TR: Dr. Cecil H. Fox/Science Source; 008: Andrew J. Martinez/Science Source; 009 CL: Steve Gschmeissner/Science Photo Library/Getty Images; 009 CR: Cultura RM/Alamy Stock Photo; 011: Biophoto Associates/Science Source; 013: Stegerphoto/Getty Images; 014: David M. Phillips/Science Source; 018: Don W. Fawcett/Science Source; 020 BCL: Don W Fawcett/Getty Images; 020 BCR: Biophoto Associates/Getty Images; 020 BL: Porter K/Getty Images; 020 BR: Biophoto Associates/Getty Images; 021 BCL: Professors Pietro M. Motta & Silvia Correr/Science Source; 021 BCR: Panther Media GmbH/Alamy Stock Photo; 021 BL: Biophoto Associates/Science Source; 021 BR: David McCarthy/Science Photo Library/Getty Images; 022 : John Lund/Drew Kelly/Glow Images; 023: Keith R. Porter/Science Source; 024: Tom Brakefield/Getty Images; 027: Microfield Scientific Ltd/Science Source; 028 B: Eric BVD/Fotolia; 028 TR: Science Source; 030 BL: Gary Carlson/Science Source; 030 BR: Gary Carlson/Science Source; 032: Jozef Polc/Alamy Stock Photo; 033: ZEPHYR/Science Photo Library/Getty Images; 036: Ed Reschke/Oxford Scientific/Getty Images; 037 BCL: Jennifer Waters/Science Source; 037 BCR: Jennifer Waters/Science Source; 037 BL: Jennifer Waters/Science Source; 037 BR: Jennifer Waters/Science Source; 038 BR: Frank Fox/Science Source; 038 TL: Ed Reschke/Getty Images; 041 B: Andrey Nekrasov/Image Quest Marine; 041 BL: David Courtenay/Getty Images; 041: Biophoto Associates/Science Source; 042 BC: Leena Robinson/Alamy Stock Photo; 042 Bkgrd: Shutterstock; 042 C: ArtTDi/Shutterstock; 042 TR: Charlie Summers/Nature Picture Library; 043: Steffenboessl/Fotolia; 046: Redma/E+/Getty Images; 047: Iphoto/Shutterstock; 051 B: Michael Reusse/Getty Images; 051 CR: Melinda Fawver/Shutterstock; 055 BR: Ramon Espelt/AGE Fotostock; 055 CR: Ramon Espelt/AGE Fotostock; 055 TR: Ramon Espelt/AGE Fotostock; 058: Antonio Olmos/Alamy Stock Photo; 064 BC: Nikola Rahme/Shutterstock; 064 BR: Matauw/Fotolia

Topic 2

068: Stefan Schurr/Getty Images; 070: Michael Svoboda/Getty Images; 072: imageBROKER/Alamy Stock Photo; 075 BL: Christopher Meade/Shutterstock; 075 CL: Biophoto Associates/Science Source; 075 CL: Martin M. Rotker/Science Source; 075 CR: Biophoto Associates/Science Source; 077: 3Dstock/Shutterstock; 081: © 2016 Takashi Tsuji, RIKEN Center for Developmental Biology; 082: Dsafanda/Getty Images; 084 BR: SPL/Science Source; 084 C: Steve Gschmeissner/Getty Images; 086 BL: Jorg Hackemann/Shutterstock; 086 BR: Jorg Hackemann/Shutterstock; 087: Bikeriderlondon/Shutterstock; 090: Kateryna Kon/Shutterstock; 092 BL: Giovanni Cancemi/Shutterstock; 092 TL: PA Images/Alamy Stock Photo; 094: SolStock/Getty Images; 095 BC: Yossi James/Shutterstock; 095 BL: Amenic181/Shutterstock; 095 BR: Artphotoclub/Shutterstock; 096: Anna Hoychuk/Shutterstock; 100: Anna Pustynnikova/Shutterstock; 105 B: NASA; 105 T: Phanie/Alamy Stock Photo; 106: Colin McDonald/Getty Images; 116: Zia Soleil/Getty Images Inc.; 118: David Fleetham/Alamy Stock Photo; 123: Chernomorets/Shutterstock; 124: Bettmann/Getty Images; 132: OJO Images/Getty Images

Topic 3

136: Robert Harding/Alamy Stock Photo; 138: Rickyd/Shutterstock; 141 Bkgrd: draleksun/Fotolia; 141 C: Biosphoto/Superstock; 141 CL: Alan J. S. Weaving/Ardea/AGE Fotostock; 142 CL: Laurent Geslin/Nature Picture Library; 142 TL: cbimages/Alamy Stock Photo; 144: Les Gibbon/Alamy Stock Photo; 145 BL: Sujata Jana/EyeEm/Getty Images; 145 TR: Visions Pictures/AGE Fotostock; 146: Kadmy/Fotolia; 147: Danita Delimont/Alamy Stock Photo; 148: kali9/Getty Images; 150: Gino Santa Maria/Shutterstock; 152: Blickwinkel/Alamy Stock Photo; 154 B: Inga Spence/Science Source; 154 CR: Barsan ATTILA/Shutterstock; 155 C: WILDLIFE GmbH/Alamy Stock Photo; 155 TR: Krystyna Szulecka/Alamy Stock Photo; 159 CR: NASA; 159 TR: NASA; 160: Paula French/Shutterstock; 163: Shawn Hempel/Shutterstock; 164: Kitch Bain/Shutterstock; 165: Tony Wu/Nature Picture Library; 166 B: Tony Wu/Nature Picture Library; 166 C: Morley Read/Alamy Stock Photo; 169 B: Tim Laman/Nature Picture Library; 169 CR: Tim Laman/Nature Picture Library; 170: Aodaodaodaod/Shutterstock; 172 BC: Cathy Melloan/Alamy Stock Photo; 172 BL: Martin Shields/Alamy Stock Photo; 172 BR: Haru/Shutterstock; 173 BL: Patjo/Shutterstock; 173 BR: Artens/Shutterstock; 174: Panuwat Kanisarn/Shutterstock; 177: Alex Staroseltsev/Shutterstock; 180 Bkgrd: WILDLIFE GmbH/Alamy Stock Photo; 180 TL: Blickwinkel/Alamy Stock Photo; 184: Nina B/Shutterstock

Topic 4

190: Brian J. Skerry/National Geographic/Getty Images; 192: Helen H. Richardson/The Denver Post/Getty Images; 194: Steve Allen/Photodisc/Getty Images; 196: Ephotocorp/Alamy Stock Photo; 199: Martin Harvey/Alamy Stock Photo; 200: Awie Badenhorst/Alamy Stock Photo; 202: Steve Byland/Shutterstock; 204: Fritz Rauschenbach/Corbis/Getty Images; 211: Oliver Smart/Alamy Stock Photo; 213 Bkgrd: Christopher Berkey/EPA/Alamy Stock Photo; 213 CR: STILLFX/Shutterstock; 213 TR: Christoph Gertler/Bangor University; 214: Somkiet Poomsiripaiboon/Shutterstock; 216: Paul Lemke/Fotolia; 218 Bkgrd: Jovannig/Fotolia; 218 BL: Cvalle/

Shutterstock; 218 BR: Aleksander Bolbot/Getty Images; 219 BC: Blickwinkel/Alamy Stock Photo; 219 BL: Steven Widoff/ Alamy Stock Photo; 219 BR: Yeko Photo Studio/Shutterstock; 221: Mikeexpert/123RF; 223 B: Jonathan Plant/Alamy Stock Photo; 223 CR: Kuttelvaserova Stuchelova/Shutterstock; 223 T: Olha Insight/Shutterstock; 226 Bamboo: Gnek/Shutterstock; 226 Civet: Miroslav Chaloupka/CTK Photo/Alamy Live News CTK/Alamy Stock Photo; 226 Cobra: FLPA/Alamy Stock Photo; 226 Douc: Bee-Eater/Shutterstock; 226 Dove: Luis Castaneda Inc./Getty Images; 226 Fig: Sarama/Shutterstock; 226 Insect: Deposit Photos/Glow Images; 226 Jambu: David Bokuchava/ Shutterstock; 226 Mango: Apiguide/Shutterstock; 226 Rhino: Terry Whittaker/Alamy Stock Photo; 226 Tiger: Biosphoto/ Alamy Stock Photo; 226 Viper: Biosphoto/Alamy Stock Photo; 228: Mlorenz/Shutterstock; 229 L: WILDLIFE GmbH/Alamy Stock Photo; 229 R: Loop Images Ltd/Alamy Stock Photo

Topic 5

232: Kong Act/Shutterstock; 234: Skyward Kick Productions/ Shutterstock; 236: Twomeows/Moment/Getty Images; 238: Frank Slack/Moment Open/Getty Images; 239 TC: Chloe Kaudeur/EyeEm/Getty Images; 239 TCR: Russell Burden/ Stockbyte/Getty Images; 239 TL: Alessio Frizziero/EyeEm/ Getty Images; 239 TR: Steve Leach/Moment Open/Getty Images; 240: Horh/Fotolia; 242: Dorling Kindersley/Getty Images; 243 BR: Shaen Adey/Gallo Images ROOTS Collection/ Getty Images; 243 CL: Bryan Knox/Papilio/Alamy Stock Photo; 243 TR: Ktsdesign/Shutterstock; 244 BL: WaterFrame/ Alamy Stock Photo; 244 BR: Stephen Bonk/Fotolia; 246: Erich Schmidt/imageBROKER/Getty Images; 248 BL: Tusharkoley/ Shutterstock; 248 TL: Jim Corwin/Alamy Stock Photo; 249 BR: Picsfive/Shutterstock; 249 T: Hellen Sergeyeva/Shutterstock; 252: Frans Lemmens/Alamy Stock Photo; 253 B: Jan Martin Will/Shutterstock; 253 TR: Photodiem/Shutterstock; 254: Elvis Antson/Shutterstock; 256: Boezie/Getty Images; 257: Ludmila Yilmaz/Shutterstock; 258: Frieda Ryckaert/Getty Images; 259: Paul & Paveena Mckenzie/Getty Images; 260: 2630ben/ Shutterstock; 261 Bkgrd: Charles Knowles/Shutterstock; 261 BR: Zhai Jianlan/Xinhua/Alamy Live News; 261 CL: Zeljko Radojko/Shutterstock; 261 CR: VCG/Getty Images; 261 TL: Georgy Rozov/EyeEm Creative/Getty Images; 261 TR: William Silver/Shutterstock; 262 B: Stocktrek Images, Inc/ Alamy Stock Photo; 262 T: Reinhard Dirscherl/Alamy Stock Photo; 263 BL: Michael Doolittle/Alamy Stock Photo; 263 BR: Goodluz/Shutterstock; 263 CR: Ariel Skelley/Getty Images; 264: Leonardo Gonzalez/Shutterstock; 266: Chris Fourie/ Shutterstock; 268: Design Pics Inc/Alamy Stock Photo; 269: 123RF; 270 BC: Holbox/Shutterstock; 270 BL: Ammit Jack/ Shutterstock; 270 BR: Kletr/Shutterstock; 270 C: PointImages/ Shutterstock; 270 CL: Hero Images/Getty Images; 270 CR: Pink Candy/Shutterstock; 271: Melpomene/Shutterstock; 273: Pawe/Shutterstock; 274: Nik Wheeler/Alamy Stock Photo; 275: Michael Willis/Alamy Stock Photo; 277 B: Michael Willis/Alamy Stock Photo; 277 T: Commission Air/Alamy Stock Photo; 283 BR: Redmal/E+/Getty Images; 283 T: Jose A. Bernat Bacete/ Moment Open/Getty Images

Topic 6

286: Panpilas L/Shutterstock; 288: Philipus/Alamy Stock Photo; 292: Aleksandr Pobedimskiy/Shutterstock; 294: Louisiana Governors Office/Alamy Stock Photo; 296: National Geographic Creative/Alamy Stock Photo; 298: Everett Historical/Shutterstock; 300: Raulbaenacasado/Shutterstock; 304: Chris James/Alamy Stock Photo; 308: Henryk Sadura/ Shutterstock; 310: WaterFrame/Alamy Stock Photo; 311 B: Siim Sepp/Alamy Stock Photo; 311 T: Shu-Hung Liu/ Shutterstock; 314: The Natural History Museum/Alamy Stock Photo; 316: Pulsar Imagens/Alamy Stock Photo; 320: Larry Geddis/Alamy Stock Photo; 323: Bennyartist/Shutterstock; 325: World History Archive/Alamy Stock Photo; 330: Haizhen Du/Shutterstock; 331 B: Anton Starikov/Alamy Stock Photo; 331 T: iStock/Getty Images

Topic 7

334: KPG Payless2/Shutterstock; 336: ThavornC/Shutterstock; 338: Justin Lambert/Getty Images; 343: Fotokostic/ Shutterstock; 344: Kletr/Shutterstock; 346: Por Nahorski Pavel/ Shutterstock; 350: Karol Kozlowski/Shutterstock; 352: Mark Kauzlarich/Bloomberg/Getty Images; 353: Science Source; 355: Vadim Petrakov/Shutterstock; 356: Brian A. Jackson/ Shutterstock; 358 BCL: Chad Ehlers/Alamy Stock Photo; 358 BCR: Jiri Foltyn/Shutterstock; 358 BR: Rob Crandall/Alamy Stock Photo; 359: Perytskyy/iStock/Getty Images; 360 CL: Kletr/Shutterstock; 360 CR: Blickwinkel/Alamy Stock Photo; 361: JurgaR/iStock/Getty Images; 364: lowsun/Shutterstock; 366: George Clerk/Getty Images; 368: Philip Duff/Alamy Stock Photo; 370: iStock/Getty Images; 374: Rosanne Tackaberry/ Alamy Stock Photo; 376: US Navy Photo/Alamy Stock Photo; 377: ZUMA Press Inc/Alamy Stock Photo; 384: Philipp Dase/ Shutterstock

Topic 8

388: Paul Melling/Alamy Stock Photo; 390: Losevsky Pavel/ Shutterstock; 392: Mark Leary/Getty Images; 393: NOAA; 394: Wavebreak Media Ltd./123RF; 400: imageBROKER/Jim West/Newscom; 402: Brian Maudsley/Shutterstock; 405 BCL: Science Source; 405 BCR: Kenny10/Shutterstock; 405 BL: Roberto Lo Savio/Shutterstock; 405 BR: Nublee bin Shamsu Bahar/Shutterstock; 407: Denis Gladkiy/Fotolia; 409: Sergey Nivens/Fotolia; 411 CR: Graham Oliver/123RF; 411 TR: Lionel Le Jeune/Fotolia; 413: LightField Studios/Shutterstock; 414: Lipsett Photography Group/Shutterstock; 416 B: Andrey Kuzmin/Shutterstock; 416 C: Mike Flippo/Shutterstock; 416 T: Pukach/Shutterstock; 417: Goran Djukanovic/Shutterstock; 418: Mr_sailor/iStock/Getty Images; 419: Vvoennyy/123RF; 422: U.S. Navy; 427: Gaspr13/Getty Images; 428 B: Arno Vlooswijk/TService/Science Source; 428 TL: Chuck Franklin/ Alamy Stock Photo; 429: Anton Petrus/Fotolia; 431 B: Andrey Armyagov/123RF; 431 TR: Blend Images/Alamy Stock Photo; 433: Sirtravelalot/Shutterstock; 434: Yellow Cat/Shutterstock; 435 B: Falk/Shutterstock; 435 C: Havoc/Shutterstock; 436 B: Anne08/Shutterstock; 436 T: Tusharkoley/Shutterstock; 437 B: Yuelan/123RF; 437 T: TLF Design/Alamy Stock Photo; 438 B: Mediaphotos/iStock/Getty Images; 438 T: Science Source; 446: Amirul Syaidi/Fotolia; 447: EpicStockMedia/Shutterstock

Topic 9

450: Perry Van Munster/Alamy Stock Photo; 452: Tingimage/ Alamy Stock Photo; 454: Ali Kabas/Alamy Stock Photo; 459 BCR: Boonchuay1970/Shutterstock; 459 BR: All Canada Photos/Alamy Stock Photo; 459 TCR: Bokeh Blur Background/ Shutterstock; 459 TR: Rassul Azadi/Shutterstock; 461: Andy

ACKNOWLEDGEMENTS

Crawford/Dorling Kindersley/Science Source; 463: Radius Images/Alamy Stock Photo; 465: Siiixth/Shutterstock; 467: Claire Cordier/Dorling Kindersley/Science Source; 469: Bart Sadowski/Shutterstock; 470: Steve Bloom Images/Alamy Stock Photo; 472: Karl-Friedrich Hohl/Getty Images; 477 BR: Valentinrussanov/Getty Images; 477 CR: China Images/Alamy Stock Photo; 477 TR: Simon Turner/Alamy Stock Photo; 479 B: Dave Higginson/Getty Images; 479 TR: Hero Images Inc./Alamy Stock Photo; 481: Tom Wang/Shutterstock; 486: Martin Shields/Alamy Stock Photo; 490: NASA Graphic/NASA Langley/Advanced Concepts Lab, AMA, Inc.

Topic 10

500: Raimundas/Shutterstock; 502: Smolaw/Shutterstock; 504: Room27/Shutterstock; 508: F.G.I. Co., Ltd./Alamy Stock Photo; 514: imageBROKER/Alamy Stock Photo; 516: Everett Collection/Shutterstock; 517 CR: Sirtravelalot/Shuttertock; 517 TL: Monkey Business Images/Shuttertock; 517 TR: Pressmaster/Shutterstock; 522: Marcio Jose Bastos Silva/Shutterstock; 527: CSP_Elly_l/AGE Fotostock; 528: Dotshock/

Shutterstock; 530 BL: Tempura/Getty Images; 530 CR: Ruslan Ivantsov/Shutterstock; 530 TCR: Gallofoto/Shutterstock; 531 CR: Asharkyu/Shutterstock; 531 R: David Ducros/Science Photo Library/Getty Images; 535 B: Bettmann/Getty Images; 535 T: Jacob Lund/Shutterstock; 541 TL: Doug Martin/Science Source; 541 TR: Richard Megna/Fundamental Photographs

End Matter

544 BCL: Philippe Plailly & Elisabeth Daynes/Science Source; 544 BL: EHStockphoto/Shutterstock; 544 TCL: Cyndi Monaghan/Getty Images; 544 TL: Javier Larrea/AGE Fotostock; 545: WaterFrame/Alamy Stock Photo; 546: Africa Studio/Shutterstock; 547: Jeff Rotman/Alamy Stock Photo; 548: Grant Faint/Getty Images; 549: Ross Armstrong/Alamy Stock Photo; 550: Geoz/Alamy Stock Photo; 553: Martin Shields/Alamy Stock Photo; 554: Nicola Tree/Getty Images; 555: Regan Geeseman/NASA; 556: Pearson Education Ltd.; 557: Pearson Education Ltd.; 558 BR: Pearson Education Ltd.; 558 CR: Pearson Education Ltd.

Take Notes

Use this space for recording notes and sketching out ideas.